# Beyond a Shadow of a Diet

# BEYOND A SHADOW OF A DIET

## The Therapist's Guide to Treating Compulsive Eating

*Judith Matz and Ellen Frankel*

Brunner-Routledge
Taylor & Francis Group

NEW YORK AND HOVE

Published in 2004 by
Brunner-Routledge
29 West 35th Street
New York, NY 10001
www.brunner-routledge.com

Published in Great Britain by
Brunner-Routledge
27 Church Road
Hove, East Sussex
BN3 2FA
www.brunner-routledge.co.uk

Library of Congress Cataloging-in-Publication Data

Matz, Judith, 1958–
    Beyond a shadow of a diet: the therapist's guide to treating compulsive eating
by Judith Matz and Ellen Frankel.
        p. cm.
Includes bibliographical references and index.
    ISBN 0-415-94609-3 (hardback)
    1. Compulsive eating. 2. Compulsive eaters — Rehabilitation. I. Frankel, Ellen,
1961– II. Title.
RC552.C65M243 2004
616.85'26—dc22

                                                                    2003027252

# DISCLAIMER

The information contained in this book is not intended as a substitute for medical
treatment. The information presented offers a perspective to inform decisions related to food and health. Clients should always be advised to seek care from a doctor for any concerns related to medical conditions.

The case examples used in this book reflect a composite of the many clients
with whom we have worked over the past twenty years. All names have been
changed.

Cover Image: ©2004 Dave Cutler c/o theispot.com

# DEDICATION

*For David,*
*Laura, Ethan, and Jordan*
*and*
*For Steve,*
*Allison, and Matt*
*May your hearts be full*
*And your stomachs satisfied*

# CONTENTS

# FOREWORD

*Beyond a Shadow of a Diet* is an inspiring, innovative, and practical non-dieting guidebook that provides an optimistic alternative to the seemingly neverending stream of diet-book mania that dominates the best-seller lists today. In this book, Judith Matz and Ellen Frankel offer uncommon clarity by defining "The Problem," "The Treatment," and "The Solution" to chronic dieting and compulsive eating. They do this in a straightforward, well-written, and humanistic style.

All therapists, whether specialists in the field of eating disorders or those in a more general practice, will benefit from exploring their own beliefs about eating and weight. The need for self-examination that this book promotes is also reflected in a recent study indicating that even professionals whose careers emphasize clinical management of obesity show very strong "pro-thin" and "anti-fat" weight bias suggesting strong and pervasive stigmatization.[1] Steps offered in this book will help professionals assist their clients in transforming their lives as they begin to understand why diets fail and learn about other effective interventions; in fact, therapists may want to pass this book on to their clients as well.

The title *Beyond a Shadow of a Diet* has a connection with one of the first feminist anti-dieting books, *Shadow on a Tightrope: Writings by Women on Fat Oppression*, by Lisa Schoenfeld, published in 1983.[2] The first *shadow* caught my attention 20 years ago because it was becoming increasingly apparent that weight loss, whether it occurred in connection with anorexia nervosa or in those labeled as clinically obese, produced certain negative symptoms such as depression, mood swings, anxiety, and binge eating.[3] Although my primary interest was individuals with anorexia and bulimia nervosa, I gradually recognized that many of those with eating disorders were actually "successful dieters" who had begun their weight loss at a body weight that earned them the label "obese." At that point, my own interest in body weight and fat stigmatization began to intensify and culminated in companion reviews with renowned clinician, Susan Wooley.[4,5] Writing this foreword to *Beyond a Shadow of a Diet* has reminded me of how far we have come, as well as the challenges that remain ahead.

Scientists still remain sharply divided on the fundamental question of whether traditional behavioral and dietary treatments should be the standard offered to larger individuals. It is of interest that, despite evidence to the contrary, the debate still rages over the effectiveness of dietary and behavioral treatments. Perhaps it is partly a problem of semantics. It is without question that most diets "work" in the short term. However, the reality is that restrictive dieting: (1) is ineffective in producing *lasting* and *clinically significant* amounts of weight loss for most people; (2) is no match for the genetic and biological factors that regulate weight; (3) may aggravate health risk factors associated with obesity, health risks that may have been exaggerated in the first place; (4) can lead to serious side-effects such as binge-eating and depression; and (5) may reinforce the myth that weight loss is the preferred route to improve self-esteem for women.[6] The traditional approach of dieting as a means of improving physical and emotional health is sharply challenged in *Beyond a Shadow of a Diet.*

It is very difficult for a person who has spent years trying to lose weight to suddenly accept the notion that diets don't work. The recommendation to abandon the traditional weight-loss paradigm has been criticized as a pessimistic and even irresponsible view. A common objection to voicing doubts about the universal mandate for weight reduction is that this may unleash an epidemic of obesity. It has been argued that promoting "self-acceptance" among those at the heavier end of the weight spectrum might lead them to relax their dietary vigilance and gain weight. However, there is little evidence for these contentions. The literatures on the biology of weight regulation and the heritability of body weight suggest that the vast majority of individuals will settle at a weight that is natural for their genetic predisposition. Moreover, the past two decades have witnessed the height of diet preoccupation among women living in North America and Western Europe. This is the same timeframe that has been associated with a marked increase in the body weights for young women.

An alternative to this approach is provided by *Beyond a Shadow of a Diet.* Judith Matz and Ellen Frankel propose that current evidence should compel greater effort in exploring alternative methods for improving lifestyle, health risk factors, body image, and the self-esteem of compulsive eaters without requiring significant amounts of weight loss. This book advances the anti-diet movement (also known as the Health at Every Size paradigm) that has been cast in a somewhat radical light when, in fact, it is based on very conservative principles that govern decision making in other areas of science and medicine. It is based on the principle that *safety* and *efficacy* should be demonstrated *before* there is wide endorsement of a particular intervention. It is also grounded in the corollary that when there is compelling evidence that a treatment is either unsafe or ineffective, it should not be recommended. At the very least, the public should be fully informed regarding information available on safety and efficacy, and this should be clearly displayed or described for all commercially available products or programs.

More than ever before, women are dissatisfied with their weight and are fighting it through the use of relentless dieting and exercise. Thinness is the preeminent yardstick for success or failure for women, a constant against which every woman can be measured, a gauge that has slowly permeated the male mentality. Matz and Frankel provide practical advice aimed at improving self-esteem, self-acceptance, quality of life, and health for individuals of all sizes, using a model that ends the restrictions that lead to overeating.

The images that we have of our bodies are both reflected and affected by the things we do to alter those images, and altering body image has a long and honorable history. From the most primitive to the most advanced cultures, people have tried to both distinguish themselves from others and conform to social customs by camouflaging, enhancing, and adorning body parts via clothes, jewelry, hairstyles, makeup, and body markings. Our so-called advanced society has added extreme exercise, dieting, body building, and cosmetic surgery to the list of body enhancing activities — and these activities make a crucial difference in creating unhealthy, but normative behaviors.

The result of these preoccupations is a negative body image, which is undoubtedly detrimental to mental health. It also seems to be a metaphor for our culture of mass consumption that encourages narcissism, a new kind of self-consciousness or vanity through which people have learned to judge themselves not merely *against* others but *through* others' eyes. The "image" projected by possessions, physical attractiveness, clothes, and "personality" replaces experience, skills, and character as gauges of personal identity, health, and happiness. We are thrown into a chronic state of unease, perfect prey for an array of commercial "solutions." There's always been a payoff for those with the most alluring features, but nowadays we are bombarded nonstop from outside with recommendations on how to change, control, nurture, and interpret our body.

*Beyond a Shadow of a Diet* shows how improvements in health and self-image do not have to wait for a thinner physique, contrary to the relentless declarations by the weight-loss industry. Even modest exercise has a profound effect on health and longevity.[7,8] There are now exercise programs designed specifically for large women.[9] Giving up weight loss as a goal may be viewed by some as a surrender to self-loathing, and relinquishment of hope for a degree of self-acceptance that thinness supposedly promises. However, the focus on weight loss delays positive lifestyle changes that can improve health and well-being. In fact, the suggestion that weight loss should be abandoned is often met with a grieving reaction: denial, anger, bargaining, depression, and finally, acceptance. Parting with the weight-loss myth is painful, but perhaps not as painful as the lifelong pursuit of false hope and the delay of positive lifestyle changes that can improve health and well-being. Dignity, self-respect, and happiness can be achieved at any weight.

A few years ago, a well-known obesity researcher stated that subjecting the obese to restrictive dieting to lose weight is "the modern day equivalent of beating the insane to keep them quiet." Not much has changed since this blunt simile except that the public grows ever more weary and confused by the torrent of contradictory health claims. Every chapter of *Beyond a Shadow of a Diet* conveys liberating insights and effective approaches for those struggling with food, weight, and body image issues. These insights and practical suggestions provide an easy-to-read roadmap through the maze of inner emotional turmoil created by the conflict between cultural propaganda about weight loss and biological reality. The result is a formula for ending compulsive eating and achieving genuine self-confidence through self-acceptance.

David M. Garner, Ph.D.

Dr. David M. Garner is a clinical psychologist and the Director of the River Centre Clinic in Sylvania, Ohio. He is an Adjunct Professor in the Department of Psychology at Bowling Green State University. Dr. Garner is a Founding Member and Fellow of the Academy for Eating Disorders and has served as a scientific advisor for two civil rights organizations for large people: National Association to Advance Fat Acceptance (NAFFA) and Association of the Health Enrichment of Large People (AHELP).

# ENDNOTES

1. Schwartz, M.B., Chambliss, H.O., Brownell, K.D., Blair, S.N., & Billington, C. (2003). Weight bias among health professionals specializing in obesity. *Obesity Research*, 11, 1033–1039.

2. Schoenfeld, Lisa. *Shadow on a tightrope: writings by women on fat oppression.* Iowa City: Aunt Lute Press, 1983.

3. Garner, D.M., & Garfinkel, P.E. (1980). Socio-cultural factors in the development of anorexia nervosa. *Psychological Medicine*, 10, 647–656.

4. Garner, D.M., & Wooley, S.C. (1991). Confronting the failure of behavioral and dietary treatments of obesity. *Clinical Psychology Review*, 11, 729–780.

5. Wooley, S.C. & Garner, D.M. (1991). Obesity treatment: The high cost of false hope. *Journal of the American Dietetic Association*, 91, 1248–1251.

6. Kassirer, J. P., & Angell, M. (1998). Losing weight — an ill-fated New Year's resolution. *New England Journal of Medicine*, 338(1), 52–54.

7. Blair, S.N., Kohl, H.W., III, Paffenbarger, R.S., Clark, D.G., Cooper, K.H., & Gibbons, L.W. (1989). Physical fitness and all-cause mortality. A prospective study of healthy men and women. *The Journal of the Amerian Medical Society*, 262, 2395–2401.

8. Gaesser, G. A. (1997). *Big fat lies: The truth about your weight and health.* New York: Fawcett Columbine.

9. Lyons, P. & Burgard, D. (2000). *Great shape. The first fitness guide for large women.* Palo Alto, CA: Bull Publishing Co.

# PREFACE

With great enthusiasm, we set out to write a book for therapists that would address the problem of compulsive eating. Our motivation stemmed from a variety of factors. As clinical social workers, we have both worked in the field of eating problems using a non-diet approach since the mid-1980s. On the one hand, we repeatedly observed that therapists were acutely aware that many of their clients struggled with eating and weight issues but lacked clear and effective clinical strategies to address these problems. In our experience, this scenario was compounded by the fact that many excellent therapists wrestled with their own relationships with food and their bodies which, in turn, had profound ramifications as to how they approached these issues with clients.

At the same time, therapists are in an extraordinary position to understand and implement a treatment of compulsive eating that offers lifelong, positive results for their clients. The psychological perspective that therapists have allows them to consider problems of overeating and body dissatisfaction on intrapsychic, interpersonal, and cultural levels. Their willingness to examine personal beliefs and experiences and their impact on the treatment situation offers therapists a basis for reconsidering their ideas. Throughout this book, our readers will be asked to do just that.

We are sisters who, typical of females in this society, struggled at varying points in our lives with food and weight. Bonding together in "sisterhood" has given us a wonderful opportunity to share with others what we have learned, both professionally and personally. Although the issues were different for each of us, we reached the same conclusion: Diets don't work, and the obsession with thinness never leads to a positive body image. These principles, which we have incorporated into our work as therapists, have been substantiated over time by a growing body of research that exposes the harmful effects of dieting and offers new guidelines to help people achieve physical and psychological well-being. Despite the research and the experiences of most people that diets fail in the long run, Americans still turn to diets at a fervent pace, contributing to the $50 billion a year industry. Many of these consumers are our clients. The question arises: If diets don't work, what can a person do instead? This book answers that question.

The majority of individuals seeking treatment for eating problems are women. Therefore, in order to simplify the text, we chose to use the female pronoun throughout the book. In no way do we mean to imply that men are immune from these issues and, in fact, their numbers are increasing. The information presented throughout this book can be used with male as well as female clients.

Another major tenet of our work with clients who eat compulsively is that people naturally come in different shapes and sizes. The word "fat" has become a four-letter word in our language, implying moral failure and creating shame. We view the word "fat" merely as a description of size, and therefore use it at times in the text as an appropriate adjective. In fact, we view the word "overweight" as more arbitrary and judgmental because of its implication that a correct weight exists, which someone is above; we therefore do not use this term unless it is part of a quote.

This book will teach you how to help your clients end their compulsive eating. However, this book is about more than just what people eat and weigh. As clients discover how to cure compulsive eating rather than control it, they pave the way for physical, emotional, and spiritual well-being. Energy freed up from the preoccupation with food and weight can be directed toward more productive endeavors, including relationships, work, hobbies, and general self-care. Learning to tune into needs related to physical hunger leads to an ability to recognize and respond to other kinds of psychological hungers. Taking pleasure in food and one's body leads to a fuller, more satisfying life. These benefits will empower your clients. They may also empower you.

As therapists, we have a duty to promote practices that enhance the lives of our clients, rather than supporting mainstream viewpoints that may cause damage. Evidence of the harm caused by dieting is seen in the explosion of eating problems, body hatred, and weight cycling. As therapists, we can become knowledgeable about scientific research, the dynamics of compulsive eating, and the relationship between food and emotions, while questioning cultural messages about diet and weight that have become ingrained in our culture. The process of helping a client find freedom from the pain of compulsive eating is profound and rewarding.

We recognize that some of you will already be familiar with many of the concepts offered in this book, while others will be learning about this approach for the first time. Interspersed throughout the book we will ask you to examine your attitudes and their effects on clinical treatment. We hope that you will find information and case examples that will enrich your professional, and perhaps even personal, life.

If we come together as a therapeutic community to understand how a non-diet, size-accepting approach improves the lives of our clients and the public at large, our potential to create societal change will be immense. Full of research and theoretical and practical information, we hope that *Beyond a Shadow of a Diet* will become an invaluable resource for you.

# ACKNOWLEDGMENTS

Our immense appreciation goes to Laura Goodman, Deb Werksman, and Linda Edelstein for their support and wisdom in helping us launch this project.

For their invaluable comments on our manuscript and their understanding of our purpose, we would like to thank Carol Grannick, Linda Glass, Pam Duhl, Barbara McCollough, Ellen Reifler, and Sue Fligor.

We are deeply grateful to our colleagues who contributed their expertise in their related fields, adding to the richness of this book: Cheri Erdman, Jon Robison, Paul Ernsberger, Dana Armstrong, Elisa D'Urso-Fisher, Sally Strosahl, and Marilyn Glielmi.

For their clinical contributions and personal reflections, we thank Rachel Lurie, Paula Fried, and Maureen Morrison.

For their pioneering work in the non-diet movement, their support of this project, and for their friendship, we thank Jane Hirschmann and Carol Munter.

We are indebted to our clients and workshop participants who have honored us by sharing their stories, taught us through their experiences, and inspired us with their courage. We hope that this book will give you further support along your journey.

Our heartfelt thanks go to Brunner-Routledge for its commitment to this project and its ongoing support of our work, especially to George Zimmar for having the vision, Shannon Vargo for her enthusiasm and wisdom, and Mimi Williams for her diligence.

To our many friends, family, and colleagues, too numerous to name, who offered encouragement through their actions, questions, and continuous support, we thank you for
the gift of friendship.

To our parents, thank you for keeping food plentiful,
along with your love.

To our husbands, David and Steve, we thank you for
your help with tracking down articles, recovering misplaced
chapters from the computer, ordering pizza, giving us the
space to write, and most of all, for your unconditional love.

For Laura, Ethan, Jordan, Allison, and Matt, our next generation, thanks for your curiosity about our work, your
awareness and celebration of diversity, and the wonderful
ways in which you listen to and trust your bodies.

# I WANT TO LOSE WEIGHT

## Identifying the Problem

A new client arrives at your office. "What brings you here?" you ask. "I need help losing weight," she replies. "If only I could control my eating and be thin, I know my life would be better. This isn't the body I was meant to have. I want to have more energy and I know my marriage would improve if I looked more attractive. I've tried every diet and lost a lot of weight, but I've always gained it back. I've never been this heavy before. It's been a really stressful time. I know I turn to food when I'm unhappy. Can you help me?"

You've worked with a client for the past 10 months. During this time, he has achieved many goals, including managing his depression and choosing a career path. He is a large man but has never referred to his body size. You know that he would like to begin dating. Do you bring up his weight as a therapeutic issue?

After many months of therapy, a client tells you that she feels great shame about her body. This comes as a surprise to you because she appears to be average weight and physically fit. She explains that she works very hard to keep herself this size. She follows a strict food plan and doesn't allow herself any "junk" food. "It works pretty well for me," she tells you. "I couldn't stand myself if I gained any weight. But, whenever I go to a party or out with a friend, I get really worried. What if there's nothing for me to eat? Sometimes I want what they're having so badly, and I do eat it. I feel so guilty afterwards. Sometimes I'm really good while I'm out, but on my way home, I stop at the store and buy some candy or cookies. They're usually gone before I walk in my house. That is the worst feeling in the world."

These scenarios are typical of the different ways in which clients bring food and weight issues into treatment. Compulsive eating problems may be the presenting problem, or they may arise as a client moves deeper into the treatment relationship. Conversely, they may never be mentioned during the course of therapy.

## ASSESSING YOUR REACTIONS

Take a moment to reflect on your reactions to each of these scenarios. How might you respond in the session? Your assessment of these vignettes depends upon your own experiences with food and weight. Messages about the desirability of thinness and controlled eating habits are strong in our culture, and they influence everyone, including therapists.

Think about yourself for a moment.
- Are you now or have you ever been on a diet?
- Do you worry about your body size?
- Do you engage in diet conversations with friends or family members?
- Do you think dieting is a healthy behavior?
- Do you feel good when someone says that you look like you've lost weight?
- Have you ever commented on someone else's weight?

Each of these behaviors may seem innocuous at first, but they have profound ramifications in terms of what you will bring to the treatment setting. Turning back to our case scenarios, there are, of course, many possible reactions. Here are some of the common responses of therapists.

"*I know exactly what she means.*" In this situation, the therapist identifies with the client. She has also struggled with compulsive eating and understands immediately the pain and suffering of her client. She may feel a sense of helplessness in this area or may try to get her client to succeed with diets where she herself has failed.

"*It's a matter of self-esteem. If she felt better about herself she would do something.*" This belief often comes from the therapist who has not encountered significant problems with food and weight. The therapist wonders why her client doesn't just "do something" if it bothers her so much.

"*She's not fat. I don't understand what she is complaining about.*" In this scenario, the therapist may be uncomfortable with her own body size. She worries about her appearance and can experience countertransference in her work with thinner clients. She may also be unaware of how clients with body image problems present their experience.

"*My client hasn't told me that she has food and weight issues. It's not relevant to our therapy.*" The therapist feels uncomfortable exploring the possibility that these issues have meaning in the client's life. Or, she may assume that food and weight concerns pose no problem for the client and may, in fact, be correct. However, the therapist may not know how to ask about these topics or know what to do if, in fact, they require intervention.

"*The solution is for my client to understand the emotional triggers of her eating through our work together. Then her overeating will diminish.*" This response stems from the therapist's training in helping cure clients of symptoms by exploring the underlying causes of a problem. Although ultimately the client does need to understand the emotional components of overeating, if there is in fact a connection in her life, the therapist may be less versed in the need to intervene directly with compulsive eating patterns.

"*I conquered my weight problems. If my client develops more willpower and stops sabotaging herself, she can do it too.*" The therapist has had success with a particular method of weight control. She expects her client to be able to follow the same plan.

Most therapists identify with one or more of these responses. As your reactions occur, either consciously or unconsciously, you must decide how to proceed in treatment. Some therapists will encourage diet or lifestyle programs designed to help the client lose weight. This recommendation can take the shape of a formal program, a diet philosophy based on a book, or a self-imposed restricted food plan and exercise regime. The therapist also may take the route of trying to help the client understand why she overeats. In this case, the underlying belief is that once the client understands and resolves the emotional issues triggering the compulsive eating, she will no longer need to turn to food. While both of these strategies may seem logical, they usually fail. A successful treatment for compulsive eating lies in an approach that combines direct interventions regarding food, body image, and psychological insight.

## Defining Compulsive Eating

How do you conceptualize compulsive eating? Does it depend on how much food you eat? Can you tell from looking at someone if she is a compulsive eater? A compulsive eater is a person who repeatedly reaches for food when she is not physically hungry. This contrasts with a "normal eater" who eats most of the time in response to physiological hunger. Everyone eats occasionally for reasons other than hunger. A person may take a bite of food because it looks good or may overeat at a holiday meal. The natural eater usually notices that she ate too much, feels uncomfortable, and then waits for the next indication of physical hunger to eat again. The compulsive eater, on the other hand, experiences the overeating as evidence of being out of control. She begins to yell at herself internally for her transgression and thinks of ways to counteract the overeating such as tightening food restraints. For the compulsive eater who has many overeating experiences throughout the day, this type of thinking consumes a large portion of her mental energy and contributes to feelings of low self-esteem, guilt, and depression.

Compulsive eaters come in all shapes and sizes. There are large people who do not eat compulsively, and there are thin and average size people who struggle with compulsive eating problems. The amount of food eaten can vary for compulsive eaters from small amounts of "too much" food throughout the day to binges characterized by large amounts of food consumed in a short period of time. The key factor, however, is that eating has little to do with physical hunger. In fact, the person may no longer know what it feels like to be hungry.

## THE DIETING FACTOR

Dieting is commonly viewed as the solution to compulsive eating. However, dieting necessitates tuning into external cues with regard to food intake and disconnecting from internal cues of hunger, fullness, or satiety. A meal plan for weight loss typically specifies the timing of meals and a predetermined amount of permissible foods. Invariably, the food restrictions placed on the dieter eventually result in breaking the diet with consumption of the once forbidden foods of the diet plan, often in the form of a binge.

A classic study by researchers Janet Polivy and Peter Herman at the University of Toronto illustrates the way in which dieters, or restrained eaters, have lost touch with the internal hunger and fullness cues that are necessary for normal eating. In the experiment, a group of dieters and non-dieters were given the task of comparing ice cream flavors. Participants were divided into three groups. Those in the first group were given two milkshakes to drink before eating the ice cream. The second group was asked to drink one milkshake before eating the ice cream, while the third group was not given any milkshakes prior to the ice cream. Next, the researchers offered the groups three flavors of ice cream and asked participants to rate the flavors, eating as much ice cream as they desired.

The results revealed that the non-dieters ate more ice cream when they had not had any milkshakes, less ice cream when they had one milkshake, and still less ice cream when they had consumed two milkshakes. The dieters reacted in an opposite fashion. The restrained eaters who were offered no milkshakes prior to the taste testing ate small amounts of ice cream, those who drank one shake ate more ice cream, and the dieters who had consumed two milkshakes ate the most ice cream! The researchers call this process "disinhibition," and it occurs as a result of a "diet-mentality." The milkshake "preload" has a different effect on the dieter than on the non-dieter. Non-dieters, eating in a nonrestrained and normal fashion, regulate their food consumption according to internal physical cues of hunger and satiety. In this case, non-dieters regulated the amount of ice cream consumed based on the intake prior to the ice cream; the more milkshake, the less ice cream, and vice versa. Restrained eaters, or dieters, react in the opposite manner. According to the researchers, counterregulation occurs because of the psychological dieting dynamics where the milkshake preload serves to disinhibit the dieter's usually inhibited or restrained eating.[1] In other words, "I've blown it anyway, so I might as well keep eating before I go back on my diet."

## PREVALENCE OF EATING PROBLEMS

Compulsive eating affects millions of people, but its causes and treatment are not necessarily taught in the professional schools where therapists receive training. Therapists often learn about anorexia nervosa and bulimia, both of which have become increasingly widespread. Current estimates are that 1.1 to 4.2% of females will suffer from bulimia at some point in their life.[2] Additionally, 13 to 19% of female college students display subclinical features of the disorder.[3] Up to 3.7% of women will struggle with anorexia nervosa during their lifetimes.[4] A person struggling with bulimia typically binges and then compensates for that intake through vomiting, laxative abuse, or excessive exercising. Anorexia nervosa occurs when a person severely restricts food intake, and her weight falls into a dangerous range. Both disorders may result in serious physical consequences, including death. Compulsive eating has physical and emotional costs as well, yet on a continuum of eating problems, it is considered less severe.

## BINGE EATING DISORDER

Compulsive eating is a significant problem, and it is important that the therapeutic community recognizes its impact on the lives of clients. Just as therapists routinely evaluate new patients for drug or alcohol use, compulsive eating problems deserve the same attention. In an attempt to lend credence to the seriousness of overeating, Binge Eating Disorder was added to the *Diagnostic and Statistical Manual 4th edition* (*DSM-IV*) as a subtype under the category of Eating Disorder Not Otherwise Specified (EDNOS). The criteria for a diagnosis include:

> Recurrent episodes of binge eating. An episode of binge eating is characterized by both of the following: a) eating in a discreet period of time (e.g., within any 2-hour period) an amount of food that is definitely larger than most people would eat during a similar period of time in similar circumstances; b) a sense of lack of control over eating during the episode (e.g., feeling that one can't stop eating or control what or how much one is eating).
> The binge eating episodes are associated with at least three of the following: a) eating much more rapidly than normal; b) eating until feeling uncomfortably full; c) eating large amounts of food when not physically hungry; d) eating alone because of being embarrassed by how much one is eating; e) feeling disgusted, depressed, or very guilty after overeating.
> Marked distress regarding binge eating.

The binge eating occurs, on average, at least 2 days a week for 6 months.
The disturbance does not occur exclusively during the course of anorexia or bulimia nervosa.[5]

In keeping with the criteria stated above, it is estimated that binge eating disorder affects up to 4% of all adults, or about 4 million Americans.[6] People struggling with binge eating disorder may be large or more average in body size. About 10 to 15% of people who try to lose weight on their own or through commercial weight loss programs struggle with binge eating disorder.[7] Furthermore, it is estimated that 30% of people who use hospital-based weight control programs also meet the criteria for this diagnosis.[8] Yet it is important to note that many more people who struggle with compulsive eating do not meet the above criteria.

The description of Binge Eating Disorder fits the symptoms of many clients who present with compulsive eating problems. At the same time, some of the criteria are subjective. For example, it is difficult to quantify what constitutes a normal amount of food in a 2-hour period. Also, people vary greatly in their rates of eating and in their experiences of being out of control. Regardless of any flaws with the proposed definition, the benefit of diagnosis includes the recognition of the seriousness of a client's eating problem in the absence of restricting and purging behaviors. The diagnosis also allows clients to receive insurance benefits for their treatment.

## DISORDERED EATING

Not everyone who overeats meets the criteria for a psychiatric diagnosis. The prevalence of compulsive eating in the general population is huge, as evidenced by the number of consumers who yearly support an approximately $50 billion diet industry.[9] In 2000, the number of American males and females dieting to lose weight or maintain weight totaled nearly 116 million adults, representing about 55% of the total adult population.[10] With more than half of the population dieting at any given time, the cultural norm has shifted to a point where dieting behavior and body dissatisfaction have become the common experience for many.

Nutritionist Debra Waterhouse uses the term "disordered eating" to encompass the extent to which compulsive eating affects the lives of people, particularly women. She maintains, "any woman who has some form of an unhealthy relationship with food and her body is a disordered eater. She may be caught in the diet–binge cycle, restricting 'forbidden' foods, feeling guilty after eating or in a semi starvation state from chronic under eating, fasting, skipping meals or over exercising."[11] Francis Berg, an internationally known authority on weight and eating problems, proposes the following definition: "Dysfunctional eating is eating in irregular and chaotic ways — dieting, fasting, bingeing, skipping meals — or it may mean consistently undereating much less or overeating much more than your body wants or needs. Dysfunctional eating is separated from its normal controls of hunger and satiety, and its normal function of nourishing the body, providing energy, health and good feelings. Instead, it is regulated by external and inappropriate internal controls and seeks to reshape the body or relieve stress."[12]

This definition would describe Julie. Last year she lost 30 pounds on a commercial weight loss program. Recently, she began to crave sweets and started to binge on candy and cookies. The pounds returned, and Julie felt increasingly depressed and ashamed. The definitions proposed by Waterhouse and Berg also fit a client named Bob. He explained that he eats all day, regardless of hunger. "The more I think of trying to lose weight, the more I seem to eat. What's wrong with me?" he asked.

The broadness of both definitions extends beyond individual psychopathology. At the same time, a significant number of people who seek counseling each year do not meet the criteria of Binge Eating Disorder but engage in compulsive eating behaviors. The current cultural climate that idealizes extreme slenderness, abhors fat, and encourages dieting contributes greatly to the problem of compulsive eating as a social problem, affecting the emotional lives of millions of people. As the terms "compulsive eating," "disordered eating," and "Binge Eating Disorder" describe a similar clinical picture, albeit with varying intensity, for the purposes of this book, the phrase "compulsive eating" will be used the majority of the time. The treatment approach described in this book applies to clients at all points on the continuum of overeating.

Therapists are in a unique position to help people solve the problems of compulsive eating and body hatred. Through both individual and social interventions, clinicians can positively affect the attitudes and behaviors of clients, resulting in greater physical and emotional well-being. At the same time, however, therapists can also harm their patients, albeit unknowingly, by using interventions based on faulty information. Laura Fraser, author of the book *Losing It*, highlights this problem. In her article "The Diet Trap," Fraser writes:

> I believe that our obsession with dieting is a cultural sickness. It induces chaotic emotional states and eating patterns that deprive people of the ability to naturally regulate themselves. In fact, dieting worsens the problems — overeating, overweight, food obsession and body shame that it purports to solve. And it wreaks havoc on moods, lives and emotions.

> The research supporting this view has been known for decades. Yet there are still plenty of therapists who assume, like mine did, that obesity is a pathological state and the obvious antidote is to diet to lose weight. Year after year, they prescribe hypnosis, nutrition education, appetite suppressants, diets and behavior management, even though study after study has shown that for the vast majority, none of this works for long. Many therapists assume that people must be fat because they were sexually abused as children or have other emotional problems; once those are cleared up, these therapists seem to think, the pounds will melt away. Both of these views are simplistic and reflect profound ignorance of human behavior, physiology and genetics.[13]

*Beyond a Shadow of a Diet* offers a sane and sound approach that will help you provide services to clients suffering with compulsive eating problems. These techniques are based on solid research that diets do not work and draw from years of clinical experience.

## The Experience of Compulsive Eating

By the time a client walks into your office, chances are she has already tried to solve this problem on her own. The first step is to understand the experience of the compulsive eater.

---

## THE CASE OF CORY

Cory is a 45-year-old woman who reported that her food issues began at age 12. Looking back at pictures, she observed that her weight was "normal." But, as she moved toward puberty, her hips became wider and her stomach wasn't as flat as it used to be. Her mother, who struggled with her own weight, told Cory that she needed to lose weight before "it really becomes a problem." Together they agreed that Cory would cut out all desserts at dinnertime and eat only "healthy snacks" during the day. This seemed to work at first and Cory found that she lost 10 pounds, "enough to make me feel better," she added.

During high school, Cory found it harder to follow her mother's regime. When she went out with her friends, she couldn't resist the late night snacks of pizza and ice cream. She started to gain more weight. Her mother took her to the pediatrician who recommended that Cory be placed on a restricted 1,000-calorie-per-day diet. Cory tried to follow this plan, but she found herself increasingly uncomfortable. From the moment she woke up in the morning, she worried about whether she would have a "good" or "bad" day. She resented the fact that her family and friends could eat cookies and candy. She found herself using some of her spending money to stop at the local food mart, and she began sneaking the "forbidden foods" into her bedroom. Sometimes her mother discovered an empty candy wrapper and yelled at Cory for her transgression. Cory remembered feeling ashamed of her behavior. "I really wanted to be good and lose weight. But I couldn't control myself. I felt guilty, but the harder I tried, the worse things seemed to get."

During her first year of college, Cory joined the first of many commercial diet programs she would try over the years. She liked the camaraderie of the other dieters and felt encouragement from the group leader. She successfully lost 25 pounds and felt pleased with herself.

When Cory was a junior in college, she married the man she had dated for the past 18 months. There were problems in the marriage from the start. Cory began to gain weight, regaining all she had previously lost, plus some. She believed that her feelings about her marriage caused her to eat more and put on pounds.

Despite their difficulties, Cory and her husband decided to have a child. Cory viewed her pregnancy as a "license to eat." During the course of the pregnancy she gained 55 pounds, which she then found impossible to lose after the birth of her child.

The family moved to a new city because of a job opportunity for Cory's husband. She felt hopeful that life would be better on the East Coast and immediately rejoined the commercial program. Again, Cory followed the structure of the program and was able to lose 50 pounds. Unfortunately, the problems continued between Cory and her husband. Of particular concern to her was the increase in his alcohol use. The couple sought marital counseling and eventually decided to divorce.

Following the divorce, Cory found her weight at a higher point than ever before. She attempted to follow the diet plans in a few books that her friends had recommended. She also tried another national weight loss program, hoping that prepared food would help her stay in better control. Several times she lost weight, only to regain it back again.

Cory and her daughter returned to Cory's hometown. She began individual therapy in an attempt to understand how she had allowed herself to marry an alcoholic. She hoped to remarry at some point and wanted to solve her problems with intimacy. Cory found the therapy to be helpful. She did not address her eating issues at the time. In fact, she had stopped focusing on her weight as she struggled to work full time and be a good mother to her daughter. Without trying, her weight dropped by about 60 pounds.

Cory began to date again and married a man who was very different from her first husband. He provided much love and support for Cory and was accepting of her body size. Cory, however, decided to return to therapy, this time to look at why she found herself feeling "depressed and overburdened" at times. Her preoccupation with food surfaced as an important issue.

Cory explained to her therapist that while she felt okay about herself at her current weight, she still did not know what to do about her food problems. One day she could eat "healthy" just fine, and the next day she felt out of control. She wanted to make peace with food. Her therapist was supportive and tried to help Cory examine the emotional triggers of her overeating. Cory was able to identify some issues, such as feeling that she always had to please everyone. But the eating behaviors still did not change.

Cory's therapist suggested that she go back to a commercial weight loss program. However, Cory knew that her dieting days were over. She couldn't stand the roller coaster anymore; the thrill of weight loss followed by the shame of weight gain. She couldn't stand the discomfort of physical hunger that came when she managed to control herself. But she also couldn't stand the emotional daily toll of worrying about food. She believed there must be some way out of this problem.

Cory and her therapist looked for alternative ways of treating overeating. Cory was referred to a therapist who specialized in the treatment of overeating at a well-respected hospital. He advised her to stop all diets. Instead, he said that she should follow an eating plan that was low in fat. For example, if she wanted pizza, she could just pull off the cheese. Or, if there was a birthday celebration at work, she could substitute carrots or apples for cake. Cory was also told to add exercise to this regime. She already walked several times a week, which she loved, and the therapist agreed that this was sufficient. By following this healthy lifestyle, Cory was told that she could expect to lose weight and that she would have an eating plan that she could comfortably follow for the rest of her life.

Cory did her best to follow this expert's recommendations. She saw him weekly for six sessions, reviewing her progress each time. When she reported that she still found herself turning to food, especially in the evenings, he told her to take all cookies and ice cream out of the house. Instead, she could substitute frozen yogurt and Snackwells to get the flavor without the fat. Cory found herself canceling her last two appointments with this therapist. She felt shame about her failure to stick with this lifestyle change and anger because she felt she was being blamed for her difficulties.

Several months later, Cory came across an advertisement for a workshop on ending overeating without diets. Fed up with dieting, tired of her compulsive eating, and ready to find a solution to her predicament, Cory, with the support of her individual therapist, joined a group that would eventually help her work her way out of her problems with food and body image.

## The Diet–Binge Cycle

Every person is unique, and each story a client brings to therapy speaks to the pain of living as a compulsive eater and dieter. Conflicts with food and weight have profound effects on the individual's life. But in many ways, the stories are the same. In her groundbreaking book, *Fat is a Feminist Issue*, Susie Orbach identified the dynamics of compulsive eating within a cultural context.[13a] In her books *Feeding the Hungry Heart* and *Breaking Free from Compulsive Eating*, Geneen Roth was a pioneer in describing and validating the experience of compulsive eaters.[14] The similarities that almost universally describe the compulsive eater's experience, including negative thoughts, dieting, and overeating, make up the diet–binge cycle. Here's how it works.

### NEGATIVE THOUGHTS

Chances are you have never heard someone say, "I look wonderful today. I think I'll start a diet!" Instead, like Cory, a person usually looks in the mirror and has negative thoughts about her body. An internal dialogue begins. "My stomach sticks out too much, my thighs are too fat, and my hips are too wide." As the lamenting continues, she eventually reaches a conclusion. "I must do something about my weight. I need to get myself back in control. I cannot continue to eat so much. As of today, (or tomorrow, next week, on New Year's Day) I will start a diet." *Every diet begins with negative body thoughts.* The prospective dieter engages in what Jane Hirshmann and Carol Munter, authors of *When Women Stop Hating Their Bodies*, call "bad body thoughts."[15] Without this kind of thinking, there would be no incentive to ever begin a diet.

The current cultural climate, with its idealization of extreme slenderness, encourages negative body thoughts and contributes to the profitability of the diet industry. The average fashion model is 17 to 26 years old, 5'9" tall, and weighs 110 to 118 pounds. The average American woman is 44 years old, with a height of 5'4" and a weight of 142 pounds. Media messages suggest that with enough determination and by purchasing the proper products, this ideal image is attainable. Advertising is a $130 billion industry. The average American watches 30 hours of television per week and spends 110 hours a year reading magazines. This adds up to an exposure rate of 1,500 advertisements daily.[16] One of the main messages conveyed through television, magazines, billboards, and movies concerns the ideal female body, which is very tall and very thin. Yet only 3 to 5% of the population would naturally fall into this body type. The average fashion model has a weight of 13 to 19% below "expected weight" for her height, meeting the criteria of 15% below "expected weight" for a diagnosis of anorexia nervosa. At the same time, there has been a significant increase in the number of diet articles in popular women's magazines suggesting that with the right plan and enough willpower, the "perfect" body is attainable.[17]

Researchers have reported that a mere 3-minute exposure to photographs of models taken from popular women's magazines led to increases in depression, stress, shame, insecurity, and body image dissatisfaction.[18] Four years later, these findings were replicated in a study that measured the body dissatisfaction of female college students. The women were divided into two groups; one viewed slides of slim fashion models while the other group viewed neutral images. The results revealed that women who viewed the slides of fashion models showed a significant increase in body dissatisfaction and weight concern as compared to the group who viewed the neutral slides.[19] Women are repeatedly encouraged to compare themselves to an unrealistic and unhealthy view of thinness and taught that dieting and weight loss result in happiness, success, and love.

## THE DIET

Once the dieter has reached the conclusion that weight loss is the way out of her body discomfort and negative image, she feels much better. With this new resolve, she already feels a sense of control. She may choose a diet plan from one of the latest books on weight control or perhaps join a program. Or, she may choose to cut back on certain types of foods or follow a restricted, low-calorie diet. She won't be alone. On any given day, almost half of the women in the United States are on a diet and one in four men are on a weight loss plan.[20] Dieters have a menu of over 30,000 diet plans from which to choose. Whichever plan the dieter follows, the key ingredient is some type of food restriction in which weight loss is the anticipated goal. She understands that she will need to give up some of the foods that she loves but believes that the result will make it worthwhile.

With great excitement and hope, this person shares her decision to diet with friends and coworkers. She receives praise from them. They tell her it is great that she is going on a diet. "Just think how much better you'll feel carrying around less weight. It is so good that you are taking care of yourself," they say.

As the diet begins, she meticulously follows the plan. She feels virtuous when passing up certain foods at a party. She shops carefully and prepares meals using all the correct ingredients allowed in her diet. "This time it will really work," she thinks. After 2 weeks, she can see the results. Her jeans already feel looser around her waist.

## OVEREATING

Fast forward a week, a month, or even 6 months of adhering to a restricted food plan, and our dieter finds herself overeating. In fact, this is the inevitable result for the great majority of dieters. As she breaks out of the restraints, she goes for her "forbidden foods." You will never hear someone say, "Oh, I broke my diet and couldn't stop eating carrots." Instead, she finds herself bingeing on ice cream, chips, pizza, or any number of foods that she had labeled as "bad."

As the overeating continues, many feelings surface. Guilt, depression, anxiety, and low self-esteem are common during this time. Particularly painful to this once hopeful dieter is the shame that accompanies the perceived failure. After all, her friends told her that dieting was the right thing to do. They supported her and complimented her on her weight loss. As the overeating continues and the weight is regained, no one says a word.

The now frustrated dieter continues to eat in a way that she experiences as distressing. As she reaches for the donuts someone brought into the office, she reasons, "I might as well have them now while I'm not on a diet. Starting Monday, I'm going to have to begin a new diet because I am getting so fat." She eats the donuts, and just about anything that she "shouldn't" all weekend long. This way of thinking is supported in our culture. At a popular chain restaurant, a standing dessert menu advertising a chocolate peanut butter cup pie adorns each table. The text reads, "Suddenly Tomorrow's A Better Day To Start Your Diet."

### NEGATIVE THOUGHTS REVISITED

On Monday, she glances in the mirror, steps on the scale to confirm her worst fears, yells at herself for how she has let herself go and, with new determination, begins her next diet. The cycle continues.

Does this sound familiar to you? You may be one of the millions of people caught in the vicious dieting trap. Or, you may know someone or many people who follow this pattern, including some of your clients. Once people are caught in the diet–binge roller coaster, breaking the cycle becomes very difficult. In order to help clients get out of this trap, you must understand why diets fail as well as the causes of overeating.

## Why Diets Fail

If weight gain is the result of excess caloric intake, as the common belief goes, then the obvious solution for losing weight is to cut back on calories. Initially, this strategy will produce a decrease in weight. However, for approximately 95% of dieters, the pounds will be regained, with some people exceeding their original weight. Why, when people over and over claim how much they want to lose weight, are they unable to diet their way to a smaller size to fit into that coveted pair of jeans? The answer lies, in part, with a different set of genes, and the fact that *DIETS DO NOT WORK!*

## GENETICS

Our bodies are not as malleable as the diet and advertising industries would have us believe. Researchers estimate that approximately 50 to 80% of our weight is the result of genetics; nearly 80% of identical twins raised in separate households develop adiposity to the same level.[21] Other findings from identical twin studies indicate that genetic inheritance has a substantial impact on weight, while the environment during childhood has minimal or no impact.[22] Researchers estimate that between 40 to 70% of our Body Mass Index (BMI) — a measure of weight relative to height — is determined by our genes. Moreover, our metabolism, a major component of weight maintenance, is largely determined by our genetic makeup. Resting metabolic rate refers to how much energy we burn when we are not active. Our resting metabolism rate accounts for approximately 70% of the fuel we burn each day. Researchers suggest that 40 to 80% of this resting rate is inherited. Finally, even the distribution of fat on our bodies is approximately 40% due to our genes.[23] Just as genetics contributes to height and intelligence, our genes are an important component in determining our weight.

## EVOLUTION

Evolution also plays an important role in the physiology of weight. Our ancestors were hunters and gatherers, always in search of food to ensure their survival. At times food was plentiful, and sometimes it was scarce. The human body had to find a way in which it could survive during periods of famine. Those whose bodies were able to adapt to the scarce conditions were able to successfully reproduce. The legacy passed on through human evolution is a body designed to ensure survival in times of feast or famine. Our bodies now have a genetic predisposition to hold on to fat after each period of scarcity; our bodies fail to distinguish whether the cause of that deprivation is from a famine or from a weight loss diet.

An example of the body's efficient biological programming is evident during puberty. To ensure that females will be well prepared for fertility and pregnancy, a girl's body will create fat cells to be stored in her stomach, thighs, hips, and breasts. According to Debra Waterhouse, dieting during adolescence mimics a time of famine, putting her body on alert and stimulating the overproduction of fat cells. "Instead of producing 5 million fat cells in her left thigh, her body retaliates and increases its inventory to 6 million — just in case. Instead of making her fat cells the size of a dime, her body will make them the size of a quarter. . . . [Dieting] also overstimulates the production of fat storage enzymes so that when your daughter goes off the diet and starts eating again, she'll quickly fill her fat cells to their maximum capacity. In other words, your daughter's body becomes twice as efficient at taking every extra little calorie traveling around in her bloodstream, scooping it up, and storing it in one of her fat cells. Dieting doesn't burn fat, it builds fat and boosts its stubborn, rebellious nature."[24] The current idealization of thinness and attempts to lose body weight through dieting is but a blip on the evolutionary radar screen. The body, for its own survival, is programmed to defend its weight and resist a decrease in pounds.

## ADAPTATION

Each person has a weight range known as a set point that the body tends to maintain over an extended period of time. The set point, or set point range, is the place where weight is steady when a person eats when physically hungry, stops when full, and engages in some amount of daily movement. Body weight, like body temperature, has a natural point that, similar to a thermostat, it seeks to maintain. When a person takes in less fuel (food), the body attempts to deal with the reduced intake by slowing down. Conversely, when the body takes in more fuel, it speeds up. The set point is maintained in this manner.

When a body is deprived of the food it demands, it defends itself by shutting down to conserve energy. It does this by lowering the metabolism, or the rate at which calories are burned through energy expenditure. Within 24 to 48 hours of beginning a calorie-restricted diet, the metabolic rate decreases 15 to 30%.[25] In a recent study by Leibel, Rosenbaum, and Hirsch, the effect of dieting on metabolism was explored. The researchers recruited people of varying sizes. The participants were studied at their initial weight and during periods of subsequent weight changes. The researchers found that when weight is lost, total energy use drops and stays reduced for as long as weight remains at that lower level. Subjects in the study who maintained a weight of 10% below their initial weight showed a 15% drop in metabolic rate.[26] This means that their bodies slowed down to compensate for the decrease in food intake.

Furthermore, when caloric intake is decreased to a certain point, the body, thinking it is experiencing a famine, feeds off fat and muscle. With every diet, a person will lose both fat and some lean tissue. Muscle is the part of the body that is metabolically active. In other words, the more muscle a person has, the more calories that person burns in energy. Conversely, the less muscle she has, the lower the metabolism and, therefore, the fewer calories she utilizes. Losing lean muscle not only renders one weaker, it also lowers metabolism. Paradoxically, this causes the body to burn fewer calories, making it easier to gain weight and resulting in an even higher fat-to-muscle ratio. Therefore, the chronic dieter may significantly change her percentage of body fat over time. *Going on a diet automatically lowers a person's metabolism every time.*

At the same time the metabolism is lowered, the body sends out urgent red flags indicating the need for more fuel. As intake is reduced, the body fights against this starvation mode by conserving energy (lowering metabolism), instructing fat cells to store more fat, and by increasing the appetite, compelling the person to eat. Falling levels of the recently identified protein named Leptin boost chemicals circulating around the brain such as neuropeptide Y, a powerful eating stimulant that induces cravings, particularly for carbohydrates. As long as food restrictions are in place, the body will continue to defend itself through conserving energy, storing fat, and creating a desperate hunger.

Glen Gaesser, author of *Big Fat Lies*, states, "A number of studies have shown the inescapable consequences of repetitious cycles of weight loss and gain appear to be ever greater accumulations of fat."[27] Virtually any diet program that involves food restrictions will produce short-term weight loss. However, the great majority of people who lose weight will regain the weight, often plus some, within 1 to 5 years. The "failure" rate of diets is actually a "success" in terms of species survival. However, for the millions of people who are trying to lose weight, the physiological defense mechanisms of the body are overwhelming. According to eating disorders specialist David Garner, "The best way to gain weight is to lose weight."[28]

## The Dieter's Predicament

Let's return to our dieter who decides that losing weight will help her feel better about herself. After days, weeks, or months of deprivation and denying her increasingly strong hunger signals, she eventually breaks the food restrictions. Because of her level of deprivation, her body demands increasing amounts of food, which she experiences as overeating. It is a truism that for every diet, there is an equal and opposite binge. But now her metabolism is lowered and she has lost some muscle. After breaking her diet, she quickly gains back the pounds as fat. Proportionately, her body now has more fat and less muscle than before the diet. You may have heard clients say that they weigh more after the diet than when they began their food restrictions. Evolution has ensured this process.

An article in the *Chicago Sun-Times* titled "Obesity experts suggest putting end to dieting" features the work of David Garner. The story shows a before and after picture of a female dieter. Unlike the ads for commercial diet companies, this picture shows the dieter larger after the program is over. The caption reads, "Quick weight-loss ads may show obese people becoming svelte and happy, but obesity experts describe a different picture: Dieters nearly always regain the weight — and then some."[29] This is understandably upsetting to clients who discover that their years of yo-yo dieting have altered their metabolism and body composition. As a result, their weight will likely be higher than if they had never started to diet in the first place.

## THE KEYS STUDY

The knowledge that the human body will rebel against unnatural weight loss and that dieting is a major trigger of binge eating has been available for quite some time. In 1944, Ancel Keys, a physiologist at the University of Minnesota, conducted a study of 36 conscientious objectors. Interested in the effects of semi-starvation, Keys placed the group of physically and emotionally healthy men on a 6-month diet that was adequate in vitamins, minerals, and protein, but amounted to half of the calories they were used to eating. The men were allowed about 1570 calories per day. In fact, the restricted meal plan they followed was similar to diets marketed by commercial weight-loss programs today. As these men lost approximately 25% of their body weight, they underwent profound personality changes. They became irritable, lethargic, distracted, depressed, and apathetic. In addition, they became obsessed with food. Berg notes, "They talked of little else but hunger, food and their weight loss."[30]

What these men experienced as a result of their semi-starvation is typical of feelings and behaviors exhibited by dieters. When the men entered the refeeding portion of the study, the food restrictions were lifted. Free to eat what they wanted, the men engaged in binge eating for weeks yet continued to feel ravenous. They overate frequently, sometimes to the point of becoming ill, yet they continued to feel intense hunger. The men quickly regained the lost weight as fat. Most of the subjects lost the muscle tone they enjoyed before the experiment began, and some of the men added more pounds than their pre-diet weight. Only after weight was restored did the men's energy and emotional stability return.

## Diets Don't Work

According to William Bennett and Joel Gurin, authors of *The Dieter's Dilemma*, "People who have dieted long enough to lose weight, only to succumb to a binge of guilty eating, may recognize their own experience in this story. They will recall the ceaseless hunger that a single indulgence cannot relieve and the internal pressure to continue eating until all the pounds so triumphantly shed have returned."[31]

The power of our physiology is unmistakable, yet most dieters feel it is their fault that the lost pounds are regained. The common perception is that if a person had more willpower, she could succeed. The reality is that as a group dieters do have more willpower than most people. They can give up favorite foods for long periods of time while those around them continue to partake. They can go on liquid fasts and eat nothing for 3 months. They can exercise 7 days a week for 2 hours at a time. The extremes to which dieters go are sometimes mind boggling and usually require great effort and restraint. The real problem for dieters is not willpower but the solutions that are offered to them. It is not that people fail diets, but rather, diets fail people. Garner and Wooley state, "Virtually all programs appear to be able to demonstrate moderate success in promoting at least some short-term weight loss. . . . [T]here is virtually no evidence that clinically significant weight loss can be maintained over the long-term by the vast majority of people."[32]

### THE GOVERNMENT GETS INVOLVED

Beginning in 1989, Congressman Ron Wyden, a Democrat from Oregon, held hearings investigating the marketing and advertising practices of diet programs. "While expert after expert testified that fewer than 1% of people are able to maintain a weight loss for five years, the diet companies insisted their programs were effective."[33] In 1992 and 1993 the Federal Trade Commission (FTC), which is in charge of regulating advertising and marketing, charged 17 companies, including the five biggest in the United States — Weight Watchers®, Jenny Craig, Nutri/System®, Physicians Weight Loss Center®, and Diet Center — with making false and deceptive claims about the safety and effectiveness of their weight loss plans.[34] Moreover, in 1992, the National Institutes of Health (NIH) held a 2-day conference to examine why more Americans are gaining weight despite the fact that more people are dieting in search of weight loss. In attendance were medical professors, physicians, and researchers and experts in obesity and public health. After examining all of the evidence on weight loss programs, the conclusion reached was that diets don't work. The NIH panel also proclaimed that dieting itself may cause serious physiological and psychological problems.

## DIETS IN DISGUISE

As various diet programs and gurus have caught on to the idea that diets don't work, they have eliminated the word "diet" from advertising. Instead, they offer "lifestyle plans" as an alternative. Don't let yourself or your client be fooled. Usually this means low-fat eating and exercise or some other imposed food restrictions for the purpose of losing weight. These are diets in disguise and have the same physiological and psychological consequences.

# The Causes of Compulsive Eating

In order to help your client break through the diet–binge cycle and discover a more normal way of eating, you must both understand the causes of overeating. The two major factors that lead people to reach for food when they are not physically hungry are deprivation and the use of food for affect regulation.

## DEPRIVATION

Imagine you are sitting in a room full of people. The speaker tells you not to think about a pink elephant. Think about anything else in the world, but don't think about a pink elephant! What happens? When you are told not to do something, or want something, it is hard to stop thinking about it.

The same is true with food. Researchers Polivy and Herman state, "Dieters' deprivation — whether real or imagined — has been identified as a contributor to overeating and eating binges."[35] When a client is told, or decides, that she cannot eat a particular food, she will find herself thinking about it more than she normally would. When that particular food is around, she will become constantly aware of its presence. She will feel a sense of deprivation; there is something she wants but she cannot have. The reason she cannot have it comes from her negative thoughts. She feels she is too fat to fit into the cultural ideal, and depriving herself of what she loves is her penance. When she breaks through the restraints of this food prison, she will go straight to the restricted or forbidden foods. She will eat more of those foods than her body actually needs.

Perhaps you have a client who describes a binge. She may tell you that she had a box of cookies in the house. She thought that she shouldn't have them around and therefore finished them so they wouldn't be there the next day to interfere with her self-control. Or, a client describes his overeating on the weekends. He explains that he controls himself all week at work, but when he is at home, he allows himself to eat whatever he wants. A client may tell you that she plans to begin a new diet program on Monday. In preparation for the restrictions, she explains, "I ate everything I could get my hands on because I knew I could never eat it again." In all of these examples, the notion of deprivation initiates the binge.

Finally, imagine you are told that starting tomorrow *you* can never have ice cream again. Take a minute to think about what you would do and how you would feel.

Most people respond that they would go out today or tonight and eat a lot of ice cream. This is a *natural* reaction to deprivation. Every time a client decides to diet, she creates this situation. Whether she eats these foods in anticipation of a diet, or as the result of breaking through the restraints of a diet, she will consume these forbidden foods regardless of whether or not she is actually physically hungry for them. Every time a client imposes restrictions on herself for the purpose of losing weight, she ensures a feeling of deprivation. Deprivation inevitably leads to overeating. Dieting is the major cause of deprivation, and deprivation is the leading cause of overeating.

The men in the Keys study demonstrated the insatiable hunger that follows a period of deprivation. When the participants were allowed access to food during the refeeding process, they would binge beyond fullness, sometimes licking their plates. The men consumed an average 5,218 calories daily, with some consuming 8,000 to 10,000 calories on the weekend. Moreover, some men reported a loss of control in their eating, followed by self-reproach and shame. Polivy states, "Starvation and self-imposed dieting appear to result in eating binges once food is available and in psychological manifestations such as preoccupation with food and eating, increased emotional responsiveness and dysphoria, and distractibility. Caution is thus advisable in counseling clients to restrict their eating and diet to lose weight, as the negative sequelae may outweigh the benefits of restraining one's eating."[36]

## AFFECT REGULATION

The second major cause of overeating is the use of food by compulsive eaters to regulate their affect. Many overeaters state that they turn to food for all kinds of emotional reasons. Anger, stress, loneliness, boredom, and happiness are among the common feelings mentioned by clients as triggers for overeating. Yet, upon deeper examination, it becomes clear that it is not actually the feeling itself that leads to the overeating. Rather, the person has a calming problem in which her inability to manage certain emotional states leads to overeating. Food is used in the moment to soothe her as she struggles, sometimes unconsciously, with unacceptable or overwhelming feelings. This process is explored in depth in chapter 5.

### Understanding the Language of Fat

Clients use words such as numbing, distracting, comforting, soothing, and calming to describe the function of food in their lives. At the same time, clients will also express distress about their use of food for emotional reasons, which typically results in feelings of being out of control and weight gain. Judith Lightstone, a psychotherapist specializing in eating disorders, explains:

> The binge is initially triggered by an event or thought that may also be associated to an earlier less conscious experience. The earlier experience may have included a great deal of shame. That experience is then transferred to feelings of body shame, and self-critical thoughts. At this point the person reaches for food to help salve the pain. The shaming thoughts are then redirected onto the eating behavior, which puts the eating in a paradoxical role. While it is soothing the person, it also acts as a scapegoat for the bad feelings that triggered the binge to begin with. The eating behavior, and the soothing it brings, then becomes the enemy. The person then believes, "I feel bad because I am eating" rather than "I felt bad and so I ate," because they no longer remember what made them reach for the food in the first place.[37]

Jane Hirschmann and Carol Munter have named this process the translation of the language of feelings into the language of fat.

The food deprivation of a diet will lead to a normal and healthy reaction: a binge. But the binge triggered by deprivation looks behaviorally the same as a binge triggered by emotions that have nothing to do with physiological hunger. The shame and low self-esteem the person experiences as a result of this confusion lead to further dieting behavior and the continuation of the diet–binge cycle.

---

## THE CASE OF GAIL

Let's take a deeper look at the process of the compulsive eater who uses food to manage uncomfortable feelings. Gail had a terrible day at work. Her boss gave her a new project that requires much of her time. She already feels overwhelmed by the amount of work that several other people in the office have asked her to do. Her evaluation is 1 month away, and she does not want to jeopardize her chances for a promotion. She agrees to take on the project. When Gail arrives home, she heads for the refrigerator. She begins to eat some ice cream, followed by the half bag of chocolate chip cookies she has in the house. As she eats, she begins to yell at herself. "You pig! You are completely out of control. Your stomach is so fat and here you go again. No wonder you can't even fit into the clothes you bought last summer. No wonder people treat you so badly — look how you treat yourself. You have got to stop eating like this. You are just getting too big. You had better do something right now. You had better go back to the weight loss clinic and get this under control."

---

Gail has just made a translation from the language of feelings to the language of food and fat. Polivy and Herman state, "Binge eating appears to relieve anxiety, possibly through distraction from one's problems or by displacing feelings of distress from other, more threatening issues onto the seemingly more manageable problem of overeating."[38] When Gail's boss gave her a new project, she felt angry. She felt she was being treated unfairly, but she could not speak up for herself. However, it was not her anger that led to her overeating. Rather, it was her inability to tolerate the feeling that caused her to start eating. Reaching for food at that moment was an attempt by Gail to calm herself because her anger was unacceptable to her. She may have had a clue that she was upset but could not handle her emotions. Or, like many compulsive eaters, she may have found herself eating but had no idea what was bothering her, or even that something was bothering her at all.

As Gail finds herself overeating, the yelling begins. In fact, the yelling is a necessary part of the process for the compulsive eater. This is because the negative internal dialogue immediately and effectively takes Gail away from her real problem. Of course, she does not sit and think, "I am angry at my boss. I feel taken advantage of and do not like that about myself. But, I cannot tolerate this feeling so I will go have some cookies and ice cream to distract myself." Instead, Gail finds herself overeating but does not know why.

As the yelling progresses, Gail defines the problem as the size of her body, caused by her overeating. She believes that it is her weight and eating issues that deserve her attention. Gail views her main obstacle as being out of control with food rather than acknowledging that she feels out of control at work. She contends that she is treating herself badly with food rather than admitting that she feels treated badly at work. Gail assumes that if her weight and overeating are the significant problems for her, then dieting is the obvious solution. Gail has effectively made a translation from the language of feelings to the language of food and fat. This process is common for compulsive eaters. The culture at large — family, friends, the media, and often the medical and mental health communities — supports this translation by saying, "Yes, dieting is a good idea. You will feel much better about yourself if you lose weight and control your eating."

### Consequences of Emotional Eating

Unfortunately, the compulsive eater who relies on food to regulate difficult emotions loses out in several ways. Feelings are an important pathway for people to understand themselves and their world. Therapists, of course, devote much of their work to helping people identify their feelings and use them as a road map to solve difficulties that occur in life. Yet the minute the compulsive eater turns to food to calm herself, she loses access to these feelings. When she calls her problem one of food and weight, she distances herself even further from the real issues in her life. Every time a client reaches for food to manage a feeling, she misses out on an opportunity to learn something important about herself and deal directly with a difficult problem or situation.

This aspect of overeating is significant in the lives of many compulsive eaters. Because of the psychological nature of this type of overeating, therapists can be of great value to clients. In fact, an entire chapter will be devoted to emotional overeating later in the book.

## The Seeds of Compulsive Eating Behavior

Some clients begin eating compulsively as an attempt to use food to manage feelings. As a result, they gained weight, began dieting, experienced deprivation, and got caught in the diet–binge cycle. Other clients may have begun their diet careers as the result of some sort of deprivation. Perhaps a family member commented that they looked a bit pudgy. Or, a female client may have begun dieting after the birth of her child to "get back in shape." As they tried to restrict foods, they began to overeat more. The negative thoughts and yelling began and resulted in another diet. For all clients, and for all of us, the backdrop of these scenarios is a culture that promotes thinness as the only acceptable body type. This belief is so insidious that most people, including therapists, may assume it is a fact.

## The Role of the Therapist Treating Compulsive Eating

As the result of training as mental health professionals, therapists are already in a unique position to help people solve their problems with compulsive eating. There are principles of psychotherapy that lend themselves to providing the atmosphere needed to assist clients in the process of creating a normal relationship with food and their bodies.

## CHALLENGING ASSUMPTIONS

As you begin to educate your clients about the causes of overeating, you will need to question and examine your assumptions about body size. This is a monumental and necessary task if your client is to experience freedom from the obsession with food and weight. Throughout this book, we will provide information and ideas to help you do just that. From the outset, however, appreciating how the cultural environment of body hatred fuels the diet–binge cycle will help you to further understand your client's compulsive eating. Deprivation occurs only because people believe their size is unacceptable and therefore begin to manipulate their food. The translation from the language of feelings to the language of food and fat occurs only because people are strongly supported in their belief that losing weight solves complex personal issues.

The power of culture to influence dieting and weight behaviors may seem less relevant to your clients than other causes of overeating. As clients come to your office and try to work their way out of their preoccupation with food and weight, they will probably be more interested in their own situation than in challenging the cultural norms about size. Ultimately, however, changing the climate of our society is crucial to ending the epidemic of dieting disorders and eating problems.

## UTILIZING THERAPEUTIC SKILLS

Basic to the therapeutic relationship is the establishment of trust between client and therapist. The compulsive eater who experiences shame in her life because of food and weight must know that she can share her situation with you without fear of blame or judgment. Because of her own notions that a thin body is a better body, she is likely to expect you to agree with her that she is "bad" for "letting herself go" and for being unable to control her obsession with food. Your existing therapeutic skills, such as the ability to communicate a non-judgmental attitude, starting where the client is, and active listening, combined with a compassionate stance built on your new understanding of the causes of overeating, will promote a supportive environment conducive to using the techniques provided in later chapters.

Therapeutic training also aids in understanding the psychological aspects involved in the process of ending overeating. Many clients find that as they try to implement new behaviors aimed at normalizing their relationship with food, they get stuck. As clients face these obstacles, you will be able to help them understand their resistances so that they can work their way through any roadblocks. By exploring with your client the patterns, defenses, and self-soothing techniques she brings to life's challenges, she will be in a better position to develop adaptive coping skills. Through the compassionate attitude you communicate to your client, she will learn that there are understandable reasons for her struggles, and that together you can resolve issues that arise so that she can move closer to her goals.

As your client breaks the diet–binge cycle and develops a healthier relationship with food, she will be in a position to begin to deal directly with her feelings. At this point in the process, your therapeutic knowledge becomes crucial. For many clients, food and negative body thoughts have served as distractions from problems they have avoided for many years. For the first time, they must look directly at their issues without using food as a buffer. Perhaps they struggle with depression or anxiety. Maybe they must come to terms with a failing marriage. Some clients may discover intimacy issues that they never knew existed. Memories of sexual abuse may surface. Of course, not all compulsive eaters bring deep psychological problems to the treatment situation. Sometimes the diet–binge pattern is the result of repeated deprivation and the cycle that ensues in the climate of a culture that fears fat. At the same time, however, there is a strong link between compulsive eating and emotions. The combination of knowing how to treat compulsive eating and being a skilled therapist provides the optimal treatment situation.

## EMBRACING A NEW PHILOSOPHY

Learning the non-diet approach to ending compulsive eating is exciting and often life changing for the therapist as well as for the client. Yet in order to successfully teach this process to your clients, you must first have an attitude that genuinely encompasses acceptance of the philosophy that people of equal value come in all shapes and sizes. Although you now have new information regarding the problems of the diet–binge cycle and the causes of overeating, are you really convinced that dieting and weight loss are not the solution for the compulsive eater? If not, you will find implementing treatment strategies offered in later chapters difficult at best and often impossible. As your clients struggle with their own feelings about stopping the diets that exacerbate compulsive eating problems, they will turn to you with their concerns and fears. Your consistent non-diet attitude and acceptance of a range of body types will help to reassure your clients as they embark on this new path.

The cultural messages about the desirability of thinness run deep. Your task is to confront any biases you take with you, perhaps unknowingly, to treatment. Identifying your beliefs about body size and eating habits, exploring your own issues with food and weight, and becoming familiar with the current research on dieting, weight, and health are necessary steps for you, as the therapist, to take at this juncture. When you cultivate an attitude of acceptance, the potential to positively impact your clients becomes limitless.

## ENDNOTES

1. McFarlane, T., Polivy, J., & McCabe, R. (1999). Help, not harm: Psychological foundation for a non-dieting approach toward health. *Journal of Social Issues, 55* (2), 262.
2. American Psychiatric Association Work Group on Eating Disorders. (2000). Practice guideline for the treatment of patients with eating disorders (revision). *American Journal of Psychiatry, 157* (Suppl. 1), 1–39.
3. Nash, J. D. (1999). *Binge no more: Your guide to overcoming disordered eating.* Oakland, CA: New Harbinger Publications, Inc., p. 4.

4. American Psychiatric Association Work Group on Eating Disorders. (2000). Practice guideline for the treatment of patients with eating disorders (revision). *American Journal of Psychiatry, 157* (Suppl.), 1–39.

5. American Psychiatric Association. *Diagnostic and statistical manual of mental disorders* (Fourth ed.), Text Revision. Washington, D.C.: American Psychiatric Association, 2000, p. 787.

6. American Psychiatric Association. *Diagnostic and statistical manual of mental disorders* (Fourth Edition), Text Revision. Washington, D.C.: American Psychiatric Association, 2000, p. 786.

7. Binge eating disorder. [Online]. (2003). Diet Information. Available: www.diet-i.com/eating-disorders/binge-eating.htm [2002, October 14].

8. Fairburn, C. G., & Wilson, G. T. (Eds.). (1993). *Binge eating: Nature, assessment, and treatment.* New York: Guilford, p. 29.

9. Berg, F. M. (2000). *Women afraid to eat: Breaking free in today's weight-obsessed world.* Hettinger, ND: Healthy Weight Network, p. 24.

10. Gaesser, G. A. (2002). *Big fat lies: The truth about your weight and your health.* Carlsbad, CA: Gurze Books, p. 29.

11. Waterhouse, D. (1997). *Like mother, like daughter.* New York: Hyperion, p. 12.

12. Berg, F. M. (2000). *Women afraid to eat: Breaking free in today's weight-obsessed world.* Hettinger, ND: Healthy Weight Network, p. 53.

13. Fraser, L. (1997, May/June). The diet trap. *Networker,* p. 47.

13a. Orbach, S. (1994). *Fat is a feminist issue.* New York: Berkley Books.

14. Roth, G. (1982). *Feeding the hungry heart.* New York: Signet; (1984). *Breaking free from compulsive eating.* New York: Plume.

15. Hirschmann, J., & Munter, C. (1995). *When women stop hating their bodies.* New York: Fawcett Columbine, p. 9.

16. Fallon, P., Katzman, M., & Wooley, S. (Eds.). (1994). *Feminist perspectives on eating disorders.* New York: Guilford Press, p. 4.

17. Garner, D. M., Garfinkle, P. E., Schwartz, D., & Thompson, M. (1980). Cultural expectations of thinness in women. *Psychological Reports, 47,* 483–491.

18. Stice, E., & Shaw, H. E. (1994). Adverse effects of the media/portrayed thin/ideal on women and linkages to bulimic symptomatology. *Journal of Social and Clinical Psychology, 13,* 288–308.

19. Posavac, H., Possavac, S., & Posavac, E. (1998). Exposure to media images of female attractiveness and concern with body weight among young women. *Sex Roles, 38* (3/4), 187–201.

20. Has your perspective of your body weight been distorted by the media? [Online]. (2003). Ideal Fitness. Available: http://www.inch-aweigh.com/dietstats.htm [2003, March 15].

21. Kratina, K., King, N. L., & Hayes, D. (2002). *Moving away from diets.* Lake Dallas, TX: Helm Publishing, p. viii.

22. Stunkard, A. J., Harris, J. R., Pedersen, N. L., & McCleam, G. E. (1990). The body mass index of twins who have been reared apart. *The New England Journal of Medicine, 322* (21), 1483–1487.

23. Vogel, W. H. (1999). *The skinny on fat.* New York: W.H. Freeman and Company, pp. 23–24.

24. Waterhouse, D. (1997). *Like mother, like daughter.* New York: Hyperion, pp. 46–47.

25. Omichinski, L. (1993). *You count, calories don't.* Winnipeg, Manitoba: Tamos Books, Inc., p. 28.

26. Leibel, R., Rosenbaum, M., & Hirsch, J. (1995). Changes in energy expenditure resulting from altered body weight. *The New England Journal of Medicine, 332* (10), pp. 621–628.

27. Gaesser, G. (2002). *Big fat lies: The truth about your weight and your health.* Carlsbad, CA: Gurze Books, p. 33.

28. Gubernick, L. R. (1995, March). Why dieters aren't biting. *Allure,* p. 189.

29. Van Vynct, V. (1991, November 14). Obesity experts suggest putting end to dieting. *The Chicago Sun-Times,* p. 3.

30. Berg, F. (2000). *Women afraid to eat: Breaking free in today's weight-obsessed world.* Hettinger, ND: Healthy Weight Network, p. 137.

31. Bennett, W., & Gurin, J. (1982). *The dieter's dilemma.* New York: Basic Books, p. 16.

32. Garner, D. M., & Wooley, S. C. (1991). Confronting the failure of behavioral and dietary treatments for obesity. *Clinical Psychology Review, 11,* 733.

33. Gubernick, L. R. (1995, March). Why dieters aren't biting. *Allure,* 189.

34. Gubernick, L. R. (1995, March). Why dieters aren't biting. *Allure,* 189.

35. Fairburn, C. G., & Wilson, T. G. (Eds.). (1993). *Binge eating.* New York: Guilford, pp. 175–176.

36. Polivy, J. (1996). Psychological consequences of food restriction. *Journal of American Dietetics, 96,* 589–592.

37. Lightstone, J. (2000). The binge and diet cycles. [Online]. Psychotherapist.org. Available: www.psychotherapist.org/BingeCycles.htm [2003, February 17].

38. Fairburn, C. G., & Wilson, T. G. (Eds.). (1993). *Binge eating.* New York: Guilford, p. 181.

# CHAPTER 2

# THE THERAPIST TRAP

You've heard it a thousand times at parties, during office conversation, or from your friends. "I'm too fat. I can't eat this. I'm on a diet. I'm being bad today." Chances are your clients voice similar comments.

Therapists, like all members of society, may struggle with their relationship with food and weight. Many years ago, a presenter at an eating disorders conference told a story about a survey she took of therapists during a similar conference. She told the attendees, all mental health professionals, that at the lunch break there would be two lines. The first line contained a selection of lasagna, garlic bread, salad, drinks, and dessert. The second line consisted of salad and a beverage only. The majority of anonymous, written responses revealed these therapists' own concerns with food. Typical comments included, "I want the lasagna but my colleagues would think I'm a pig," and "The lasagna sounds good, but I promised myself I'd be good today." Clearly, many of these therapists struggled with eating issues. Of course, therapists who are comfortable with food and their bodies will still have personal opinions about weight and food. Usually, therapists are trained to look at their own issues and beliefs and put them aside when treating their clients. Unfortunately, this concept has been largely ignored in the area of body size and compulsive eating.

The problem is compounded by the fact that there is so much contradictory information about these topics that can influence the therapists' attitudes in the treatment setting. Almost no literature exists on therapists' attitudes toward clients' weight and related countertransference issues.[1] One exception is two chapters in the book *Eating Problems: A Feminist Psychoanalytic Treatment Model*. Contributing author Susan Gutwill states, "The underpinnings of compulsive eating and body image distortion problems are socially normative and, therefore, easily escape analytic attention. . . . Underlying assumptions about eating and body size thus may be hard to see in their fullest importance and insidiously difficult to question because of their general social acceptance. Even though these aspects may be repressed and unarticulated, both client and therapist experience transferences to these cultural practices and to the discourse about eating and body image."[2]

## Evaluating Therapists' Attitudes

Let's take a look at where you stand on the issue of body size. Consider the following statement and choose your response.

### IT IS BETTER TO BE THIN THAN TO BE FAT

| Strongly Agree | Agree | Neutral | Disagree | Strongly Disagree |
| --- | --- | --- | --- | --- |

There is a good chance that you picked strongly agree or agree as your answer. After all, this attitude reflects the predominant belief in our culture. The statement that it is better to be thin than fat may seem like a fact to you. However, we maintain a different point of view. Our preferred response to the statement is neutral. We do not assume it is better to be thin any more than we assume that it is better to be fat. People naturally come in a variety of shapes and sizes. Large, average, or small people may enjoy physical and mental health, just as it may be compromised in people belonging to each of these groups.

People offer many reasons to support their belief that it is better to be thin than to be fat. As you consider your own views and attitudes, check off the factors that contribute to your beliefs.

__health issues
__easier to fit in the culture
__more attractive
__higher self-esteem

Each of these factors is worthy of consideration. By exploring each topic, you may deepen your awareness of some different ways to think about the meaning of being thin, average, or fat and discover that appearances can be deceiving.

## Health Considerations

Simply by assessing body size, we often assume that the thin person is healthy and the fat person is unhealthy. Kara is a very large woman in her early 40s. She has had a series of health problems, including diabetes. For years doctors have told her that she must lose weight to be healthy. Kara has tried diet after diet but has repeatedly gained back the lost weight. She eventually followed the suggestion of her support group to look for a doctor who would attend to her medical problems without demanding that she change her size. Her new doctor helped her by finding appropriate medications. Kara also consulted a dietician who follows a non-diet philosophy and learned techniques to address her diabetes without feeling deprived. As a result of these actions, Kara is in good health. She recently had a physical and passed with flying colors. She has not lost an ounce of weight.

Anna, on the other hand, has recently lost weight. Although she was never particularly large, she is now slimmer than ever before. People at work compliment her for her weight loss, noting that she must be doing something right. Actually, Anna is dying of cancer.

These examples illustrate how quickly we, as a culture, judge fat and thin. In fact, health reasons are often cited as a major reason to lose weight. Problems such as high blood pressure, high cholesterol, and diabetes are frequently tied to obesity. As this point of view is espoused by the majority in the medical and scientific community with the media serving as the messenger, it would seem hard to dispute the notion that in regard to health issues, it is absolutely better to be thin than fat. But does the research support this assumption? Berg reports, "Currently, U.S. health policy exaggerates the risks of obesity, and ignores or minimizes the risks of under nutrition, disruptive eating, eating disorders and hazardous weight loss. It often repeats the false and misleading media messages that thin people live longer and larger people are unhealthy, that we should enjoy only low fat or no fat food, that most Americans should keep dieting to lose weight."[3]

## THE MEDICALIZATION OF FAT

The obsession with thinness and the belief that a thin body equals a healthy body are relatively recent notions. Prior to the twentieth century, excessive thinness, rather than excessive fatness, was seen as a potentially greater threat to health. In her book *Losing It*, Laura Fraser notes that in the 1870s, when plumpness was in vogue, physicians typically encouraged patients to gain weight. She states, "Two of the most distinguished doctors of the age, George Beard and S. Weir Mitchell, believed that excessive thinness caused American women to succumb to a wide variety of nervous disorders and that a large number of fat cells was absolutely necessary to achieve a balanced personality."[4] During the late nineteenth century, doctors advocated increased weight because a heavier body was seen as a defense against disease. Physicians saw many patients suffering from diseases where thinness appeared to be a major risk factor.

Toward the end of the nineteenth century, insurance companies were seeking to increase profits and to determine which applicants proved a greater risk, thus decreasing revenues. The thinking was that if the insurance industry could identify those variables that were associated with early death, they could charge higher premiums to applicants identified as high risk or refuse to cover them all. Weight was a variable that could be measured cheaply and easily, with data examined over the years to determine the relationship between body weight and mortality. In 1897, the first height/weight chart was introduced. Modifications have occurred over the decades. It is both interesting and important to note that in the initial height/weight charts, a person had to weigh 20 to 30% above the average before his body weight was thought to increase mortality rates. The number of applicants that fell into this group was relatively few, and being overweight was not, at that time, considered to be a public health concern. But, as Gaesser notes, "The weights at which risk supposedly set in would drop and the national hysteria about weight as a health problem would rise accordingly."[5]

During the late 1940s a biologist named Louis Dublin, working with Metropolitan Life Insurance Company, developed the "Ideal Weights" chart, which had an enormous impact on the current belief that thin equals health, and fat is synonymous with disease. Dublin's statistical research claimed a relationship between increased weight and mortality rates. However, there were serious problems with his data and conclusions. First, the people in the study were not representative of the population as a whole. The weights that were used in Dublin's work were a select group of mostly white, wealthy men whose Northern European roots tended toward a tall, lean build. Moreover, these men could afford to buy their own private policies, while men who received insurance through their employer were not included in the sample. However, the data were used to draw conclusions about the entire population, including women and diverse ethnic groups. Because there was no standard method implemented for collecting weights, many men underreported their weight, which meant that men who were actually overweight were in the "normal" category of the data. In addition, weight was reported only once, when the policy was initially purchased. Therefore, any weight fluctuation over the person's life was not included in the data, nor was their weight recorded at the time of death. The fact that there is a natural tendency for people to gain weight with age was never factored into the research. The ideal weights Dublin identified were based on self-reported weights of men in their 20s.

According to Cheri Erdman, a psychologist specializing in the area of size acceptance and self-esteem, "Dublin changed the definition of overweight to 10% above *ideal* (not average) weight, and obesity as 20 to 30% above *ideal*. In one move Dublin reclassified average weight people as over-weight, and slightly over-average weight people as obese — a term that implies an extreme and severe medical condition."[6] Dublin spent his career telling Americans that the greatest risk to their health was being overweight. The medical community jumped on board and promulgated the myth that thinness equals health. In subsequent alterations of the height/weight charts, the weights that were reported to increase mortality rates would decrease, and the population as a whole would be encouraged to reach lower weights through dieting.

The notion latched onto by doctors was that weight gain over one's lifespan was the result of overeating. This belief, in turn, led to the popularization of dieting as the key weapon against public enemy number one: fat. It ignored other factors that would later prove to be important aspects of health. Despite research to the contrary, the notion of fat as unhealthy and dieting as the solution to fat prevails to this day.

## THE EFFECT OF PROMOTING IDEAL WEIGHT

In addition to an increasingly sedentary lifestyle, rising "obesity" rates over the years resulted from the weight charts changing their standards so that more Americans suddenly fall into an "overweight" category. Also, as explained in the previous chapter, dieting tends to increase rather than decrease body weight over the long run. Still, dieting is encouraged and continues to exacerbate the situation. Gaesser refers to a survey in *Prevention Magazine* and states, "97% of the nutritional experts indicated that controlling weight by caloric intake was their highest priority. A decade later nothing has changed. The annual meetings of the American Dietetics Association are dominated by a 'weight loss mentality.'"[7]

The height/weight charts have become sacred, possessing the power to render a person healthy or unhealthy all from a single range that has become a pronouncement of sorts. Such thinking encourages us to believe that a simple number on a scale is sufficient information to determine who is healthy and who is not. Yet, that weight tells us nothing about the person's level of fitness or dietary habits. Is it possible that a man who meets the "ideal" weight drinks six cups of coffee per day, eats predominately at fast food chains, with few, if any, fresh food, and lives a sedentary lifestyle? What about his wife in the "overweight" category, who enjoys a high level of physical activity and a wide range of food including adequate amounts of fruits, vegetables and grains? What about the weight of a woman who falls in the "ideal" category, living in a state of semi-starvation, with a daily dose of diet pills, in order to maintain what is for her, an artificially low body weight?

In *Women Afraid To Eat*, Berg writes,

> The official policy view is that all large people can and should lose weight. Health and medical professionals who promote this view assume that any excess weight over a narrow "ideal" is unhealthy, dangerous and expensive. They believe that weight loss is always desirable and healthy for persons over this ideal, no matter how it is accomplished, and that all large persons can successfully lose at least 10–15 percent of their weight and maintain it. These assumptions are not supported by research.[8]

Where does that "ideal" stand today? The current U.S. government guidelines for body mass index (BMI) are as follows:

BMI under 18.5 = underweight
BMI of 18.5–24.9 = normal
BMI of 25.0–29.9 = overweight
BMI of 30.0 and up = obese

BMI is calculated by multiplying weight in pounds by 703 and dividing the result by the square of height in inches. These definitions place 55% of American adults, or 97 million people, into the overweight and obese categories. The U.S. Centers for Disease Control and Prevention estimates that 61% of Americans are overweight and 26% are considered obese using these standards. Many in the medical and scientific community, as well as the media, have exaggerated the risks of being moderately overweight, as defined by such changeable guidelines. The diets encouraged as a solution to the supposed sequela of being overweight are more risky than the pounds people carry.

## RECONSIDERING OBESITY RESEARCH

Obesity experts have highlighted a host of diseases that are more common in the obese population, and have made the assumption that obesity *causes* these health problems. Jeanine Cogan, a social psychologist, and Paul Ernsberger, an associate professor of nutrition, medicine, pharmacology, and neuroscience at Case Western Reserve, reflect on this reasoning. They state a "common misperception in the area of obesity, health and dieting is that obesity directly causes disability and death and should be considered a disease itself. . . . Currently there are no data from controlled trials showing that weight loss reduces disease or extends life expectancy. . . . Indeed, such trials are impossible owing to a lack of effective treatments."[9]

While obesity may be considered a risk factor for some health problems, it is not itself a disease. In fact, research reveals that any increased risk associated with being fat decreases with age. This is the opposite of what one would expect if obesity were a degenerative disease.[10] Moreover, research suggests that weight gain over time may be normal and healthy. For example, by the time a woman reaches her 60s, a BMI of 27.3 (considered to be overweight) is associated with the lowest mortality rate. As will be explored in chapter 8, research that supports the thin as healthy/fat as unhealthy bias is overreported, while the consistent and expanding research refuting this notion is typically underreported.

Current studies show that obesity is unrelated to the presence of atherosclerosis (clogged arteries) or to the progression of this disease overtime. In addition, body fat, depending on its location, can be beneficial. For example, fat on the thighs and hips has been associated with a lower risk of cardiovascular disease and possibly type 2 diabetes, especially in women.[11] In addition, obesity is a poor predictor of high blood pressure; typically over 85% of the variation in blood pressure within the population is found to have nothing to do with body fat. Obesity is also a poor predictor of high cholesterol and hyperlipidemia (high blood fats).[12] Obesity has been associated with a lower incidence of stomach and colon cancer, chronic bronchitis, tuberculosis, mitral valve prolapse, anemia, type 1 diabetes, premature menopause, and osteoporosis. Furthermore, obesity is associated with improved survival in a variety of diseases.[13]

According to Paul Ernsberger, "Osteoarthritis is the only disease that has been proven to be directly caused by high body weight. It should be noted, however, that thin persons are not exempt from osteoarthritis."[14] Thin people are at greater risk for osteoporosis, a bone wasting disease that affects 20 to 25 million Americans, mostly middle-age women. Physicians often encourage patients to lose weight due to supposed health risks. The reverse is less common. How many people have been advised by their doctors to gain weight, thereby reducing their risk of osteoporosis?

Many clients struggling with compulsive eating have reported that at a young age, their doctors advised them to lose

5 or 10 pounds because their weight fell into a higher range than the height/weight charts advocated. This directive began a cycle of dieting and binge eating behavior that eventually contributed to increased weight and decreased self-esteem. Conversely, some clients who are diagnosed with anorexia nervosa have commented that they were struggling with their eating disorder for years without any comment from their physician. In the eyes of culture, including physicians and medical personnel, these girls represented the culturally sanctioned ideal; namely, they were growing taller and thinner. Gaesser echoes this bias, stating: "Our belief that 'thinner is better' often has nothing to do with health, even when it is a member of the health establishment itself who is promoting it."[15]

## THE RELATIONSHIP BETWEEN WEIGHT AND MORTALITY

For the population as a whole, is it more dangerous to be overweight or underweight? Most studies have shown a U-shaped relationship, with both extremes of the tail ends putting the person at risk. Ernsberger and his colleagues offer several examples. A Finnish Study looked at women ages 25 to 64 and found both the leanest one fifth and the fattest one fifth of the population were most at risk. In the Ontario Longitudinal Study of aging, mortality was found to be highest in underweight men with a BMI less than 20, and lowest in the overweight group with a BMI of 25 to 30. In this study, the most obese men had a lower mortality rate than those in the underweight group. In Italy, the groups with the lowest mortality rate were women with a BMI of 32 and men with a BMI of 29.[16] A Norwegian study followed 1.8 million people for 10 years. The results revealed that those in the underweight category (BMI equal to or less than 18) had the highest risk of death, and women with a BMI greater than 40, the morbidly obese group, faired better than those in the lowest weight category.[17]

Ernsberger and Koletsky, in their review of many long-term studies finding a U-shaped risk pattern, report, "The consistent pattern appears to be that individuals in the lowest weight category are at greatest risk, those in the highest weight category are also at risk, and those at average to slightly above were at least risk in terms of mortality."[18] Moreover, research has shown that a weight gain program for the extra lean in the population may decrease their risk of early death. On the other hand, dieters are eight times more likely to develop an eating disorder and risk becoming yo-yo dieters, both conditions with serious physical consequences.[19]

The current guidelines that define normal weight as a BMI of 18.5 to 24.9, with anything over that range a risk, appear not to be borne out in the research. Nor does it take into account the individual's set point or set point range, marking that person's *natural* weight rather than the medically and culturally determined ideal. At any given time, 40 to 70% of the U.S. population is trying to lose weight in pursuit of health. But the reverse appears to be the outcome, especially when dieting is used in the quest to achieve slenderness.[20]

In 1992, the NIH reported that weight loss is associated with an increased risk of death, rather than increased longevity, as had originally been hypothesized. In an 18-year follow-up from The Framingham Heart Study, the largest running epidemiological study in the United States, men and women who lost weight throughout the 10-year period had the highest death rate. Dr. Reuben Andres, clinical director of the National Institute of Aging, reviewed 10 studies examining the relationship between dieting and mortality. The results showed that weight loss is associated with an increase in mortality rate.[21] In fact, in *The New England Journal of Medicine* (1998) doctors Marcia Angell and Jerome Kassirer stated, "Until we have better data about the risks of being overweight and the benefits and risks of trying to lose weight, we should remember that the cure for obesity may be worse than the condition."[22]

## FITNESS IS KEY

Steven Blair, director of research at the Cooper Institute for Aerobic Research in Dallas, has challenged previous studies that have pegged obesity itself as a killer. He states, "It has become abundantly clear to me that in terms of health and longevity, your fitness level is far more important than your weight. If the height/weight charts say you are 5 pounds too heavy or even 50 or more pounds too heavy, it is of little consequence health wise — as long as you are physically fit."[23] Blair explains that the health risks commonly associated with obesity are similar to those associated with a sedentary lifestyle and a nutritionally inadequate diet. To support this notion, he cites the fact that health problems commonly associated with obesity, such as hypertension, diabetes, and blood lipid disorders, can be controlled without weight loss.

Blair followed 26,000 men and more than 8,000 women between the ages of 20 and 90 for a 10-year period. Subjects were admitted to the study if their health passed a variety of diagnostic tests. Fitness level was measured by a standard stress test — how long people could walk on a treadmill at increasing intensity levels. What Blair discovered was that obese-fit men and lean-fit men both had low death rates, and that the obese-fit men had death rates half that of lean-unfit men. Lean-unfit men, with a BMI of 25 or less, had twice the risk of mortality from all causes compared to fit men with a BMI of 27.8 or greater. The research supports the idea that fitness is more important than body weight in terms of longevity and disease for both men and women. Blair maintains that 30 minutes of moderate, daily walking (3 to 4 MPH) would make most fat people fit. In a meeting with the Association for the Study of Obesity in London, he declared, "There is a misdirected obsession with weight and weight loss, the focus is all wrong. It's fitness that is the key."[24]

Numerous studies show an inadequate diet and sedentary lifestyle adversely affect health for people of all body sizes, not just those who are fat. Because of fat prejudice in our society, heavier people are often uncomfortable joining a gym or taking an exercise class, thereby missing out on fitness opportunities. According to Blair's research, being fit offers health benefits whether or not weight is lost. Moreover, his research highlights the deleterious effects of dieting. He found that men risk heart disease, hypertension, and diabetes by "always" dieting. In a sample of 12,025 men with a mean age of 67 years, those who said they were always dieting had a 23.2% rate of heart disease compared to 10.6% for men who never dieted, regardless of initial weight. Rates of hypertension and diabetes were higher for the men who were always dieting versus men who never dieted.[25]

## WEIGHT CYCLING

Despite evidence that dieting is associated with health risks, Berg notes that the "traditional paradigm 'control model' holds that all bodies should be at an 'ideal' weight, and large people must lose weight to be healthy, even though they cannot do this in a healthy, lasting way."[26] Indeed, many strategies for weight loss include very low-calorie diets, liquid fasts, and diet drugs, all of which have proven to be unsafe, resulting in dire physical consequences, including death. It is important to note that fat men and women are likely to have tried the most severe diets, including fasting and diet drugs. The extreme measures taken to lose weight, rather than the weight itself, can result in serious medical problems, even death.

As discussed in the previous chapter, the majority of dieters regain the lost weight, plus some. The most common response to this outcome is to begin yet another weight loss plan, moving the dieter into a weight cycling paradigm. Along with the emotional toll of losing and regaining weight are the physical risks associated with yo-yo dieting. Gaesser notes that the vast majority of dieters in the United States whose weights fluctuate considerably throughout their adult lives have a risk of cardiovascular diseases and type 2 diabetes that is up to twice that of overweight people who remain fat.[27] In the Framingham Heart Study, a 32-year analysis of weight fluctuations in 3,130 men and women revealed that those with high weight variability, many weight changes, or large changes were 25 to 100% more likely to be victims of heart disease and premature death. These risks were evident in all individuals regardless of whether they were initially thin or fat and held true regardless of physical activity, smoking, and other health risks.[28]

These findings are consistent with the fact that in populations that accept body fat as normal, or more readily tolerate it, obesity is not a risk factor for higher mortality rates.[29] While the public is often warned of the dangers of "excess" pounds, research increasingly points to the dangers of dieting and weight cycling, rather than a particular body weight. Of course, it is those in the heavier BMI range that continue to be encouraged to lose weight, and who subsequently run an increased risk for physical complications as a result.

Ernsberger and Cogan state that "research has consistently shown that weight loss programs do not have long-term positive outcomes. Continued participation in weight loss programs is associated with repeated weight loss and regain. This may cause problems, as weight fluctuation is associated with increased mortality and cardiovascular disease. Additionally, chronic restrictive dieting is a significant risk factor for the development of binge eating behavior and eating disorders."[30] Studies show that it is possible to significantly improve diabetes, hypertension, and elevated blood fats while remaining in the overweight or obese range. The alarming message that obesity is a killer is an unsubstantiated hypothesis, not a fact. Gaesser explains that no published report of the alleged annual death toll attributed to obesity has satisfactorily eliminated the possibility that higher death rates are the result of physical inactivity, low fitness levels, poor diet, risky weight-loss practices, less than adequate health care, or weight cycling. The myth that dieting is a healthy method of decreasing weight and that being thin will translate into optimal health must be challenged.[31]

## REASSESSING WEIGHT LOSS FOR HEALTH

Canadian dietician Linda Omichinski, founder of the non-diet program HUGS, poses five important questions. She asks:

1. If there is no proven method of achieving weight loss, then why do we continue to prescribe it?

2. Are many of the health problems associated with obesity the result of repeated attempts at weight loss?

3. Is it ethical for us to assist clients in another attempt at weight loss only to set them up for failure as the inevitable weight gain returns?

4. For the 2–5% who maintain the weight loss, are they constantly preoccupied with food and weight? Are they undereating and/or overexercising to maintain this artificial lower weight?

5. If losing and regaining weight is more harmful than stabilizing at a higher weight, why do we continue to focus on weight as a measure of success?[32]

## Easier to Fit in

The next assumption on our list includes the idea that being thin makes it easier to fit into our culture. We cannot argue with the idea that thin people have a much easier time in our society. Yet the reality is that genetically, people come in a variety of shapes and sizes.

### WEIGHT PREJUDICE

Imagine your child comes home from school one day saying, "Mommy, the kids were making fun of me because I'm Jewish. What should I do?" "That's easy," you respond. "We'll convert." Sound absurd? It is always easier to become like the mainstream group, yet Jews, African Americans, Hispanics, and numerous other minority groups have sought to preserve and, ultimately, celebrate their differences. While a Jewish person could choose to convert to Christianity, a person who is African American cannot simply choose to become white; while it may be "easier," it is basically impossible. The problem for the fat person is the culturally pervasive belief that it is possible for anyone to become thin, if only the willpower is there.

The following question must be raised: Should we attempt to change the size of a person exemplifying a subjectively less desirable shape, or should we attempt to change the cultural attitude that translates into the condoned behavior of discriminating against people of a certain body size?

Weightism, or fat oppression, is one of the last socially sanctioned prejudices of our time. Fat people are teased, shunned, denied jobs, and subjected to various forms of abuse in our culture. According to Charisse Goodman, author of *The Invisible Woman*, "Weight prejudice is a true form of bigotry in every sense of the word. Like racism, it is based on visible cues, i.e., the fat person is discriminated against primarily because of the way she looks."[33] Not many people would choose to be fat over being thin in this day and age. But therein lies the point. This current ideal of slenderness is culturally subjective and changeable over time. As Goodman quotes, "Every society has promoted a certain ideal of beauty over all others. What that ideal is is unimportant, for any ideal leaves the majority out. Ideals, by definition, are modeled on rare qualities. . . . [I]f and when, by artificial methods, the majority can squeeze into the ideal, the ideal changes. If it were attainable, what good would it be?"[34]

### FASHIONABLY THIN

Fashion models today are thinner than 98% of the women they parade in front of, contributing to 80% of American women reporting that they feel dissatisfied with their bodies.[35] The tall, thin ideal of today represents only 3 to 5% of the population, yet millions of people try each day to manipulate their bodies into the tail end of the bell-shaped curve.

This wasn't always the case. During most of the nineteenth century, fat was in. In this land of opportunity, plumpness exemplified wealth, status, and superiority. Laura Fraser notes, "Women were sexy if they were heavy. In those days, Americans knew that a layer of fat was a sign that you could afford to eat well."[36] Fat held status. As the agricultural economy shifted to an industrial one, the ideal body image was thrown a curve. Of the late 1800s Fraser writes,

A huge influx of immigrants — many of them genetically shorter and rounder than the earlier American settlers — fueled the industrial machine. . . . Food became more accessible and convenient to all but the poorest families. People who once had too little to eat now had plenty. . . . When it became possible for people of modest means to become plump, fat no longer was a sign of prestige. Well-to-do Americans of Northern European extraction wanted to be able to distinguish themselves physically and racially from stockier immigrants. *The status symbol flipped: it became chic to be thin, and all too ordinary to become overweight.*" (our italics)[37]

As a nation obsessed with thinness, this ideal body type has been celebrated as a means to affirm one's value and success. Conversely, fat has become equivalent to the notion of failure. Our society views fat people as exhibiting a loss of control and tends to attribute a host of negative characteristics to the larger person based solely on his or her body size. Studies over a 20-year period have found that Americans view fat people as "unattractive . . . aesthetically displeasing . . . morally and emotionally impaired . . . alienated from their sexuality . . . and discontent with themselves."[38]

## THE BIRTH OF BIAS AGAINST FAT

Children are not born into this world believing that thin is better than fat. Think about a small child curled up in the lap of her soft, plump mother. She loves the squishiness of her mother's body and finds her to be beautiful. She is content and in love. When she becomes older, however, she may hear her mother complain that she is "too fat" as she views her reflection in the mirror. The female characters on the television screen are thin; the few fat people in the shows are often teased about their shape. The programs are interrupted with commercials for weight loss centers and diet products. The "before" picture for the advertisement is a fat woman claiming she was depressed until embarking on a weight loss plan and now, newly slim, she is also newly happy and newly successful in every aspect of her life. Tall, thin models sell viewers cars, perfume, vacation packages, and high fashion. Our previously neutral child now learns that it is better to be thin than fat. And she learns it early in life.

Fat prejudice and stigmatization have been seen in children as young as 6 years of age. In one study, young girls and boys described silhouettes of an overweight child as "lazy, dirty, stupid, ugly, cheats and lies." When these 6-year-olds were shown drawings of a child of normal weight, an overweight child, and children with various disabilities, including facial disfigurement and missing hands, children rated the overweight child as the least likeable. These responses were seen from all children, regardless of being thin, average, or overweight them- selves.[39] In a replication of this study 40 years later, the strongest bias was once again directed toward the fat child. This preju- dice was more pronounced than in the original study.[40]

This bias favoring thinness and abhorring fatness contin- ues throughout childhood and beyond in a profound way. According to The Council on Size and Weight Discrimination, young girls are more afraid of becoming fat than they are of nuclear war, cancer, or losing their parents.[41] In her film *Slim Hopes*, reknowned lecturer Jean Kilbourne reported that when a group of girls age 11 to 17 were asked what they would wish for if they were to be given three magical wishes, almost all of these young females' first wish was to lose weight and keep it off. When a group of middle-aged women were asked what they would most want to change about their lives, ap- proximately half of the respondents said they would lose weight.[42] What would these girls and women be thinking about and hoping for in their lives if they weren't preoccu- pied with weight? What if the female body wasn't seen as an object of endless manipulation in an attempt to meet an ex- ternal ideal? How would life change if the female body was honored for what it is, rather than for what it could sell?

In their book *It's Not About Food*, Carol Normandi and Laurelee Roark write,

> There was a time when women's bodies were not treated like objects but were honored by their spiritual proper- ties . . . the miraculous ability to give birth and nurture new life. . . . But over time this connection has been lost and repressed. . . . Goddess images with all different body types

have been found; for example the earth mother of Laussel with huge breasts and belly honoring the sacred female, the vegetation goddess with small breasts and large thighs representing the fertility of the earth, the goddess of Mesopotamia who offers her breasts as a sacred gesture honoring the milk of life, and the tall, thin bird-faced goddess with her arms raised high, bringing the life-giving energy of the sun to the earth."[43]

A range of female body shapes celebrate life, renewal, and growth.

## THE CONSEQUENCES OF FAT PREJUDICE

But this is not what we teach our children, nor what we tell ourselves. And the result? The National Eating Disorder Association reports that 42% of elementary school students between the first and third grades want to be thinner, and 80% of 10-year-old children are afraid of being fat. Of 9- and 10-year-old girls, 51% feel better about themselves if they are on a diet, and 80% of all girls have been on a diet by the time they reached the fourth grade. According to Anorexia Nervosa and Associated Disorders (ANAD), 11% of high school students have been diagnosed with an eating disorder. One study found that over half of the females between the ages of 18 and 25 would prefer to be run over by a truck than be fat, and two thirds surveyed would rather be mean or stupid than fat.[44] Moreover, 2 out of 5 women and 1 out of 5 men would trade 3 to 5 years of their lives to achieve their goal body weights. Gaesser reports that fat people are routinely described as "ugly, disgusting, sloppy and gross" and characterized as "weak-willed, self-indulgent, lacking in self-respect, and emotionally disturbed."[45]

Mental health-care professionals often share these feelings. In *Love's Executioner and Other Tales of Psychotherapy*, psychiatrist Irvin Yalom acknowledges this prejudice in his chapter titled "The Fat Lady." "I have always been repulsed by fat women. I find them disgusting: their absurd sideways waddle, their absence of body contour — breasts, laps, buttocks, shoulders, jaw lines, cheekbones, *everything*, everything

I like to see in a woman, obscured in an avalanche of flesh. . . . How dare they impose that body on the rest of us?"[46] Charisse Goodman makes an important point about the skewed process of fat prejudice and size bias. She states, "One of the most curious contradictions of weight obsession is that if a woman succumbs to it and keeps her weight unnaturally low by even the most desperate means, she is popularly considered in our culture to be an attractive person who 'cares about herself,' even if she risks her health in the process. On the other hand, a heavy woman who shuns this mania and refuses to waste her life fixated on her figure is characterized as unattractive and lacking in self regard."[47]

In the context of our cultural climate, it is hard to find many fat men and women who accept their size. The socially sanctioned fat prejudices, along with the belief that willpower and dieting can permanently alter body weight, make living fat in this culture a difficult prospect indeed. Furthermore, these prejudices are institutionalized within our culture. Fat people are less likely to be admitted to elite colleges, are less likely to be hired for a job, make less money when they are hired, and are less likely to be promoted. With few exceptions, there is no state legislation to protect against employment discrimination because of size. The diet industry encourages weight prejudice in the workplace because it turns a nice profit. Goodman cites a 1992 letter sent out by a national weight loss program advertising their At Work Program: "Absenteeism, poor job performance, low productivity, depressed morale, these are just some of the potential consequences of having overweight employees."[48] This blatant misinformation promotes the myth that people of a larger size are lacking in physical and emotional health.

The prejudice extends from the workplace to other areas of life. Fat people have told researchers that strangers accost them on the street and admonish them to lose weight, and that many doctors find fat people disgusting and refuse to treat them. Dr. Esther Rothblum, a psychologist at the University of Vermont, researched the consequences of being fat. She found that 90% of fat men and women reported that friends or relatives had ridiculed them about their weight, and three fourths stated that colleagues had laughed at them because of their size. One quarter of fat men and 16% of fat women said that they had been hit or threatened because they are large.[49]

In another study, college students rated fat people last as marriage partners, after embezzlers, cocaine users, shoplifters, and blind people.[50] A 1984 *Glamour* survey reported that a majority of respondents said that they would be willing to give up a spouse, career, and money to achieve an ideal body.[51] And it gets worse. In 1990, *Newsweek* reported a study that found 11% of parents polled admitted they would have an abortion if the child they carried were predisposed to obesity.[52] Given the social and economic discrimination against people of size, is it any wonder that most fat people want to lose weight and fear life as a fat person?

## CHALLENGING THE FEAR OF FAT

The fear of fat is culturally induced. As a society, we have created this thin/fat bias. This is merely a cultural decision, a subjective view. It is easier to fit into this culture when you are thin simply because we have decided to celebrate this particular body type at this particular time. There is nothing inherent in a body type that makes one size better than another. It is, rather, the collective decision to exalt one ideal over all other variations and sanction the discrimination against others based on body size.

The purveyors of fat prejudice need to become conscious of their attitudes, which are ingrained into the cultural fabric, in order to challenge and change their beliefs and behaviors. It is the prejudicial attitudes that must be altered, not the individual bodies that are the targets of discrimination. Recognizing that people come in different shapes and sizes, and passing that message on to our children, is a step toward changing the culture. Just as other groups have become accepted and integrated into our society, it is time to develop a climate of size acceptance in which large people are welcomed fully and equally in society.

As therapists, we must acknowledge that weight oppression, fueled by ignorance, is one of the last acceptable prejudices in our society. We can help our clients challenge aspects of the culture that reinforce these prejudices. For example, jokes and comments are often made about fat people that could never openly be made about other groups. Your client may come to understand that rather than internalizing these remarks, which usually lead to feelings of shame, she can reject them. She can begin to challenge overt and covert messages that tell her she must be thin to be acceptable. This option is empowering and leads to improved emotional well-being.

Most importantly, as therapists we can stop participating in the cultural dictates that demand thinness as a prerequisite for mental health. Our psychological training promotes concepts of diversity and enhances our ability to treat and respect people with different backgrounds, abilities, and needs. We like the term *size diversity* to describe an attitude toward weight that contains no judgments and assumptions. Rather, size diversity connotes the idea that people come in all shapes and sizes, and that one size is not intrinsically better than another. As therapists, we can be on the forefront of embracing the concept of size diversity for our clients and for ourselves.

## Attractiveness

The lesson taught to most people from a very early age is that the attractive person is the successful person. Images throughout the media tell us both implicitly and explicitly that it is the attractive woman who will find love and happiness. Today, the attractive woman is the thin woman. If thinness equals attractiveness, and attractiveness paves the road to success, who would want to be fat? A girl living in Nigeria would.

### CROSS-CULTURAL PERSPECTIVES

Margaret Bassey Ene has one mission in life, gaining weight. The Nigerian teenager has spent every day since June in a "fattening room" set aside in her father's mud-and-thatch house. Most of her waking hours are spent eating bowl after bowl of rice, yams, plantains, beans and "gari," a porridge-like mixture of dried cassava and water. After 2 months of starchy diet and forced inactivity, Margaret will be ready to reenter society bearing the traditional mark of female beauty among her Efik people: fat. In contrast to many western cultures where thin is in, many culture-conscious people in the Efik and other communities in Nigeria's Southeastern Eastern Cross River State, hail a women's rotundity as a sign of good health, prosperity and allure.[53]

Cross-cultural differences point toward the subjective nature of beauty images as well as the changeable nature of those ideals. Dr. Ann Becker and her colleagues at Harvard University studied the population of Fiji, where food is plentiful and rounded figures are admired. In 1995, just after television was introduced, 3% of Fijian girls vomited to control their weight, and 13% scored in the high-risk group for disordered eating. Thirty-eight months later, 15% of the girls reported vomiting to control their weight, and 29% scored in the high-risk group for disordered eating. Moreover, 74% of Fiji teens surveyed said they felt "too big or too fat" some of the time, and two thirds reported dieting in the past month.[54] Exposure to the Western view of the ideal, thin body encouraged a rise in body dissatisfaction and in behaviors aimed at more closely approximating that image. The Fijians have named this disease *macake*, a desire to "go thin."

In the Western world where food is abundant, weight loss programs and diet products are commonplace, but this is not so in developing countries. In countries in Southeast Asia such as Nepal, products such as diet soda are found only in hotels catering to Western tourists. In a country where poverty is the norm, the idea of purposely decreasing caloric intake for appearance sake is ludicrous.

## A HISTORICAL PERSPECTIVE

Take an afternoon to wander through an art museum. The female body is portrayed in a variety of ways that honor her lushness, spirit, and form. Artists such as Rubens and Renoir glorify the round, abundant woman. On your way home from the museum, take time to notice the billboards dotting the highways, the advertisements on the buses rushing by. The female image exalted today is an ultrathin physique. That ideal is ingrained to such an extent in our collective psyche that the preference of thinness over fatness goes unchallenged. Yet it is merely a subjective, cultural decision. Within our own culture, the ideal body has changed over time. The popular axiom that the personal is political and the political is personal is exemplified in the increasing number of people struggling with some form of an eating disorder. Societal messages about the ideal body type are dictated by the political, economic, and social climate of the period. The manifestation of these forces is often played out in a personal struggle with the body. Each struggle, in turn, speaks to the politics of body size.

During the late 1800s, a full, fleshy body was a sign of prosperity, health, and success. Thinness was equated with poor health and a nervous temperament. A framed poster in an antique shop from the turn of the century asks, "Are you too thin?" The advertiser, Susanna Cocroft, states, "You can be round, plump, wholesome, rested and attractive. Nature intended you to be — why should you not?" One satisfied pupil declares, "Just think Miss Cocroft, I have gained 25 pounds."

The plump Victorian ideal of the late nineteenth century served as a reflection of women's traditional role as housewife and mother, bound and dependent on her husband. Her full body, highlighted in her breasts and hips, was accented by the corset that cinched in her midsection. This body type was valued as a sign that her husband had achieved financial success and could amply provide for his wife and family. The popularization of corsets during this era encouraged women on both the physical and metaphorical levels to be constricted in movement and tied to hearth and home. Corsets damaged the lungs, liver, intestines, bladder, and stomach. Like Chinese foot binding, the physical mutilation ensured that women remained passive and unable to move freely. This Victorian image, exemplified by the actress Lillian Russell, began to change just prior to World War I. Thinness and dieting started to become a female preoccupation during the suffragette movement in the 1920s when women received the right to vote. The flapper look became popular by emphasizing a thin, boyish body with bound breasts. As women were gaining political equality, the ideal woman's body became more male-like.

During the Depression and World War II, when threats of food shortages occupied Americans, a fuller figure was once again acceptable. In the 1950s Marilyn Monroe, who would be considered fat by today's standards, was the famous sex symbol. Naomi Wolf, author of *The Beauty Myth*, states, "During the repressive 1950s, women's natural fullness could be briefly enjoyed once more because their minds were occupied in domestic seclusion. But when women came en masse into male spheres, that pleasure had to be overridden by an urgent social expedient that would make women's bodies into the prisons that their homes no longer were."[55]

In 1965, Twiggy made her debut in *Vogue* during a time when women were increasingly gaining economic and political power. Wolf describes how *Vogue* introduced the new model: "Twiggy is called Twiggy because she looks as though a strong gale would snap her in two and dash her to the ground."[56] The ultrathin ideal encouraged women to take up less space in the world rather than more, to be weak rather than powerful, and to be concerned about the minutia of their bodies. Instead of fostering bonds of sisterhood in the fight for women's equality, the new ideal body encouraged competition between women and an obsession with being thin as the marks of true success.

In the 1970s, the thin ideal merged with increasing numbers of women in the workforce, and the androgynous, dress-for-success look was popularized. The notion was if women were going to enter the world of men, then they'd best look male. By the 1980s, Elle McPherson typified the strong, lean look. Women were to be thin, yet also muscular and athletic, an imitation of the male physique. In the 1990s, Kate Moss popularized the emaciated "heroin chic" look. The "mature" female ideal looked like a prepubescent boy. Though women were more fully integrated in the world both economically and politically, the cultural discomfort with powerful women led to a backlash, a glorification of weakness and passivity. The dictates of an ultrathin ideal spurred the eating disorder epidemic and fueled the body hatred and food and weight obsessions of today. The questions played out on the body are typically struggles with power, control, identity, and one's place in the world. Yet women are encouraged to focus on their bodies as the place for implementing change, rather than upon society at large, which continues to place women in a subordinate role. They are taught to count calories rather than count themselves.

In September 2002, Twiggy returned to the runway and, 30 years after her initial fame, commented that compared to the new generation of models, she feels short (5'6") and fat (116 pounds), having gained 20 pounds in the interim. Will the comparisons and relentless drive to attain an elusive ideal ever end? The fashionable body is ever-changing. Unlike the hemline of a skirt, which changes, as fashions will, the body is not easily altered. The personal struggle of a client needs to be addressed, but that struggle is part of a broader context that must not be ignored. Fraser notes, "As a society, we have yet to develop an image of femininity that conveys women's real power. . . . [W]e have yet to acknowledge how different women's bodies are from men's and how diverse we all are, size wise, from each other."[57]

## A MALE PERSPECTIVE

Traditionally, men and their bodies have not been a cultural focus. Men's identity was typically defined through career and financial success. However, in recent years, with the roles of men and women increasingly overlapping, the tide has turned. Body-building magazines, along with an increase in male fashion magazines that include articles on body sculpting, have created a new generation of males experiencing body dissatisfaction. The message is for men to take up more space in the world, with an emphasis on a lean and muscular body. The implicit message is a commitment to male power and dominance. Joni Johnston, author of *Appearance Obsession*, notes, "Advertisements and men's fashion magazines have changed in style, both to accommodate and emphasize changes in men's physique toward a more trim and muscular body. The newest window dummies are 6'2" tall, have 42-inch chests and need a size 42. Compare these measurements to the old industry standard of a 38 regular."[58] Moreover, diet programs are increasingly targeting men and using famous sports figures as spokespersons. While fewer males than females develop eating disorders, boys and men spend millions of dollars a year on the black market on steroids in an effort to bulk up, risking serious physical consequences, including death. Men spend still more money on over-the-counter supplements purporting to enhance muscle mass and burn fat.

## ADOPTING A NEW PERSPECTIVE

It is not easy for most clients or therapists to quickly dismiss their belief that attractiveness equals thinness. In fact, redefining ideals of beauty and attractiveness is probably the most difficult part of the work we are proposing. Our chapter on body image offers suggestions for working with clients on these issues. The essential step at this point is for you to question your assumption that attractiveness equals thinness, and to understand the subjective nature of one ideal over another.

## Self-Esteem

Clients often seek treatment with a wish to improve their self-esteem. As a therapist, you understand that many factors over a client's lifespan contribute to her self-concept. Factors such as trust, unconditional love, and a sense of control over one's environment are building blocks to a positive sense of self-esteem. Where does body image fit in?

## THE PREVALENCE OF BODY DISSATISFACTION

Each of us carries a mental image of our own self, which may or may not closely approximate our actual appearance. While body image is a psychological phenomenon, it is comprised of physiological and sociological aspects. If your client has a positive body image, one in which she views herself as healthy, strong, and attractive, she will feel better about herself than if she envisions herself unhealthy, weak, and unattractive. In today's cultural climate, it is difficult to emerge with an accurate and affirming sense of body image due to the unrealistic standards of the times.

Consider, for example, the 1984 *Glamour* survey of 33,000 respondents. Of women between the ages of 18 to 35, 75% believed they were fat, while only 25% were medically overweight. Of the underweight women, 45% thought they were too fat. The women surveyed indicated that losing 10 to 15 pounds was more important than success in work or in love, and achieving this weight loss was noted as their most desired goal.[59] In a 1997 body image survey of 4,000 men and women conducted by *Psychology Today*, 89% of the women wanted to lose weight. Is it any wonder, considering the ultrathin ideal to which we are taught to compare ourselves? In a society that emphasizes the external rather than the internal, conforming to subjective standards of appearance holds the elusive notion of acceptance, praise, and success.[60]

We have already discussed the idea that it is easier to be thin in our culture, even though it is not always possible. We believe this for ourselves, and we teach this message to our children. Parents often express great concern about their children's weight. With the best of intentions to help their kids fit into a world where thin is best, a parent of a larger or even average-sized child may make comments meant to encourage their offspring to slim down. Statements such as, "If you don't lose weight, no one will want to date you," or "Do you really think you ought to be eating that dessert? Your stomach looks fat," are familiar to many. Consider the effect of these words, often made repeatedly over an extended time, on a person's self-esteem. These negative comments about weight lead to a poor body image and contribute to a lack of self-esteem. Moreover, such comments about weight and body size often trigger dieting behavior. As diets typically end in failure, this leaves people feeling helpless and hopeless. What was meant as an attempt to improve self-esteem (i.e., losing weight) leaves people feeling worse than before.

## DIETING AND SELF-ESTEEM

Let's explore more fully the effects of dieting on self-esteem. Reducing caloric intake to achieve weight loss is condoned in our culture as a method of self-improvement. Embarking on a diet is commonly seen as an indication that the person is "taking care of herself." In developing countries, the starvation level of food is considered to be less than 1,300 calories per day. Most commercial weight loss plans are really semi-starvation diets. As Laura Fraser notes, "Whether the calories are consumed in milkshakes, prepackaged microwave meals, or precisely measured exchanges of real food, they all add up to 1,000 to 1,200 calories a day. . . . [M]ost semi-starvation diets promise a weight loss of up to 2 pounds a week."[61] Liquid and other low-calorie diets typically provide only 300 to 800 calories per day. In the United States today, many men and women are living on starvation levels of food in order to feel good about themselves. Common goals for weight loss include improved health, appearance, energy level, and chances for relational and occupational success. Is dieting, or self-enforced semi-starvation, able to produce such positive results?

Typically, the effects of calorie restriction have emotional and physical consequences such as depression, fatigue, weakness, irritability, social withdrawal, and reduced sex drive. The potential dieter is already experiencing body dissatisfaction and has been taught to believe that weight loss is the panacea for all good fortune. Berg states, "For a time they [di-eters] are buoyed by a false sense of hope. Then hopes are dashed once again by the inevitable transgressions and weight gain. Their self-esteem drops lower. Yet as one diet fails, another beckons them on again with false hope. It's a downward spiral of negative self-esteem marked by repeated failure, depressed mood, loss of hope, worsened self-image and commonly, an even stronger resolve to begin another, better diet."[62] This process is further complicated by the fact that the dieter tends to attribute her success, as measured by lost pounds, to the diet — but considers her eventual break-ing of the diet and subsequent regaining of pounds as her personal failure. The dieter believes it is her lack of willpower and her own inadequacies that have led her away from her goal weight. She is well on her way to losing self-esteem.

In her book *Why Women Need Chocolate*, Debra Waterhouse notes the physiological consequences of dieting that can lead to emotional consequences. She explains, "Dieting causes brain turbulence. It decreases your brain chemicals and brain sugar supplies, increases your food crav-ings, and depresses your mood."[63] Dieting contributes to decreases in serotonin levels, which are necessary for main-taining a sense of calm and stabilizing mood. The body re-acts to this serotonin depletion by craving carbohydrates, which boosts serotonin levels in the brain. However, the di-eter once again attributes the urge to break her deprivation as a personal failure rather than as a biological response to her restrictions. Omichinski explains that dieting can cause fatigue and insomnia as well as decreased sex drive. This is due to the brain's impulse to conserve energy during times of famine. As a result, dieting can lead to mental and physical depression.[64]

The fact that diets typically fail means that people often lose and gain weight repeatedly. One telephone survey of 2,031 adults found that the more diets women had been on, the more severe were their symptoms of depression.[65] Moreover, research has found that people with weight fluctuations have more emotional problems, and that these findings hold regardless if these people were thin or fat. Recent studies found that adult women who diet frequently, (five or more times per year) were 50% more likely to be depressed, and young women who diet frequently were 62% more likely to be depressed than those who did not diet.[66] Yo-yo dieters also run an increased risk in a range of psychopathology and decreased life satisfaction. Dietary restraints result in people scoring higher on measurements of stress, depression, maladjustment, and neuroticism compared to unrestrained eaters. In addition, laboratory studies have revealed that restrained eaters, or dieters, report feeling more anxious and depressed than non-dieters.[67]

The notion that a diet will lead to increased self-esteem and a happier life is more fantasy than fact. The Keys study, discussed previously, shows evidence that dieting itself creates psychological disturbances. The 36 conscientious objectors who lost approximately 25% of their former body weight in a 6-month period were all psychologically healthy prior to the semi-starvation experiment. As David Garner and Susan Wooley report, "Most experienced dramatic attitudinal, behavioral and emotional changes during weight loss. Most experienced periods of depression, anxiety, irritability, anger, mood swings, transitory for some but protracted for others. Almost 20% experienced extreme emotional deterioration and some had to be hospitalized as a result of debilitating psychological distress. . . . Personality testing confirmed clinical impressions, with some of the men showing dramatic changes in their personality profile after losing as little as ten pounds."[68]

It is important to remember that these men were participants in an experiment and were not seeking weight loss for personal reasons. The dieter who undergoes these emotional changes during the weight loss process must also deal with the depression, anxiety, anger, and self-loathing that accompany the unwanted return of pounds. For example, in a 3-year follow-up study on the treatment of obesity through a very low calorie diet and behavioral therapy, the researchers found that after initial treatment and at the 1-year follow-up, participants reported significantly reduced depression. However, at the 3-year follow-up, there was a reemergence of initial symptoms, and subjects reported that regaining the lost weight had "untoward consequences on their self-esteem, self-confidence, happiness and on other areas of physical and psychological health."[69]

Dieting also impacts the mind. With fewer calories for the body to use, energy level is decreased. The brain is less alert. Studies have shown that people on diets exhibit slower reaction times and are less able to concentrate than people who are not dieting and are consuming adequate caloric levels. Research has shown that short-term diets can have a negative impact on study and work.[70] Remember the commercial weight-loss company's marketing plan that promised companies that their employees would improve performance through their weight loss program? Dieting actually creates some of the problems it purports to solve.

Berg notes that normal, unrestrained eating promotes clear thinking and the ability to concentrate. It promotes mood stability as well as healthy relationships with family, peers, and community. Conversely, dysfunctional eating, including dieting behavior or restrained eating, contributes to decreased mental alertness and ability to concentrate and a narrowing of interests. It may cause greater mood instability, irritability, and anxiety, and contribute to a lowered sense of self-esteem. The dysfunctional eater may become withdrawn, isolated, and disconnected from others.

### NON-DIETING AND SELF-ESTEEM

While dieting negatively impacts a person's emotional life, research is finding that participating in programs that focus on both improving women's body image and teaching natural eating as opposed to restrictive eating is associated with improved eating behaviors and psychological well-being. The emphasis is on weight stability rather than weight change.[71] Other research concurs. For example, in a psychoeducational group that focused on helping large women stop dieting, measures of self-esteem and body image improved. Members in the group normalized eating behaviors without increasing weight or blood pressure.[72]

Challenging the myth that dieting and weight loss increase self-esteem is not only necessary for adult's mental health, but for children's as well. In her book, *Like Mother, Like Daughter,* Debra Waterhouse explores how dieting and body image problems are passed down from generation to generation. Families have the greatest impact on a child's developing self-esteem, and they can begin to break the pattern of teaching messages that reinforce dieting behavior and negative body image. Many clients who are in the process of working on their own body images consciously end their negative self-talk about their bodies in front of their children. They realize that the way they speak in front of their children will have a significant impact on the formation of their sons' and daughters' self-esteem. As they feel ready, these clients try to talk about their bodies in positive ways in order to promote good feelings for themselves and serve as role models for their children.

In our current cultural climate, a large person is likely to face some obstacles because of size that can affect self-esteem. However, the manner in which a person's size is treated by family, teachers, health practitioners, and therapists, as a child or an adult, will go a long way in determining how that person feels about herself. If she is treated with respect based on an acceptance of size diversity, she will feel better about herself; if she is blamed and shamed for her size, she will feel badly. Self-esteem is only related to size because of cultural messages that deem fat to be bad. Without these messages, a large person would be no more or less at risk for a decrease in self-esteem than a thin person.

At the start of the chapter, we asked you to consider the following statement: *It is better to be thin than to be fat.* We hope that you will now understand the reason we chose "neutral" as the best response. Our goal is to challenge the assumptions that form the basis of your point of view. You may also wish to consult some of the many resources available that further explore the issue of body size. As you engage in this process, you will see your clients, and perhaps even yourself, in different ways. This will enable you to listen differently, question differently, and respond differently during the course of therapy. Questioning your assumptions about weight will set the stage for exploring your beliefs about food and helping your clients solve their compulsive eating problems.

# ENDNOTES

1. Elder, J. (2001, August). Anti-fat attitudes and the incidence of restricted eating/dieting among mental health practitioners. Dissertation. Santa Ana, CA: College of Behavioral Sciences, Southern California University for Professional Studies.
2. Bloom. C., Gitter, A., Gutwill, S., Kogel, L., & Zaphiropoulos, L. (1994). *Eating problems: A feminist psychoanalytic treatment model.* New York: Basic Books, p. 147.
3. Berg, F. (2000). *Women afraid to eat: Breaking free in today's weight obsessed world.* Hettinger, ND: Healthy Weight Network, p. 20.
4. Fraser, L. (1997). *Losing it: America's obsession with weight and the industry that feeds on it.* New York: Dutton, p. 19.
5. Gaesser, G. (2002). *Big fat lies: The truth about your weight and your health.* Carlsbad, CA: Gurze Books, p. 40.
6. Erdman, C. K. (1995). *Nothing to lose: A guide to sane living in a larger body.* New York: HarperSanFrancisco, p. 11.
7. Gaesser, G. (2002). *Big fat lies: The truth about your weight and your health.* Carlsbad, CA: Gurze Books, p. 45.
8. Berg, F. (2000). *Women afraid to eat: Breaking free in today's weight-obsessed world.* Hettinger, ND: Healthy Weight Network, p. 24.
9. Cogan, J. C., & Ernsberger, P. (1999). Dieting, weight, and health: Reconceptualizing research and policy. *Journal of Social Issues, 55* (2), 194.
10. Erdman, C. K. (1995). *Nothing to lose: A guide to sane living in a larger body.* New York: HarperSanFrancisco, p. 16.
11. Gaesser, G. (2002). *Big fat lies: The truth about your weight and your health.* Carlsbad, CA: Gurze Books, p. xviii.
12. Gaesser, G. (2002). *Big fat lies: The truth about your weight and your health.* Carlsbad, CA: Gurze Books, p. 59.
13. Ernsberger, P., & Koletsky, R. J. (1999). Biomedical rationale for a wellness approach to obesity: An alternative to a focus on weight loss. *Journal of Social Issues, 55* (2), 236–238.

14. Ernsberger, P., & Koletsky, R. J. (1999). Biomedical rationale for a wellness approach to obesity: An alternative to a focus on weight loss. *Journal of Social Issues*, 231.

15. Gaesser, G. (2002). *Big fat lies: The truth about your weight and your health.* Carlsbad, CA: Gurze, p. xix.

16. Ernsberger, P., & Koletsky, R. (1999). Biomedical rationale for a wellness approach to obesity: An alternative to a focus on weight loss. *Journal of Social Issues, 55* (2), 234–236.

17. Cogan, J. C., & Ernsberger, P. (1999). Dieting, weight, and health: Reconceptualizing research and policy. *Journal of Social Issues, 55* (2), 194–195.

18. Ernsberger, P., & Koletsky, R. (1999). Biomedical rationale for a wellness approach to obesity: An alternative to a focus on weight loss. *Journal of Social Issues, 55* (2), 195.

19. Patton, G. C., et al. (1990). Abnormal eating attitudes in London school girls — prospective study: Outcome at 12-month follow-up. *Psychological Medicine, 20,* 383–394.

20. Cogan, J. C., & Ernsberger, P. (1999). Dieting, weight, and health: Reconceptualizing research and policy. *Journal of Social Issues, 55* (2), 188–189.

21. Berg, F. M. (2000). *Women afraid to eat: Breaking free in today's weight-obsessed world.* Hettinger, ND: Healthy Weight Network, p. 150.

22. Kassirer, J. P., & Angell, M. (1998). Losing weight — An ill-fated new year's resolution. *The New England Journal of Medicine, 338,* 52–54.

23. Gaesser, G. (2000). *Big fat lies: The truth about your weight and your health.* Carlsbad, CA: Gurze Books, pp. xiii–xiv.

24. U.S. scientist: Fat can be healthy. [Online]. (2001, July 18). CNN.com/ HEALTH.Available: http://www.cnn.com/2001/HEALTH/diet.fitness/07/ 18/fat.fit/[2002, October 2].

25. Berg, M. (2000). *Women afraid to eat: Breaking free in today's weight-obsessed world.* Hettinger, ND: Healthy Weight Network, p. 68.

26. Berg, M. (2000). *Women afraid to eat: Breaking free in today's weight-obsessed world.* Hettinger, ND: Healthy Weight Network, p. 22.

27. Gaesser, G. (2002). *Big fat lies: The truth about your weight and your health.* Carlsbad, CA: Gurze Books, pp. xviii–xix.

28. Lissner, L., et al. (1991). Variability of body weight and health outcomes in the Framingham population. *The New England Journal of Medicine, 324,* 1839–1844.

29. Ernsberger, P., & Koletsky, R. J. (1999). A biomedical rationale for a wellness approach to obesity: An alternative to a focus on weight loss. *Journal of Social Issues, 55* (2), 246–247.

30. Cogan, J. C., & Ernsberger, P. (1999). Dieting, weight, and health: Reconceptualizing research and policy. *Journal of Social Issues, 55* (2), 187.

31. Gaesser, G. (2002). *Big fat lies: The truth about your weight and your health*. Carlsbad, CA: Gurze Books, pp. 79–80.
32. Omichinski, L. A paradigm shift from weight loss to healthy living. [Online]. Available: http://www.hugs.com/01facilitator/corp/Milestones/aparadigmshift.htm [2002, October 25].
33. Goodman, C. (1995). *The invisible woman: Confronting weight prejudice in America*. Carlsbad, CA: Gurze Books, p. 7.
34. Firestone, S. (1970). *The dialectic of sex: The case for feminist revolution*. New York: Bantam Books, p. 152.
35. Statistics: Eating disorders and their precursors. [Online]. Respecting and understanding body image. Available: http://www.msu.edu/~rubi/rubistats.html [2002, December 10].
36. Fraser, L. (1997). *Losing it: America's obsession with weight and the industry that feeds on it*. New York: Dutton, p. 16.
37. Fraser, L. (1997). *Losing it: America's obsession with weight and the industry that feeds on it*. New York: Dutton, p. 18.
38. Crandall, C. S. (1994). Prejudice against fat people: Ideology and self-interest. *Journal of Personality and Social Psychology, 66*, 882–894.
39. Stafferi, J. R. (1967). A study of social stereotype of body image in children. *Journal of Personal Social Psychology, 7*, 101.
40. Puhl, R., & Brownell, K. D. (2001). Bias, discrimination, and obesity. *Obesity Research, 9*, 788–805.
41. Normandi, C., & Roark, L. (1998). *It's not about food*. New York: Grosset/Putnam, p. 4.
42. Jhally, S. (Producer and Director), and Kilbourne, J. (1995). *Slim hopes: Advertising and the obsession with thinness*. [Videotape]. Northhampton, MA: Media Education Foundation.
43. Normandi, C., & Roark, L. (1998) *It's not about food*. New York: Grosset/Putnam, p. 69.
44. Eating disorders statistics. [Online]. Alliance for Eating Disorder Awareness. Available: http://www.eatingdisorderinfo.org/eating_disorders_statistics.htm [2003, January 6].
45. Gaesser, G. (2002). *Big fat lies: The truth about your weight and your health*. Carlsbad, CA: Gurze Books, pp. 27–28.
46. Yalom, I. (1989). *Love's executioner and other tales of psychotherapy*. New York: Basic Books, pp. 87–88.
47. Goodman, C. (1995). *The invisible woman*. Carlsbad, CA: Gurze Books, p. 13.
48. Goodman, C. (1995). *The invisible woman*. Carlsbad, CA: Gurze Books, p. 151.
49. Kolata, G. (1992, November). The burdens of being overweight: Mistreatment and misconceptions. *New York Times* [Online] Available: http://www.naafa.org/press_room/burdens.html [2003, January 5].

50. Tiggemann, M., & Rothblum, E. D. (1988). Gender differences in social consequences of perceived overweight in the United States and Australia. *Sex Roles, 18* (1–2), 75–86.

51. Wooley, W., & Wooley, S. (1984, February). Feeling fat in a thin society: 33,000 women tell how they feel about their bodies. *Glamour,* p. 198.

52. Cowley, G. (1990, Winter/Spring). Made to order babies. *Newsweek Special Issue,* p. 98.

53. Simmons, A. M. (1998, October 18). In Nigeria, girls learn that big is beautiful. *The Boston Globe,* p. A20.

54. Goodman, E. (1999, May 27). The culture of thin bites Fiji teens. *The Boston Globe,* A23.

55. Wolf, N. (1991). *The beauty myth: How images of beauty are used against women.* New York: Anchor Books, p. 184.

56. Wolf, N. (1991). *The beauty myth: How images of beauty are used against women.* New York: Anchor Books, p. 184.

57. Fraser, L. (1997) *Losing it: America's obsession with weight and the industry that feeds on it.* Dutton: New York, p. 49.

58. Johnston, J. E. (1994). *Appearance obsession: Learning to love the way you look.* Deerfield Beach, FL: Health Communications, Inc., p. 63.

59. Wooley, W., & Wooley, S. (1984, May). Feeling fat in a thin society: 33,000 women tell how they feel about their bodies. *Glamour,* p. 198.

60. Garner, D. (1997, Jan–Feb). The 1997 body image survey results. *Psychology Today, 30,* 30.

61. Fraser, L. (1997). *Losing it: America's obsession with weight and the industry that feeds on it.* Dutton: New York, p. 146.

62. Berg, F. (2000). *Women afraid to eat: Breaking free in today's weight-obsessed world.* Hettinger, ND: Healthy Weight Network, p. 64.

63. Waterhouse, D. (1995). *Why women need chocolate.* Hyperion: New York, p. 42.

64. Omichinski, L. (2000). *Staying off the diet rollercoaster.* Washington, D.C.: AdviceZone, p. 18.

65. Ross, C. (1994). Overweight and depression. *Journal of Health and Social Behavior, 35,* 63–78.

66. Kenardy, J., Brown, W. J., & Vogt, E. (2001). Dieting and health in young Australian women. *European Eating Disorders Review, 9* (4), 242–254; Patton, G.C. (1997). Adolescent dieting: Healthy weight control or borderline eating disorder? *Journal of Child Psychology and Psychiatry, 38,* 299–306.

67. McFarlane, T., Polivy, J., & McCabe, R. (1999). Help, not harm: Psychological foundation for a nondieting approach toward health. *Journal of Social Issues, 55* (2), 265.

68. Garner, D. M., & Wooley, S. C. (1991). Confronting the failure of behavioral and dietary treatments for obesity. *Clinical Psychology Review, 11,* 757.
69. Wadden, T. A., Stunkard, A. J., & Liebschutz, J. (1988). Three-year follow-up of the treatment of obesity by very low calorie diet, behavior therapy and their combination. *Journal of Consulting and Clinical Psychology, 56,* 925–928.
70. Wilson, T. (1996). Acceptance and change in the treatment of eating disorders and obesity. *Behavior Therapy, 27,* 423.
71. Higgins, L., & Gray, W. (1999). What do anti-dieting programs achieve? A review of research. *Austrian Journal of Nutrition and Dietetics, 56* (3), 128–136.
72. Ciliska, D. (1998). Evaluation of two nondieting interventions for obese women. *Western Journal of Nursing Research, 20,* 119–135.

# CHAPTER 3

# PRINCIPLES OF THE NON-DIET APPROACH

Regardless of the reasons why your client eats compulsively, the first step in the process of ending her overeating requires direct intervention with her symptoms. Common to all human beings is our need to have a relationship with food. Eating is one of our most basic needs, from the moment we arrive in the world until the end of our lives. You may think about food consumption all the time, or you may rarely give it a thought. Regardless of how conscious or unconscious this process is for you, you make decisions about food on a daily basis. Although eating is a pleasurable experience for most people, it is really a physiological process that involves a need and satiation of that need. Consider the following questions:

- Do you know when you are hungry?
- Do you eat when you are hungry?
- Do you ask yourself what you are hungry for?
- Do you do your best to get what you are hungry for?
- Do you stop when you are full/satisfied?

To the extent you answered yes to these questions, you are in tune with your body's natural hunger signals. To the extent that you replied no to these statements, you may be out of touch with your true hunger needs. When a client comes to you to work on compulsive eating, her response will be "no" to these questions as they apply to the majority of her eating.

The non-diet approach to treating compulsive eating helps clients return to a normal relationship with food. These concepts of normal eating address the questions of when to eat, what to eat, and how much to eat. Researchers, dieticians, and therapists who developed these ideas agree that human beings have natural, internal instincts that can reliably direct them in regulating their food choices. Clients who display symptoms of compulsive eating have lost their innate ability to regulate their hunger and satiation. Regardless of whether this lack of attunement comes from years of dieting, the use of food for affect regulation, or both, the first step in the process of curing compulsive eating is for clients to relearn how to accurately listen to and trust their bodies' signals.

Consider for a moment whether you are a "natural" eater who responds most of the time to your internal cues for hunger and satiation. Or, do you make food choices based on other external factors such as what you believe is "good" or "bad" to eat. Like clients, therapists are constantly bombarded with messages from family, health practitioners, and the media about what and how to eat. This information may influence you because of concerns about weight and health. Adjustments to eating that stem from outside sources and still conform to natural hunger signals can enhance physical and emotional well-being. However, if these recommendations, which are often contradictory and change substantially over the years, undermine the connection to your body's needs, the ability to self-regulate diminishes.

The Renfrew Center, a major eating disorder treatment facility, offers a simple checklist to help you reflect more thoroughly on your own attitudes toward eating. This tool can be used with clients to determine their relationship with food.

Yes   No

___  ___   1. Can you eat when you are hungry and quit when you are satisfied?

___  ___   2. Do you stop eating because you *think* you should (as opposed to because your body is satisfied)?

___  ___   3. Do you make food choices based on foods you enjoy?

___  ___   4. Do you become physically uncomfortable (such as weak, tired, dizzy, a headache) when you under-eat or diet?

___  ___   5. Do you feel that your food selections are a combination of "healthy foods" and pleasurable foods?

___  ___   6. Do you *have* to eat in a certain pattern — *always* three meals a day or *always* at a certain time of day?

___  ___   7. Do you trust that if you eat when you are hungry and stop when you are satisfied, you will *not get fat?*

___  ___   8. Do you feel guilty when you eat to the point that you are stuffed and uncomfortable?

___  ___   9. Can you balance the time you give to thoughts about food, weight, and dieting with other important aspects of your life, such as relationships, work, and self-development?

___  ___  10. Do you watch what other people eat to determine what you will eat?

___  ___  11. Can you leave some cookies on the plate because you know you can have some again tomorrow?

___  ___  12. Do you usually pick foods based on their calorie content?

Scoring: Add up all the "no" responses to the **odd-numbered** questions. Give one point for each "no" and put that number here ___

Add up all the "yes" responses to the **even-numbered questions.** Give one point for each "yes" and put that number here___

Total both the above numbers here ___

Interpretation:

**Scores between 0 and 3.** These scores indicate a healthy attitude toward food and eating.

**Scores between 4 and 8**. These scores suggest that cultural pressures about appearance and ideas about how much and what kinds of foods to eat may be negatively affecting self-acceptance and overall happiness. Exploring these issues may be helpful.

**Scores between 9 and 12.** These scores suggest serious issues with food, ranging from food obsession to an eating disorder. These issues could be interfering with daily life and may negatively affect overall health. Professional assistance is recommended to deal with thoughts, feelings, and behaviors related to food and body image. Medical evaluation and intervention may also be needed to address health concerns. (Copyright: The Renfrew Center, 2003. Reprinted with permission.[1])

# A Paradigm for Normal Eating

The notion that people can be trusted to be in charge of their own eating, without outside interference, was first documented by Clara Davis in 1928. A researcher in the area of child development, Davis found that infants displayed an innate ability to regulate their food intake, both in terms of caloric content and nutritional value, when they were allowed to select their own diets over a period of several months. At the same time, however, eating patterns varied greatly from feeding to feeding, so that at times a child "ate like a bird" while at other times she "ate like a horse." Yet all of these children showed good health and growth patterns.[2]

More recently, researcher Leann Birch and her colleagues have demonstrated repeatedly that children are born knowing how to regulate their food intake. One study, which appeared in *The New England Journal of Medicine*, found that while children's caloric intake varied greatly from meal to meal, the daily amount of energy consumption remained relatively consistent over a 24-hour period as children adjusted the amount they ate at successive meals.[3] Another research study found that the more parents tried to control their children's eating behavior through practices such as food rewards, threats, and bribes, the less able these preschoolers were to self-regulate their own food intake. This research suggests that when children are left to their own devices, they are extremely capable of knowing how to eat, but that external influences negatively affect this innate ability. The authors further conclude that parents who are concerned about their own weight and attempt to control their food intake with dieting behavior are more likely to attempt to control their children's eating patterns.[4] The message from this type of research is that human beings have an innate capacity to respond to internal cues for hunger and satiation that can persist if supported by the familial environment, but that can also diminish or disappear when external sources interfere. For the compulsive eater, reconnecting with these natural cues is essential in the process of making peace with food.

Therapists Jane Hirschmann and Carol Munter have written extensively on the process of demand feeding for adults. They borrow a familiar concept that has widespread acceptance regarding the care of infants. Demand feeding for newborns directs that when a baby cries in hunger, the parent or caretaker offers the breast or bottle. The infant sucks until she is satiated, and then turns away. The intake of milk will vary from feeding to feeding. The length of time between feedings will also vary; the infant may signal hunger again in 30 minutes, an hour, or several hours, at which time sustenance is offered again. Rather than adhering to a rigid schedule, the child is trusted to accurately communicate her needs. The adult who responds to these needs helps the child establish trust and experience the physical and emotional satisfaction of good caretaking. According to Hirschmann and Munter, this attunement teaches the child that she can trust the outside world to take care of her. She learns that her needs are important and responded to, creating a sense of safety and security.[5]

As the child grows older, numerous factors can interfere with her natural ability to identify hunger needs and ensure an attuned response. Parents concerned about nutritional needs may "force" the child to eat foods she does not like or restrict foods that she does enjoy. The structure of family meal times and school may prevent the child from eating when she is hungry or demand that she eat when she is not hungry. As she becomes more aware of her body size and the culture of dieting, she may become caught in the diet roller coaster at a young age, thereby compromising her body's ability to self-regulate. Compulsive overeating to manage emotions can further move this child away from her own internal signals to tell her when, what, and how much to eat.

Hirschmann and Munter offer a method of eating for adults that helps clients reestablish the body–hunger connection. When compulsive eaters can move in the direction of eating when they are physically hungry, eating exactly what they are hungry for, and stopping when satisfied, they will experience tremendous satisfaction, both physically and psychologically. The collection of these experiences, which we refer to as *attuned eating*, helps clients end the diet/binge cycle and normalize their relationships with food. They can return to the natural process of eating that they most likely enjoyed at an early age, in which they can fully trust themselves and feel calm around food.

The benefits of regaining this attunement with eating do not end with this accomplishment, but extend to psychological aspects of clients' functioning. "Each time you feed yourself when you are hungry, you demonstrate that you are able to care for yourself in an attuned way. The more reliable you are as a self-feeder, the more emotionally secure you will feel and the less likely you will be to turn to food for reasons other than hunger. You will have less anxiety in general, and you will feel better equipped to name your problems and deal with them directly."[6]

Helping clients end compulsive eating often involves exploring emotional issues and developing new ways of coping with problems. It is through the process of learning to eat in a normal, attuned fashion that clients strengthen their *internal* resources. Increased self-esteem, trust in the ability to care for and nurture the self, and entitlement to identify and respond to needs are all aspects of the client's sense of self that are positively influenced just through the process of learning to eat in an attuned manner. As her compulsive eating decreases, the therapist and client are ultimately placed in a strong position to address the underlying issues and conflicts that may exist. The process of understanding the relationship between compulsive eating and managing feelings will be addressed in-depth in a later chapter.

The ideas presented in the following chapters are meant to be guidelines that help people work their way out of compulsive eating problems. Unlike diets, where rules must be strictly followed to achieve results and the dieter is judged as good or bad based on her adherence, we offer a process whose principles form a solid basis toward normalizing eating and resolving psychological issues. Clients have a tendency to want to turn these guidelines into a new set of rules, preferring the structure of an external source to the idea of relying on themselves to direct their eating. There is frequently a wish to make the non-diet into a new diet.

At each step of the way, implementing non-diet principles furthers the client toward her goal of ending compulsive eating. Yet both client and therapist must understand that her difficulties in making use of these guidelines at various points in the process signal her trouble spots and warrant exploration. She is not "bad" for eating past fullness; rather, there is meaning in her behavior that is important and worthy of understanding. The non-diet guidelines offer a road map, and the path for each client will be unique to her own set of circumstances.

# HUNGER

The first step in helping your client become an attuned eater is to help her identify physiological hunger. If you ask a compulsive eater how she decides when to eat, you will find that her food intake has very little to do with internal cues. She may tell you that she tries to eat at certain times of the day, that many foods in her world are too hard to resist, that various feelings trigger emotional eating, or that she just loves to eat. Some compulsive eaters will say that they know what it feels like to get hungry, and that they do get hungry sometimes. However, many compulsive eaters will tell you that they rarely or never experience physical hunger; in fact, they are no longer sure how true hunger feels in their bodies. Your task at this point is to assist your client in defining the signs of physiological hunger so that she can begin to reconnect her bodily needs with the act of feeding herself.

## Identifying Physical Hunger

Hunger, which is controlled by the hypothalamus, is a physiological event that is generally experienced in the stomach. It is useful to check in with your client to make sure she knows that her stomach is located in the abdominal area. Some clients point below the area, while others may confuse feelings of anxiety experienced above the stomach as signs of hunger.

If you ask people how they know when they are hungry, typical responses include:
- Growling stomach
- Weakness
- Emptiness in stomach
- Light-headedness
- Headache
- Irritability
- Fatigue
- Shakiness

All of these answers indicate physical sensations, and the ability to recognize these sensations is essential in your client's ability to move in the direction of attuned eating.

Symptoms such as weakness, light-headedness, headaches, irritability, and shakiness indicate that a person is well beyond hunger because she has waited too long to feed herself. While a growling stomach can indicate physical hunger, stomachs can growl at other times, such as during digestion. Therefore, presenting the concept of emptiness in the stomach provides a more accurate cue for clients returning to normal eating.

As clients first attempt to identify physiological hunger, they often recognize their hunger only once it has reached an extreme, and they feel they are "starving." Thus, they experience the unpleasant effects of a body that is desperate for sustenance. If waiting for hunger means headaches, weakness, or crabbiness, there is not much incentive to hold out for these signals.

In an attempt to help clients recognize and identify different degrees of hunger, Matz and Grannick developed the Hunger Scale. The purpose of this instrument is to teach compulsive eaters how to notice variations in the physical sensations of their stomach.

## HUNGER SCALE

Starving

Very Hungry

Hungry

Somewhat Hungry

Not Hungry/Not Full

Somewhat Full

Full

Very Full

Stuffed

The designers of this scale intentionally avoided the use of numbers, such as a scale of 1 to 10, because of the propensity of former dieters to turn information about eating into a new set of rules. They wanted to avoid the problem of clients reporting that they were "good" because they ate "at 3" or "bad" because they ate until they were "a 10." Rather, the goal of the scale is to offer clients a set of words that they can apply to their internal states.

Consider the scale for a moment and think about your own eating. Where do you usually fall when you make a decision to eat? Does this level represent an attunement to your physical hunger? If yes, do you acknowledge the importance of this response? If no, can you imagine trying to move in the direction of responding more accurately to your physical cues? How can you best use this information to assist your clients in their own process?

Probably everyone has had the experience of waiting too long to eat and reaching the range of "starving" on the Hunger Scale. We've already discussed the physical discomforts that accompany this state of hunger. When a person reaches the "starving" range, she feels desperate to put food in her body. At this point, she can no longer determine what foods her body craves — anything will do. This level of deprivation places your client at a very high risk of overeating. She is likely to eat whatever is available and more than her body needs.

In the center of the scale is a state called not hungry/not full. This was included because of the discovery that many compulsive eaters assume that if they are not full, they must be hungry. It seemed difficult for them to consider that there were times when their body maintained a perfect balance.

Between "starving" and "not hungry/not full," there is wide range of possible physiological signals. Although at first your client may say that she cannot tell the difference in her degree of hunger, over time she will begin to recognize the nuances in her hunger signals. People vary in where they prefer to respond to their hunger, and this variation can occur for the same person on different days or at different times of the day. The optimal times for making a decision to eat fall into the ranges of "somewhat hungry," "hungry," or moving into "very hungry." Under these conditions, your client can begin to recognize her body's message that she needs to be fed, without the unnecessary discomfort that comes from waiting too long. She will now be in a position to discriminate the type of food her body craves.

In order to help illustrate this process to clients who are relearning hunger and fullness, it is useful to have them imagine a glass of water that is half full. As the level goes down, this represents increasing stages of hunger. Their task is to bring the level back up to half full, or perhaps a bit higher. Eventually, the level decreases again, and the experience is repeated.

## Relearning Physical Hunger

Another reason your client may have difficulty identifying hunger is because she cannot wait for a physical signal. The nature of compulsive eating can mean that she is compelled to reach for food when her emotional needs become too great, and therefore she cannot wait for her physical cues for hunger. Reassure your client that this is to be expected at this phase. Her task for now is to ask herself when she is reaching for food, if she is physiologically hungry.

In their book *Overcoming Overeating*, Hirschmann and Munter use the term "stomach hunger" to refer to physiologically based eating and "mouth hunger" to refer to all other forms of eating. These terms are easy for clients to understand and help them clearly distinguish the different types of eating they engage in by offering a way to label the experience. Furthermore, the repeated use of the phrase "stomach hunger" by both client and therapist reinforces the body–food connection for the compulsive eater.

## Responding to Nonphysical Hunger

Let your client know that you expect most of her eating will be mouth hunger at this early stage of normalizing eating. Even though you understand that this is upsetting to her, by definition, a compulsive eater cannot wait until physical hunger; if she could simply begin to eat out of physiological hunger because you suggested the idea, she would not need to work on this issue in therapy. In the past, your client has reprimanded herself for overeating. Yet each time she yells at herself, she prolongs the overeating experience. While her negative self-talk takes her further away from her real problems, she creates a state of anxiety that fuels her overeating. Her continued yelling allows her to effectively translate intrapsychic issues into a belief that her eating and body are the real problems.

As you teach your client about the difference between physiological and psychological hunger, it is important to offer her another way to respond to her mouth hunger. "I'm out of control" and "I'm fat and disgusting" can be replaced with words such as, "I'm reaching for food and I'm not physically hungry. Something must be making me uncomfortable right now and this is the best way I know to calm myself." She might add, "I look forward to the day when I no longer need to turn to food to manage my uncomfortable feelings." Although she will quickly return to the familiar, critical voice, over time she will come to believe that she is not inherently bad because of her need to turn to food. In part, the messages that you convey to her will help her internalize a new voice that is compassionate and nonjudgmental. This new way of being with herself will decrease her anxiety and, therefore, the number of times she must turn to food to soothe herself.

*Entitlement*

If your client checks in with her stomach and finds that she is truly experiencing hunger, she can commend herself. "This is terrific. I'm hungry. I get to eat." These words are novel for the compulsive eater. For example, Hayley reported that she always feels guilty when she eats. Although she binges frequently, she never truly feels entitled to eat anything at all. "If I eat three carrots, I probably should have only eaten two." While her words seem extreme, many compulsive eaters share the feeling that they are not entitled to eat.

Up until now, your client has judged herself negatively for her appetite. As a dieter, she considered herself virtuous when she felt very hungry but avoided eating, thereby maintaining great control. Of course, this stance ultimately backfires for all dieters when they return to food, guaranteeing a binge to make up for the deprivation. When your client begins to experience physical hunger and she learns that the correct response is to feed herself, she has a new and reliable way of organizing her eating. As the body becomes hungry numerous times throughout the day, she will never need to wait long for the chance to go to food.

### Responding to Physical Hunger

The primary goal for your client early on in the treatment is to check in with her stomach and try to wait for hunger. Clients sometimes assume that their hunger will become obvious to them, but this is not always the case. Suggest to your client that she can check in with her stomach every so often, perhaps in 15-minute intervals. If she notices physiological hunger, instruct her that she must respond by eating. Developing the hunger/food connection is essential to breaking into compulsive eating patterns.

Everyone can eventually rediscover physical hunger, but the process will vary from person to person. In order to help your client find that attunement, she will need to give up preconceived notions about when she is supposed to eat. If she is not hungry first thing in the morning, let her know that it is okay to await a cue from her body. If she notices her hunger at 10:30 A.M., she will need to respond by eating. Her eating will proceed in this manner throughout the day. If her lunch break occurs at 12:00 and she is hungry, she will eat; if not, she will wait until later. Attuned eating means letting go of the concept of mealtimes and replacing external structure with internal cues.

---

## THE CASE OF CARY

Cary learned from her diet programs that she should never eat past 7:00 P.M. She did her best to follow this rule. She recalled that when ordering a pizza for dinner one night, she ate three quarters of it. She explained that she felt stuffed and uncomfortable afterward. She reasoned, however, that she would not be able to eat again until tomorrow morning. She feared becoming hungry later in the evening and, therefore, ate more than she needed. In the course of a 6-week workshop that included the concepts of attuned eating, Cary tried an experiment. With the encouragement of the therapist, she told herself that she could eat whenever she was physically hungry. This meant that if her stomach signaled hunger at 10:00 P.M., she could and would respond. Cary found that she needed only a couple of slices of pizza to satisfy her when she ate early one evening. She trusted that she would attend to her needs for food if hunger arose. That night, Cary became hungry again around 9:00 P.M. There was plenty of leftover pizza, which appealed to her. Cary ate half a slice of the pizza, and she put the rest away.

---

As you discuss the concept of using physiological hunger as the best indicator of when to eat, clients may express concerns about the feasibility of eating when they are hungry because their lifestyles specify certain times of day that they are supposed to eat or are able to eat. First and foremost, your client must understand that in order to have a good chance of eating when she is physically hungry, she must have food available to her. If she allows herself to wait for hunger but cannot get something to eat, she will become very uncomfortable. As a result, she will engage in prophylactic eating in which she turns to food in order to prevent hunger at some future time. She must think about herself the way she might think about a young child. When parents know they will be away from home for a period of time, they bring a bottle or food for the child. No one expects the child to suffer through her hunger; in fact, both parents and child end up miserable when unprepared. The client must also view her own hunger as so important that she will go to the trouble of bringing food with her when she is away from home.

Perhaps your client tells you that she only has a certain time to eat at work or wants to have dinner with her family. These concerns are very important and need to be addressed. As with all aspects of the guidelines presented for normalizing eating, it is useful to start with a problem-solving approach to difficulties. If these ideas fail to help your client implement the behaviors useful in ending compulsive eating, then it may become necessary to explore deeper meanings.

The organization of our society into three meals a day is not necessarily in sync with the individual's physical needs. For example, in other cultures people eat a large meal in the afternoon, followed by a "siesta" and something lighter to eat in the evening. Eating three meals a day is not necessarily the ideal for an individual, but rather meets the needs of the workplace. Some research suggests that our bodies actually prefer smaller amounts of food throughout the day. Many clients report that they will graze during the day, and this style of eating may actually fit their body's natural rhythm, once they can successfully attach their eating to hunger. Giving your client this information may help her feel that eating in response to her body is acceptable.

In general, people can be very creative in finding ways to allow themselves to eat when they are hungry, if they truly believe that they are entitled to do so. For example, Sheila used the refrigerator provided to the staff at her office to keep yogurt, bread, and lunch meat. In addition, she kept a couple of cans of soup and some frozen entrees at work. Now that she no longer needed to go out to a restaurant to order food, she was able to eat when she noticed she was hungry, rather than becoming constricted to her 1-hour lunch break. As a teacher, Gwen decided to eat in front of her second grade class if she became hungry. With a sense of fairness, her students were also allowed to keep a snack at their desks. Greg called his wife prior to leaving work to let her know whether he thought he would be hungry when he arrived home. Although the family mealtime was usually around 6:00 P.M., the couple agreed that if Greg was not hungry, he would join the family for conversation, and put together his own meal later in the evening when he was ready to eat.

These solutions are not meant to be rigid, but reflect the idea that the more meticulous a compulsive eater can be in feeding herself in an attuned manner, the more quickly she will end her overeating. As your client feels more entitled to eat when she is physically hungry and experiences the benefits of this process, she will become more likely to develop strategies that allow her to eat on her own schedule.

## MAKING THE MATCH

The next task in becoming an attuned eater requires your client to identify what she is hungry for when her physiological hunger occurs. Previously, your client chose what to feed herself primarily in response to what she "should" or "shouldn't" ingest. Foods such as apples, salads, or raw vegetables were deemed "good" while she considered pizza, cake, and ice cream to be "bad." Eating rarely had to do with what her body actually craved, and the idea that she can trust her body to tell her what to eat is likely to feel frightening to her.

### The Wisdom of the Body

By understanding the wisdom of the body and its amazing capacity to self-regulate, your client may become more willing to trust herself when it comes to listening to internal cues. When a mother breastfeeds her baby, her milk supplies the perfect amount of nutrients for optimal growth, and the more milk the baby drinks, the more milk the mother produces. Yet even more remarkable is research that shows women who birth premature babies produce milk that is different from the milk of mothers who deliver full-term infants. The milk from mothers of premature babies has a higher concentration of protein, fat, sodium chloride, and iron to fight infection.[7] The research of Leann Birch and her colleagues consistently reveals that when children are presented with a wide variety of healthful foods, they are capable of self-regulating their nutritional needs on their own, without external guidance.[8]

In their book *Intuitive Eating*, dieticians Evelyn Tribole and Elyse Resch also speak to the wonderful adaptability of the body as they emphasize that nutritional recommendations for adults will balance over a period of time rather than require precise monitoring each and every day. They offer examples such as the fact that if a person consumes more vitamin C than is necessary, the body begins to excrete more of it, or that if a person does not take in enough iron, the body starts to absorb more of it.[9] Nutritionist Debra Waterhouse highlights the wisdom of the body as she explains that chocolate cravings serve a physiological function in premenstrual women. She points out that chocolate contains ingredients that increase both serotonin and endorphins into the brain, which promotes a sense of happiness and well-being.[10] These examples support the notion that responding to internal signals and choosing from a wide variety of food lead to choices that frequently meet nutritional needs, and that the body will naturally compensate for imbalances.

*Presenting the Concept*

Initially, your client is likely to have a difficult time making matches. Reassure her that this is to be expected, and that you understand that it will take her time and practice to re-learn how to listen to her body's natural cues. Eventually, the ability to recognize her hunger and decipher the food(s) she needs will become second nature. At the same time, even normal eaters usually must stop for a moment and give some thought to what they are hungry for. While as a dieter she has been quick to negate her true hunger, she must now feel entitled to spend time thinking about her needs. It is important for you to convey to her that you trust that over time she will develop her natural ability to recognize what her body craves.

You can begin the process of helping your client understand the concept of matching by asking her if she can remember a time when she was hungry and got exactly what she wanted. Most people can recall an experience, either recent or in the past, when they clearly knew what they wanted. Explore that memory with your client so that she can begin to connect her own desires with eating and satisfaction. For example, Lisa reported that when she was on vacation with her partner, she just had to have a steak and potatoes. After checking with the hotel concierge, they found a restaurant known for its steaks. Because she was on vacation, Lisa relaxed her diet rules and allowed herself to get exactly what she wanted. The steak tasted great to her and felt very good in her stomach. She remembers this as a very satisfying eating experience, although she also remembers telling her partner, "I probably shouldn't have eaten a steak because it's so fattening. When we get home, I'm really going to have to get back on my diet."

You can explain to the client that this is exactly the type of experience she will want to try to collect. Congratulate her for listening to her body so well, and emphasize that this is an excellent example of how listening to her body provides great satisfaction both physically and psychologically. Physically, she had the feeling that she had eaten just the right food and her stomach felt good as a result. Psychologically, she demonstrated that she can listen to herself, trust herself, and care for herself.

Unfortunately, at the time Lisa allowed herself the steak, she felt guilt because of her belief system that includes steak as a "bad" food. As she becomes an attuned eater, she will have a new way to evaluate her food choices. Eating steak in response to a physiological craving for meat is a good match; a steak eaten in response to a craving for soup is a poor match. This method of organizing her eating gives Lisa a reliable, internal structure that she was previously lacking.

Opportunities for matching occur only when there is a signal of physiological hunger to match. Therefore, when your client turns to food for reasons other than stomach hunger, she will continue to pick foods that have nothing to do with her internal needs. Again, reassure her that although you understand that she wishes she could end her compulsive eating quickly, you expect her to continue to have mouth hunger. The important focus for her at this juncture is to notice her physical hunger and experiment with responding as accurately as possible.

### Learning the Strategies

You can share several strategies with your client as she begins this challenging task. At the moment she experiences physical hunger, she can ask herself, "If I had a magic wand and could summon whatever I wanted to eat, what would I choose?" This question eliminates obstacles, either real or the result of resistances, such as not having the food available or not having the time to prepare a particular dish. Instead, the client has made a first step toward identifying a food preference at a particular moment. Ideally, she will be able to get the exact food she craves; regardless, she has begun to realize that her body can speak to her, if only she can listen.

Often, clients will find that even after asking what they truly want to eat, they are still unable to discriminate among food options. Teach your client that she can ask herself a series of questions that will help her in the process of learning about herself as an attuned eater. Specifically, does she want something:

- Hot
- Crunchy
- Smooth
- Spicy

- Cold
- Mushy
- Salty
- Bland

Your client's choice will have something to do with how she imagines the food will taste in her mouth; after all, there is no reason to consume food that does not taste good to her. However, she must also think beyond her mouth and imagine how the food will feel in her stomach. Is it too light or too heavy? Can she tell if her body craves protein, fat, or carbohydrates? The idea of truly paying attention to her body is a novel idea for the compulsive eater. At first she may say that she just does not know what she really wants to eat; she loves all food. However, over time and with gentle prodding to listen to herself, your client will discover that she can collect attuned eating experiences.

## THE CASE OF MICHELLE

Michelle, a new group member, told the other participants that she never knows what she wants to eat. In fact, she was noticing some hunger as she sat in the group, but "didn't have a clue." The therapist took this opportunity to work with Michelle on the process of identifying the match.

**Therapist:** Michelle, can you tell if you want something hot or cold?

**Michelle:** I don't know.

**Therapist:** Think about how the food will feel in your body. Temperature is usually the easiest to figure out.

**Michelle:** Something warm would feel better.

**Therapist:** Okay. Can you tell if you want something substantial or solid, like meat, or something mushy?

**Michelle:** (responding immediately) Soft.

**Therapist:** Soft like soup, or soft like pasta?

**Michelle:** I actually want something more like a burrito. That's soft and warm, but the spicy sounds good, too.

**Therapist:** Fine. Now take a moment to imagine the burrito in your stomach. Does it seem just right?

**Michelle:** It feels pretty good.

---

The therapist asked Michelle if she would be able to provide herself with a burrito following the group, and Michelle assured the group that she knew a restaurant that had just the kind that she liked. Hopefully, Michelle identified the correct food to satisfy her craving. If so, she will have collected an attuned eating experience, which will serve as a building block toward her new way of feeding herself. Unlike diets in which one "binge" means failure and starting over, encourage your client to view her hunger and matching as a process of gathering experiences that she will carry with her forever. Whether she collects one, five, or ten experiences between sessions with you, she has begun to move in the direction of attuned eating, and these experiences cannot be undone.

*Collecting Experiences*

Jane Hirschmann and Carol Munter describe this collection of stomach hunger experiences as similar to having "money in the bank." When a compulsive eater first seeks treatment, most of her eating will fall in the column of mouth hunger. Over time, she will gather stomach hunger experiences here and there. Thus, she makes a deposit in the column of good caretaking, where it remains. The client automatically feels an incentive to repeat these experiences because of the physical and emotional rewards. The stomach hunger account builds over time as the compulsive eater accumulates attuned experiences. This metaphor reassures the client that you expect her compulsive eating to continue, and that she is not bad for reaching for food when she is not hungry. At the same time, you also communicate that she makes a significant accomplishment each and every time she eats out of physiological hunger and makes a match.

Returning to Michelle, let's consider the possibility that the burrito did not satisfy her craving. Instead, she reports at the next meeting that her stomach felt upset. Michelle needs help processing the experience to understand what happened. She explains that the burrito felt too greasy after all; the cheese did not sit well in her stomach. By asking her if she can remember what would have made the food more correct in her stomach, Michelle reveals that she thinks a fajita would have been a better match because she liked the warmth and spiciness of the burrito, but didn't need the cheese. In this manner, Michelle learns to listen to herself and see that her stomach provides important feedback. Rather than berating herself for not making the perfect match, Michelle can adopt a compassionate view of herself. She is engaged in relearning how to eat, which will take some time after the many years of ignoring herself and looking toward external sources. Furthermore, Michelle will need to hear repeatedly from the therapist that each eating experience provides an opportunity to learn something about herself as an eater. If she feels satisfied, she gains the knowledge that she can tune into her physical hunger. If she misses the mark, she can ask herself where she misinterpreted her signals so that she is in a stronger position to make a match the next time she feels stomach hunger. After years of dieting, there is no longer any good or bad, just a process of listening, experimenting, and learning.

Encourage your client to make use of this process of matching each and every time she is hungry. Rather than searching the refrigerator or cabinets to see what is available, or looking at the restaurant menu first, your client will benefit from checking in with her stomach before she limits herself.

---

# THE CASE OF ESTHER

Esther reported that she came home from work tired and hungry. She had not gone shopping recently so there were few foods available in her home. She went to her pantry and found a can of soup. Although this did not seem like the best match to her, it was quick and easy. When Esther was asked to try to remember how her stomach felt and what type of food she really wanted, she was able to recall that she wanted something warm and substantial. After some reflection, Esther identified that lasagna would have been the perfect match. She was able to articulate that she had not allowed herself to really tune into her needs because she would have felt too disappointed by her inability to match her food preference with her hunger needs.

Given the reality of Esther's situation, why was it so important that she notice her desire for lasagna? First, identifying food preferences can guide her shopping list when she goes to the grocery store. Esther may buy the ingredients to make lasagna so that they are on hand the next time she desires this dish; perhaps she will even make one over the weekend and freeze it so that she could have some with little effort when her body craves it again. Or she may choose to buy a frozen lasagna. Esther can now ensure that in the future she has a better chance of getting what she is hungry for when she is hungry. Furthermore, by pinpointing the lasagna, Esther can attempt to make a "good enough" match. The reality is that situations will occur that make it impossible for a person to make a precise match each and every time. By asking herself exactly what her body needs, Esther can make some adjustments. When she notices she wants lasagna, Esther can ask herself what the most important part of the food is for her. Is she craving some pasta, or did she really desire the feel of the melted cheese? In the former case, she could have cooked some noodles along with jarred spaghetti sauce, both of which she did have in her pantry. If the melted cheese felt crucial, she could have made a grilled cheese sandwich or a cheese omelet. These options will bring her more satisfaction than the soup that had little to do with her internal cues. Finally, Esther may have found that the lasagna sounded so right to her that she decided it was worth calling the local Italian restaurant and ordering this item to take out.

When your client dines at a restaurant, she can approach the menu in the same manner. Hopefully, the restaurant offers the type of food that will match her needs. By checking in with her stomach before opening the menu, she can use the same process described above to pick out the most important aspect of this eating experience. She may realize that a salad is the main interest for her and have it as her meal. She may choose to have the salad as an appetizer, electing not to order other items. Or, she may order a main dish, feel satisfied by the salad, and take the rest of the food home to add to her stock of food. The ability to act on these decisions requires your client to believe that she is entitled to have exactly what she craves, and that if she does not desire something at a particular moment, she can always have it at a later time. As your client becomes more comfortable asking the question, "What would feel just right in my stomach," and listens to the answer, she will have made a solid step in the direction of ending her compulsive eating.

---

## LEGALIZING FOODS

As you encourage your client to listen to her body to tell her what to eat, she faces a major obstacle. She has already categorized foods as good and bad, fattening and unfattening, or healthy and unhealthy. This division of food interferes with listening to her body's true needs because she judges the food before allowing herself to have it. Therefore, the next task in the process of helping your client return to normal eating is to work with her on the process of "legalizing" foods.

As we said earlier, normal eating means eating a wide variety of foods. Sometimes our body craves protein; at other times we want something sweet. Sometimes we need vegetables; at other times we require starchy foods. Imagine for a moment that what you ate would have no effect on your weight. What would stay the same about your food choices? What might change? This is a question that can be useful to your clients. Although the initial fear may be, "I would only want junk food," most people realize very quickly that their bodies naturally desire a wide variety of foods.

Among professionals using a non-diet philosophy, there is unanimous agreement that the restrictions of dieting cause overeating and that diets must stop. There is also agreement that people need to eat a wide variety of foods in conjunction with their internal signals. There is disagreement, however, as to exactly how to help the compulsive eater learn to trust her body. The issues center on how to help compulsive eaters reach the goal of normalizing their eating. While some experts revert back to healthy eating and incorporate some of the previously forbidden foods, others leave the field wide open to the compulsive eater's own ability to self-regulate. On the one hand, it is our belief that clients who can truly overcome their overeating by ending their fear of food and trusting their bodies to dictate their eating achieve a freedom from their compulsiveness that they never dreamed was possible. The "Overcoming Overeating" approach as developed by Jane Hirschmann and Carol Munter has guided much of our work with compulsive eaters. At the same time, we recognize that there are clients who are uncomfortable with some of the guidelines suggested by these non-diet experts. As social workers, we are trained to "start where the client is." This tried and true principle needs to be applied to your client and her unique situation as you decide together the best way to proceed in treatment.

## Presenting the Concept

In order to help your client stop the judgments about food that prevent her from considering her body's needs, instruct her that *for the purpose of ending her compulsive eating*, she will need to view all foods as equal. This means that a candy bar equals an apple, which equals a chicken breast, which equals pizza, and so on. Obviously, foods are not nutritionally equal. However, she will need to temporarily put aside these concerns in order to normalize her eating, which will ultimately provide her with a balanced diet. As a therapist, it is important for you to trust that she will eventually provide herself with a wide variety of foods and a nutritionally sound diet. After all, the deprivation your client currently experiences as the result of trying to stay away from "illegal" foods actually causes her to eat more of them than she needs when she breaks her food restraints. Conversely, the pressure she feels to eat certain foods causes her to reject them, even if she actually craves them. Ultimately, as your client learns to listen to her body tell her what to eat, she will find that she wants to eat all types of food, without the anxiety that accompanies her current food choices.

---

## THE CASE OF DEVIN

Devin, the newest client in the group, is trying to learn to listen to her hunger. With the encouragement of her therapist, Devin tells herself that all foods are now legal. When she is hungry, her task is to ask exactly what she is hungry for and do her best to obtain that food. When Devin arrives home from work, she realizes that her stomach feels empty. She asks herself what would feel just right at that moment. The chocolate cake that she often eats is available; however, when Devin really checks in with her stomach, she finds that some pasta with sauce would feel better in her body. She reassures herself that if she gets hungry again later in the evening, she will once again make a match. If chocolate cake is what her body craves at that time, she can have some. The pasta tastes very good to her and feels just right in her stomach. Devin has made a match and collected a stomach hunger experience, without feeling any deprivation. After all, if she was hungry for the cake, she could have had it. If she becomes hungry for the cake, she will have it.

---

One of the biggest misinterpretations of this method of normalizing eating is a false belief that the instruction to clients is to eat whatever they want whenever they want. The true goal of attuned eating is for people to *eat what they are hungry for when they are physically hungry.* The results of these statements are dramatically different. A person who eats whatever she wants whenever she feels like it will move no closer to ending her compulsive eating. She will feel out of control and possibly gain weight because she skipped over the step of connecting her eating to internal, physiological cues.

On the other hand, a client who begins to link her hunger with her food choices will feel an immediate sense of calmness in relation to these attuned eating experiences. She will discover that she does not always crave the foods that make her feel out of control. She will probably be surprised by some of the foods that make good matches for her. Because this process is usually fraught with psychological meaning for the compulsive eater, the guidance of a therapist can prove invaluable as she navigates her hunger signals and all of the complicated issues and obstacles likely to be associated with her eating.

### Forbidden Foods

As your client tries to legalize all foods, she must confront another dilemma. As the result of years of deprivation, certain foods "call" to her. These foods are her "forbidden" foods. She knows she is not supposed to eat them and that makes her want them that much more. If there are M&M's® available, she feels compelled to eat them. When her colleagues bring donuts to work, she is unable to resist. She may have no sign of hunger, or she may feel some hunger and crave other foods but eat the forbidden food anyway. Afterward, she may feel uncomfortably full. Or she may have interfered with the possibility of attaining some physiological hunger in the near future. How can she stop this cycle?

Ideally, your client will begin to apply her new way of considering food choices. Thus, when the donuts appear at work, she asks herself if she is hungry. If the answer is yes, she asks herself what she is hungry for. If the answer is a donut, she eats the amount of the donut(s) needed to satisfy her. If she is hungry but her body craves something different, she does her best to have that item. If the answer is no, she does not eat.

In order for your client to make the decision to pass up the donut without feeling a sense of deprivation, she must believe that donuts are always available to her. When she is hungry for a donut, she will absolutely supply this food for herself. A donut is a donut; when you are hungry for one, it can be a great match, but if not, why eat it? If she does not believe that she can have a donut when she desires one, she will feel compelled to eat the donut because "it is there," or she will restrict herself and make up for the deprivation at a later time in the form of overeating.

## STOCKING

The first step in this process was to legalize donuts. Now your client must prove to herself that she can be trusted around all types of foods. This process, referred to as "stocking" by Hirschmann and Munter, is the key to ending compulsive eating. "The issue of quantity is integral to the process of legalizing. Scarcity makes people anxious; surplus creates a sense of well-being and relaxation, the state of mind necessary to feed yourself in an attuned way."[11] If you are learning about this concept for the first time, there is a good chance that you will question whether this method could possibly work. It can also be helpful to tell your clients that you understand that what you are about to propose may sound a bit bizarre. Ask them to bear with you as you explain the purpose of stocking to them. We ask the same of you!

Stocking is the process of bringing an abundance of foods, including forbidden foods, into the home. Stocking is a paradoxical intervention. In the past, your client tried to keep the foods she binged on away from her home to control her overeating. Yet this restriction backfires over and over. Sooner or later she comes in contact with the food — at a party, during a secret run to the convenience store, or when she relaxes her restraints enough to bring the food into her kitchen. She tells herself that she should not have this food and she is not supposed to eat it. She makes this food scarce for herself, but scarcity creates anxiety. Feeling that she cannot get what she wants or needs makes her anxious. In an attempt to calm her anxiety and get what she can while it is available, the principle of scarcity guarantees the binge.

At the opposite end of the continuum is abundance. If what she needs is always available, she can relax. In fact, she can even forget about what food is around because at the moment she becomes hungry, the abundance ensures she will get what she needs.

Let's take this concept outside of the realm of food. Imagine that a very popular performer whom you have always wanted to see is coming to your area for one night only. You become anxious as you consider how to get tickets. Will you wait in line early in the morning or rush to your computer to order online? Will you be able to get them at all? It doesn't matter that you had a meeting that evening; you will miss it for this event. Perhaps the concert is more exciting because tickets are scarce.

Now imagine that the event you want to see is a play with a very long run. There are shows almost every night with no plan for it to close. You can wait for the exact date to see the show that works well with your schedule. You feel relaxed when you think about purchasing tickets; again, you can do it at a time and in a way that is most convenient for you.

Scarcity makes people anxious, and abundance makes people calm! The paradox for your client is that the more food she has around, the less she will need to go to it when she is not physically hungry. Although the concept of bringing a large amount of food into the home may seem radical at first, it is an effective solution to the casualties caused by dieting. Dieting, after all, is radical. People deny themselves food when their bodies are hungry, yet food is available.

*Teaching the Concept*

A compulsive-eating client may relate an experience to you where she has, for example, a half bag of potato chips in her pantry. She considers the chips to be a "bad" food, but wants to have some. As she eats, she tells herself, "I might as well finish the whole bag. That way there won't be any left tomorrow and I will be safe again." Thus, she ensures her overeating in order to get rid of the forbidden food. Or, she tells you that she was at a party where the host served mashed potatoes. Even though she was full, she ate them since she never allows herself to make them at home because they are too fattening. In these situations, your client's judgment that a food is bad makes it forbidden. Her perception that it will not be available again fuels her overeating. An effective solution for many clients to intervene with their compulsive eating involves creating an abundance of food that is so large that they cannot see the end in sight.

---

## THE CASE OF PAIGE

Let's consider Paige, who binges on potato chips. Every so often she brings a bag into her house and eats it. This overeating confirms her perception that she cannot be trusted with chips and reaffirms her conviction that she will not buy them again. Yet sooner or later Paige gives in to her desire for this snack and repeats the cycle. With careful instruction, Paige decides that she will never deprive herself of potato chips again. She likes the idea of being able to keep them in the house because she notices that sometimes she craves a few chips with her turkey sandwich. Paige will need to prove to herself that she can be trusted with potato chips and that she will never be deprived of them again.

Paige buys her favorite brand of potato chips during her next grocery shopping trip. She actually follows the advice of her therapist and buys eight bags. This amount of chips gives her the feeling that no matter how much she binges, she cannot possibly eat her way through her supply. Undoubtedly, Paige will overeat some of these chips. After all, they have been forbidden for a very long time and she will "make up" for some of that past deprivation. Yet at the same time, another interesting phenomenon takes place. Paige cannot finish the eight bags of chips. There are too many and she cannot make them go away. Unlike in the past where she finished all of the chips so that she would not have to face them tomorrow, at some point Paige must make an internal decision to stop eating. She will actually feel safe stopping because the chips are not going anywhere. She has promised herself to keep them available at all times. If she wants them again later, they are there for her. When her supply begins to diminish, she will buy herself more. Over a period of time that is usually fairly brief, Paige will shift her thinking about overeating. She will find that there are times she notices the chips but just does not want them, and there are other times where she actually forgets that they are in the house. Paige discovers that the technique of limiting food, which was supposed to help her stay in control, actually caused her to be out of control when confronted with that food. When she keeps the food around her with full permission to have it, she finds that she does not always want it. She begins to feel in charge of her eating. She can eat when she is hungry, eat what she is hungry for, and not feel at the mercy of her "forbidden" foods. She develops a sense of calmness that is reassuring to her and allows her to continue the process of normalizing foods.

---

When a client is first learning about the concepts of legalizing foods and stocking them, it is helpful to ask her to use her imagination. The dialogue may go as follows:

**Therapist:** Tell me about a food that you often turn to when you overeat.

**Client:** I love chocolate chip cookies.

**Therapist:** Is there a particular brand you prefer?

**Client:** I like them all. (She then mentions a store brand that she likes.)

**Therapist:** If you were to leave here today and binge on those cookies, approximately how many do you think you would eat?

**Client:** Oh, I could easily eat a box.

**Therapist:** Okay. Let's imagine that you went to the store and bought six boxes. And tonight you eat a box, leaving you with five boxes. How many do you think you could eat tomorrow?

**Client:** Probably another box.

**Therapist:** So now you're down to four boxes. Let's have you go back to the store and get two more boxes so that you are back up to six. How many cookies do you think you will eat the next day?

**Client:** Well, I'm starting to get a little tired of them. Maybe half a box.

**Therapist:** And the next day?

**Client:** Probably a couple of cookies. Or maybe none. I get it! I'm going to get sick of them.

**Therapist:** People often think the idea is that you'll get sick of the food, but that's not really the goal. The point is that when you are hungry for a cookie, a cookie is great. But, when they're always around, they stop glittering like they do for you right now. After awhile, you'll find that you can have the cookies around, but it won't occur to you to eat them unless they are exactly what you want.

**Client:** That makes sense to me, but I don't know if it could really work for me.

**Therapist:** If it makes intellectual sense, that is enough. It's scary for everyone at first because you're being asked to bring into your home the very foods that frighten you. If you can make a leap of faith and do it, you'll find that your bingeing will slow down very quickly. Close your eyes for a moment and imagine an abundance of food in your kitchen. What do you experience?

**Client:** I feel scared, but there's something calming about it, too.

## Taking Stock of Your Reaction

Whether you are learning about these ideas for the first time or have heard of them from another source, there is a good chance that your initial reaction to these concepts is that they seem extreme. Can *you* imagine having an abundance of food in your home? Your answer to that question affects the way you will view this process. If you do, in fact, keep your house well stocked with a variety of food, you may understand instinctively how maintaining a stocked home creates a calm and nurturing environment. At the same time, however, many therapists learning about the concept of stocking wonder if this process can really work. If the idea of having all types of food available in your home makes *you* anxious, then, understandably, it will be difficult for you to suggest this method to your clients.

### Taking Stock of Clients' Reactions

Just as therapists will vary in their reaction to the concept of stocking, so will clients. Keep in mind that the purpose of bringing large quantities of food into the home is in the service of ending the compulsive eating. Once your client truly believes that she is entitled to eat what she is hungry for and no longer subjects herself to deprivation, she will reduce the amount of food she buys. As she sees that the chips are stale because they have been in her pantry for so long, your client has accomplished the step of legalizing, and she no longer requires the previous volume. At the same time, assuming chips are a food she enjoys, she will still need to buy a bag or two so that they remain available to her when her body craves a salty, crunchy match.

In order to ensure that stocking will be an effective intervention for your client, you must consider several factors. First, you must evaluate whether your client has truly forsaken diets forever. If she views herself as "trying" this method with the option of going back to restrictions when she overeats, *it will not work.* The reason for the failure is that at some level, your client perceives that deprivation is just around the corner. As she makes her forbidden foods available, she will eat her way through them in anticipation of their eventual disappearance.

Also, in order for this method to succeed, your client must keep up supplies of her "illegal" foods. If she buys many candy bars and watches her supply diminish over time as she consumes them, she will become anxious. She must figure out how many candy bars she needs to have so that the end is not in sight, and keep her stock well above that amount.

Finally, your client must refrain from judging herself when she eats the very foods she attempted to avoid for so long. Reassure her that it is completely natural to "make up for lost time," but if she remains consistent in her stocking, you trust that her bingeing will slow down. After all, ice cream sundaes and chocolate cake lose their appeal after awhile if you can truly have them whenever you want. Your client will discover that she naturally craves a wide variety of food. Unlike in the past where the diet told her she was good for eating "healthy foods," she will find — on her own — that she naturally craves these foods. Of course, when your client goes grocery shopping, she must buy all types of foods, not just her forbidden ones, so that she can make good matches. If your client craves an apple but only has candy bars on hand, she will consume the candy bar despite the fact that this is not a good match for her.

### The Mechanics of Stocking

In order to begin stocking, explore with your client what types of foods she likes and what she currently provides herself. Many clients report that despite their overeating, there is actually very little food in their homes. A quart of milk, some eggs, and spoiled lunch meat occupy their refrigerators. There are some cans of soup and a box of pasta in their cabinet. No wonder they feel anxious about food! Others buy for their families but do not consider their own needs. It is important that your client begin to identify her food preferences. She can begin by writing or imagining a list of all the foods she might enjoy. You may also introduce her to Hirschmann and Munter's visualization known as the Food House Fantasy, which helps identify her specific interests (see appendix). If your client is comfortable bringing all of her forbidden foods into her home at once, she can do so. If she is very frightened and wants to proceed cautiously, she can bring in just a few of her illegal foods at a time. Once she experiences how the process works, her fear will decrease and she will feel more comfortable with the process of stocking.

## THE CASE OF CANDACE

After hearing about this idea of stocking, Candace felt very excited. She said that she was a bit nervous, but it really made sense to her. Candace planned to go to the grocery store on the following Saturday. Because she felt anxious about whether this method would work for her, she decided to start with one item: Milky Way® bars. She bought five bags for herself and emptied them into a large bowl on her counter. She found herself munching on them for several days. Although she felt upset by the fact that she was eating the candy, she reminded herself that she was not supposed to yell. In the next meeting with her therapist, she was instructed to buy more candy bars even though she continued to overeat. The therapist reassured her that even though she may feel physically uncomfortable as the result of eating Milky Ways when her body was not hungry, going to the store and buying more Milky Ways would help her end the overeating. The therapist informed Candace that she could never go wrong by having too much — only by not having enough. Candace accepted the therapist's instructions and bought several more bags, which she promptly added to her bowl. The next week, Candace reported that her consumption of Milky Way Bars had slowed down to a trickle.

Several months later, as Halloween approached, Candace stated that for the first time that she could remember, she was not afraid to have candy in her house. In the past, she bought types of candy that she did not like or waited to the last minute to purchase the trick-or-treat candy. "This time," she laughed, "I already have all of the candy in my home and I don't even want it. I hear other mothers discussing their fears about Halloween candy, and I think, 'That was me last year.' I am so relieved."

*A Misinterpretation of Stocking*

Let's compare Candace's experience to a personal vignette reported by a woman struggling with her compulsive eating.

Periodically I also tried an inverse approach to weight management. By that I mean I totally gave in to my food whims and desires. I would feed myself whatever I wanted whenever I wanted it. If I wanted a KitKat bar, no problem. Rush out to a 24-hour convenience store and get three or four of them. I thought I should respect my cravings and respond to them. After all, my cravings were telling me something about my innermost need for love and acceptance. I believed that the root cause of my compulsion stemmed from a long-term denial of the foods I most love. The solution then was to stop denying myself and to give myself what I wanted when I wanted it. If I wanted chewy chocolate chunk cookies for dinner, then I should have chewy chocolate chunk cookies for dinner. If I wanted a quart of Ben & Jerry's exotic ice cream for breakfast, then I should have a quart of Ben & Jerry's ice cream for breakfast. This practice was supposed to diffuse and quench my desire. Theoretically my desire was supposed to gradually decrease in a natural way until it completely disappeared or until it operated in a more or less normal range. I tried this approach over and over and over. I wanted it to work. I wanted it to be true. Yet my cravings never lessened. The craziness never went away. All I got was fatter and more out of control and more afraid that Kit Kats and other foods that I loved had some kind of abnormal power over me. Giving in to the desire for food did not work for me.[12]

In this scenario, several factors contributed to the problematic outcome for this woman, and they are not uncommon pitfalls for people attempting to legalize food on their own. First, she reports that she tried this approach periodically, suggesting that she never truly accepted that diets do not work. By adopting a "wait and see attitude," she unintentionally set up a situation in which the prospect of deprivation always existed as a future possibility. There is no evidence that she tried to attach her eating to any internal signals to tell her when, what, and how much to eat; rather, she used the non-diet approach as a license to eat anything at anytime. This woman also failed to implement the process of legalizing and stocking within her home. Therefore, she describes running out to the food market to buy whatever she craves and consuming these foods until they are gone. She does not allow herself the opportunity to create abundance within her home so that she can collect the experience of the "forbidden" foods beginning to lose their power that comes over a period of time. It is unclear from this example whether she yelled at herself when trying to follow her cravings; to the extent that this judgment was present, it would have also fueled her compulsive eating.

This example illustrates the worst fears of people who doubt the validity of this approach. While the use of stocking is extremely effective with clients, as in the example of Candace, it will never work when a client does not feel that she can meet the criteria for its use. Likewise, as the therapist, you must feel comfortable with the concepts and able to coach your client through this process. It is better for both of you to move through the guidelines of the non-diet method at a pace that meets the needs of the treatment situation.

As your client considers the process of stocking, she will raise all sorts of questions, such as the cost of the food, her concerns about wasting food, health issues, and family issues. These important factors will be addressed in the chapter on obstacles.

### Is Stocking Necessary?

As stated earlier, there is some variation in the literature as to how clients can move from a stance of restricted eating to a position of trusting their body's internal cues to tell them what to eat. Hirschmann and Munter promote the necessity of stocking, as described above. Tribole and Resch, authors of *Intuitive Eating*, also advise that the client must stop all restrictions and bring into their homes any food that they enjoy. "While for years many health professionals have agreed that there should be no forbidden foods, very few will go the distance and say to eat whatever you want. Eventually there is a limit imposed. And knowing there is a limit can impart a food lust of sorts — better eat it now."[13] These authors do go the distance and support the notion that the client must be completely in charge of her eating. Unlike Hirschmann and Munter, they do not recommend specific guidelines for completing this task.

Other non-diet authors make an excellent case for ending restrictions and relearning normal eating. Yet at some later point in their book, they introduce recommendations for eating in a healthy manner. Of course, they include the suggestion that other foods such as chocolate or fats are now considered acceptable; yet there is still a tone of moderation. While their intentions are understandable, these suggestions can have a similar effect on the client who is sensitive to signs that she is supposed to eat in a particular way, thereby leading to rebellion through the binge.

The goal of all non-diet advocates is to help people end the negative physiological and psychological consequences created by the diet–binge cycle. No one wants to see their client eat only foods high in fat and sugar and low in nutrients. Health is the central concern of all experts, and the issue is how to best help clients get there. Does giving complete permission to eat all foods in response to hunger help people end their bingeing quicker? Our clinical experience tells us that this is, in fact, the case. At the same time, there are clients for whom this method is not possible. This does not mean that the client cannot benefit from the non-diet approach to solving compulsive eating. Rather, the therapist must work with her based on her needs. The following case illustrations show examples where stocking was the key to ending a client's compulsive eating and where stocking was not the solution for a client.

---

## THE CASE OF SHAY

Shay began a non-diet group after attending a workshop on this approach and doing some additional reading. She felt excited about the prospect of stocking and finally ending all the deprivation from past diets. It just made sense to her. She embraced the concept of stocking and over a period of 18 months worked her way out of her compulsive eating. She became an attuned eater, feeding herself when hungry, delighting in her matches, and stopping when satisfied. She examined her psychological hunger and managed, in the majority of circumstances, to let herself feel whatever bothered her, without turning to food. When she left the group, she reported that after 25 years of struggling with food and weight, she never thought she would reach the point of such comfort with food. She felt convinced that stocking was the most important factor in enabling her to stop using overeating as a tool for covering up her emotions.

---

# THE CASE OF JAMIE

Jamie also understood that diets were not the solution to her problem. At the age of 55, she had tried just about every possible plan. She learned about legalizing and stocking and believed they made sense. Yet she also reported that she felt very guilty when she ate anything sweet, particularly if she thought another family member might see her. Therefore, when she brought cookies or candy into the house, she felt the need to hide these items and felt as though she was sneaking food when she decided to eat them. Under these circumstances, the therapist advised her not to stock at this time. Instead, Jamie focused on learning to honor her hunger, rather than ignoring her physical cues as she tended to do. She practiced the idea of matching and required much support with determining what types of foods were important for her to prepare. She tended to wait to find out what her husband and adult daughter desired rather than respecting her own needs, which were often different. Jamie found that when she listened to her hunger and made a match, she could usually stop when satisfied. Sometimes she would identify a need for something sweet and go to a local ice cream parlor, feeling very pleased with herself. At other times, she might want something sweet as the result of mouth hunger. If there was candy in the house, she might eat more than she needed or she might go to a store and buy a box of cookies, resulting in a binge. Overall, Jamie overeats less often than she did in the past and has a reliable method to determine when, what, and how much to eat during those periods of time in which she can sustain this level of self-care. She struggles with the concept of legalizing foods and continues to work on that issue.

---

With practice and experience, you will be able to evaluate when the method of stocking is appropriate and when it is not in the client's best interest. Your understanding and flexibility will help you and your client develop the most effective treatment plan possible for her circumstances.

## FULLNESS

So far, we have addressed the when and what in the process of normalizing eating. The final aspect of physiological-based eating involves knowing when to stop. While packaged foods provide serving portions, these amounts do not necessarily correspond to your client's hunger needs. Restaurants, which offer varying serving sizes, cannot predict the exact amount of food patrons require on a particular visit. It is by tuning into her stomach that your client will discern when she is ready to stop eating.

### Identifying Fullness

Earlier in the chapter, we provided the Hunger Scale, which gives a range of experiences that your client will have as she tunes into her stomach. Her task is to notice how her stomach feels when she stops eating. Your client will discover that if she pays attention, she can learn much about her overeating. When a client first comes to see you for help, chances are that the majority of her eating experiences leave her in the very full to stuffed range. Point out to her that for now, she needs to be aware of how this makes her body feel. Is she uncomfortable? Is this okay with her?

Most clients find that they have an easier time recognizing their signals for hunger than noticing their signals for satiation. For all attuned eaters, in order for there to be a signal to stop, there needs to have been a signal to start. If your client turns to food for reasons other than physical need, she will be unable to rely on an internal cue to stop her overeating. Likewise, matching plays an important role in the ability to stop. If your client eats exactly what she is hungry for when she is hungry, she will find a moment when her stomach feels satisfied. If she can pay attention to this signal, she will accomplish the task of stopping when full.

Compulsive eaters will often describe eating experiences where they actually know what their bodies crave. However, they judge the food as "bad" and try to eat their way around it. Ultimately, they do not feel satisfied by their other choices and either return to the forbidden food after all or keep eating the undesired foods in an attempt to become satisfied. As a result, their stomachs become overfull, but they do not feel satisfied.

---

## THE CASE OF ROSE

Rose revealed that as a dieter she sometimes wanted macaroni and cheese for dinner. Since this was not allowed on her food plan, she ate all the foods she was "supposed" to have — chicken, baked potato, and some vegetables — in order to stave off her craving. After dinner, she discovered that she felt unsatisfied. She opened and shut the refrigerator, searched her cabinet, and settled on a brownie. She started with one brownie, and then finished off another half dozen.

---

Rose's story is typical of compulsive eaters who try to ignore their cravings in order to eat by external rules. Clearly, she ate beyond her physical hunger. There is a good chance that if Rose felt able to eat exactly what she wanted, she would have felt satiated after her meal. Perhaps she needed some dessert to top off her meal, but she would have been at less risk of bingeing.

*Teaching the Strategies*

As your client focuses on the task of learning to stop when full, you can offer her some suggestions to aid in this process. In the past, the biggest cause of her overeating was a belief, conscious or unconscious, that certain foods would be taken away from her — either literally by the next diet or in her mind as the result of her judgment that she should not be eating them. Now, she can remind herself that the food she desires will always be available to her. Nothing and no one will ever take it away from her again. This will help her feel safe enough to begin to consider putting down her fork or spoon when she feels satiated.

Furthermore, you can advise your client to remind herself that the sooner she stops eating, the sooner she will become hungry again, leading to the next eating experience. This is a very important concept to your client who, by definition of being a compulsive eater, needs to go to food often. She may prefer to stop when she is no longer hungry, or she may choose to stop when she feels a full feeling in her stomach. Her choice of where to stop may vary throughout the day or on different days. On the one hand, if she stops sooner, she will collect more eating experiences throughout the day. This frequent contact with her internal cues promotes her attuned eating. At the same time, sometimes people prefer a full feeling. These guidelines are meant to be flexible, so your client should determine when she feels satisfied. If, however, she feels physically uncomfortable, she has clearly eaten more food than her body needs.

Clients usually report that once they eat in accordance with their bodies' signals for hunger and satiation, they are surprised by how little food it takes to feel satisfied. This presents clients with an interesting dilemma; on the one hand, they feel much more in charge of their eating and achieve physical and psychological satisfaction, yet they must also grieve the loss of consuming more food. The ability to tolerate this situation varies among clients who often feel that they are giving up a "best friend." Even as clients mourn the loss of the amount of food in their lives, the incentive to continue to move in the direction of attuned eating stems from the quality of these new eating experiences in comparison to the distress of their compulsive eating and bingeing. It is useful to remind your clients that while they may need less food during any given eating experience, another opportunity to eat is just around the corner. Unlike other addictions such as smoking or alcoholism where the goal is to completely give up the substance, people cannot live without food. With this approach to ending compulsive eating, clients do not have to give up the very thing they love. Instead, they get to have exactly what they want day in and day out.

As you teach or support your client in the process of learning to eat when she is hungry, eat what she is hungry for, and stop when she is full, you enable her to build an internal structure by which she can organize her eating. She is no longer as susceptible to the latest diets and fads that eventually lead to the next binge. She can replace her chaotic eating style with a consistent and reliable method of evaluating her food choices. Yet even as she collects these stomach-hunger experiences, she is bound to run into some obstacles along the way. As her therapist, it is your job to help her explore the meanings and solutions to these obstacles so that she can continue to intervene with her compulsive eating patterns.

## ENDNOTES

1. The Renfrew Center (2003). The Renfrew Center was established in 1985 as the nation's first free-standing facility created exclusively for women with eating disorders. Since then, it has treated more than 35,000 women and adolescent girls aged 14 and older. For more information about eating disorders, treatment, and professional resources, please call The Renfrew Center at 1-800-RENFREW or visit its web site at www.renfrew.org.
2. Davis, C. M. (1928). Self-selection of diet by newly weaned infants: An experimental study. *American Journal of Diseases of Children, 36,* 651.
3. Birch, L. L., Johnson, S., Andersen, G., Peters, J. C., & Schulte, M. C. (1991). The variability of young children's energy intake. *The New England Journal of Medicine, 324,* 232.
4. Johnson, S., & Birch, L. (1994). Parents' and children's adiposity and eating style. *Pediatrics, 94,* 653–661.
5. Hirschmann, J., & Munter, C. (Eds.). (1995). *When women stop hating their bodies.* New York: Fawcett Columbine, p. 98.
6. Hirschmann, J., & Munter, C. (Eds.). (1995). *When women stop hating their bodies.* New York: Fawcett Columbine, p. 98.
7. The benefits of mother's own milk. [Online]. Rush University Medical Center. Available: http://www.rush.edu/rumc/page-P02339.html [2003].
8. Birch, L., & Fisher, J. (1995). Appetite and eating behavior in children. *Pediatric Nutrition, 42* (4), 931–950.
9. Tribole, E., & Resch, E. (1996). *Intuitive eating.* New York: St. Martin's Paperbacks, p. 237.
10. Waterhouse, D. (1995). *Why women need chocolate.* New York: Hyperion, p. 110.
11. Hirschmann, J., & Munter, C. (1988). *Overcoming overeating.* New York: Fawcett Columbine, pp. 98–99.
12. Bentley, K. A. (2000). *Stop out-of-control eating.* Concord: Lovejoy and Lord Publishing, p. 80.
13. Tribole, E., & Resch, E. (1996). *Intuitive eating.* New York: St. Martin's Paperbacks, p. 103.

# CHAPTER 4

# OBSTACLES

After working with the non-diet approach for several months, a client stated, "This is the simplest and the most complex thing I've ever done in my life." She understood that the concept of eating when hungry and stopping when full is so basic that it should take place naturally and easily. At the same time, as a result of years of dieting and compulsive eating, she no longer knew how to listen to her physiological cues; furthermore, eating and weight were now fraught with meaning that needed to be unraveled so that she could move in the direction of attuned eating.

As clients move through the process of attuned eating, they often encounter obstacles to implementing various guidelines. Many of these issues are logistical and require a problem-solving approach. However, when clients attempt to use suggested strategies and repeatedly stumble, the therapist must help the client explore deeper psychological explanations for their resistance.

Each of the principles discussed in the previous chapter is subject to obstacles as your client ends her dieting. These include responding to physiological hunger, matching food choices with physical cravings, ending judgments about "good" and "bad" foods, stocking, keeping food available at all times, and stopping when full. Your client will also face obstacles as she deals with her body image. Chapter 6 will be devoted to working with these issues.

The goal of this chapter is to offer a therapeutic stance that will help your client navigate through obstacles as she tries to implement the guidelines of the non-diet approach. The sections of this chapter are arranged according to the three basic tenets of attuned eating; identifying physiological hunger, matching the correct food, and stopping when satisfied. However, these categories are not always discreet. For example, a client may experience difficulty making a match with food because she is too hungry by the time she decides to eat. In this case, she must first address the issue of identifying hunger in order to successfully make a match. Along the same lines, the issue of ending judgments about good and bad foods may overlap different categories. One client may find that she failed to listen to a craving because she told herself that she shouldn't eat the pumpkin pie she truly desired, while another client ate past fullness because she binged on cheeseburgers at a barbecue. Although the cheeseburger was, in fact, the perfect match, she ate more than her body needed as the result of her judgment that this was a "bad" food. A mother who frequently eats from her child's plate may do so because she is already hungry but has not taken the time to eat, or she may crave chicken salad on a bed of greens but does not take the time to make the match. Finally, she may view the grilled cheese and chips served to her child as forbidden food and, therefore, feel compelled to eat them while she can.

There are as many scenarios of possible roadblocks during the process of normalizing the relationship with food as there are clients seeking treatment for compulsive eating. Yet common themes emerge for people as to why they become stuck at various points along the way. As you become more familiar with the dynamics of compulsive eating, you will develop your own style of integrating responses, including education in the form of information, suggestions and reassurance, and psychological exploration, which frees your client to move beyond any obstacles that she encounters in her own unique process.

## Identifying Physiological Hunger

If your client reports that she cannot identify physiological hunger, review the Hunger Scale with her. Reassure her that everyone can eventually locate this physical cue. She may have done such an excellent job of suppressing her hunger signals over the years that it may take her some time to coax them back and believe that it is safe to experience this sensation. Many clients state that they feel the most hunger in the morning. Let your client know that this is a good place to start her process of relearning how to eat in an attuned manner. Remind her that accumulating even one hunger experience counts as an important event in her treatment.

Emphasize to your client that she must stay present with her hunger in order to accurately respond. This requires her to put aside her preoccupation about when and what she will eat later in the day or when and what she ate previously, and instead focus on a particular moment.

### OBSTACLES TO IDENTIFYING HUNGER: CASE EXAMPLES

Clients will often protest that their real life situations prohibit them from eating whenever they feel hungry. As a therapist, it is necessary to listen carefully to your client's objections. Are there concrete solutions to her predicament? Is there a psychological meaning for her concerns? Is she presenting a situation that requires a reasonable adaptation?

*Waiting for Hunger*

Liz revealed that she is not hungry first thing in the morning, but eats anyway because she cannot take time to eat when she gets to work. Further exploration found that Liz has a 45-minute train ride to work. The therapist asked Liz to consider taking her food with her on the train. Liz agreed to this experiment and discovered that she became hungry about 20 minutes into her ride. She had brought a container of cereal, a piece of fruit, some yogurt, and cookies with her. Liz ate the fruit and cereal and felt satisfied.

Liz liked the way she felt by waiting until she was truly hungry and decided to continue to provide for herself in this manner each morning. Of course, if Liz became hungry before leaving her house, she would eat at home. Eventually, Liz reported that on an occasional morning, she did not become hungry by the time her train arrived at the station. However, as Liz realized her strong preference for waiting until hunger to eat, she allowed herself to bring the food to her office. Her workplace permitted employees to have food at their desks, so eating at work was an option. Upon reflection, Liz realized that her initial concerns about eating in her office had several underlying meanings. She said that she hadn't really understood how important it was to eat at the moment of hunger. At first, this seemed silly to her and somewhat self-indulgent. It also felt like a hassle to go to the trouble of packing up her food to take on the train or bring to work. Liz had wondered if she was truly entitled to make such a fuss over herself. However, as Liz took the time to stay present with her hunger and respond in an attuned manner, she felt very good and enjoyed the self-care her actions represented.

## Becoming Entitled

The issue of entitlement is a common theme among compulsive eaters and often requires deeper exploration. Unlike Liz, Amy had a much more difficult time believing that she was entitled to eat when she was hungry. Amy's therapist began by making concrete suggestions over a period of several weeks, yet Amy continually reported that she was unable to wait for hunger before eating.

> **Therapist:** When you think about getting hungry, what comes to mind?
>
> **Amy:** I shouldn't get hungry.

**Therapist:** That's an interesting response. It's natural for people to get hungry. (Amy nods in agreement.) I wonder why it's okay for everyone else, but somehow it's not alright for you.

**Amy:** I wasn't supposed to.

**Therapist:** Can you explain that to me?

**Amy:** My mother had the four of us children and by the time she came home from working all day, she was exhausted. It was all she could do to put some food on the table for us. If I told her I wanted to eat something before dinner was ready, she said, "It's not time to eat." But that was true about anything I wanted. After my parents' divorce, I think my mom was pretty depressed. My brother became a rebel, but I just tried to stay quiet and out of the way. I've never let myself need much of anything.

**Therapist:** It's very helpful that you are making the connection between your fear of upsetting your mother and your inability to experience hunger in the present. This is an issue that's going to take time to work on. I can hear that growing up it felt dangerous for you to notice your needs. I want to point out to you that in the present, if you notice when you are hungry, it really won't have an effect on your relationships with other people in your life. After all, when you reach for food, no one really knows whether you are eating because you are physically hungry or for other reasons. Our goal is to help you feel that you deserve to notice your needs and respond to them. We'll start with your hunger, and over time you are likely to find that this sense of entitlement will transfer to other areas of your life as well.

Over the next 6 months, Amy struggled to allow herself to become hungry. Amy's successes at responding to her physiological cues were followed by strong feelings of guilt related to the damage she felt she would cause in the relationship with her mother by tuning into her own needs. The therapist weaved between checking in with Amy about her actual eating experiences and exploring the feelings triggered by her attempts to take care of herself. Amy reached the point where she ate out of stomach hunger the majority of time, and continued to work on her internal conflicts related to her mother.

*Fearing Hunger*

Susan also struggled with allowing herself to become hungry. The therapist asked Susan what she imagined would happen if she became hungry. Susan replied by describing the great discomfort she associated with physical hunger, reminiscent of her dieting days when she went without eating for extremely long periods of time. Susan's therapist reminded her that with a non-diet approach, there was no reason to become so hungry; in fact, she was to feed herself the moment she noticed her physical signals. Susan developed a phrase for herself: "I will keep myself comfortably fed." This became a mantra for Susan, enabling her to wait for hunger rather than to reach for food in the service of preventing any anticipated unpleasant sensations.

*Experiencing Shame*

Gloria faced a different psychological obstacle in regard to her hunger. Gloria reported to her treatment group that she felt fine waiting for physical hunger at home, but she often waited too long at the office. The consequence of ignoring her hunger was fatigue and crabbiness at work, and a binge when she arrived home. Group members offered helpful suggestions to Gloria, such as ideas for making sure she had enough food with her so that she knew she could eat when hungry, and putting a post-it on her computer that read, "Am I hungry?" which would remind her to check in with her stomach. Gloria tried to implement these ideas, but found that she was still waiting too long to eat. The therapist asked Gloria what her fantasy was of eating when she became hungry at work. Gloria immediately responded that she would feel shame if other people saw her eating. She believed that her officemates would think that she had no right to eat at her current size. At the same time, Gloria noted that there were several larger people in her office who ate at work.

The therapist asked Gloria to elaborate on the theme of shame, and she talked about her experiences of going shopping with her mother for clothes as a child. Gloria explained that her mother was very fashion conscious and took her to stores that had clothes that did not fit Gloria's body. Gloria asked her mother if they could try a store for "big girls," but her mother told her that she didn't need those stores; as soon as she dropped a few pounds, the regular clothes would fit fine. Gloria felt physically uncomfortable in her tight clothes and extremely self-conscious of the way they stretched across her body. She was made fun of by other children, and to this day Gloria does not like to call attention to her body. The shame she felt as a child remains with her as an extremely vulnerable affect, and Gloria realized that she hides much of herself from other people to the detriment of these relationships. After reaching this insight, Gloria decided to pursue individual treatment for these psychological issues while continuing to work on her compulsive eating in the group setting. For the time being, she continues to build her positive eating experiences when she is by herself, and understands that her sense of shame makes it impossible to be watched by others when she eats. She accepts that this is where she is in her process of ending overeating and will continue to work on this issue in treatment. The group suggested to her that she consider going out to eat by herself at work so that she can still try to make a good match without feeling she is under the scrutiny of others.

## FINDING SOLUTIONS

As your client describes her difficulties in responding to hunger, she may need to develop creative solutions. Clients experimenting with hunger almost always agree that it is worth the trouble to wait for physiological hunger and then respond. Yet the reality of life means that various factors can impinge on her ability to feed herself when she is hungry. By exploring these situations, which can occur at work, in social settings, or at home, your client can develop strategies to promote her attuned eating.

### At Work

Melissa is a librarian who cannot eat while working because food is prohibited anywhere near the books. She has a set lunchtime but often becomes hungry prior to her break. Melissa decided to keep a snack in her purse. She can usually take a quick bathroom break when needed, and on her way there she will take a bite or two of her snack in order to take the edge off her hunger. This plan helps her remain physically comfortable until her scheduled lunchtime.

Unlike Melissa, Andrew works at home. He spends most of the day on his computer in his upstairs office. He explains that even though the kitchen is only a flight of stairs away, sometimes he becomes so engrossed in his work that he doesn't want the interruption of getting food. However, Andrew also notices that by late afternoon he often gets a headache and realizes that he is extremely hungry. After some discussion, Andrew decided that the best solution for him is to prepare food early in the morning and bring it upstairs with him to his office. If he checks in with his stomach and discovers that he is hungry, he can simply reach over to his supply of food and respond without losing his concentration on his current project. Of course, if Andrew craves something that he did not bring to his office, he is free to go to his kitchen and get it. The flexibility of his plan ensures that he can stay focused on his work and respond to his physiological needs.

### In Social Situations

In the course of life, there are times when people want to be able to eat at a specific time. Your client may have plans to meet her friends for dinner or be invited to a holiday meal or wedding. The non-diet approach encourages normal eating, and participating in social occasions is a part of everyday life. As your client becomes more comfortable recognizing and responding to her physical hunger, she may want to consider manipulating her hunger at times to conform to other social needs. This process involves anticipating a future eating experience and planning accordingly so that she does not compromise her body's requirements for feeding.

For example, Ariel is having dinner with her boyfriend at 7:00 P.M. She finds herself feeling hungry at 5:00. Ariel realizes from past experience that if she waits until she arrives at the restaurant to eat, she will be ravenous and overeat. She currently craves the leftover pasta that she has in her refrigerator, but knows that if she eats it, she will not be hungry when she arrives for her date. Ariel knows that she must respond to herself in the present because she is hungry now. She decides to have a small amount of pasta, just enough to ease her hunger pangs. Ariel has practiced this method of attuned eating for sometime, so she can predict fairly accurately how much pasta she needs to eat in order to feel hunger again in a couple of hours. In this way, Ariel has "arranged" her hunger to satisfy her needs for both physical sustenance and sharing a meal with her boyfriend.

The concept of manipulating hunger is a flexible tool for clients that can be evaluated as each situation arises. One week later, Ariel was meeting a friend for lunch. She woke up late and was hungry for eggs and a bagel with cream cheese. Ariel realized that if she ate this amount of food, she would not feel hunger when she met her friend. However, Ariel decided that her craving was strong enough that she needed to satisfy her hunger by eating the breakfast. At the restaurant, Ariel explained to her friend that she wasn't hungry and ordered a cup of coffee. The two friends talked for a long period of time, and at some point Ariel noticed some hunger and ordered a bowl of soup.

In a similar situation, Denise was having lunch at a restaurant with her sister and was not physically hungry.

Unlike Ariel, she was uncomfortable with the idea of not ordering food. She chose to order a Chinese chicken salad, ate a few bites, and had the waitperson wrap up the rest for later. She felt pleased to know that when she did become hungry, she would have the option of eating this luscious salad.

In all of the above examples, the most important aspect of the person's decision-making process is acknowledging her entitlement to eat when she is physically hungry. From this starting point, your client will be in a sound position to decide if and when she wants to manipulate her hunger in order to guarantee her appetite at a particular time.

*At Home*

Clients who live alone are able to adhere to their internal schedule of hunger without pressures and concerns about reactions from roommates, significant others, or family members. A frequent issue for clients moving in the direction of attuned eating is the fact that they may not be hungry at the same time when others are sitting down to eat. The significance of this problem varies widely among clients.

Sharing food is viewed culturally as a way to connect with friends and family. Sitting at a table together, enjoying a bountiful meal, and engaging in conversation can provide a pleasurable, satisfying experience. However, mealtime can also be a source of conflict and dissension in many families. There is nothing magical about the food in and of itself that creates connection; rather, the quality of the experience is the result of what each person brings to the table.

If your client feels that it is important for her to sit down with others at home for a meal, support her wish to maintain this structure. However, she must also consider giving herself permission to eat only when she is hungry. If her husband arrives home at 7:00 P.M. but she is hungry at 6:00, she can eat in advance and still sit at the table with him while he eats. Conversely, if her family eats at 6:00 P.M. but she is not hungry, she can join them at the dinner table to talk about the day. Remind your client that it is conversation that connects people, not eating the exact same food at the exact same time. If your client reports that she feels a sense of deprivation when everyone else is eating, or that others at the table pressure her to eat, remind her that this choice is always up to her. If she feels she needs to eat, she can go ahead and do so; as always, she should pay attention to the way she ends up feeling physically. She can also make a plate for herself and put it away for later so that she feels secure that there will be plenty of food for her at the moment she becomes hungry. Many clients will reveal that as children, there was competition with siblings to get enough food. This feeling of deprivation over the possibility of not getting a fair share often leads to eating when not hungry, eating food that is not really desired, and eating more food than necessary.

Over time, your client may find that as she gets to know herself better as an attuned eater, she can predict more reliably when she will become hungry. She may use this information to make adjustments so that, for instance, she eats half a sandwich on her way home from work when she is somewhat hungry, allowing her to be physically hungry once again when her family sits down for dinner at 6:45. Without this sandwich, she would have walked in the door famished and eaten an amount of food that would have prevented physiological hunger at the time her family gathered to eat.

It is important to emphasize to your client that in the beginning of her work with the non-diet approach, the more meticulous she can be in responding to her physical signals, the more progress she will make in ending her overeating. Therefore, she may need to eat at times that do not seem particularly convenient but correspond to her internal cues. As she feels more comfortable with her hunger and reaps the benefits of meeting her needs, she will discover that it is less tolerable for her to ignore her physiological cues that tell her it is time to eat. At the same time, she will become more adept at figuring out ways to accommodate her internal needs to the external situations that are important to her.

# Making the Match

When your client identifies physical hunger, her next task is to ask herself exactly what she is hungry for. This concept is probably very new to your client, and at first it will take a significant amount of effort for her to accurately decide just what type of food her body needs at a particular moment. Reassure your client that if she continues to ask herself what she craves and practices this behavior over a period of time, she will eventually find that this process becomes integrated and natural. At the same time, even normal eaters must take a few moments to check in with themselves about what they desire in order to determine their hunger needs.

## OBSTACLES TO MAKING THE MATCH: CASE EXAMPLES

In the last chapter, we offered techniques to enable your client to identify what she is hungry for by asking herself questions related to the temperature and texture of the food. We also described the importance of keeping a wide variety of foods available to ensure that your client has a reasonably good chance of obtaining what she desires. However, the ability to keep plenty of food available often creates a significant obstacle for clients pursuing this work.

### The Empty Refrigerator

Gretchen felt comfortable with the idea of using a non-diet approach. However, she realized that she had very few supplies in her refrigerator. She currently had half a bottle of apple juice, some old eggs, a container of yogurt, and leftover Chinese food. The therapist asked her what it felt like to have so little food in her home. Gretchen stated that she found this to be the best way to control her eating. In fact, she told her group that she felt terrified of bringing food into her house because she knew she would gobble it up immediately. Gretchen explained that because she did not feel ready to bring large amounts of food into her house, the idea of having more of a particular food available than she could possibly finish was not useful to her at this time. Group members provided support to Gretchen by sharing their initial fears about stocking their refrigerators, and they asked Gretchen what foods she thought she could allow in her kitchen. Gretchen made a list of foods that felt safe to her, including bread, turkey, fruit, salad ingredients, juice, eggs, milk, cereal, soups, pasta, and sauce. She went to the grocery store during the week and reported to the group that she did feel calmer knowing there was food in her house. She did not find herself overeating any more than usual. Over the next several weeks, Gretchen allowed herself to increase the variety of foods she bought at the grocery store. She realized coming home to an empty kitchen had actually made her extremely agitated. As she continued to maintain her well-stocked supply, she noticed that she was able to listen to her physical hunger and often make a successful match.

*The Grocery Store*

Ivy confronted a different type of problem as she considered going to the grocery story to buy food. As a very large woman, Ivy often felt she was under the scrutiny of others as she put food in her grocery cart. While she knew she had to buy enough food to keep her family fed, she felt great shame at the idea of stocking certain foods that were just for her. Ivy reported that when she went to the grocery store last week, she became so overwhelmed with shame that she abandoned her cart and left the store. The therapist empathized with her feelings, and Ivy elaborated on a previous experience in which another customer actually commented on the items she planned to buy in an judgmental and hostile manner.

> **Therapist:** I can hear how painful these experiences have been for you, and I certainly understand that you are afraid of the intensity of these feelings. At the same time, it is so important that you feel entitled to eat the foods you want. Otherwise, you create

a sense of deprivation, and we know from your past history that eventually you will binge on the very foods you tried to avoid. What are your thoughts about that?

**Ivy:** I do feel that this approach is right for me. I really know that diets don't work. But what if I can't bring myself to actually buy them? I know it shouldn't matter to me what other people think, but when a child is pointing at me and saying something to his mother, I just can't bear it.

**Therapist:** At this stage, let's try to think of some concrete ideas that will help you get the food you need in your house and keep you as comfortable as possible. Can you think of any ideas?

**Ivy:** Well, I was actually considering going to a grocery store in a different neighborhood. That way at least I won't run into anyone I know. But then I thought maybe that was too extreme and I just need to get over it.

**Therapist:** I think your idea is fine. As long as you have the time to go to a different grocery store, our main concern is that you have the food. It's worth going out of your way on behalf of yourself. At some point in the future, you may feel more comfortable with what you need to buy at your local grocery store, but for now it sounds like this idea appeals to you.

**Ivy:** I was even thinking that if someone comments on the number of boxes of cookies I was buying, I would just say I'm having a party. I don't usually lie, but really, they have no business asking.

**Therapist:** I just want to mention a couple of other ideas that clients have used who felt the way you do about grocery shopping. One person asked her husband to do the shopping, and he was very agreeable to helping her in this way. Other clients have found grocery stores where they can order food on the Internet and have it delivered.

Some group members also discussed visiting stores where there is a discount for buying in bulk; that way they feel people expect them to buy large quantities of food!

Ivy took her own advice and shopped in a different neighborhood. After several weeks, she came to an interesting conclusion. She realized that while shame about her body size made the experience of shopping more anxiety provoking, she really does not like to go to the grocery store. She began to have her groceries delivered to her home on a regular basis. Ivy's belief that she was entitled to have food for herself allowed her to experiment with different methods of grocery shopping until she found a way of procuring food that felt good to her.

As your client considers what she will buy at the grocery store, remind her that she needs to purchase a wide variety of foods. Sometimes a client will become excited by the concept of bringing forbidden foods into her home but neglect to purchase other foods that she may also crave. If she only has cookies and ice cream but discovers she desires a salad, she will turn to the sweets because they are her only option. Remind her that her goal is to create an abundance of all types of food so that she can choose freely at the time she experiences her physical hunger.

For example, Phyllis reported that she visited the grocery store and gave herself full permission to buy whatever she wanted. She found that just knowing she could have the Twinkies that she had enjoyed so much as a child was enough to make her decide that she really wasn't very interested in them. She opted not to buy them and continues to describe them as "awful" even though she now believes she can have one whenever she wants. "I can't believe that I've spent years thinking about how much I wanted to eat Twinkies, but they were completely unacceptable on any diet I've ever been on. Now that I can have them, it's the last thing I want." As the therapist, it is important to accept Phyllis' experience without judging her outcome as better or worse than another client who buys and eats many Twinkies before reaching a similar conclusion, or yet another client who decides that when she craves something sweet and soft, sometimes a Twinkie is the perfect match. Each client will need to discover her own food preferences through the process of legalizing all foods and then experimenting with which items satisfy her when she becomes hungry.

### Food Preparation

As your client discovers what types of foods she craves and enjoys, she may struggle with the concept of cooking. While some clients look forward to preparing meals for themselves, many clients state that they do not have the time or interest to cook the foods they desire. Brainstorm with your client about the many possible ways to address this problem. If your client knows that she likes chicken stir-fry but does not want to cook, she may decide to buy it frozen rather than make this dish from scratch. She could also order this item from a local Chinese restaurant. If time is the main issue for her, she can consider cooking over the weekend and freezing foods so that they are readily available during the week when her schedule is busier. If your client rejects these suggestions or finds herself unable to implement these ideas, you will need to use your therapeutic skills to explore other possible psychological issues such as themes of entitlement and self-care.

### Judgments

Letting go of judgments about food creates another significant obstacle for many clients. As the result of spending years memorizing the fat gram and caloric counts of most foods, your client may find that this information returns to her thought process unbidden as she attempts to legalize formerly forbidden foods. Furthermore, the constant bombardment of information about food from friends, family, and especially the media, often portrayed in the context of "good" and "bad," intensifies her doubts about abandoning her guilt when she eats certain foods. On the one hand, it is important to empathize with your client about how difficult she finds the process of approaching food in a manner different from the dictates of mainstream culture. At the same time, remind your client that when she avoids her forbidden foods because of a fear of fat, history shows that she eventually overeats. Both you and your client must remember that giving herself permission to eat exactly what she is hungry for is in the service of normalizing her relationship with food. Once your client accomplishes this task, she may choose to make adjustments in her food choices to accommodate nutritional needs, a concept that is described in chapter 8. At this point, however, her negative judgments about her food preferences actually fuel her compulsive eating.

For example, Tanya worked with the non-diet approach for a 9-month period and felt she had legalized the majority of foods. Yet she reported that she consistently ate a Reuben sandwich and chips for lunch, even though she realized that sometimes this combination did not feel quite right in her stomach. Her group therapist asked her to think back to the last time she ate this sandwich but did not feel that it was the correct match. Tanya recalled that she had been at work and knew she was hungry. As she reflected on the experience, Tanya remembered that at the time the Reuben sandwich was actually too heavy in her stomach, and a turkey sandwich would have felt better physically. That day, Tanya had stopped in a deli that offered all types of sandwiches, so availability was not an issue. Tanya's therapist advised her to continue to pay attention to what she was hungry for and notice what she experienced as she attempted to make a match.

Over the next several weeks, Tanya concluded that even though she agreed in theory with the idea of listening to her body, at a subtle, emotional level she continued to believe that it was "better" to eat low fat foods. Tanya now understood that at the moment she made this judgment, she felt compelled to prove to herself that she could eat the "illegal" food. As this idea became conscious, Tanya was able to talk herself through these experiences more consistently by reminding herself that she really would have a Reuben sandwich when she craved one, that the most important goal was to satisfy her hunger, and that yelling at herself for eating "bad" foods never leads to positive change. Over time, Tanya became more comfortable tuning into her hunger needs and reported that she felt better physically and psychologically.

## Legalizing "Healthy" Foods

Another interesting dynamic arises for many clients with a long history of dieting. While compulsive eaters feel attracted to the very foods that were limited on diet programs, they often develop an aversion to the foods that were mandated by these plans, such as fruits, vegetables, and salads. Valerie told her group that sometimes she notices that an apple would be the perfect match in her stomach, but she still goes for a piece of candy. Valerie has legalized foods over a period of many months, and her bingeing has decreased significantly. However, she explained that the minute she thinks about having the apple, she feels as though she is "being good," which causes her to experience some deprivation and want to rebel. This is a natural reaction to being compelled to eat a certain food; even former president George Bush Sr. once said that his mother made him eat broccoli as a child, and now he refuses to eat it! Several members of the group related that they also experience this sense of being controlled when they turn to healthful foods. At the same time, all agreed that their bodies really did desire the foods that had been part of their diet plans in the past. Valerie had essentially stopped buying fresh foods because she usually threw most of them away.

The therapist instructed Valerie to continue to buy fruits and vegetables so that they would be available to her if she craved them. The therapist also advised Valerie that she could buy smaller amounts to decrease the amount of waste, but reminded her that if she stopped providing healthful foods to herself, she would ensure an incorrect match at certain times. Valerie agreed that she needed to "legalize" her former diet foods. By recognizing her resistance to certain food types, she was more able to listen to her body's needs.

## FINDING SOLUTIONS

Remind your client that keeping a wide variety of food available is essential to making a match. Stocking the kitchen ensures that there will be plenty of food at home. However, clients often need to eat when they are away, such as at work, running errands, or traveling, and therefore they must find a means to provide food for themselves at these times. Also, in the course of examining strategies to support their abilities to make a match, clients may discover internal conflicts that need to be understood.

### Using a Food Bag

In the previous section, Liz took food with her on the train and Melissa took food with her to the library. Each of these clients carried a supply with them so that they could respond to their physiological hunger when it arose. Hirschmann and Munter label this idea, "carrying a food bag." Just as a parent would not leave home without sustenance for her small child, encourage your client to provide this type of care for herself.

Alana is in the early stages of becoming an attuned eater. She reported that over the weekend she was able to wait for hunger several times before eating. She found herself craving toast and an orange in the morning, which felt great in her stomach. She experienced hunger a couple of hours later and made a match with a cheese omelet. During the afternoon, she went to the circus with her niece and nephew. She found herself becoming hungry and considered her options. She would have preferred a tuna sandwich or tuna salad, but the only type of food offered was on the heavy, greasy side. The children ordered hot dogs and fries, so she decided these would be the simplest items to buy. Alana ate the hot dog and fries and found that she felt slightly nauseous for the next several hours. It was clear that this was not the food she would have picked if there had been more choices.

Packing a food bag will solve this dilemma for Alana the next time she is in a similar situation. The food bag is meant to provide a wide variety of eating options. If a client packs only cookies, this guarantees she will eat the cookies whether they are the correct match or not. Instead, a food bag might include items such as a sandwich, pasta salad, chips, fruit, carrots, cereal, candy, yogurt, cookies, or drinks. Each client will decide what types of foods she likes to have with her. If your client is at work and a group of colleagues decides to go out for lunch, she is in no way obligated to eat from her food bag just because she brought it with her. Instead, she can go to the restaurant and make a match for herself. If she has any leftovers, she can add them to her food bag for a future eating experience. If she is very hungry before it is time to meet for lunch, she can eat something out of her food bag ahead of time to take the edge off of her hunger until she meets her friends. If the chosen restaurant does not provide foods that would create a match, she can figure out a way to eat what she really wants from her food bag and join her colleagues anyway, perhaps ordering coffee or dessert.

The food bag is like a security blanket; it is there for a person when she needs it. Clients can use different methods to carry their food, such as a lunch box, paper bag, backpack, cooler, thermos, briefcase, or tote bag. The most important element for your client is that the container accommodates the amount and type of food she plans to bring with her in a comfortable manner.

After Alana considered the idea of a food bag, she reflected that if she had brought a sandwich with her to the circus, she would have ended up feeling much more physically comfortable by making a better match. She carries a backpack with her most of the time and thinks she can easily add food to her pack.

*Worth the Trouble*

The notion of carrying food is often met with resistance by clients. Your client may complain that it is too much trouble to pack food in the morning, that nothing sounds good to her when she wakes up, or that there are plenty of places nearby to get food if she should become hungry. Let your client know that while you understand her concerns, if she experiments with carrying a food bag, she will discover how invaluable this tool can be in certain situations.

**Elizabeth:** When I leave my home in the morning, the thought of most foods makes me sick. I have no idea what I will crave later in the day.

**Therapist:** I agree with you that a lot of times certain foods do not sound good in the morning. Many times when people leave the house, the food they bring with them sounds unappealing. But they know from experience that later in the day they will become hungry and be very glad that they brought the food with them. You might want to try to place a wide variety of food in your bag anyway and see what happens. Hopefully, you'll find that at some point when you are hungry, you have exactly what you need. If not, you can use that experience to adjust what you bring with you. What do you think about that idea?

**Elizabeth:** You know the truth is that it just seems like too much trouble. Mornings are already so rushed getting the kids off to school before I go to work. It's enough that I have to make their lunches.

**Therapist:** I understand that you have a very hectic schedule. But it's interesting to me that you find the time to make your children's lunches but not your own. What do you make of that?

**Elizabeth:** Well, they have to have lunch for school. I can always run out later to get something.

**Therapist:** Yet sometimes you don't. We've talked about how hard it is to get away from your desk sometimes. I remember you telling me that you were eating your secretary's candy because you felt so desperate for food. I can't help but think that if you knew you had food available to you at work, you'd feel better.

**Elizabeth:** You're probably right, but I just don't think it's going to happen.

**Therapist:** What would it be like to pack the lunches for you and your children the night before?

**Elizabeth:** At night there is so much going on: dinner, homework, sports practice. It's too much trouble to think about tomorrow.

**Therapist:** You've used the phrase "it's too much trouble" a couple of times now. Sometimes it can be helpful when you look at an obstacle to implementing the guidelines of the non-diet approach to apply the words you are using to something about your past. If you were to say, "I'm too much trouble," I wonder what comes to mind.

**Elizabeth:** When I was a child, I was too much trouble to my parents. After my dad lost his job, my mother took on overtime at work. Since I was the oldest, I was expected to take care of myself because my little brother and sister were just too young. (With a smile) I had to make my own lunch everyday and I hated it. That's why I promised myself that my children would never have to make their own lunches.

**Therapist:** And you've followed through on that promise! But let's talk more about your own feeling of being too much trouble.

**Elizabeth:** My mom seemed so sad. And my dad was de-pressed. He should have had the time to help us more, but he just sat in his study and read his books. Eventually he was hospitalized. I did everything I could to help my mom with Joe and Molly. But I hated it. I wanted to be out with my friends, and instead I had to come home every-day after school to get dinner started. Truthfully, I'm sick of taking care of everyone else. Why can't someone take care of me for once?

**Therapist:** It sounds like you are feeling angry.

**Elizabeth:** Absolutely. When does my turn come?

Elizabeth and her therapist continued to discuss these dynamics over several sessions. Elizabeth realized she still held out hope that one day her mother would provide the care she felt cheated out of as a child. She imagined her mother coming over and preparing her food bag for her, although at the same time Elizabeth knew that the level of care she craved would be inappropriate at this stage of her life. As Elizabeth understood that her opposition to preparing food for herself represented her anger at not getting previous needs met, she continued to explore her longings from the past. Elizabeth concluded that if she were to take the time to make a food bag for herself, she would be acknowledging in a significant way that she had to let go of her familiar wishes for being rescued. Over time, Elizabeth understood that by holding on to her fantasies, she ensured that she would continue to feel deprived of caretaking; if she felt others should do for her, she could not do for herself. New memories emerged for Elizabeth as she explored the theme of feeling like "too much trouble" to her family. However, she also became able to take care of herself and ask for what she needed from her husband and close friends. Elizabeth began to carry a food bag with her and experienced the pleasure of being worth the trouble.

## Unexpected Situations

Clients often state that there are plenty of restaurants near their workplaces or on the routes they are using to shop, do errands, or travel, therefore eliminating the need to carry a food bag. When a client becomes hungry and one of these food establishments offers the right match, your client can obtain what she needs. However, life can be unpredictable, and people often find themselves in circumstances that they did not anticipate. For example, a delayed flight left Julie caught on a plane out on the runway with no means of procuring food for herself. She had counted on the meal served on the flight to take care of her hunger needs, but developed a severe headache as a result of this situation. Greg looked forward to the pasta and salad he planned to eat when he arrived home from work. However, an emergency situation developed at work, and he was stuck at his office for several more hours than he expected. Leaving to obtain food was impossible. Lynn had lost track of time and had exactly 20 minutes to eat before she had to give a presentation. She knew precisely what she was hungry for, but the restaurant that sold this food was 10 minutes away by car, if traffic was good. She could not take the risk of being late and had to settle for eating something available at the take-out restaurant next door. This action took care of her hunger, but did not provide a satisfying eating experience.

In all of these examples, a food bag would have prevented the discomfort that occurred for each person. Julie, Greg, and Lynn might have packed some of the foods that would have adequately satisfied their hunger, or they might have chosen to eat a few bites of something until their situations were alleviated, and they could return to the foods previously anticipated. There is never a disadvantage to keeping food available at all times for both compulsive eaters and normal eaters alike. As people develop the habit of bringing food with them, they usually discover that it is quite a convenience. Anne reported that she did not realize the value of her food bag until she forgot to bring it with her on her last business trip. She arrived at the hotel late at night, completely exhausted and with no interest in going down to the coffee shop. She thought about the tote bag she had forgotten on her kitchen counter containing a banana, sandwich, some chips, and a granola bar, and wished she could make it appear at that moment! Carrying food is not meant to be a rigid expectation, but rather expresses a statement about the practical and psychological benefits of providing for oneself.

*Processing the Reactions of Others*

Your client may worry that if she brings her food to work, other people will think she is out of control or self-indulgent. Office settings are usually ripe with diet talk, from discussing the latest weight loss plans to actual weight loss contests. Yet when Marie placed a large bowl of candy on her desk, people were constantly in and out of her office partaking in her supply and thanking her for sharing with them. Marie eventually had to set a limit when a coworker began to use the frozen meals she kept in the company's refrigerator without replacing them. Clients who bring food into work often become popular very quickly as other people who do not provide food for themselves know that they can always count on this person to have something to eat. The important point is for your client to develop the stance, as Marie successfully did, that she deserves to have food with her. To the extent that other people make judgments about her eating, she can view their reactions as projections of their own discomfort with food.

Esther worried about the reaction of her friends when she joined them at a resort for a reunion weekend. The eight women shared two rooms. Esther was the only one who brought a supply of food with her because she knew, from past experience, that she could not always get what she wanted when she needed it. Historically, Esther and her friends spent much time discussing food and weight. Esther planned to share her new approach with her friends but was anxious that they might be critical of her end to dieting because she was still at a large size. She received mixed reactions to her explanation of trying to eat what she was hungry for when she was hungry, but at the end of the weekend, the group of women realized that they had all made use of Esther's food supply.

Cynthia is less comfortable letting her parents know about the non-diet approach. For her entire life, Cynthia's parents focused on "healthy" eating, and they did not keep any dessert foods in the house. Cynthia debated going along with their restrictions during her week-long stay. Her therapist asked her to consider speaking with them about her needs to have different types of foods available before she arrived at their home. Cynthia explored this possibility, but felt that for now, she was still too afraid of their judgments to risk this type of openness. The therapist asked Cynthia to imagine how the week would go in terms of being able to make good matches while she was visiting her family. Cynthia concluded that she would ask her parents to buy a brand of frozen whole wheat waffles she often likes in the morning because this choice would be acceptable to them. She realized that she would feel deprived without her supply of chocolates and become more at risk of overeating if she was unable to have a sweet when she needed one. Cynthia settled for keeping the chocolates in her suitcase away from her parents' scrutiny but easily available in case a craving should arise.

### The "Good Enough" Food Match

Despite your client's best efforts, she is bound to find herself in situations where it is impossible to get exactly what she wants at a particular moment. Psychoanalyst D. W. Winnicott developed the concept of the "good enough" mother to acknowledge the fact that no parent can always be perfect. Likewise, your client may need to settle at times for a "good enough" match when she cannot get the exact food she craves. As explained in the previous chapter, suggest to your client that she identify the most important flavor or texture and then choose a food as close as possible. If she is successful, the food should feel good enough in her body to keep her physically comfortable.

### Taking a Deeper Look

If your client cannot identify what she wants at all, she may eat something bland, such as pasta or bread, which is unlikely to create physical discomfort. However, if she repeatedly fails to determine a match, further exploration is warranted.

> **Lauren:** I can tell when I'm hungry, but I just can't seem to identify what I want.
>
> **Therapist:** Do you have a wide variety of foods at home?
>
> **Lauren:** Yes, in fact I just went to the grocery store yesterday and got all sorts of stuff. It's there if I need it, but I just don't ask myself what I want.

**Therapist:** What do you think gets in the way of asking your-self that question?

**Lauren:** What if I want something, but I can't get it?

**Therapist:** You just told me that you really do have a lot of food. When you think about listening to your-self, what feeling comes to mind?

**Lauren:** It's funny that you ask that. I've noticed that every so often when I do make a match I feel sad.

**Therapist:** Sad?

**Lauren:** Yes, it's strange because it's happened when I'm perfectly fine. I notice I'm hungry, eat what I crave, and then instead of feeling good, I get very sad. I hadn't really made the connection until I said it out loud just now.

**Therapist:** Do you have any idea about what might make you sad when you get what you want?

**Lauren:** Actually, I do. I was just talking with a friend of mine yesterday. We met for a cup of coffee. She is one of my closest friends, but it's been months since I've seen her. We were talking about how hectic our lives are now with children and hus-bands and jobs. I have all the things I wanted, but it seems like I just can't find the time to do some pretty basic things for myself. I know I shouldn't complain, but it makes me feel very sad.

**Therapist:** As you talk, I hear the parallel between your sit-uation with food and the circumstances of your life: You have what you think you want, but you still can't quite seem to tune into what you need for yourself. Let's think about what that means in terms of letting yourself eat exactly what you want. After all, it may be difficult for you and your friend to plan the time to see each other, but the food is literally right in your kitchen.

**Lauren:** Somehow getting what I want with food reminds me that I often ignore my needs. That's what the

> sadness is. I didn't realize that by tuning into my
> needs with food, I automatically think about
> other areas of my life. I guess it just seems eas-
> ier to ignore those needs completely than to
> have to think about them.

Following this discussion, Lauren may find that her new insights allow her to match her food needs more accurately and tolerate any sadness that follows. She may also use this acknowledgment of distress as an opportunity to work on "making matches" in other areas of her life. If Lauren remains unable to tolerate the feelings that occur when she makes a match, she and her therapist will need to focus on this issue in further sessions, perhaps exploring the meaning of meeting needs in her family of origin.

Bruce related a different sort of issue with his difficulty in making matches. He explained that when he is at home where he lives by himself, he consistently identifies what he is hungry for and provides that food for himself. However, Bruce finds that when he is out with his friends or colleagues, he often misses any cues about what would feel good in his stomach. Bruce is acutely aware of the difference between making a match and being off the mark, and he is anxious to solve this problem. Bruce listed interventions he had already tried on his own, such as trying to decide what he was hungry for before joining others. However, he felt that a deeper reason existed for his inability to pay attention to himself when eating with a group of people.

As Bruce analyzed his situation with his therapist, he talked about his long-standing concern of pleasing other people. He is aware that he often suppresses his own thoughts and feelings in order to keep people around him from feeling angry, a dynamic that stems from his early relationship with his volatile father. Bruce has learned that it is easier to go along with what other people expect of him rather than express his own desires and risk the anticipated abuse he received from his dad. Although Bruce knows intellectually that his friends will not be angry with him for ordering what he wants at a restaurant, he feels compelled to go along with whatever they eat. If Bruce wants an appetizer but his colleague does not suggest this idea, Bruce will suppress his own cravings. Initially, Bruce felt calmer at his understanding of this pattern, even though he continued to follow the food preferences of his friends. As Bruce grew angrier at their ability to control his eating (of course, they had no idea that this was how he experienced these meals), he connected this reaction to his anger toward his father for treating him so poorly. Ultimately, Bruce was able to strengthen his inner self and feel more secure in the boundary between himself and others. Ordering what he was hungry for at a restaurant became a relatively nonthreatening situation for him to begin to assert his needs. He realized that his friends were not particularly interested in what he ate and felt much more satisfied physically and socially by his improved ability to respond to his hunger signals.

When your client listens to her hunger and provides herself with a wide variety of foods both at home and away, she will gather experiences in which she makes matches that feel great. Clients use words such as "fabulous," "excellent," and "perfect" to describe those moments that support their physical and psychological well-being. After all, it was through their own careful attunement to their bodies and their ability to accurately respond to themselves that they created this sense of satisfaction. Not all matches will generate this excitement, but your client will develop the crucial ability to determine whether a food match was right for her. You can communicate the importance you place on your client's entitlement to take care of herself with food in this way by frequently asking her to share and analyze her eating experiences with you.

## Stopping When Full

As your client identifies her hunger and eats what she is hungry for, she must make a decision about when to stop. Although experts moving away from the diet paradigm may use the term "moderation" to suggest how much food a person should eat, this concept connotes an external parameter of deciding when to stop. For the compulsive eater who is already sensitive to any implication of deprivation, the idea that she should eat a particular amount feels like a restriction, even if her body craves less than the recommended serving. Therefore, the most important factor in accomplishing the task of stopping when full is for your client to pay attention to the way her stomach feels. As she becomes increasingly adept at listening to her physiological cues, she will naturally regulate her eating patterns so that her food intake may match views of moderation, without requiring her to exert control.

## INITIAL STRATEGIES

Frequently, a compulsive eater will find that it is easier at first to recognize the cues that tell her when to start eating than it is to tell when to stop. Therefore, your client may find that she has an increasing number of experiences where she can identify her hunger and make a match, but she continues to eat past satisfaction. Reassure your client that this is natural, but that over time it will feel less tolerable to her when she eats past fullness.

As your client imagines how a particular food will feel in her stomach, she can also visualize how much she believes her body requires in order to feel satiated. Ask her to think about how her stomach will feel not only immediately after she finishes eating, but 15 or 20 minutes later. As your client becomes an attuned eater who is increasingly in touch with her stomach, she will also become an accurate predicator of the amounts of food her body needs to achieve her desired level of fullness.

In the beginning of treatment, ask your client to simply notice the way her body feels when she eats more than her body requires. She can also remind herself that the sooner she stops, the sooner she will become hungry and be able to eat again. As described in the last chapter, this idea is very important for the compulsive eater who often needs to go to food.

## OBSTACLES TO STOPPING WHEN FULL

As your client becomes more proficient at recognizing her physical hunger and making matches, ask her what happens when she thinks about stopping at the point of satisfaction. Your client may tell you that the food tastes so good that she does not want to stop. Invite her to consider putting down her fork or spoon at the moment of satiation, with full permission to return to the food a few minutes later or whenever she desires it again. Often, the act of breaking her intake of food helps her realize that she is ready to be finished with a particular eating experience. Explain to your client that this suggestion is not meant to make her feel that she must control her overeating. Many diet programs recommend strategies such as leaving the table or even pouring salt or pepper over a food to force a person to stop eating. Your intervention is aimed at helping her pause long enough to reflect on her internal needs. If she realizes that she is physically comfortable, she can choose to stop eating. If she determines that she must use all of her willpower to refrain from continuing to eat, she can go back to the food. It is important for you and your client to always remember that the goal of the non-diet approach is to help her move naturally in the direction of attuned eating rather than to control her compulsive urges. Clients eventually discover that as they eat past satisfaction, the food no longer tastes as good, and the physical discomfort is no longer worth experiencing. The key to reaching this state is your client's knowledge that she can return to a particular food when a physical craving occurs.

### *"But If I Don't Eat It Now . . ."*

In order for your client to truly believe she can get what she desires when she is hungry, she must keep that food available. Your client may tell you that she ate past fullness while at a restaurant because she could never recreate this dish at home.

> **Andi:** I ordered pasta Alfredo, which is a specialty at this restaurant. I have tried to make this sauce at home, but it just doesn't taste the same. It's hard to stop when I know I can't have it again.
>
> **Therapist:** What about the possibility of taking home whatever is leftover once you notice you are full?
>
> **Andi:** It just doesn't taste the same when I heat it up.
>
> **Therapist:** How far is this restaurant from your home?
>
> **Andi:** It's about half an hour away.
>
> **Therapist:** Could you consider the idea that if you have a strong craving for pasta Alfredo from this restaurant, you will either go to the restaurant or order it out so that you convince yourself that you can have it again when you need it?
>
> **Andi:** There would be times that I could do that, but it's not always possible to get there with my schedule.
>
> **Therapist:** It's worth going out of your way on behalf of yourself whenever possible while you are engaged in this process. Of course, there is the reality that sometimes we just can't get what we want. At times, you may need to eat something as close as possible to the restaurant's meal so that you make sure you respond to your physical hunger, but it would be useful to promise yourself that if the craving continues, you will make sure that you get back to the restaurant when time allows.

Eating past fullness will decrease significantly for your client as she truly gives herself permission to eat what she is hungry for when she is hungry. Andi's commitment to be meticulous in this endeavor will help her feel safer at the prospect of stopping to eat something she loves. By repeatedly demonstrating that she will cook, buy, and order the foods she craves, she will find that stopping no longer feels so dangerous. In the past, Andi continued to eat beyond satisfaction because of the deprivation she experienced when she told herself that she would not be able to have the pasta again. Now she can eat exactly the amount she needs, which, Andi discovered, was sometimes a smaller portion than the restaurant served.

## FINDING SOLUTIONS

There will be times when it is impossible to recreate an eating experience, such as a unique food experienced while on vacation, and if your client overeats under these circumstances, she should not become overly concerned. After all, normal eaters overeat on occasion also. However, there is an important difference between the reactions of these two groups. An attuned eater is likely to notice that she ate too much because of the discomfort in her stomach, and acknowledge this distress to herself and perhaps her companions. Then she will automatically wait until the next time she is physically hungry to consume more food. The compulsive eater, on the other hand, will berate herself for overeating. She may promise to abstain from food for a long period of time in order to repent for her transgressions. She will either succeed in waiting until she is extremely hungry to eat again, creating a high risk of overeating, or she will eat prior to becoming hungry again, either because the wait feels too long or because of the perceived deprivation.

As you try to help your client interrupt this cycle, instruct her to be gentle with herself. She can notice the way her body feels when she overeats and register the discomfort. She can also tell herself that she is doing her best to work her way out of this problem, and that the nature of compulsive eating is that, at times, she will eat more than her body physiologically requires. She can do her best to wait until she experiences physical hunger to eat again. In past programs, your client viewed her bingeing as breaking her diet. This led to more overeating while she was "off" her plan in anticipation of future restrictions. Reinforce the concept with your client that her eating past fullness is part of the process and not a failure of willpower. Her goal is to continue to notice and analyze these experiences. Simply by ending the internal yelling, your client will find that her overeating slows down significantly because of the decreased anxiety she experiences when she is compassionate with herself.

## STOCKING: OBSTACLES AND SOLUTIONS

Another important aspect of supplying enough food to reduce overeating relates to the concept of stocking. We already discussed the importance of keeping a wide variety of food available in order to increase the chances of making a match. Next, your client must consider the amount of food she keeps available so that she can feel secure at the prospect of letting herself stop eating when her stomach signals satisfaction.

If your client is not ready to consider the possibility of bringing large amounts of food into her home, suggest that she continue experimenting with paying attention to hunger, making matches, and noticing how her body feels when she reaches fullness. As she gradually discovers that she can trust her body to organize her eating, she will become more comfortable integrating her binge foods into her life. Continue to emphasize that as she eliminates the diet mindset that creates deprivation, she will find the task of stopping when full more natural. However, if your client is willing to engage in the process of stocking, she will learn in a profound manner how having more than enough food actually allows her to stop eating when she feels satisfied.

Imagine for a moment that you are at the end of a meal that you have thoroughly enjoyed. There are only a few pieces of the stir-fry beef left, so you decide that you will finish them. After all, it is only a few more bites and hardly worth the effort of putting it away for a future time. Now imagine that there is so much stir-fry beef left that you could not possibly make it go away. You place it in a container to store in the refrigerator where it will remain available if you become hungry later in the evening or in the next few days. When there is more food available than can be consumed, a person must make an active decision about when to stop eating. While many diet programs recommend that an overeater should put small amounts of food on her plate or practice leaving some food at each meal, these behaviors reinforce feelings of deprivation, which lead to overeating. The act of providing more food than needed offers a sense of security to the compulsive eater, which allows her to focus on her body's natural needs rather than rebel against her sense of being controlled.

### Removing the Boundaries

Gail reported that everyday after she returned home from her teaching job she made one bag of microwave popcorn and ate it all. While this snack usually felt like a good match in her stomach, Gail felt unsure about the amount she needed to eat. Her therapist agreed that it was curious for Gail to require the exact amount of popcorn each and every day. Together, they developed a plan where Gail would actually make three bags of popcorn when she returned from work, and place them in a large bowl. In a short period of time, Gail learned that on many days her body needed less than a bag of popcorn to feel satiated, while on other days she needed more than one bag to fulfill her hunger needs. Eliminating the boundaries of the wrapper helped Gail tune into her natural fullness.

The technique of removing the boundaries of packaging supports your client's movement in the direction of taking charge of her own eating. Andrea often felt upset if she noticed that she ate a whole bag of Snickers® bars. She discussed these concerns in her group.

> **Andrea:** I feel like I'm completely out of control. I think that maybe this process isn't right for me. I'm not sure what to do.
>
> **Therapist:** I know that you feel upset about your bingeing. We can make a decision together about whether

the concept of stocking is best for you. Based on my experience, you are a good candidate for this method. I know it feels scary when you eat the candy. But I also know that when you didn't allow yourself to bring sweets into your home, you were stopping at the convenience store to get them or bingeing on other foods. Remember that bringing in the abundance is in the service of ending your compulsive eating. The goal is not to encourage overeating, but to help you truly tune into your needs without exerting control.

**Andrea:** For a few weeks, this was really working for me. But as I saw my supply getting low, I thought that maybe it was just beginner's luck. I feel afraid that I will just keep eating and eating and never stop.

**Cindy:** That's exactly the way I felt when I first started working with this approach. I thought there couldn't possibly be enough chocolate chip cookies to satisfy the amount I craved. But, I did what was suggested and it really worked! I have chocolate chip cookies in my pantry and I often forget that they are there. I've also gotten very picky. I used to say any chocolate chip cookie was fine, but now when I crave one, I want the gourmet kind.

**Therapist:** Does anyone else have an experience they would like to share with Andrea?

**Elyse:** I started the group when Cindy did. She was able to just go ahead and trust this process. But it was different for me. I was extremely frightened and decided not to stock at first. My individual therapist helped me explore the meaning of my anxiety. I learned that for me, I believed there could never be enough supplies to meet my needs. I've been working on understanding the emotional emptiness I carry around with me. I never had the love I wanted as a child, and it makes me feel very needy as an adult. But now I know that there really is enough food to satisfy my stomach and that has been an important step. I feel much

safer knowing that there is plenty of food available to me whenever I am hungry so that at least
in one way, I can count on myself to meet my
own needs.

**Andrea:** I do think I'm ready to do this. I want to be able
to feel more comfortable around food. It reminds
me that when I used to work in a restaurant and
could have whatever I wanted, I lost interest
pretty quickly.

**Pat:** I remember that one time we talked about this
concept using toilet paper instead of food. If
you're down to your last roll and don't have any
more in your home, it creates anxiety. After that
discussion, I stocked up on toilet paper the next
time there was a big sale at the grocery store! It
really makes a difference to know there are
plenty of rolls there, so I never have to think
about it. It was easier to think about abundance
with toilet paper or laundry detergent because it
had no meaning for me, unlike the food. But the
result was the same — I felt calmer and could
forget it was there until I needed it.

**Andrea:** That makes sense to me.

**Therapist:** Andrea, there are certain guidelines you will
need to follow if you decide to proceed in this
direction. The main thing is to never let your
supply run out, and that's what has been happening for you. As funny as it may sound, you
can never go wrong by having too much of a
particular food, only by not having enough.
What will help you work your way out of your
overeating is to buy more Snickers® than you
need — let's say 10 bags. Put them all in a huge
bowl, so that you can no longer tell how many
you eat. That will help you to stop counting how
many candy bars you consume. As the amount
in your bowl gets lower, to about two thirds, add
some more from extra bags in your pantry. That
way, your supply will never be drained.

Andrea agreed to follow these instructions, and to her relief, her interest in candy waned very quickly. Of course, she still wanted Snickers bars on occasion, but she was able to listen to her body tell her when and how much to eat, thereby eliminating the physical and psychological discomfort that occurred in the past.

*Waste Considerations*

Clients often express concern about wasting food as they engage in the process of stocking. If a client buys more food than she can possibly eat, she will certainly need to throw some of the food away. Your client may relate to the idea that when she is overeating, in a sense she is also wasting food by putting more into her body than she needs. Remind your client that stocking is only for the purpose of ending compulsive eating. At some point in the future, she will no longer need to buy large amounts of particular foods, and she will be in a stronger position to gauge how many groceries she needs to buy. Yet she will always need to keep her kitchen well supplied. When shopping, it is impossible to buy the exact amount of food needed for one person or a family. Therefore, there will always be too much or too little food. Your client will find that she prefers to have a feeling of abundance, even as her compulsive eating diminishes.

*Cost Considerations*

The process of stocking food costs money, and this causes an obstacle for clients who are unable to afford a consistent, large supply of groceries. Talk with your client about creative ideas to help her build a sense of abundance within her financial means. For example, she may bake cakes or muffins at home rather than buy these goods at a bakery. She can attempt to shop at stores that sell products in bulk to reduce the cost. She may rotate which items she stocks each week so that she buys ice cream during a 2-for-1 sale 1 week and frozen pizzas on sale the next. She can search for food ideas that use lower cost ingredients such as rice or beans. If your client decides that a particular food is too costly to stock, help her focus on the fact that her action is based on budgetary concerns rather than a fear of fat.

### Family Considerations

If a client lives with her family, she may worry that other people will consume her supply of food. Some clients make sure that they stock enough food to cover themselves and family members at all times, while other clients find a special shelf or cabinet to store the foods they want to stock. The main goal is that your client builds a sense of safety regarding her supply of food. Many clients report that their families are thrilled when they begin to provide a greater abundance of food. The entire family benefits as each member trusts that plenty of food is available to meet their needs. However, clients may also confront situations in which significant others object to the new approach, such as when one member of a couple continues to diet. If your client believes that stocking is in her best interest, she will need to consider possible solutions to meeting her own needs while respecting those of others. You may also help your client explore whether the conflict that arises in an important relationship is only about food, or whether deeper issues exist.

### Stocking Considerations

The use of this guideline to solve the problem of stopping when full will create the most controversy in the non-diet approach for therapist and client alike. This method goes against the cultural notions of the need to control food intake or risk complete abandon with food. However, if you or your client has the opportunity to talk with someone who has used this process to make peace with food, you will find that her level of calmness around food is significantly greater than people who rely on restraint to decrease overeating. Although some weight control experts may counsel that certain foods should be avoided to prevent overeating, the reality is that for the most part, food is plentiful in our culture. While your client may be able to control which foods she brings into her home, when she attends celebrations, eats at restaurants, or participates in work-related functions, all types of foods will become available to her. To the extent that these foods remain illegal, she will find herself preoccupied with her decision about what to consume. She may overeat at the event or control her urges only to overeat later in the day. The advantage of the stocking method is that clients have the opportunity to live in a world of food without fear, attaining a freedom from compulsive eating that they never dreamed was possible.

Claire became concerned about whether to continue using the stocking method. She found that despite her commitment to bring a large supply of her forbidden foods into her kitchen, she continued to eat past fullness. Claire discussed this problem with other group members whose overeating has lessened considerably during the several months since she joined the group. Claire realized that while the other women gave themselves full permission to eat exactly what they craved, she judged her desire to eat higher fat foods as bad. As a result, she told herself that she shouldn't eat them again, which created a feeling of deprivation and led to consuming more than she needed. Claire agreed to focus on ending her judgments about the quality of foods she desired and to trust that her eating would become nutritionally sound over time. As she continued to consciously reassure herself that it was acceptable to eat butter on her baked potato or cheese and crackers, she discovered that she needed less of these foods than she previously ate.

Janine confronted a different concern. She realized that when she implemented the guidelines of a non-diet approach, her body naturally preferred healthful foods. While this felt good to her in many ways, she had always liked sweets and began to feel deprived when she no longer found a place for them in her daily eating experiences. She paid attention to her fullness so well that while dessert sounded appealing, she was no longer hungry and therefore refrained. "My stomach never craves dessert when I'm physically hungry. Will I ever get to eat these foods again?" Janine's therapist suggested that she consider eating a bit less of her main meal so that she could "save room for dessert," an old saying that fits quite well with the process of attuned eating. Across cultures, dessert is part of the eating experience, indicating a natural tendency for people to end a meal with something sweet. This technique allowed Janine to solve her feeling of deprivation without the discomfort of eating past her physical fullness.

## WHEN EATING PAST FULLNESS PERSISTS

If your client continues to find that she eats past fullness after she has stopped judging her choices, listened to her hunger, made a good match, and ended her sense of deprivation by providing plenty of food for herself, consider exploring the psychological meaning of overeating. For example, Rose reported that while she was aware of the discomfort in her stomach when she became stuffed, her overeating allowed her to stop moving. After a long day at work, followed by the responsibilities of parenting two young children, Rose would become so full that she literally could not do anymore chores. Instead, she would sit on the couch and "shut down" both her body and her mind. Rose continues to work on the meaning of her eating past fullness in treatment, as well as other solutions to the overwhelming demands in her life.

## TAKING A DEEPER LOOK

Carol Grannick, a clinical social worker and specialist in the non-diet approach, developed a visualization that can help clients identify unconscious reasons that may cause them to eat past physical hunger. First, instruct group members to close their eyes, take a few deep breaths, and relax their body. Next, ask them to imagine that they are watching a video of the last time they ate past fullness or of a recent overeating experience that comes to mind. Instruct them to imagine it in their minds as it happened at the time. Now, have them return to the beginning of that eating experience and this time they should notice the exact moment they reach satisfaction. Instead of continuing to watch themselves eat, ask them to imagine putting down the fork or spoon. What do they notice? Are there any thoughts or feelings that emerge? As they notice these reactions, can they find a caretaking voice to help them get through that moment?

As a result of this visualization in a group, Stacey found that she was crunching very hard on chips as she ate past satisfaction. When she stopped eating the chips in her fantasy, she noticed that she was very angry with her brother for the way he treated her at a recent family get together. She imagined the voice of the group therapist telling her, "It is okay to be angry with him. You have a very good reason to feel this way." Ginny learned that her overeating contained a punitive aspect. She found herself noticing how good she felt right at the moment of satisfaction. However, she was feeling guilty about her recent decision to place her elderly father in a nursing home, and concluded that she had no right to feel so good herself when her father was in so much pain. Ginny imagined her sister's voice reassuring her that they were making the best decision possible. She also heard her own voice saying that it was all right to feel bad about putting her father in a nursing home; the feeling would pass. During future eating experiences, both Ginny and Stacey continued to ask themselves, "What would be on my mind if I stopped eating right now?" They found at times that they could tolerate the feelings that occurred. The process of learning to manage feelings without food will be considered at length chapter 5 on emotional eating.

Through the process of paying attention to the feeling of fullness in their stomachs, clients typically report that they can no longer tolerate the stuffed feeling that used to be commonplace. Your client may continue to eat a bite or two past satiation or even allow herself to become too full, and ongoing analysis of these situations remains worthwhile. However, as your client looks back over her progress with attuned eating, she is likely to indicate the amount of food consumed in an overeating episode has decreased considerably now that she has established a connection with her stomach.

## EVALUATING THE PROCESS

Clients vary in the amount of time required to institute the guidelines of the non-diet approach. Remind your client that her eating patterns developed over a long period of time, and likewise it will take time to relearn normal eating. Many compulsive eaters engage in perfectionist thinking in which they expect their overeating to end immediately, otherwise they consider themselves a failure. This type of thinking was reinforced in past diet programs that fostered beliefs of being "good" and "bad" based on adherence to a restricted plan. The road to ending compulsive eating is not straightforward. The change in paradigm requires that both client and therapist understand that the process of curing compulsive eating includes bumps and turns. These obstacles serve as signposts that attention to a particular area is warranted and guide the direction of treatment.

Emphasize to your client that she is engaged in a process of working her way out of compulsive eating, and that you expect her to have all types of experiences. The fact that she collects some experiences that are in response to her physical hunger should feel encouraging to her and give her hope that she can cure her overeating problem. Clients often continue to use expressions reminiscent of their dieting days, such as, "I was good this week with food." Explain to your client that the semantics are important as she learns to listen to her internal cues. Therefore, rather than communicating a statement that suggests an external, judgmental stance, she can reframe her assessment to say, "It felt good to me this week when I was able to listen to myself with food."

As your client attempts to meticulously follow the guidelines to normalize her eating, she may state that she feels even more obsessive about food than before. Remind her that careful attention to her internal hunger states is in the service of solving her compulsive eating. As she collects experience after experience of becoming hungry, making matches, and feeling satiated, this new way of approaching food will feel natural to her and become integrated into her psyche. All eaters must take a moment or two to check in with their stomachs and determine what, when, and how much to eat. The tremendous amount of mental energy used in the past to control her compulsive eating will fade away as your client feels increasingly in charge of her satisfying and anxiety-free eating experiences.

# CHAPTER 5

# EMOTIONS

Clients differ in their knowledge of psychological factors related to their compulsive eating. While one client may tell you that she is aware of all sorts of emotional issues that trigger her overeating, another client may state that all is fine in her life, and that she is unsure as to why she reaches for food when she is not hungry. We never assume that compulsive eaters must have serious, psychological problems that create the need to reach for food. In fact, some clients who seek treatment specifically for their overeating find that once they end their dieting patterns that stemmed from cultural pressures to be thin, their anxiety levels decreased significantly. At the same time, many clients do use food as a form of affect regulation. As their compulsive eating diminishes, they must confront problems directly by learning new ways to manage uncomfortable feelings.

Up until now, we have focused on the failure of diets and on a method of normalizing eating that allows your client to become an attuned eater. Although your client may accurately be aware that underlying issues fuel her bingeing, when she first tackles her compulsive eating she cannot truly determine the reason for her actions. Does she go to the

French fries because she is anxious or because they are a forbidden food and "call" to her? She must first solve the problem of deprivation in order to reach the stage where she can truly identify when she is eating due to emotional triggers. As she legalizes foods and listens to her body to tell her what, when, and how much to eat, her overeating will lessen appreciably. She is now in a strong position to examine her overeating experiences in relation to her emotional life.

## Affect Regulation

Compulsive eating is a prevalent form of self-soothing because it works so well. Reminiscent of an earlier time in life when food equaled care, overeating provides clients with a means of trying to help themselves in moments of emotional distress. Like a true friend, food is always there. We frequently tell clients that reaching for food to take care of themselves is not the worst thing they could do. After all, many people turn to drugs, alcohol, gambling, or perhaps become very depressed when they are unable to regulate intense emotional states. While overeating has the unwanted side effect of weight gain, in the scheme of possible solutions to psychological conflict, overeating is an understandable choice. Discussing this idea with your client promotes a compassionate stance to help her move from berating herself to understanding her behavior in a different light. At the same time, as much as her compulsive eating helps her through difficult situations, your client is likely to be in great pain regarding her eating and weight, and it is important to empathize with her distress.

When your client reaches for food to manage an uncomfortable feeling, she is reaching for comfort. She may describe the food as distracting, calming, or even numbing, and counts on this function to regulate her affective states. Perhaps she feels overwhelmed by anger, or perhaps she had a thought that was unacceptable to her. At the moment she begins eating, she redirects attention away from whatever created internal discomfort and may lose access to the original feeling. In this regard, her attempt at self-care is misguided. While the ice cream may move her away from whatever truly bothers her, it is no more effective at solving her problem than it would be for her to apply ice cream to a scrape on her knee. The attempt to respond to herself is admirable, but the use of food is an ineffective response. As she normalizes her relationship with food, your client must now learn more appropriate ways to deal directly with her internal conflicts.

## TEACHING THE CONCEPT

During the initial phase of treatment, instruct your client to notice whether her eating is the result of stomach hunger or mouth hunger — that is, eating that is not connected to a physical need. While she will welcome and respond to her physiological hunger, she must give herself permission to eat even when she is not hungry. After all, if she could simply begin to eat only from physical hunger after hearing about this concept, by definition, she is not a compulsive eater. If she forces herself to eat only out of stomach hunger because of your instructions, she will exert great control over the problem but will not truly solve it. Eventually, the restraint she exercises will break down, causing her to return to compulsive eating. Therefore, the initial goal for your client is to move in the direction of physiological hunger, while remaining compassionate about her need to turn to food for other reasons.

Clients who are aware that their overeating is sometimes elicited by emotional issues will list a wide range of feelings that trigger their reach for food, such as anger, sadness, loneliness, boredom, and happiness. It is important to help your client understand that the feeling itself does not actually activate her overeating response; rather, it is her inability to tolerate a particular feeling that prompts her to turn to the food in an attempt to provide self-soothing. Of course, she does not literally say to herself, "I'm feeling angry at my sister, but I cannot tolerate this feeling. I think I will go eat something to calm myself." Instead, your client finds herself at the refrigerator, reaching for food when she is not hungry. This action sets off a chain of events that serve to take her even further away from whatever is bothering her at the moment.

As she continues to eat, your client often talks with herself about her behavior. "I'm so fat." "I'm out of control." "I'm a pig." "My thighs are disgusting." These are all examples of phrases typical at this stage of overeating. These reprimands lead your client to the conclusion that she must do something soon to solve her problem. Usually, that solution is the next diet. However, a diet cannot solve the real problem for your client, which was her discomfort with a particular feeling or feelings. As stated earlier, Hirschmann and Munter label this process a translation from the language of feelings to the language of food and fat. As you describe this dynamic to your client, she will have greater insight about her need to go to food to manage emotions, allowing her to experience more empathy toward herself regarding her compulsive eating. At the same time, your client can begin to understand that her situation encompasses more than a food and weight problem. She must come to realize that some of her compulsive eating is a manifestation of her difficulty in regulating certain feelings. Now that she has ended her overeating that resulted from deprivation, she is ready to tackle the psychological causes of her compulsive eating.

## BUILDING A STRONGER SENSE OF SELF

When your client can stop yelling at herself about overeating and replace these self-recriminations with compassionate words that reflect her new understanding, her anxiety about overeating will decrease, and she will actually find herself stopping the binges sooner. She is now able to identify the true nature of her eating issues. "I'm reaching for food because something is making me anxious" has a very different quality from "I'm fat and disgusting and need to lose weight." As she continues to reframe the meaning of her compulsive eating, she is simultaneously engaged in the process of normalizing her eating. As she gathers experience after experience in which she notices physical hunger and responds in an attuned manner, she creates structure in her inner world that is more secure and affirmative than what she experienced in the past. It is this greater sense of internal consistency that will ultimately allow her to manage affective responses without her dependency on food, or the translation of these issues into eating and weight problems.

Think about a person who is a normal eater. Each time she eats, she conveys an important message to herself that she has needs and that these needs can be met in a reliable fashion. Rather than creating anxiety, eating brings the physical pleasure of satiation and the psychological satisfaction of self-care reminiscent of an earlier time in her life when others provided for her. Now consider the internal life of a compulsive eater and dieter. Each decision about what to consume is fraught with anxiety. She experiences constant noise in her mind as she struggles with guilt over eating too much, making "bad" choices, eating the "right" thing but feeling deprived, or wondering whether it is okay to eat at all. These thoughts take up space in her mind and drain her mental energy from other endeavors including work, relationships, and hobbies. Unlike the natural eater who gains constant positive feedback from her eating experiences, the compulsive eater feels psychologically weakened by her obsessive thoughts. Her tremendous, ongoing anxiety about her eating experiences reduces her capacity to tolerate other uncomfortable affects, creating feelings such as insecurity, lower self-esteem, depression, and hopelessness.

In previous chapters, we identified deprivation as a major cause of overeating along with the use of food for affect regulation. Initially, your client cannot really sort out which cause motivates her compulsive eating, and therefore we emphasized the importance of ending restrictions before looking at emotional factors. However, the reasons for postponing the exploration of psychological factors have another aspect. Not only must your client rule out deprivation as the trigger for her compulsive eating, she must also build a stronger sense of self that will enable her to do the therapeutic work of learning to cope with feelings without her reliance on food.

This strengthened inner self evolves through her accumulation of attuned eating experiences. Each time your client eats when she is hungry, she conveys to herself that she has needs. Each time she makes a match with a particular food, she communicates to herself that her needs are important and specific. Each time she stops when she is satisfied, she lets herself know that her needs can be fulfilled. These basic but significant acts provide your client with a consistent and reliable internal structure — important aspects of good caretaking. The positive, internal feedback she garners as she accurately responds to her hunger fosters trust and confidence in herself that was not possible when her eating patterns, and her perceptions of those behaviors, created havoc in her mind. As this internal transition occurs, your client will feel psychologically bolstered in a way that allows her to consider facing underlying issues.

As your client moves in the direction of listening to her internal cues to tell her when, what, and how much to eat, she collects more and more attuned experiences. She will find that compared to her disorganized, compulsive eating these experiences bring her greater satisfaction both physically and psychologically, providing her with a huge incentive to continue on the path of listening to her physiological hunger.

Check in with your client occasionally to learn where her eating falls at a particular point in treatment. When she first consults with you, the majority of her eating will be described as mouth hunger. A month later, she may tell you that 20% of her eating is out of stomach hunger, and that percentage may increase to 50% several months later. The use of percentages should in no way be viewed as a rigid scale to measure progress. Each client will proceed in the direction of attuned eating at a different pace. However, this tool provides a convenient and quick method to help you and your client reflect on her eating. When your client reports that the amount of eating that falls into the stomach hunger category reaches somewhere in the range of 80%, she is in a position to examine her psychological issues through her compulsive reach for food during the remaining 20% of the time. Again, perhaps her proportion of stomach hunger eating to mouth hunger eating is 75 to 25%, or 85 to 15%; the key factors are that she has ended much of her deprivation-triggered eating, increased her attuned eating, and developed a calmness around food that supports her goal to become able to tolerate difficult feelings directly.

## MOVING AWAY FROM COMPULSIVE EATING

In chapter 3, we discussed how to help your client stop yelling about overeating and develop a more compassionate stance toward herself. Now she must use these experiences to discover what is bothering her at a particular moment by actively intervening. When she notices that her eating is not associated with physical hunger, she can ask herself, with a curious mind, "Can I wait?" The knowledge that her next opportunity to eat is just around the corner may allow her to pass up the food in favor of a more satisfying, future experience. Yet the nature of compulsive eating means that often the answer to her question will be, "No, I can't wait." If that feeling is extremely powerful, your client will proceed to eat, and she can remind herself that although she may feel sad or disappointed about her compulsive eating, this is the place she is at with food at the moment. She must continue, however, to ask herself whether she can wait for the next signal of physical hunger each time she finds herself reaching for food when she is not hungry.

Eventually, your client will find that a time comes when she asks if she can wait until she is hungry and the answer is yes. Perhaps she waits just a minute or two longer than in the past, or perhaps she gets through the urge until she becomes physically hungry again. The fact that she could postpone her compulsive reach for food is a positive sign of her progress. However, in order to help herself move away from her use of food for self-regulation, she must actively push herself to learn about what is bothering her. Your client can accomplish this task by asking, "I'm reaching for food and I'm not hungry. I wonder what I might think about or feel right now if I didn't eat?" Thus far, her compulsive eating actually interfered with her ability to discover what she was feeling because it covered her emotions and took her down the path of body hatred. Now, she has a perfect opportunity to gain access to her internal experience as it occurs.

---

# THE CASE OF ALYSSA

Alyssa told the group about a recent experience in which she attempted to use food to deal with a difficult situation but found that it no longer worked.

**Alyssa:** I was so mad at my husband. We had a huge fight because once again, he didn't fix the leak in the bathroom like he promised he would. I'm so sick of him breaking his promises to me, and I told him that maybe it was time for him to move out. He stormed out of the house, and I didn't know what to do with myself. I was so mad. I opened my candy drawer, which is full of every kind of candy I like, and it was the weirdest thing. I just didn't want any.

**Therapist:** How did you feel about that?

**Alyssa:** I didn't like it. I was enraged with Kurt, but I couldn't bring myself to eat the candy. It's always there, and it just doesn't glitter for me anymore. I even tried to take a bite anyway, but I could see it wasn't going to help. So I just had to handle it.

**Therapist:** Your reaction is fairly common. On the one hand, you are solving the problem you came here for — you are no longer eating when you are not hungry. But you've depended on food for a long time, and it can feel like a loss when you give up food as a way to help yourself through difficult times.

**Alyssa:** Food has always been my best friend. Maybe I'd rather use food than feel as bad as I did the other night.

**Therapist:** In the long run, it's really much better to deal with your problems directly than disguise them with overeating. What happened for you once the candy didn't work?

**Alyssa:** I just cried and cried once Kurt left. I thought about calling my sister, but I really didn't feel like talking to anyone. Kurt finally came home and we slept in separate rooms. But the next day we were both calmer. I know we have to figure this out. We talked about the possibility of getting some couples counseling.

---

Alyssa's experience illustrates how a client will begin to let go of her compulsive eating as a natural outgrowth of the non-diet approach. While she may feel distressed by the emotions that emerge, she will generally find herself at this juncture only when she is psychologically ready to tolerate her affective states. There is a delicate balance for your client between pushing too hard in the direction of experiencing all of her uncomfortable feelings versus a wish to avoid any emotional discomfort. Part of her treatment involves encouraging her to expand her understanding of her internal dynamics as she develops the capacity to do so. You can promote her curiosity about herself by asking her to think about her overeating experiences and delve into the thoughts and feelings that led to that moment. Occasionally, a client will feel satisfied by the decrease in overeating as the result of ending the deprivation of dieting and choose to let herself continue to use food as a means of self-regulation. While this outcome may be acceptable for a client who eats in accordance to her body's signals a majority of the time, a client who uses this approach to justify eating whatever she wants, whenever she wants, is not truly engaged in attuned eating. In our experience, most clients are interested in learning about their internal life and fine-tuning their eating so that they no longer rely on food to manage their emotions.

---

## THE CASE OF ERICA

Erica worked with the process of normalizing her eating for a year and reached the point where she gave herself permission to eat exactly what she craved when she was hungry. Despite her success in attuned eating, she continued to binge on homemade brownies from time to time. As she explored this situation in her group, Erica recognized that she did not feel completely ready to face her problems without food. She realized that at an unconscious level, she maintained the idea that brownies were too fattening and, therefore, she should never eat them. By keeping this dessert forbidden, Erica explained that they still "worked" for her when she felt that she desperately needed to escape an intolerable feeling; she could move away from uncomfortable emotions by yelling at herself about her overeating. Erica accepted that she had made progress in acknowledging and dealing with her psychological issues, but was not yet ready to give up her reliance on compulsive eating in certain situations. She agreed to continue to discuss this dynamic so that she could move in the direction of letting go of her need to turn to food.

---

## THE CASE OF JOYCE

Joyce, another group member, reported a different experience than Erica as she learned to eat according to her body's cues. Very quickly, Joyce found that food no longer effectively helped her manage her affective states. While she felt grateful that her compulsive eating rapidly ceased, she was left to sort out many feelings and situations, but felt unprepared to do so. Fortunately, Joyce was already in individual therapy and received a lot of support to help her cope with her problems. While she previously spent much treatment time bemoaning her food and weight problems, she now had more insight into what was really bothering her. The group also provided aid to Joyce as they discussed their own experiences in tolerating feelings without food. Joyce found herself much sadder at times than she had been when she was eating compulsively, but she also became more effective in actively solving her troubles. She terminated her group treatment to pursue more intensive help for her specific concerns.

---

This result is much less typical for clients, who usually engage in a slow process of giving up their compulsive eating as they become better equipped to bear their emotions. Each client must learn how to get through a difficult period of intolerable feelings without using food to distance herself from the experience. Part of her ability to accomplish this task results from the calmness and confidence she developed through the process of attuned eating. However, you can also help your client learn to cope with her emotional discomfort through education regarding different aspects of managing feelings. Your training as a therapist places you in an ideal position to promote your client's mental health. At this point in the treatment, your skills as a professional will guide your work. Each client offers a different set of circumstances with their own particular dynamics. We offer examples of the types of struggles clients may bring to the treatment situation as their overeating decreases; it will be up to you to tailor your interventions to the needs of your client.

## EXPERIENCING FEELINGS

Ask your client what she imagines will happen if she allows herself to experience her feelings. This will promote exploration of the barriers that prevent her from tolerating various types of emotions. First, she must be able to label her feelings about different aspects of herself and her life, and this can become a central focus in treatment. During her childhood she may have been discouraged, either implicitly or explicitly, from expressing various feelings. As a result, she utilizes a variety of defenses, including turning to food, to keep them at bay.

---

# THE CASE OF KRISTIN

Kristin initially believed that she overate simply because she liked food. She told her therapist that she had a pleasant childhood and that everything was fine. As Kristin became able to postpone reaching for food when she was not physically hungry, she noticed some anxiety but could not put words to what she felt. As the therapist explored how Kristin's feelings were handled as a child, it became clear that Kristin learned to suppress her emotions early in life. She remembered that when she went to her mother because she was concerned about some of the girls at school not liking her, her mother said, "They like you." Her father drank wine with dinner each night and quietly fell asleep. Although she never associated his habit with alcoholism, she now realized that she knew something was amiss in her family. As she began to attach feelings to her experiences, she felt greater understanding about her childhood and the relationship of these dynamics to her current difficulties with her boyfriend. Identifying her feelings in a safe and secure environment created a feeling of calmness for Kristin that increasingly helped her tune into her affective states when reaching for food. She discovered that even when an emotion was uncomfortable, labeling her feeling provided enough relief to allow her to tolerate her mood without using food to numb herself.

---

## Intense Feelings

Often, clients believe their feelings are so intense that, if permitted to surface, they would take over and destroy them. Explain to your client that a feeling is just a feeling that will eventually pass. Like a wave, emotions gather in intensity, reach a peak, and begin to recede; your client's task is to ride the wave. This reassurance can help your client begin to consider letting herself experience strong emotions such as rage or sadness. The knowledge that she will not always feel such distress, and that the feeling cannot kill her, can lead to a greater acceptance of such emotions. Depending on the level of functioning of your client, it may be important to examine the concept of feeling a feeling versus acting on a feeling. If your client grew up in a home where family members acted on anger with physical abuse, this affect will frighten her. Or, as in the case of Ginger, who was repeatedly told not to engage in any conflict with her siblings because the noise would upset her father who had suffered several heart attacks, the message internalized was that any expression of "negative" emotions could literally result in death.

Depending on the type of relationship you have with your client, you may want to suggest some ideas about how to help her through a difficult moment. Perhaps she finds that talking with a close friend or relative gives her an essential outlet for her feelings. If she is a client who enjoys writing, she may find that journaling provides a soothing function that also helps her keep track of her reactions to various situations in her life.

Many diet and lifestyle programs suggest that people engage in activities such as taking a walk or a bubble bath as a way of avoiding the urge to eat when they are not scheduled to do so. The problem with this recommendation is that it is an attempt to control the compulsive behavior without understanding or recognizing the function of the reach for food. Explain to your client that developing the ability to tolerate uncomfortable feelings does not mean that she must experience the full intensity of her emotions at all times. For example, your client may notice that she feels extremely sad about the recent move of her closest friend to another city. She may decide that she cannot tolerate the depth of her emotion at that moment and choose to watch a movie as a distraction. In this situation, she has fully acknowledged that she is having a strong feeling and actively opts to regulate her sadness by diluting it with a movie. She knows that the feeling exists and that she will need to return to its meaning when she becomes psychologically able to do so, perhaps by discussing this situation in therapy. Unlike diet programs, which encourage people to evade their psychological motivations, clients must understand that their unconscious feelings affect their well-being, even if they are unaware of them. The only solution to this condition is for your client to actually experience these feelings directly as she develops the capacity to regulate the intensity of her emotions through the process of treatment.

### Forbidden Feelings

Another common conflict that prohibits clients from openly expressing feelings is the forbidden nature of certain thoughts and emotions. Clients often struggle with opposing sets of feelings that create internal tension. For example, Susie noticed that when she asked herself why she was reaching for food at a particular moment, she realized that she was angry with her mother.

**Susie:** How can I tell her that I'm really mad at her? She never took my feelings seriously, and sometimes she made fun of me for being so sensitive. But she had her plate full. She was working two jobs after my father stopped paying child support. She made sure I had enough clothes for school, and she came to my plays whenever possible. It would really hurt her feelings if she knew how I felt.

**Therapist:** It sounds like you are in a bind. On the one hand you've come to understand how your mother's reactions to your feelings hurt. You've said that it made you think there must be something wrong with you, and we know that it's made times rough for you in other adult relationships. At the same time, I know that you love your mother and that keeping a good relationship with her is very important to you.

**Susie:** Exactly.

**Therapist:** I wonder if you can consider the idea that it's possible to have two sets of feelings. Often, people think that if they let themselves acknowledge the angry feelings, they will undo the good feelings. It's possible, though, to have two sets of feelings. You feel angry, and you love your mother. One does not have to cancel out the other.

**Susie:** I never thought about it that way. I always thought that I would have to tell my mom how angry I am, and I don't think she could stand it.

**Therapist:** If you own your anger, you can still make a decision about how to handle it. Maybe you'll eventually decide that there is a way to talk with your mother about your experiences, or maybe you'll decide that it's best to work it out in here. What's important is that you give yourself permission to have your feelings. Otherwise you'll need to continue to reach for food when your anger gets stirred up.

**Susie:** It makes me feel disloyal when I talk to you about her faults. She would be so upset.

**Therapist:** I can understand that it makes you anxious. I also know that parents do the best they can with their children. We're not here to bash your mother.

**Susie:** I'm not sure how to even talk about it. I've never let myself go there.

**Therapist:** Can you tell me more about what you experienced when you tried to talk with your mother about your feelings?

Susie continued to explore her sense that her feelings were too powerful for her mother to tolerate. She received overt and covert messages that she should only talk about things in her life that made her mother happy, such as her excellent academic performance, and that she should avoid telling her mother about her anger over the divorce and problems with friends at school. For the first time, Susie considered her mother's experience as an immigrant who came to the United States to marry her father. Her mother had escaped a home in which her domineering father controlled much of her life. Susie speculated that her mother must also have conflicted feelings about her parents, and she felt certain that her mother would never have developed the skills to understand her own emotions. She developed empathy toward her mother's emotional fragility, and at the same time accepted that her mother's incapacity to tolerate her feelings contributed to her own current difficulties. Susie continued to admire her mother's strength in moving to a new country and raising a family on her own. She never doubted her mother's love for her. Susie's increased ability to tolerate inconsistent affective states meant that she no longer needed to eat compulsively in order to rid herself of unacceptable feelings.

Other clients may identify forbidden thoughts or feelings that seem dangerous to them, such as sexual feelings toward a boss or competitive feelings with a close friend. Helping your client distinguish between having a feeling and acting on a feeling may improve her ability to manage discomfort without turning to food. Just as she labeled food as "legal" and "illegal," she has made these distinctions regarding her internal thoughts. Using the metaphors of the non-diet approach can help a client grasp new concepts. Your client will discover that when she legalizes her feelings, comparable to the process of legalizing food, they lose some of their intensity and place her in a position to consider how to proceed. She may acknowledge the sexual attraction she feels, yet decide that acting on these impulses would be inappropriate. She may own her competitive feelings as natural, or she may look at how her low self-esteem creates excessive tension for her as she tries to make herself feel superior to others. When she perceives these feelings as unacceptable, she is compelled to eat and focus on her body dissatisfaction in order to divert herself from her discomfort. Now she can begin to identify her feelings with full permission to acknowledge them openly, decreasing the need to overeat.

### Accepting "Negative" Feelings

The use of compulsive eating by your client may represent the only form of soothing available to her when difficult emotions arise. As your client experiences the natural ups and downs of daily life, she may lack strategies to help herself through rough times. Now that she is in the process of letting go of her compulsive eating as a primary way to manage problems she is in a stronger position to develop new coping skills.

## THE CASE OF TINA

Tina believed that being an emotionally healthy person meant feeling happy and resolving all conflicts. If she felt the slightest bit of disappointment or anxiety, she turned to food to dissipate the feeling. With the help of her therapist, Tina learned to normalize her so-called "negative" feelings as part of the human condition. She was then able to integrate different aspects of herself in a manner that felt comfortable enough to tolerate without the use of food.

## THE CASE OF MIRIAM

Miriam had difficulty integrating her experience of loneliness at a conscious level. She related that as a child she came home to an empty house after school each day while both parents were at work. She knew that she was supposed to have a snack and begin her homework, but she did not want to study after a full day of classes. Instead, Miriam found herself eating more than her allotted snack. She began to look forward to these binges, but ultimately gained weight as a result. Her weight gain caught the attention of her parents, who began to restrict her food intake by making her special meals for dinner and limiting her snacks. Due to these restrictions, Miriam began to sneak food into her room for the evenings; the binges continued when she was home alone after school.

As Miriam developed the skills of attuned eating, she became ready to examine her continued but infrequent overeating. She reported that in the late afternoons she found herself eating food that she did not really want. When she attempted to postpone her urge to overeat, she felt very anxious. As her therapist asked her to describe the anxiety, Miriam further defined a feeling of loneliness. Miriam said that she could not understand this feeling because she was not aware of feeling lonely; she was content with her partner and part of a strong, supportive community. Miriam traced this feeling to the isolation she experienced when she was home by herself after school. She now recalled the anxiety she felt about being alone in the house, and how difficult it was to structure the remainder of the afternoon on her own. She did not remember trying to explain these feelings to her parents. However, she recalled that preparing and eating food gave her comfort and eased the isolation she experienced. Food became a way to comfort herself for much of her life when she experienced painful feelings, but this dynamic was obscured by the focus on diets and negative body image that accompanied her weight gain.

Miriam's ability to deal directly with most of her feelings as she solved her compulsive eating problem allowed her to become curious about the late afternoon eating that followed her into adulthood. By connecting her mouth hunger to an earlier time in her life, Miriam was in a better position to help herself through the afternoon discomfort without turning to food unless she was physically hungry.

---

## At the End of the Day

Clients often report that they are able to eat from physiological hunger during the earlier part of the day, but that they struggle with emotional eating in the late afternoon or evening. Although there is no single reason for this pattern, several themes emerge as clients explain their difficulties.

**Debra:** I've realized that I often eat at night just so I can take a break. My husband usually doesn't get home until late, so I'm left with all the responsibilities of getting dinner for the kids and helping with homework and the laundry. Even though I'm only working part-time, that stuff builds up. I'd love to just watch TV, but I can't. So sometimes I get myself a bowl of ice cream just so I can have a moment of peace.

**Therapist:** What you're describing is very common among women. Sometimes it feels that the only legitimate way to stop working is to eat. That seems more acceptable than reading a magazine or just doing nothing.

**Liza:** I used to do that when I first started working with the approach. I realized that one of the reasons I would eat at night was to give myself energy so that I could stay awake. But if I really listened to my body, I noticed that I was tired and just needed to go to bed. I don't have children like you do, so I could put on my pajamas and maybe read for a short time before I fell asleep.

**Therapist:** Debra, what do you think would happen if you listened to yourself in the moment, in a similar way to listening to yourself when you make a match with food?

**Debra:** I think I'd get really behind.

**Amy:** Maybe you would. But I find that with housework, it's never finished. If I waited until everything was done to do something for myself, I would never get to have any downtime. I've gotten to the point that when I feel like I need to relax, I give myself permission. Sometimes the house gets pretty messy and that's annoying. But the kids always get to school in clean clothes with food in their stomach. And lots of times I find that I actually have more energy to do what is needed around the house when I am taking better care of myself.

As Debra attempted to implement the advice of group members, she continued to feel guilty when she thought about or actually took time to relax. As she sat with this anxiety, Debra could hear the voice of her father, internalized throughout the course of her life, which taught her that relaxing was both unproductive and a sign of laziness. Debra began to identify the extent to which his demands and rigidity created conflicts for her, an area of her psyche not previously explored.

For many clients, evening is a time when psychological conflicts emerge. Perhaps a day was filled with a routine that took her mind away from problems, and now she must return to an empty apartment. Or perhaps reconnecting with family members creates stress. As she tries to go to sleep, perhaps thoughts and feelings emerge unbidden, causing a late-night trip to the refrigerator. It is always important to remind your client that her mouth hunger in no way undoes the stomach hunger experiences she collected throughout the day. You can empathize with the distress she experiences about her continued overeating; remind her that solving her emotional reach for food is a process that takes time.

Anna managed to meet her hunger needs throughout the day, carrying a food bag and responding accurately to herself. However, her nighttime eating felt much more chaotic. Anna reported that sometimes she would become too hungry and find herself overeating a food that did not particularly appeal to her. On other nights, she made a good match but ate more food than her body needed. Occasionally, Anna did prepare just what she needed for dinner, but found herself grazing later in the evening despite the fact that she knew she was not hungry.

Anna agreed to pay better attention to the mechanics of the approach in the evening. This meant that she would make sure that she had plenty of the foods she liked in her kitchen, and that she would become more aware of asking herself whether she was physically hungry in order to solve the problem of waiting until she was too ravenous to eat. As your client explores her psychological hunger, it is always useful to help her make sure that she maintains the different aspects of the approach that support attuned eating, such as paying attention to physical hunger, providing enough food, and ending the judgments about food. Anna began to notice that when she thought about cooking for herself or ate when she was not hungry, she experienced anxiety about being alone. Anna had lived by herself for some time and had always enjoyed the privacy. However, as Anna continued to ask herself what thoughts preceded her compulsive eating, she uncovered her deep fears about being single. Several of her friends had recently married, and Anna wondered if she was destined to always be the single one. Anna now understood that sitting down to a prepared meal in her condo stirred up her longings to share that meal with a partner. Anna began to talk directly about her concerns and consider issues about intimacy that had never been addressed. At the same time, she could now eat at home in an attuned manner, allowing the sad feelings to surface without using food to cover their meaning.

## Sexual Abuse

Some clients who struggle with compulsive eating also reveal a history of sexual abuse. Food becomes a means of providing self-soothing under extraordinary circumstances. The weight gain that results from overeating often serves a protective purpose in the mind of the survivor who believes that by becoming increasingly larger, she creates a barrier against further abuse. In a culture where fat people become invisible and/or repulsive, her size can help her feel protected from being victimized in the future. Yet the reality is that women of all sizes are vulnerable to sexual abuse. As she gains access to the complexity of her psychological make-up through the process of normalizing her eating and facing her feelings directly, she can consider both the meaning and effect of the abuse in her life, as well as other ways to protect herself as an adult.

Rita associated the start of her overeating to the age of 9 when her older brother began coming into her room in the middle of the night. She recalls that sometimes he would just stare at her, and at other times he would touch her breasts. She pretended to be asleep, hoping he would just leave her room. Eventually, she told her mother about his visits, and her mother said that she would talk with him. Rita does not know what her mother said to her brother. He stopped coming into her room for some time, but when she was 11, he began again, this time reaching under her nightgown and touching her. Again, Rita complained to her mother, and his behavior stopped. When Rita was a college freshman, she was the victim of a date rape. As the result of this history of abuse, Rita remains very distrustful of men. She has tried many diet programs, but continued to gain weight until she sought help for her compulsive eating. As Rita began to learn the process of attuned eating, she became better able to manage her feelings without reaching for food. To her surprise, Rita discovered that she felt anxious about the possibility of losing weight. Rita stated that while her weight helped her feel less vulnerable from being noticed by men, the meaning of her size felt very complicated. She felt that she had been ignored in many ways throughout her life, and that by remaining large, she made it impossible for others to ignore her now that she took up so much space. Rita realized that her size made her feel both insignificant and powerful at the same time. As Rita found that compulsive eating no longer helped her distance herself from her emotions, she continued to use treatment to talk directly about the abuse and explore the means to strengthen her sense of self.

Janet, another trauma survivor, shared with the group that as her compulsive eating diminished, she was left to figure out other ways of coping with fears elicited by the memories of being raped as a teenager. She joined a group for survivors of sexual abuse, where she felt understood and supported. She also enrolled in a self-defense course for women, where she learned techniques that helped her feel empowered. By taking action on many different levels, Janet was able to sustain a sense of security within herself and out in the world.

## THE NON-DIET APPROACH AS METAPHOR

As your client explores her need to reach for food when she is not physically hungry, the possible explanations are limitless. When you combine your therapeutic techniques with knowledge about the dynamics of compulsive eating, you can help your client gain new insights into her personal struggles as she develops the capacity to regulate feelings without food. At times, you may also find that the language of the non-diet approach provides metaphors that can better help your client understand her emotional life or translate the self-attunement she attains with food into other areas of her life.

*Discovering Inner Strengths*

Danielle described an experience in which she felt stomach hunger and considered what to eat. At first, she thought that she might need to leave her home and find a restaurant that would have the type of meal she craved. However, as Danielle further defined what she wanted, she realized that she already had the cucumbers, hummus, and bread that she needed to make the perfect sandwich. Danielle explained that this was an insightful moment because in therapy, she worked hard to figure out what career path to take, including whether to pursue further education. Danielle realized that she already has what it takes to be successful inside of her. Although she frequently diminishes her strengths, which were never mirrored by her parents, she had recently begun to reconnect with some earlier interests in fashion design. The image of already having the ingredients for a cucumber sandwich stayed with Danielle as a useful metaphor in moments of self-doubt.

*Discovering "I Matter"*

Latoya used the non-diet approach for several years and generally sustained her ability to eat in an attuned manner. She contacted her former therapist for a consultation when she experienced an increase in overeating that she could not explain.

> **Latoya:** I don't know what is going on. Usually I can figure out what is triggering any overeating that still occurs, and it becomes an opportunity to learn something about myself. This time I feel like it just doesn't matter.
>
> **Therapist:** Can you explain that to me more?
>
> **Latoya:** I don't know. It's like I've just stopped caring. I know how good it feels when I'm eating in the way I've learned with you, but I just can't seem to get back there.

**Therapist:** I'm wondering why the words "it doesn't matter" stand out for you right now. You're someone who has always valued taking good care of yourself. Can you think about whether those words describe anything else going on in your life right now?

**Latoya:** Well, yes. Just about everything. I'm still in the same situation at work. My boss had all but said I would get a promotion this spring, but it didn't happen. No matter how hard I work, I can't seem to get any further in the company, which affects my income. I was really counting on a big raise.

**Therapist:** I know that you've felt unhappy at your job for a very long time.

**Latoya:** Yes. And I haven't told you what happened with Chris. He's been attending AA like he promised, but a few weeks ago I found an empty beer can in the trash. I told him if he ever started drinking again, our marriage would be over. So now, I don't know what to do. I thought everything was going so well for us. I feel so hurt that he did this to us. It's like he's saying that our relationship isn't important. I guess that's when my eating got out of control. I'm just so tired of things not working out for me. I feel like giving up.

**Therapist:** I can hear how hurt you feel. It sounds like Chris's actions made you feel like you don't matter, and you're expressing that feeling in what you say to yourself about your eating.

**Latoya:** I think you're right. But I'm not sure what to do.

**Therapist:** You know from past experience how important it is to make sure that you have plenty of food available and to stay in tune with your hunger as much as possible. You may not have control over your husband or your boss, but you can stay in charge of how you feed yourself. I want to remind you that when you take care of yourself with your eating, you've always told me how much better you feel. You have some tough decisions to make about your job and your marriage, and you'll be in a stronger position to deal with these situations when you feel calmer with food. It really does matter that you take care of yourself.

**Latoya:** I just needed to be reminded of that. I think I'll call the marriage counselor we used to see to help me figure out the situation with Chris.

In a follow-up contact 2 weeks later, Latoya reported that she had returned to her previous level of calmness regarding her eating. She continued to feel sad about the current situation with her husband, but said that Chris had agreed to resume marriage counseling.

### Discovering a Sense of Separateness

Jill's progress with the non-diet approach helped her separate from an enmeshed relationship with her father. Jill's mother died when she was 14 years old, and as an only child, she took on a feeling of responsibility for her father's well-being. Eating was a focus in their relationship as both she and her father loved to cook. They also dieted together, and on her visits home as a young adult, Jill reported that her father often gave her contradictory messages. One minute he wanted her to eat the special, rich foods that he cooked just for her, and the next minute he criticized her for eating too much.

As Jill worked on developing her attuned eating, she struggled with the internalized voice of her father telling her what she should eat. Over time, Jill understood that her father could not know when she was hungry or what her body craved. As Jill became more comfortable feeding herself according to her body's signals, she found that she could be in the presence of her father and remain true to herself. She explained her new approach to him and requested that he stop commenting on her food choices.

Several months later, Jill announced that she had signed up for guitar lessons. She explained that she had played for a short time as a child and that her skills were just average. Her parents directed her into dance where she displayed more talent. However, Jill loved music and found it very relaxing to strum on the guitar. Jill had never returned to this hobby, but now realized that just as her father could not really know what she was hungry for when she ate he could not know what pursuits were right for her either. She enjoyed the first session of her class so much that she continued to take lessons, which gave her much pleasure.

### Discovering Needs

Like Jill, Blanca translated aspects of her experience with attuned eating into other areas of her life. Through the process of normalizing her eating, Blanca realized that there were many ways in which she ignored her needs. She had settled into a long-term relationship with a man who seemed unwilling to commit to marriage. Although she was financially successful in her career, she was not particularly satisfied with her work. Blanca felt bolstered by her ability to care for herself. As she stopped criticizing her body and ate when she was hungry, Blanca realized that much of her overeating stemmed from the dissatisfaction she felt in her daily routine. Blanca had always dreamed of living in another country and decided that embarking on this adventure would be a "perfect match" for her at this point in her life. She was able to secure a position teaching English at a foreign school. This job would provide her with enough money to support her through the year while minimizing her stress and allowing opportunities for travel. Blanca left the outcome of her relationship on hold, believing that she could better evaluate her feelings toward her boyfriend once she achieved some distance from him.

### Opportunities for Growth

Clients who sustain a period of attuned eating may find that at some point they gradually or suddenly revert back to psychological hunger. It is important to remind your client that this does not indicate that she is back at the beginning of the non-diet approach. Unlike diet programs where "getting off track" signifies undoing gains, your client is engaged in a process where she may take two steps forward and one step back. Yet all of the attuned experiences previously collected continue to reside in her psyche and provide her with a solid foundation to which she can return. As your client maintains periods of attuned eating, her mouth hunger experiences can become excellent opportunities to learn something more about herself. Rather than viewing her progress as a straight line, your client might think about a spiral, where each time she revisits a particular issue, a deeper level of understanding occurs.

## Reaching for Connection

Karla's youngest child recently left home for college. Karla feels proud of her children and excited by the idea of pursuing interests she put on hold for many years and spending more time with her husband. She felt surprised when she found herself overeating after many months of feeling connected to her hunger. Karla reported that she found herself repeatedly reaching for cookies, even though she does not particularly like them. As the therapist helped Karla explore her mouth hunger, Karla realized that baking with her children had always provided a special connection, and in a sense, she was reaching for that connection when she reached for the cookies. She talked about the bittersweet feelings of her children moving away from home and considered other ways to stay connected to them.

## Reaching for Punishment

Linda had a more difficult time identifying why her eating suddenly became chaotic after a long stretch of feeling in charge of food. Linda ultimately identified that she had begun to lose weight as the result of ending her overeating. While she thought that this would make her feel good, she felt stirred up by a variety of issues. Her mother was also large, and Linda felt afraid that her mother would resent her smaller size. These competitive feelings, however, extended beyond weight. Linda had worked hard to make sure that she felt more satisfied in her life than her mother, but at an unconscious level, Linda was unsure as to whether this was acceptable. Eating to the point of overfullness became a way for Linda to punish herself for expecting more in life than her mother. Although Linda was initially distressed by her regression with food, as she understood the conflicts behind her overeating, she was gradually able to return to the secure structure of attuned eating.

## Reaching for Freedom

The process of learning to tolerate feelings without food is both exciting and complicated. In a group session, members engaged in a discussion about what motivated them to persist with their journey.

**Felicia:** I've been telling myself that when I'm not hungry, I shouldn't eat. I should be able to get through my feelings by now. But I notice that I'm eating just a little bit more than I need when I am hungry and I think it's related.

**Therapist:** There is a fine line between control and a gentle nudge. Let's think about some different ways you might talk to yourself in the moment. For example, you could say, "The food is there to go to if I need it. But, I'm interested in seeing if I can get through these feelings without food."

**Felicia:** I like to think about the idea of wanting to know all of myself so I can live my life to the fullest. I can only do this when I can know and own all of my feelings, even my pain.

**Karen:** I've learned in therapy that my depression is related to always trying to be the "good girl" and do what I am supposed to. Part of that was always dieting so I would lose weight and fit in. But my obsession with food and my body takes away my power. When I start to turn to food to make my feelings go away, I remind myself that this keeps me from really knowing who I am. I want to feel my power and I will no longer do this to myself. That's my motivation.

**Terry:** I like to use the idea we've talked about in here about finding an internal caretaker. Sometimes I can imagine what people in the group would say to me, and other times it's just this gentle voice telling me that it is okay to have my feelings. I realize that those words really come from me, and that I've truly become my own best friend.

As the relationship between dieting, overeating, and emotions becomes clear, your skills as a therapist will enable you to help your client develop her capacity to regulate affect without the reach for food. The use of the non-diet approach as a therapeutic tool is extremely powerful and rewarding. Clients integrating attuned eating into their lives will find that their relationships to food, themselves, and the world can change in profound ways. While the path for each client will vary significantly, solving her compulsive eating will leave your client with a new freedom in relation to food, her emotions, and herself.

# CHAPTER 6

# BODY IMAGE

The formation of body image is a complicated process that begins at birth, and perhaps even earlier, as parents bring their hopes, ideals, and genetics to the life of their child. The infant experiences her world through bodily sensations such as being held and fed, and the quality of these experiences helps create her earliest sense of her body. The infant begins by experiencing the caretaking as an extension of herself, but eventually learns that she is a separate being. In her book *The Magic Years*, Selma Fraiberg, a child psychoanalyst, states, "During the early months the infant doesn't differentiate between his body and other bodies, or between mental images and perceptions, between inner and outer. Everything is undifferentiated oneness, the one being centered in the baby himself."[1] The infant feels bodily discomforts that require care from her parents or other nurturing adults, and the extent to which these needs are understood and responded to affects her bodily sense of well-being.

Consider a baby alone in her crib, cooing as she explores her fingers and toes. Her body seems to be a source of curiosity and great pleasure for her as she contentedly rolls around. Stop for a moment and think about how you feel as you picture this image.

Now imagine this female child as an adolescent looking in the mirror. What do you think she sees as she examines herself? What words do you imagine her using as she talks to herself about her body? There is a high probability that your speculation of this teenager's feelings contains her body dissatisfaction. Rapid physical changes during the teenage years require a revision of the body image at the very time the adolescent is in the midst of emotional turmoil. She typically experiences body dissatisfaction and is overly concerned with how she compares to others. The standards to which teens compare themselves and each other have become increasingly unrealistic and stringent. Kathy Kater, a clinical social worker specializing in the treatment of eating disorders, highlighted the pervasiveness of negative body image for girls at a conference. She reported that 85% of adolescent girls are unhappy with their bodies and up to 70% engage in caloric restriction.[2] As the adolescent dissects parts of her body and finds faults, she participates in behavior that is normative in our culture, but gives rise to great distress. The body is no longer a source of pleasure, but becomes an enemy to be reckoned with through dieting, cosmetic products, and perhaps even cosmetic surgery.

During adulthood, negative body image may be carried along from adolescence or, if a person was lucky enough to retain a positive self-image through her teenage years, may develop in response to lifestage events such as pregnancy and midlife changes. As noted previously, 80% of American women are dissatisfied with their bodies, and men are not immune from body image problems either. There has been a recent proliferation of men's magazines that mimic the traditional female ideals of attaining the perfect body. As mentioned earlier, unlike the image of unnatural thinness for women, the male ideal often emphasizes a body that takes up more space by developing muscles. This has lead to an increase in the amount of steroid abuse among boys and men, as well as a new, booming business in surgical procedures. Books such as *The Adonis Complex: The Secret Crisis of Male Body Obsession* illustrate men's burgeoning struggle with body image.[3] For boys and girls, and men and women, the outcome of these obsessions is increased estrangement from their bodies, along with feelings of dissatisfaction and shame.

The therapist will bring her own body image to the treatment situation. This fact is neither good nor bad; it is a reality that requires acknowledgment and exploration. Clients with compulsive eating problems will almost always feel negatively about their body. In fact, this is the major cause of their psychological distress. If a client could turn to food to manage feelings without any consequence to her body size, she would probably feel little incentive to solve this problem. However, the weight gain caused by overeating becomes the constant reminder that something is amiss, and the fear of fat compels her to intervene and seek treatment.

## External Factors

As we explore methods to repair body image, it is important to understand why a poor body image is the norm in our society and how negative body image serves a psychological function. Returning to the example of an infant completely content with her body, she comes into the world with no conceptions of the meaning of fat and thin. She is subject to the teachings of her culture, including parents and other relatives, peers, educators, health professionals, and the media to learn about the value of size. The beliefs she develops throughout childhood and adolescence are a product of what she internalizes from others rather than an innate sense of rightness or wrongness about her body. As she adopts these ideas as her own and eventually communicates them in her own roles of mother, friend, and professional, she effectively transmits these cultural beliefs and perpetuates unrealistic body ideals.

### FAMILY

Parents naturally want what is best for their children. In a culture where thin is considered best, parents usually prefer their children to be lean, and a fat child may even be experienced as a failure in parenting. This desire for a thin child is exacerbated when a parent, often the mother, has struggled with weight herself. She knows the pain of feeling "too fat" and of spending years struggling with overeating and dieting. With an understandable wish to protect her child from experiencing similar emotional trauma, she may communicate messages, consciously or unconsciously, to her child about the value of a thin body.

Molly is a college student in her early 20s. She feels hatred toward her body and recalls negative thoughts about her shape beginning at around age five. She remembers being at the swimming pool with her family and feeling happy as she ran around in her brand new, two-piece bathing suit. Her father came up to her, gave her a pat on the stomach and said, "You'd better watch it, honey. You don't want your tummy to get too big." Molly remembers that she became self-conscious in her bikini and started to notice some other girls at the pool who were fat. As she started grade school, she became more aware of her mother's comments about her own body such as, "I'd better not have any dessert because it goes right to my thighs."

As Molly entered puberty, her body became rounder. She tearfully reveals that when she came home from school one day and reached for a cookie, her mother told her that if she continued to gain weight, she would have a hard time dating in high school. She became increasingly self-conscious about her size. When her mother suggested that Molly should go with her to a local diet program, she felt she had no choice. For the past 8 years, Molly has continuously tried to diet her way to an "acceptable" size, feeling increasingly out of control with her eating and weight. She has lost her ability to recognize internal cues for hunger and satiation, and constantly berates her body for its size.

Clients often report that an off-the-cuff remark made by a family member instigated their negative preoccupation with body size. In the case of Molly, her father, whom she describes as a kind man, most likely had no idea the impact his words would have on his child. Molly's mother, who was a large woman herself, wanted Molly to have a life full of opportunities that would not be hindered by her size. Unfortunately, her attempts to help Molly actually caused her daughter great pain and contributed to a negative body image, a compulsive eating problem, and decreased self-esteem.

## PEERS

Children are subject to the opinions and pressures of their peer group, and when it comes to fat, the teasing can be extremely hurtful. Negative reactions to fat are found in children as early as the kindergarten years. Research shows how early ideas about body image emerge in children and how, when left unchecked, children are likely to communicate these negative ideas to each other. While other prejudices are likely to be interrupted by parents and teachers, this belief system is so ingrained in the general population that adults often fail to challenge or intervene in these situations.

Al is a 30-year-old man who reports that students in elementary and middle school teased him mercilessly because of his size. "Fatty" and "Pigboy" were two of the names that children used to taunt him. In sixth grade, Al began to have difficulties in school as he stopped participating in class in an effort to deflect attention from himself. He also stopped participating in sports and other extracurricular activities. His parents observed the change in his behavior and set out to understand what was wrong. Al eventually admitted to the teasing and his embarrassment about his weight. His parents, who were also large, accepted their own weight as well as their son's genetic predisposition. They spoke with him about the cause of his larger size, encouraged him to return to the sports, and helped him learn how to respond to the teasing. They also spoke with his teachers and asked them to become more sensitive to the interactions between Al and his peers, especially in gym class. Al recalls his parent's support by attending his baseball games and helping him practice how to respond to the negative comments still made by other kids. At the time Al came for treatment, he struggled with the sensitivity he felt when criticized by others. He believed that his inability to tolerate negative feedback stemmed from the hurt he still carries from childhood teasing and realized this dynamic was beginning to negatively affect his job perform-ance. At the same time, Al was fat by society's standards, but felt comfortable with his body and was in excellent physical health. He attributed his positive body image to the fact that his parents never made an issue of his size and taught him to take care of his body.

## TEACHERS

Children spend much of their waking life with teachers and other educators who also communicate their views about children's bodies. From preschool movement and dance classes to outdoor recess and gym classes, child educators gear ac-tivities to help kids explore, connect, and feel good about their bodies. Children often experience their bodies as strong and capable. At the same time, schools are ripe with messages to students about what constitutes an acceptable size. Overt pressures often occur in sports such as gymnastics, dance, and wrestling, which may require participants to maintain a certain size or risk failure. Health classes that teach nutrition may also focus on dietary restrictions based on the notion that it is important to be thin. Gym teachers sometimes weigh or measure children, which can create great shame for a fat child. As adults in authoritative positions tell the child that she is not acceptable in the body she has, or that she must ensure that her body continues to conform to a certain type, negative body image and fears compete with positive feel-ings already developed.

Covert messages occur when a teacher says in front of a student, "I can't eat the birthday treat you brought in because I'm on a diet." In this situation, it is not the fact that the teacher decides to pass on the cupcake that is important — she may not be hungry for a cupcake — but the implication that fat is bad. Likewise, a comment from one staff member to another saying, "You've lost weight. You look great," overheard by a student lets the child know what is valued by important adults in her life. When a therapist arrived at a high school to provide a program on the prevention of eating disorders, she was greeted by the principal, vice principal, and guidance counselor, all of whom commented on the importance of her work in this area. Before the meeting officially began, the therapist observed the guidance counselor congratulate the principal on his recent weight loss. The principal stood sideways, patted his stomach, and said, "Isn't it great? But I still have 15 pounds to go." The vice principal was pouring himself a cup of coffee, which he drank from a mug featuring a fat, pink pig trying to pull herself up on a chin-up bar with the caption reading, "I just pigged out." Despite the school's good intentions of implementing preventative eating-disorder workshops, the messages they sent were loud and clear.

## HEALTH CARE COMMUNITY

Health care professionals form another group of adults who influence the child's body image. Throughout their growing years, children have frequent contact with their pediatricians as well as other health experts. The views of these professionals may influence and shape the attitudes of the developing child toward her body.

A typical scenario reported by clients with compulsive eating problems relates to a parent turning to a pediatrician for help with a child's weight. At other times, it is the pediatrician herself who initiates the recommendation for weight loss. Lisa's doctor suggested that her mother put her on a 1,000 calorie diet, Rena's doctor recommended a commercial weight loss program, and Erma's doctor prescribed pills for her that were the equivalent of amphetamines. In all cases, these women recalled feeling that there was something defective about them that needed to be fixed, adding another layer of negative feeling to their body image. Even when the request to get help with weight originates from the child, the response by adults that this is a good idea reinforces the developing concept in the child's mind that her body shape is wrong, contributing to her negative body image.

Therapists comprise another group of health care professionals who come into contact with children specifically because of a parent's concern about their child's size. Philosophies and programs that focus on weight loss as the goal of success give the message that, once again, the child's body is "right" or "wrong" and can be manipulated to fit a certain standard. Of course, there can be times when a child's body size, either too thin or too fat, reflects a medical or psychological problem that must be addressed, and these issues will be discussed in the chapter 8 on redefining health.

When a child can lose weight with the assistance of a health professional, she will probably express positive feelings. Yet behind this success there remains an ongoing fear that the weight will return. In fact, it probably will. In a 1999 study, Eric Stice, a researcher at the University of Texas, investigated the outcome of dieting behavior among ninth grade girls through their high school years. He found that those girls engaged in dieting behaviors were more likely to gain weight during this 4-year high school period than their non-dieting counterparts.[4] In a prospective study conducted with a sample of 8,203 girls and 6,769 boys between the ages of 9 and 14 years, similar results were observed. Those adolescents who dieted were more likely to engage in binge eating, and at a 3-year follow-up, dieters gained more weight than non-dieters.[5] If doctors, therapists, and health professionals express pleasure with the child because she lost weight, what happens in the mind of the child as she worries about whether the weight will return? She must view her body as her enemy to be controlled and contained in order to gain acceptance from those important to her. This fuels a disconnection from her body and a vigilance regarding any signs of fat, even if it is natural sign of her maturation.

*Media*

The media plays an important role in the development of body image. The messages portrayed in ads, both implicitly and explicitly, convey the desirability of slenderness, and the bodies of superstars and models teach children what is to be emulated. Children will naturally compare themselves to these ideals and will inevitably fall short.

Given the pressures from parents, peers, health professionals, teachers, and the media, you may wonder how any child can survive with an unscathed body image. The reality is that very few children, and especially girls, reach adolescence with a positive body image intact. Children receive messages in the name of health, attractiveness, acceptance, and success from significant people in their lives who genuinely want what is best for them. Yet these imperatives have a paradoxical effect that creates anxiety and vulnerability about the body. Instead of regarding their bodies as a source of pleasure and function, children, adolescents, and ultimately adults become overly concerned with any possible imperfection and integrate these signs into a negative body image.

## Internal Factors

In her groundbreaking book *Fat is a Feminist Issue*, Susie Orbach establishes how complex social and psychological meanings are expressed through the female body in terms of "thin and fat."[6] Bloom and Kogel express this notion, stating that "having to house psychic life, the body becomes overly burdened. To the extent that the body speaks for the self, it is subject, albeit narrowly defined. However, the body is rendered object and 'thinglike' when daily practices are about control of desire and need, rather than possessing and living comfortably in the body. The greater the body/self disintegration, the riper the body is to serve as the arena and container for the displacement of emotional life and social relations."[7] This insightful observation captures the way in which clients often use their bodies to speak about their inner world.

### DEVELOPING A NEW LANGUAGE

A frequent comment made by females in today's society is "I feel fat." Although fat is not actually a feeling, this statement is usually accepted and understood with no questions asked as to what she really means. Responses generally take the form of "No you're not," "Why don't you try such and such a diet," or "Me, too." In truth, however, what is being expressed is an uncomfortable feeling that has been translated into the language of body hatred.

Kim is a 16-year-old girl with an average-sized body. Although she developed some curves at the onset of puberty, she did not focus on these changes. She was active in sports and felt pretty good about herself. Recently, her parents announced their imminent divorce. Kim knew that her parents were having marital difficulties, and she told them that she understood their decision. She leaves for college in a couple of years so she thinks that it's "not such a big deal." She adds that many of her friends' parents are divorced and now she is just like them. Although Kim's mother has reassured her that it is okay to express any negative feelings, she also feels relieved that Kim is "taking it so well."

Several of Kim's friends are dieting, and for the first time, Kim thinks she will diet too. "I feel too big" are the words she uses to describe her body. Kim's psychological state is ripe for using her body to express her conflicted feelings. By focusing on her body, Kim indirectly expresses her fear that her feelings are too big to be experienced either internally or by her family. Of course, children often have trouble putting their feelings into words, and families vary in their abilities to help their sons and daughters with their emotions. The key issue related to the development and maintenance of negative body image occurs because of the power of the culture to influence internal experience. When Kim says she feels big, her parents and other important people in her life are quick to unconsciously collude with the cultural norms that purport weight loss as the avenue to feeling better. Kim's parents are concerned with her emotional well-being and want to encourage her to take any action that will quell her anxiety. When they concur with Kim's belief that changing her body size is the solution to her problems, they have completed the translation of Kim's real problems into body language. Kim has distanced herself from her true feelings of anxiety about her parents' divorce and displaced them onto her body. Her parents have agreed that her body is the problem, which reinforces Kim's belief that dieting is the way to resolve her feelings. The language of food and fat replaces the original, difficult conflicts and creates a new realm in which to fight the battle. Kim will carry her anxiety about her parents divorce in her stomach, thighs, or whichever body part she chooses to focus on. She will begin the diet–binge cycle and most likely gain weight, which will fuel her negative body thoughts.

The translation of problems into negative body image is extremely prevalent, yet often goes unexamined. For example, a shy teenager getting ready to attend a party who says, "I feel fat," may really be expressing his fear of socializing. A student performing a solo in a music concert observes that her stomach sticks out before going on stage because she has difficulty with her competitive urges "sticking out" at the performance. An adolescent girl who has a pesty younger brother says that her thighs are disgusting because she is disgusted by her occasional thoughts that she wishes her brother had never been born. As the child uses the body language she has adopted from culture, responses that acknowledge her fat as the problem secure the continuation of a negative body image in order to contain significant, psychological distresses. She then loses access to the other sources of her discontent as she wages war against her body.

This use of the body to express feelings that are experienced as forbidden or overwhelming is common among adult clients with compulsive eating problems. The client is convinced that her weight is the issue and that becoming thinner will solve at least some of her problems. The therapist must listen carefully to understand what the client is expressing in the words she uses to describe her body. However, losing weight is not the answer to her conflicts and, in fact, any signs of weight loss may become frightening if she is unable to confront her core issues. For example, Robin is a 50-year-old woman who has been married for 25 years. Her marital relationship has always been difficult, but the couple chose to stay together in the interest of their children. One of her husband's chief complaints is Robin's weight, which he believes interferes with their sexual relationship. Robin entered a nationally known weight loss program and lost approximately 75 pounds. To her dismay, their sexual relationship did not improve. It became apparent to her at that point that her weight was not the issue, and at her insistence, the couple entered marital therapy.

## CONFRONTING NEGATIVE BODY IMAGE

Clients often find that ending their negative body thoughts is the most difficult aspect in the treatment of their compulsive eating. While overeating and bingeing often slow down quickly as clients learn to become attuned eaters, body image problems are so entrenched and reinforced by culture that they are resistant to change. As stated earlier, clients with compulsive eating problems come in all shapes and sizes. Much of the treatment we discuss applies to all clients who express negative feelings about their bodies. However, it is important to consider that the client who is very large faces many issues not experienced by her smaller/thinner counterpart. The therapist must become sensitive to the ways in which the culture shames a fat person and help her build on her own ego strengths as she confronts the realities of a culture that marginalizes her.

## RAISING AWARENESS

The language of negative body talk is so common among compulsive eaters that your client is probably unaware of the pervasiveness and effect of her thoughts on her psychological well-being. A simple exercise developed by Hirschmann and Munter asks participants in workshops to write down what they have told themselves about their bodies in the last 24 hours. A recent workshop elicited the following list of responses:

- My stomach is too big.
- I'm disgusting.
- I'm repulsive.
- I'm unhealthy.

- I'm too far gone.
- My jeans aren't as loose as I think they should be.
- Summer is coming. What will I wear?
- I'm so ugly.
- My arms are flabby.
- I'm out of control.
- Yuck.
- I look like an elephant.
- I'm a failure.

As the workshop leader read this list back to the group, the sadness in the room was palpable. The discussion of the exercise proceeded:

**Therapist:** How do you feel when you hear this list?

**Participant:** It's so sad.

**Participant:** It makes me angry. I can't believe women go around talking like this.

**Participant:** Can you imagine saying these things to anyone else?

**All:** Never, no way . . .

**Participant:** So why is it okay for us to treat ourselves this way? I wouldn't talk this way to my worst enemy.

**Therapist:** What do you make of the fact that all of you speak to yourselves this way all the time, yet you wouldn't think of treating anyone else in this way?

**Participant:** I wasn't aware that I was doing it. It bothers me, but it's the way I feel.

**Participant:** It's so familiar that I can't imagine not doing it. But, it also makes me feel so sad when I hear the rest of you. I want to say, "Stop talking like that. You are so much better than what you are saying."

**Therapist:** I think that what all of you are saying is extremely important. These thoughts have become so internalized that you are not consciously aware of them. At the same time, they do affect the way you feel about yourself, and it's easier to see how destructive they are when the rest of the group says them than to question these negative ideas for yourself. It's really important to understand that your negative thoughts never lead to change. How do you feel when you yell at yourself like this?

**All:** Sad, angry, depressed, bad, anxious . . .

**Therapist:** And what does a compulsive eater do when she has these feelings?

**Participant:** Eats!

**Therapist:** Exactly. All of these negative thoughts you tell yourself about your body make you anxious and put you at a higher risk of overeating. But, the yelling doesn't really work. After all, you've been at this a long time now. If these negative thoughts would help you lose weight, you'd be thin by now! They don't help you, but they do make you feel badly about yourself and your body.

This group exercise can be adapted to the individual client by asking her to tell you how she talks to herself about her body. It is likely that she has never shared these very private thoughts with another person. Your responses can reflect the ideas presented above.

## Strategies Promoting Self-Acceptance

As your client begins to understand that she constantly carries negative thoughts and beliefs with her and that they damage her psychological well-being, it is helpful to educate her about ways to intervene with her self-recriminations. In order to bring about self-acceptance, she will need to intervene in both her external and internal worlds.

### ADDRESSING EXTERNAL FACTORS

Explain to your client that she was not born thinking that her body size was inherently wrong, but that she has internalized cultural values throughout her life and now accepts them as truth. One incentive to change her negative thoughts is that her yelling creates anxiety, which fuels her overeating. She is entitled to feel good about herself in the body she has, rather than waiting for years, and possibly the rest of her life, to lose enough weight to become "acceptable."

In order to begin to transform her internal world from one of self-hatred to neutrality to self-acceptance and even self-love, your client can make some changes in her external world that will reinforce her attempt at countering her negative body image. As she engages in behaviors that demonstrate self-acceptance, she will begin to experience some moments of "okayness" in her body. In their book *Overcoming Overeating*, Hirschmann and Munter describe the following interventions that promote self-acceptance. Clients may express that enacting these behaviors makes them feel as though they are giving up. It is important for the therapist to understand and explain that these interventions aim to create a sense of well-being that will help the client end her compulsive eating and improve her body image and self-worth. They do not say anything about the size at which her body will stabilize. At the same time, her current behaviors, which reinforce her self-hatred, fail her repeatedly and actually lead to overeating and possible weight gain.

*Clothes*

If you ask a client with a history of dieting how many sizes of clothing she has in her closet, the answer will be at least three, and often more. Usually, she will have clothes that currently fit her, perhaps some "fat" clothes just in case, and several sizes that are too small for her but she hopes to wear again someday soon. In many diet and behavioral programs, the client was advised to keep her "thin" clothes hanging in her closet where she could see them, as this would motivate her to stay in control with food. However, if you ask your client how she feels when she looks at these clothes, chances are she will tell you that she feels awful. Rather than motivating her to follow a food plan, the fact that she cannot fit into her jeans creates anxiety, which often leads to overeating. Once again, as with the negative body talk that is supposed to move her in the direction of ending her compulsive eating, the method backfires and creates greater distress.

Imagine for a moment that you open your closet as you prepare to start your day. You see many clothes that you like but that no longer fit. There are a few outfits that do conform to your body size, but you do not particularly like them. Many of them are dark colors or black. They are not contemporary styles because you are waiting until you lose weight to buy the clothes you really want. How do you feel when you look into this closet? How do these feelings affect the way you will experience your day?

Now imagine that you open your closet and see a wardrobe in which every garment fits. The clothes reflect the colors and styles that you prefer. How do you feel when you look into this closet? How do these feelings affect the way you experience your day?

Encourage your client to consider cleaning out her closet and drawers of the clothes that no longer fit and taking an inventory of what she has left. Some clients become very excited by the possibility of getting rid of old items and begin immediately on this project. Other clients express concerns about this activity and are not ready to undertake this task. As with all aspects of the non-diet and size acceptance approach, the therapist must proceed at the client's pace, exploring her resistance as it emerges. Common concerns of clients at this juncture include a sense of giving up, financial issues, and the challenge of finding clothes that they like and that fit.

In a new group for clients working on ending their compulsive eating, a discussion ensued that illuminates the varying reactions. Claire complained that she had recently bought some new clothes; how could she justify spending more money on herself when she would be able to wear them only if she lost 20 pounds? The therapist pointed out that by keeping these clothes in her closet, she still could not get her money's worth because the reality is that they do not fit. Claire acknowledged that seeing the clothes made her feel upset. She decided that she did not want to give her newer clothes away, but was comfortable storing them in a different location out of her daily sight, in case her body became that size again. Val, on the other hand, realized that if she were ever to lose weight, the clothes she had from her "thin days" would no longer be the clothes she would want to wear. This made it easier for her to decide that she would give her clothes away to a local charity for battered women. Val wondered where she could find clothes that she actually liked and that would fit. The group was helpful in suggesting stores that had a variety of styles in larger sizes. Sally expressed her feeling that giving away her clothes meant giving up. She felt so strongly about this issue that she decided to postpone this activity. Instead, she began to explore her sadness about an earlier time in her life when she could fit into the miniskirts hanging in her closet. Tearfully, Sally revealed that while she received a lot of attention from men when she was thinner, she also felt scared by her increased sexual behavior. The therapist focused on her ambivalence about weight loss and the symbolic meaning of her "thin" clothes as both desired and feared. As Sally understands that her conflicts have been hooked to her clothes, she may find herself able to clear out the skirts that no longer fit and dress in a way that feels physically and psychologically comfortable. She will be encouraged to address her sexual conflicts in a more direct manner.

*Scales*

The scale is another tool used by clients and the diet industry that ultimately increases body dissatisfaction. Compulsive eaters, concerned about their weight, give this instrument tremendous power to determine whether they are going to have a "good day" or a "bad day." Clients often weigh themselves many times per day in hopes of seeing the number go down. They may move the scale around their homes to achieve a more favorable reading or take off jewelry prior to stepping on the scale. This behavior, which might be viewed as odd by an outsider looking in on our culture, is normative among females.

Unfortunately, the use of the scale to motivate controlled eating almost always fails. If you ask your client what happens for her when she steps on the scale and sees that her weight is higher, she will lament her lack of willpower or express other feelings of distress. Her anxiety about the number on the scale increases the probability that she will turn to food. She may eat immediately in order to soothe her feelings of failure and disappointment, or she may impose a period of restriction to undo the weight gain, thereby setting the stage for the inevitable binge. You might expect that the scale becomes more helpful to your client when she weighs herself and finds that she has lost some pounds. After all, this is the very success she craves. Yet most clients report that when the number goes down, they find themselves overeating. The client has endured the physical and psychological deprivation of the very foods she loves to achieve this goal, and now she deserves a reward. Alternately, the decrease in weight often stirs up pressure to continue losing additional pounds, which sets the diet–binge cycle back in motion. These patterns are so common among dieters that they need to be considered natural reactions to deprivation. It is helpful to explain this phenomenon to your client so that she can understand the dynamics behind her behavior rather than blame herself for her "lack of willpower."

Clients must also realize that the scale provides an inaccurate assessment of their body size. For example, muscle weighs more than fat. A client who begins an exercise regime and replaces fat with muscle could see the numbers go up even as she improves the health of her body. It would be a shame for her to conclude that she has failed in her efforts because the numbers on the scale do not meet her expectations, leading her to quit her exercise program. Also, it is natural for women's weight to vary during the month due to hormonal fluctuations and water retention. This is not a problem, but rather, a natural physiological occurrence. Yet this increase in weight can cause panic for clients who rush to restrict their intake and then eventually binge. Body size acceptance means understanding that weight is not static.

As your client strives to create an environment of acceptance, ending the ritual of weighing herself is an important step. Once a client realizes the negative impact of weighing on her self-image, she may choose to throw away her scale. However, another client may not feel ready to give up this act, which has become an integral part of her life. You can remain empathic with her difficulty in letting go of the scale and help her explore the meaning of weighing. You can also continue to point out in a gentle manner the consequences of weighing on her body image and self-esteem.

Even if your client decides to remove the scale from her home, she may confront the issue of weighing when she goes to her doctor's office. While ascertaining a patient's weight is necessary under some circumstances, this procedure is not generally indicated for routine office visits. Some clients specifically ask their doctors to forgo the weighing while others choose to step on the scale backward and not see the numbers. Many issues arise for clients who are concerned about weight when they meet with their doctors. These concerns, as well as possible strategies, are addressed further in chapter 8.

If your client decides not to weigh herself, how will she know what is happening to her body size? Clients can tell fairly accurately whether they are gaining, losing, or staying the same by the way their clothes fit. Although a client may fear that she will be out of control without the scale to rein her in, she will quickly discover that she can depend on herself to remain aware of how her body feels. The significant principle in relinquishing the scale is that she will no longer use the numbers to measure her self-worth. The way she feels about herself, her relationships, her work, and her interests are much more important and complex than the pounds read on the scale.

## Mirrors

Another helpful step in the process of changing negative body image involves the use of the mirror. Many clients who feel uncomfortable with the sizes of their bodies avoid the mirror almost completely, perhaps just glancing at their faces before they leave their homes. Others use the mirror as an opportunity to reprimand themselves mercilessly at the sight of their reflections. The goal of mirror work is to help your client learn to be able to look at herself without self-recrimination. This will help her move in the direction of acceptance as she learns to look at and describe her body in more neutral terms.

As your client looks in the mirror, she will tell herself that she is unacceptable in a variety of ways, using words such as "disgusting," "gross," or "too fat." Explain to her that these words contain judgments that interfere with the possibility of developing a positive self-image. While she will initially find it very difficult to look in the mirror and experience good feelings, she can begin to replace her negative messages with more objective descriptions. She can imagine herself as an anthropologist being curious and descriptive. For example, she may tell herself, "I am rounder in the stomach, more angular near my hips, fleshier in my thighs, and muscular at my calves," so that the harshness disappears from her internal dialogue. Of course, many clients will initially find that the yelling persists as they look in the mirror, causing distress. Let your client know that the minute she begins to feel upset by her reactions to looking at herself in the mirror, she can stop, even if she only glances for a moment or only as far as her face. However, if she pursues the task of using the mirror in an ongoing, consistent manner, over time she will notice that her relationship to the mirror changes from a negative, anxiety-provoking event to a more neutral, and perhaps even positive, action.

Your client's familiarity with her image in the mirror can help her in many ways. Clients often experience surprise and distress when they see themselves in a photograph, video, or reflected in a store window. As she learns to recognize herself more accurately, your client may become more comfortable with these situations. However, she may also report that she thought she was smaller than the pictures or reflections. In her book *Nothing to Lose*, Dr. Cheri Erdman describes a phenomenon she calls creative body image. Erdman discovered that many of the size-accepting women she interviewed reported that they saw themselves as smaller than they knew themselves to be. Rather than viewing this stance as pathological, Erdman explains that for herself and those she interviewed, "a smaller body image allows us to act as if we were 'normal' size. This 'acting as if' allows us to move through life unencumbered by the burden of fat stereotypes."[8] Erdman distinguishes the usefulness of creative body image in large clients from the need for a realistic body image with eating disorder patients, where their distortions can lead to extreme physical consequences. She also reports that as the result of a size-acceptance process, many people develop a transfigured body image in which they see a reflection of themselves in the mirror and have an accurate, non-judgmental view of their larger bodies.

Clients practicing mirror work often find over time that they enjoy looking at themselves and no longer participate in using the cultural voice of body hatred. Yet your client may report that while she can feel good about herself in the privacy of her own home, the minute she walks out the door, the yelling begins. This common experience results from the perceived judgment of others, including neighbors, coworkers, family, or friends, whom your client assumes judge her size. While she may be projecting her deep beliefs about size onto others, there is also a high probability, especially if she is large, that she is correct. It is important to help your client understand that other people's thoughts or comments reflect the extent to which they have internalized the culture, as well as their own negative body thoughts about themselves. As your client begins to feel stronger about her own body image, you can help her realize that she does not have to take in or internalize the destructive comments made by others.

### Challenging the Magic of Thinness

Another way clients use their distress about body size to reinforce feelings of low self-esteem is by putting off various hopes and goals until some time in the future when they believe they will become thin. Buying clothes, dating, career changes, increased confidence, or going to the beach are all such examples. On the one hand, this stance deprives clients of pursuing important goals, but at the same time they can avoid painful issues.

Clients with compulsive eating problems berate their bodies constantly as they express their wishes to be thin. Perhaps the biggest obstacle for your client in considering the possibility of giving up the negative feelings is her belief that if she were thin, her life would change for the better. It is important for you to explore these fantasies with your client and examine their meaning. An insightful exercise, developed by Hirschmann and Munter for their introductory Overcoming Overeating workshops, helps clients learn how they have connected psychological issues to weight. The goal of this exercise is to help clients identify what they may be putting off in their lives instead of living in the present. Clients can then determine what may be possible to do at their current size, and what may indicate deeper, psychological issues that require exploration, regardless of size.

Clients are asked to write down their reactions to the following statement: "If I were thin I would . . ." In a recent workshop, the following responses emerged from participants:

- Travel
- Wear a swimsuit/go swimming
- Date
- Go dancing
- Be more confident/have a higher self-esteem
- Stop trying to prove my self-worth
- Wear jeans/buy new clothes
- Do yoga
- See old friends
- Have sex with my husband
- Exercise/join a health club
- Wear a mini skirt

These responses fall into two categories. The first type of response includes external activities. In this example, these responses include travel, swimming/wearing a swimsuit, dancing, wearing jeans/buying new clothes, exercise, wearing a miniskirt and seeing old friends. Although your client may relate that she would feel shame if she attempted these activities at her current weight, her distress arises from internal perceptions about her entitlement to engage in these behaviors at her current size rather than an actual reality that prohibits her. You can help her consider alternatives that will allow her to engage in some of these activities in the present in ways that will feel comfortable to her. She may choose an exercise class catering to larger women; she may prefer movement such as yoga or t'ai chi, which promotes the development of the mind/body connection; or she may decide to take walks on her own and avoid the competitive atmosphere of the gym. You may also need to challenge her about her prerequisite weight loss. Is she really willing never to swim again if she remains fat? One workshop participant revealed that she loved to swim but had not done so in 30 years because of her shame around wearing a bathing suit. As group members reflected on the sadness of her loss, she realized that it was time to allow herself to buy a new bathing suit and experience the joy of the water. Another workshop participant who felt she could not wear a miniskirt unless she became thinner realized that even if she did lose weight, she would no longer want to dress in the way she did as a teenager.

The second group of responses reflects internal conflicts. These include become more confident, have a higher self-esteem, have sex with my husband, stop trying to prove my self-worth, and date. Although your client projects her deficits onto her size, in these cases her responses indicate deeper conflicts that require direct intervention regardless of her weight. For example, consider a client who feels that she cannot date until she becomes thinner. At the same time, as her therapist, you know that she struggles with her fear of intimacy. She has "hooked" this issue onto her weight and labels her "fat" as the problem, rather than stating that she is someone who has difficulties with closeness. Part of her therapy must include the work of "unhooking" these issues, otherwise the unresolved problems of intimacy may interfere with the process of her body finding its natural weight. After all, if thinness is supposed to solve this problem, and she does, in fact, begin to lose some weight, she will become distressed or frightened, causing a return to mouth hunger, followed by weight gain and a perpetuation of the belief that it is the fat that creates the difficulty.

Sometimes, answers can fall into both categories, depending on the meaning of the issue to your client. For example, having sex or seeing old friends can represent your client's difficulty with her comfort level in these areas at her size, or they can lead to deeper meaning. Your client may tell you that she cannot decide whether to attend her former college roommate's wedding because she does not have anything fancy to wear at her current size. She may need help in considering whether she could find an outfit that would feel appropriate. Does she feel entitled to have something beautiful to wear at her current size? Is she familiar with stores that cater to larger sizes and that fit her budget? If this exploration allows your client to solve her dilemma so that she can attend the wedding, you have sufficiently addressed the issue. If, however, she continues to resist the idea of buying a dress for herself, further exploration is warranted. Perhaps your client was unassertive during her college years and allowed her roommate to have control within the relationship. She has worked on taking charge of her own life in recent years and has ambivalent feelings about seeing her college friends. As she identifies this underlying reason for her hesitation, she can now discuss her conflict directly with you, rather than naming it as a problem of being "too fat."

## ADDRESSING INTERNAL FACTORS

As your client cleans out her closet, puts away the scale, engages in mirror work, and stops postponing her needs for the future, she creates a world outside of herself that reflects movement in the direction of self-acceptance. Yet she will still discover that the internalized negative body thoughts return over and over, and she must continue to intervene in order to change her relationship to her body. A series of four steps outlined in the book *When Women Stop Hating Their Bodies* offer her tools to actively work on her body image.

### Step One: Apologizing

In the first step, your client apologizes for her negative body thought. While this concept may feel contrived to some clients, it reinforces the idea that it is not all right for her to speak to herself in this way. The earlier exercise, which collected 24 hours of bad body thoughts, revealed the extent to which women criticize their bodies with little awareness of the frequency of these words and their effect on the psyche. By apologizing to herself, your client begins to challenge her own messages with an increased consciousness about how she chooses to treat herself and her body.

The treatment group provides an ideal setting to help clients realize the value of apologizing for their harsh words. Instruct your clients to think of the last time they had a negative body thought or think of a negative body thought that they often have. Next, have them partner with another group member. In succession, each group member must take their own negative body thought and say it to their partner, as if it were about them. Group members are often appalled as they turn to each other and say words such as, "You're thighs are so disgusting you make me sick." After each member takes a turn, they go around the room again, this time making an apology. These words of healing are usually very heartfelt, as clients try to repair the damage they feel they have done. At the end of this exercise, clients can discuss how they felt making and receiving the negative comments and the meaning of the apologies.

*Step Two: Confronting*

The second step in this process of confronting negative body image has the client question where her idea came from that, for example, a flat stomach is better than a round stomach. Although she may find it difficult to change her mind initially, frequent questioning of where these ideas came from and the use of other strategies to build a positive body image will help her whittle away at her ingrained beliefs.

*Step Three: Stopping*

Next, suggest to your client that she can stop her bad body thought. Remind her that the yelling she does about her body never helps her feel better about herself or end her compulsive eating. She can do her best to move her thought aside, even though both of you understand that it is likely to emerge again as she continues through the process of ending her negative body image. Sometimes, a client will report yelling at herself for yelling at herself! You can reassure her that you know how difficult it is for her to stop her negative dialogue. Ideally, you can help your client develop a compassionate stance toward herself in which she understands how hard it can be to let go of her familiar, negative self-talk, and at the same time she can give herself permission to gently push away her bad body thoughts each time they surface.

A simple visualization, developed by Carol Grannick, asks clients to close their eyes and identify a recent negative thought they had about their body.

"Imagine yourself typing that thought into the computer. Now, push the delete button! Now type in a more compassionate way to talk to yourself."

Clients often struggle with finding a compassionate voice to use toward themselves, and the therapist and other group members can provide support. For example, when Shelley deleted her thought that "the flab on my arms is gross," she drew a blank when she tried to speak differently to herself. Another group member suggested that Shelley could say, "I feel unhappy about the way my arms look, but this is just where I'm at right now." The group agreed that this statement acknowledged the feeling Shelley had about her arms without rendering the harsh judgment about the way her arm is "supposed" to look. Shelley felt that this edited version was acceptable and related that it will take a lot of practice to be able to create this new language for herself. Encouraging clients to intervene in this manner helps them establish an internal world that is size-accepting rather than self-rejecting.

*Step Four: Decoding*

The fourth step requires clients to decode their negative body thoughts. This method is extremely useful in the therapeutic process, as it promotes body acceptance and furthers the treatment process by uncovering psychological meaning. Earlier, we discussed the idea that compulsive eaters are often taught to translate their real concerns into the language of fat and food. Decoding body thoughts is an avenue through which clients can discover their original concerns and speak directly about these issues. The main principle of this technique is that a client's negative body thought is never just about her body. As the therapist, you must help your client wonder why she speaks negatively to herself about her body at a particular moment.

Lydia is a 45-year-old woman who works for a large corporation and needs to interpret a negative body thought. As the result of her recent outstanding performance, her company will feature her in their next bulletin, which is distributed to all employees. Lydia tells the group that she is very anxious about the picture because she is so fat. She wishes she could tell her boss that she does not want her picture to appear with the article, but she is afraid to do so.

**Therapist:** Is there any other reason that you don't want your picture to appear?

**Lydia:** No. I'm so fat. Nothing will look good on me. I hate having my picture taken.

**Sara:** I know what you mean. I don't like having my picture taken either. Maybe you should talk to your boss.

**Therapist:** We could talk about what it would mean to speak to your boss and whether that's what you need to do. But first, I want to explore your bad body thought. I know that you've been feeling okay about yourself lately, so I have to wonder about why this feeling that you're too fat is coming up now.

**Lydia:** Because it's my picture and everyone will see it!

**Therapist:** What exactly are you telling yourself about everyone seeing it?

**Lydia:** I hate to draw attention to myself.

**Therapist:** Those are strong words. Does the idea of drawing attention to yourself describe anything else about your life? In other words, if those words weren't about your body, what else might they be about?

**Lydia:** (Some silence, and then teary)

**Therapist:** Can you share with us what is going on for you?

Lydia went on to tell the group that she will do anything to avoid attention because of the sexual abuse she endured as a child; her history of abuse was already known to the group. As she explored her fears about receiving attention as a child, she related that she has always believed her fat would keep her invisible to the attention of others. She treaded into a new area around a particular memory and agreed to take this insight back to her individual therapist. At the same time, she realized that the picture for the corporate bulletin did not pose a threat to her in the way drawing attention to herself had as a child. She was able to allow herself the excitement she felt about being honored by her company and immediately became more comfortable with the prospect of the picture, sharing with the group the outfit she planned to wear. Lydia expressed her surprise at the shift in her feeling because she walked into the group certain that there was nothing behind her negative feelings except her dislike of pictures.

This example demonstrates how the client's language can help increase her understanding of her personality and life circumstances. Some clients are intrigued by this technique while others will argue that their negative body talk really *is* just about their body. Your own belief in this concept will help you respond to your clients' doubts.

**Abbey:** I think my stomach sticks out because it really does.

**Therapist:** Is that thought with you all the time, or does it pop up here and there?

**Abbey:** No, it's not with me all the time.

**Therapist:** Sometimes it can be useful to notice the exact moment when it does occur. You might ask yourself what you would have been thinking about at that moment if you didn't have a negative body thought. It's a lot like mouth hunger where you ask yourself what you might think about or feel if you didn't reach for food. In a sense, it's as if you're reaching for a bad body thought to take you away from the feeling.

In this scenario, the therapist plants a seed that will hopefully encourage Abbey to become more self-aware when she notices a negative body thought in the future. Clients can try to recall what was on their minds prior to the moment that the thought occurred, or they can take the exact wording of their negative thoughts and apply it to something else that is important in their life. This new way of understanding negative self-talk takes practice and insight, and your training as a therapist to listen for metaphors in a client's communication will greatly enhance this process.

Ken is a 27-year-old man who recently began therapy for his compulsive eating. The idea of decoding his bad body thoughts is a new concept. He planned to attend his high school reunion in a couple of months but is having second thoughts because of his size. He reported to his therapist that he has been consumed by negative body thoughts ever since he received the invitation. When asked about his concerns, Ken replied that his classmates are sure to think of him as a failure when they see the weight he has gained over the past 10 years. The therapist asked Ken if his words, "I'm so fat that everyone will see that I'm a failure," described anything else about his personality or situation. Ken explained that he was very popular and an excellent student in high school. However, he began having problems in college and dropped out. While many of his classmates have gone on to attain professional jobs, he works at a local retail store and lives with his parents. Ken was able to articulate that he felt like a failure, not only in comparison to his peers, but also in his own eyes. The therapist helped Ken understand that his focus on weight was a translation of his deeper concerns, which helped him avoid his true distress. As Ken identified these issues, he realized that he must come to terms with his own disappointments and consider his goals for the future. He chose not to attend his high school reunion because he felt he would experience too much anxiety. However, Ken no longer used his weight to label his problem.

As clients become familiar with this method, they often become excellent detectives when it comes to interpreting their own bad body thoughts. Over time, clients may bring in the translations rather than the original negative body thought. For example, a client may tell you that she realized how much she was dreading a meeting at work when she noticed herself criticizing her thighs for rubbing together and chafing. "I realized that I had that thought on my way to the meeting because two of my colleagues really rub me the wrong way, and I knew I was going to have to confront them about some issues." At this point, the client focuses on her assertiveness at work rather than the size of her thighs. This is an indicator that your client is well on her way to confronting her negative body image.

## CONSIDERING THE LARGER CLIENT

As mentioned earlier, very large people face obstacles that exacerbate the difficulty of improving their negative body image.

Seats in airplanes, theaters, or conference rooms can challenge the large client, who must make her way through life in a body that does not fit the cultural norms. Although many people, including therapists, believe that this is proof that a client must lose weight, the reality is that people come in different shapes and sizes. Perhaps she will eventually lose weight or perhaps she will live out her life as a large person. In either case, she is entitled to be treated with respect and seek ways to accommodate her size, just as people with other special needs deserve equal access in their daily lives. Because of the shame so often experienced by these clients, it is often difficult for them to advocate for their own needs. Clients have reported examples of having food grabbed out of their hands or shopping carts by people who have commented that they do not need the food. One client stated that her doctor told her that she didn't need to eat for at least a year because she had so much fat on her body. A major airline recently announced that it would begin to charge large passengers for two seats. These types of messages leave your client feeling hopeless about her situation. She may restrict her movement in the outside world and become, understandably, depressed.

Historically, oppressed groups such as African Americans, Jews, and other ethnic minorities have lived together in communities or neighborhoods. Fat people, however, cut across economic, class, and ethnic background and are isolated from each other as an identifiable group. They are therefore unable to unite and find strength and support from one another. To the extent that they do come together, it is usually in some type of diet group where the values and norms of the culture are reinforced. In the past, clients have typically connected with each other through their diet failures and their need to have greater willpower.

As a therapist, you have an opportunity to help your client begin to have different kinds of experiences. The fact that she often finds airplane or theater seats too small does not mean that her body is wrong; it only means that our culture fails to accommodate the variety of body sizes that exist. Your stance toward her entitlement to live in the world at her current size may surprise her, and over time it can help her create a different perspective toward her situation. For example, helping your client figure out which movie theater has the widest seats communicates your belief that she is entitled to see films and to be seen in the world. If she feels too uncomfortable to go to a theater on a crowded Saturday evening, perhaps she can consider a weeknight when the theater is less full. If this option still creates too much anxiety, she may want to rent a movie. In the past, she may have eliminated the option of seeing any movies, assuming that her needs were unimportant given her failures to control her weight. The therapeutic goal is to help her consider options to lead a fuller life in the body she has, and to decrease the amount of self-hatred and blame she experiences that prevent her access to everyday needs and desires. Groups can provide additional support as members share their experiences and problem solve with each other about the obstacles they face. Organizations such as Abundia offer weekend retreats devoted to workshops that deal with the issues of living well in a fat body.

## BUILDING A POSITIVE BODY IMAGE

The therapeutic work you and your client engage in to end negative body image is invaluable; yet you must also help her find ways to replace her negative thoughts with positive experiences related to her body. In the process of ending her compulsive eating, your client learned to collect stomach hunger experiences that became more frequent and sustained over time. In a similar vein, your client can try to collect positive body experiences in which she pays attention to the moments when she genuinely feels good in her body. Actively noticing these pleasurable feelings will help her understand that it is not an objective fact that her body is unlovable; rather she can seek to develop an attitude of care and acceptance toward herself. When she feels overcome by her negative body thoughts, she can try to remind herself that there are other moments, in the same body, when she feels good. This intervention will help your client form a more consistent, loving stance toward her body.

### Finding Affirmation within the Culture

With the growth of the size acceptance movement, there are an increasing number of resources available to your client promoting positive feelings toward people of all body shapes and sizes. Books, magazines, organizations, and Internet sites can help her discover that there are many people who live happy, healthy lives at weights above the conventional ideal, and provide inspirational stories as well as practical information. These can be particularly useful to your client when she feels isolated in her attempts to develop an accepting attitude about her body.

Encourage your client to seek role models in the culture, both in the media and closer to home. Celebrities such as Camryn Manheim, actress in the hit series *The Practice* and author of *Wake Up, I'm Fat!*, offer examples of people who are large, attractive, successful, and comfortable with themselves. There are more models who wear somewhat larger sizes than in the past.

If your client pays attention to people she knows in her own life, chances are she will be able to tell you about someone who is fat and looks beautiful or who is large and seems perfectly happy. You may also ask her to notice that there are thin people who do not look particularly great or who have many problems in their lives. The key is to help her realize that how a person looks and feels are not dependent on size. She has chosen to focus on people who she sees as fat and unhappy as a means of "motivating" herself to become thin, and to assume that thinness equals happiness. This is a cultural lesson that she has internalized very well. She can now become a curious, objective observer, noticing the way people dress, carry themselves, and present themselves to the world, independent of their size. Again, your client may also take a trip to an art museum to see how bodies are portrayed by the masters. She will find variety and roundness in the images of women rather than the stick figures of many current models. While she may already know this information on an intellectual level, any methods she can use to remind herself that bodies naturally come in different shapes and sizes will reinforce the positive experiences of herself at her current size.

## Exercises and Visualizations

In a group setting, the use of body image exercises and visualizations can offer meaningful experiences to clients as they attempt to build positive experiences. Books such as *Transforming Body Image* by Marcia Hutchinson suggest numerous techniques.[9] An example of this type of work asks your clients to write a letter to the part of their body that elicits negative feelings. After completing this task, they must have that body part respond back to them in a letter. The results of this exercise can be profound, as illustrated in the following example:

> Dear Knees up to Neck,
>
> It's hard to decide which part of you that I like the least. I feel that you are out of shape, not only by weight but by form. You make the purchasing/trying on and wearing of clothes painful and uncomfortable at times. Humiliating, to be exact. I feel ashamed of you especially when I put on a bathing suit or other summer type clothing. I look at others with slimmer bodies and long for what that might feel like. Each day when I get dressed I am reminded of your size and shape. I avoid looking in mirrors because I am afraid of what you look like. Some days the reality is too painful.
>
> Sandi
>
> Dear Sandi,
>
> We are in receipt of your letter and feel offended by the content. It seems that you are ungrateful for all the positive things that we do for you. We enable you to walk along lovely beaches, to swim in crystal blue water, and to ride a bicycle through the lovely woods, among other things. We

allow you to embrace and comfort your loved ones. There are those in the world who are disabled and cannot walk. We may not be the perfect image of what our society considers beautiful, but we are all that you have so please try to accept and love us.

Warmest Regards,

Knees to Neck

As you assess the benefits of doing experiential work with your clients, you can search for resources that support these goals, or perhaps develop your own ideas into tools that promote the end of body hatred.

A useful exercise developed by Debra Waterhouse (see Appendix B, Building Positive Body Image) asks clients to circle the words that best describe the way they feel about their bodies. Interestingly, only positive words appear! This helps push clients in the direction of understanding that they do experience positive feelings at times in regard to their bodies, and that they can actively choose to focus on these strengths rather than view their bodies as primarily defective.

In some cases, a client who makes peace with her body will express the feeling that her size does not match her vision of what someone who feels good about herself should look like. As our society expects people who are fat to be dissatisfied, your client may experience her increased sense of psychological well-being in her larger body as dystonic. The following exercise, which can be used in a group setting, will help your client integrate her view of herself. Ask clients to bring a picture of themselves to the group, or if possible, use an instant camera to take individual pictures. Next, instruct group members to write the following statement: "This is the body of a person who . . ." Clients complete this statement with positive descriptions of themselves such as:

- This is the body of a person who is smart.
- This is the body of a person who loves to laugh.
- This is the body of a person who plays tennis.

Clients can go around the room and read their responses out loud as they look at their pictures. Interestingly, clients often state that they are able to see positive qualities in other members that match their external perceptions of them, but find it harder to accept this concept in themselves. Clients can keep their photos and practice this exercise at home so that they can build an internal perception of their bodies that accurately reflects their self-definitions. This exercise also can be tailored for individual sessions.

### Reclaiming the Body

The issue of mind/body connection is extremely important to address as you help your client expand her positive self-image. Clients often disavow parts or all of their bodies in an effort to reduce anxiety over the negative self-images. Many clients describe feeling that they are "just a head," paying little attention to the needs and pleasures of the rest of their bodies. After challenging her negative body image, your client can now begin to experience her physical self in new ways. She may allow herself a massage, take a movement class, or begin to use a special lotion. Through the process of attuned eating, your client has already begun to reconnect with her internal bodily signals. Experimenting with other types of physical sensations increases her ability to know her body and feel comfortable in her own skin. In the same way she matches food to hunger, she can attempt to match her experience of her body with her own desires and preferences for self-care.

### Your Client's Journey

Clients who move through the size-acceptance process differ in how public they choose to become about their new attitudes and behavior. Some clients see their journey as very private, sharing their perspective with only their closest friends or family members. Other clients find that their personal realizations have political implications, and decide to become more public about their opinions. This can take the form of writing letters in response to articles promoting diets, objecting to company policies that discriminate on the basis of size, or joining an organization such as the National Association to Advance Fat Acceptance (NAAFA), which promotes political change. Activism allows your client to challenge the ongoing oppression toward fat people and gives her the opportunity to help others find freedom from body hatred, which can become transformative in her own process of size acceptance.

## WEIGHT

Up until now, we have purposefully avoided the subject of weight. The majority of clients who work in therapy on their compulsive eating problems express a strong desire to lose weight, even if they enter treatment with knowledge of non-diet and size-accepting approaches. The pressures to be thin in our culture are so strong that it would be surprising for a person to consciously choose to be fat. However, the major goal of treating compulsive eating is to help your client end her preoccupation with food and weight. As she cures her overeating, she may lose weight or she may stabilize at a size considered large by culture. In either case, she is successful.

The non-diet paradigm is certainly not against weight loss, yet at the same time, the number on the scale is no longer a measure of success. Instead, indicators such as eating in an attuned manner, developing a positive body image, improving physical health, and increasing self-esteem replace the scale as ways of determining progress. When a client loses weight with this approach, typically she has made peace with her eating and accepted her body size to the extent that she no longer feels particularly invested in becoming thinner. She may appreciate the fact that she can move a bit easier or that it is simpler to find clothes, but her happiness is no longer contingent on her weight. If weight loss occurs, this change can be considered a side effect of the therapeutic work taking place between you and your client, rather than the most significant outcome of the treatment.

*Responding to Your Client's Concerns*

When your client discusses her wish to lose weight, it is important to take an empathic stance toward her distress about her body and incorporate psychoeducational material. Be aware of your feelings that are triggered as your client relates her concerns. Perhaps a very large client elicits a sense of urgency that she really must lose weight quickly, while a relatively thin client makes you wonder why she feels concerned at all. In all situations, your ability to listen to your client's genuine concerns as well as the possible, unconscious meanings of her experiences will promote a sense of trust and curiosity in the treatment process. Responses such as, "I can hear that you really feel distressed," or, "You've carried this issue with you for a very long time. How do you think it has affected you?" let the client know you take her worries about her size seriously, without colluding with the idea that she must lose weight to feel better. Comments such as, "You're not fat. You don't need to worry," or "I know just what you mean" communicate support of the overly idealized value of thinness and interfere with the process of allowing the client to describe her own unique experiences.

In addition to listening to your client's concerns about weight, it is important to provide her with information about the factors that influence a person's size. First, let her know that the major factor in determining an individual's weight is her genetics. Ask her if there is anyone in her family she resembles, including parents, grandparents, aunts, and uncles. Next, explain that her size is also affected by the amount of yo-yo dieting she has done in her weight loss career. If you haven't done so already, use this opportunity to educate her about the effects of dieting on her metabolism over time, as described in chapter 1. Finally, convey to her that size is affected by the number of times she turns to food when she is not physically hungry. This is the aspect of her weight that she has the most control over as she embarks on the process of ending her compulsive eating.

## Possible Outcomes

Most clients believe that once they stop overeating, they will naturally lose weight. While this may occur for your client, it is likely to take place over a long period of time as compared to diet plans, which usually result in quick weight loss in the short run. As she starts the process of normalizing her eating, your client may actually gain some weight. This can occur for a number of reasons. If a client enters treatment following a recent diet, she will most certainly gain weight; remember that this would inevitably happen anyway as the result of breaking the restrictions imposed upon her by the diet. As your client legalizes foods that have been off limits, she will probably eat more of them than she needs in response to past deprivation. However, as your client becomes convinced that these foods are back in her life permanently and stops yelling about her food choices, her overeating will decrease as a by-product of this process. She is likely to find that her weight stabilizes rather than constantly moving up and down the scale.

Why would anyone begin a method of eating that could possibly lead to weight gain? Keep in mind that every diet program your client began ultimately led to this very consequence. Remind her that if these diet plans worked for her, she would feel satisfied with her eating and weight and would not be seeking treatment. At the point your client embarks on the process of normalizing her eating, she is convinced that diets do not work. The incentive to stop focusing on size is that the relief from the preoccupation with food and weight is greater than the distress over the actual pounds she carries. She can also maintain the realistic hope that as she ends her compulsive eating, she can have a physically healthy body and an emotional sense of well-being.

## The Paradox

Explain to your client that while she works toward learning to feed herself in an attuned manner, her weight is not her concern. She will still need to attend to her body, of course, as she concentrates on her self-image and her physical needs. Yet the moment she focuses on her weight, she creates the opposite effect. If her primary purpose in curing her compulsive eating is to lose weight, she will actually fuel her overeating because of the perceived deprivation. For example, when she reaches for a cookie, her concern about weight will lead her to calculate calories or fat grams. As she begins to tell herself that the cookies are fattening, she thinks that she should not consume them. Paradoxically, she will now eat more than she actually needs because she created an internal sense of deprivation that interfered with her ability to stop when satisfied. Let her know that while her wish to lose weight is understandable, for the purposes of ending her compulsive eating she must try to put these concerns on hold. The less concerned she can be about her body size, the more likely she is to stay present with her eating, so that her body can find its natural size.

## Conflicts about Weight Loss

As clients normalize their eating, sometimes they discover that their clothes fit more loosely, signaling a change in weight. At this point, clients have a tendency to find an increase in mouth hunger. Check in with your client to learn what she has told herself about her weight loss. A client often gets excited about the idea of becoming thinner. As a result, she tells herself that if she can just eat out of stomach hunger more often and "do it better," she will lose weight even more quickly. In a sense, she has turned her new way of eating into another diet, which we sometimes refer to as the "stomach hunger" diet. Rather than gently moving in the direction of stomach hunger, eating only when physically hungry becomes the new rule. Help her remember that her body size will take care of itself as she focuses on continuing her process of ending compulsive eating. While her good feelings about her weight loss are understandable, they are not the main event in her treatment. If she turns her attuned eating into another diet, she will begin to re-experience the deprivations and rebellions that she has worked so hard to end.

When a client notices increased eating when she is not physically hungry following weight loss, it is often necessary to explore any ambivalence she feels about becoming thinner. While most clients insist that becoming thinner would only improve their lives, unconscious, psychological factors often emerge as clients look at the meaning of losing weight.

*Fear of Losing Connection*

Karen is a 25-year-old single woman who has worked in treatment for several years on issues related to her low self-esteem and feelings of depression. She spent much time understanding the dynamics she experienced with her parents. Karen discovered how her mother's narcissistic needs interfered with her ability to get her own needs met. Karen repressed many feelings during her childhood as she learned to become the "good girl" who tried to keep peace in the family. Karen turned to food early in her life as a way to rid herself of unacceptable feelings and to soothe herself. As she began to gain weight, her mother alternately berated her and then became very concerned about her. Sometimes Karen and her mother would have huge arguments about what she could eat, while at other times they would try to diet together. Karen articulated her previously unconscious belief that if she could lose weight, her mother would finally accept her and provide the nurturance missing throughout her life. Despite Karen's insights, her overeating continued.

Eventually, Karen began a group using the non-diet approach to ending compulsive eating, and after 1 year, she noticed a significant change in her eating. Karen reported to her individual therapist that she no longer binged, and that she used her infrequent incidents of psychological eating as an opportunity to learn about an uncovered feeling. She also found that she began to lose weight, which pleased her. While she had worked on body image in her group, she welcomed the possibility of becoming thinner. However, about a month later Karen reported that for the first time in 8 months, she binged on cookies. Her overeating lasted about 3 days. She was now eating mostly out of physiological hunger again, but she could not make sense of her mouth hunger. Karen had checked in with herself to see what could be bothering her, but failed to identify any hidden feelings.

**Therapist:** I'm aware that you've been noticing weight loss over the past month. Sometimes that can trigger overeating because people often have mixed feelings about losing weight.

**Karen:** But this is what I've always wanted. It's not like it really changes anything in my life. It's just easier.

**Therapist:** I know it feels that way to you. But, I wonder if there are any ways in which losing weight creates a problem for you.

**Karen:** Like what?

**Therapist:** If you think about yourself becoming thinner, does anything come to mind that's negative or upsetting to you?

**Karen:** Well actually, I feel like my mom is winning. She'll think I'm doing it for her because it's what she's always wanted. It's like I'm giving in to her one more time.

**Therapist:** I see what you mean. In a way, being larger was a way to tell her that everything wasn't really okay with you and that she couldn't control you.

**Karen:** I think it's even more than that. I feel like I'll lose her somehow if I lose weight. (She becomes sad and tearful.)

**Therapist:** Can you tell me more about that?

Over the next several weeks, Karen elaborated on the psychological meaning of weight loss in her relationship with her mother. Karen related that her overeating and weight had become the main source of conversation between the two of them. Without this connection, Karen felt unsure as to whether any real relationship existed at all. As Karen explored this issue, she identified her core distress about becoming thin. While growing up, she longed for her mother to know her as a separate person who could listen to her and support her needs. When her needs went unmet, Karen turned to food and gained weight. As her mother focused on her weight loss, Karen developed the fantasy that if she could lose weight, her mother would finally accept her. In the present, Karen understood that her mother had done the best she could to take care of her, but because of some deficits in her own parenting capacities, had not been able to meet many of Karen's emotional needs. For Karen, her recent weight loss symbolized giving up the fantasy that her mother would ever become the kind of parent she truly desired. Allowing herself to maintain weight loss without receiving the changes in the relationship she longed for meant accepting the pain and disappointment of letting go of her hopes for a more empathic mother. At the same time, Karen's ability to understand that losing weight could never solve these deeper issues allowed her to return to her previous state of attuned eating and do some important therapeutic work of psychological separation from her family.

## *Fear of Sexuality*

Patti also discovered an unexplored fear about losing weight. She experienced difficulties in her marriage and sometimes contemplated divorce. While she knew this was an option, she felt afraid of being the single mother of four children. As Patti examined her increased overeating following recent weight loss, she realized that she worried becoming thinner would make her more attractive in the eyes of some men. She was frightened that she might have an affair outside of her marriage and believed that her fat protected her from acting on her marital dissatisfaction. After identifying her ambivalence, Patti was in a position to discuss the meaning of her fears. On the one hand, her problems with her husband needed to be addressed so that she could decide how she wanted to proceed in the marriage. At the same time, Patti was able to understand that her weight did not really protect her from her sexuality. At her current size, there were men who had expressed an interest in her. If she became thinner, she could still choose to say no. Patti's task was to unhook her internal conflicts about her marriage and sexuality from her size.

### Understanding the Ambivalence: A Visualization

The case illustrations of Karen and Patti demonstrate how core conflicts can become attached to weight loss. If your client can recognize any ambivalence toward weight loss, she will be in a stronger position to allow herself to become thinner if her body changes in that direction. If, on the other hand, she does not identify any conflicts about weight loss that do, in fact, exist for her, she will be unable to maintain a thinner size. Hirschmann and Munter developed an excellent visualization that promotes this understanding, which we have adapted as follows:

> Imagine yourself becoming larger. Where are you? Who are you with? While it may feel uncomfortable to see yourself bigger, try to think about how your larger size helps you in this situation. Now, imagine yourself at a thinner size. Again, where are you, who are you with? As pleasant as this may seem to you, see if you can identify the problem that occurs for you at this smaller size.

Clients are often surprised by the outcomes of their visualizations. Discussions of this type of work can help clients learn through their experiences how powerful unconscious fears about thinness can be. Jean found that when she saw herself as larger, less was expected of her. She communicated her fear that if she were thinner and had more energy, the demands on her time would be even greater than they are now. The therapist helped Jean identify her difficulty with boundaries and together they worked on Jean's ability to say no at her current size.

Fran revealed that when she became thin, she was like a transparent sheet of paper and could barely move. She felt she lost all sense of being and acknowledged that her fat gave "weight" to her sense of self. She continues to work on developing her internal sense of self.

Sheila found that she was at a party and felt very frightened by the sexual attention she received. She felt unable to defend herself against unwanted advances, which she related to her sexual abuse history. She stated that she is already aware that she uses her weight to keep people from seeing her. Sheila discussed the paradox of using her size as a way to be hidden and seen at the same time. Sheila's goal is to find ways to feel safe as an adult woman so that she no longer uses her body size to protect herself.

These examples further illustrate the importance of unhooking psychological issues from weight. For many clients, becoming thinner is associated with the fears and anxieties of childhood. For other clients, the wish for thinness may reflect a fear of aging, as the thinner body is often connected to the image of youth. As your client can make the connections between her wish for thinness and her associations to thinness, she can become more compassionate about her struggles. Working directly on her underlying conflicts will give her body the freedom to settle at the size it is meant to be.

*Making Peace*

There are many possible reasons why your client experiences ambivalence about weight loss, and your skill as a therapist can facilitate her exploration of these themes. While these insights can be extremely fruitful to the treatment process, we do not mean to imply that every fat person maintains her weight because she is defending against unconscious fears of thinness: people come in all sizes. As your client normalizes her eating, she may need to come to terms with the prospect that her natural body size is a larger body. Hillary expressed her feelings about accepting her body after completing her treatment for compulsive eating.

**Hillary:** I still wish I could cross my legs.

**Therapist:** You mean that your size literally gets in the way of being able to cross your legs?

**Hillary:** Yes. I don't think becoming more flexible will make it possible for me.

**Therapist:** How do you feel about that?

**Hillary:** I'm not sure what to do when I find myself frustrated that my body isn't changing in ways I wish it would.

**Therapist:** I can understand that you would like to be able to cross your legs. So, maybe you say, "It makes me sad that I can't cross my legs," or "Sometimes I wish I could go back in time to when I could cross my legs." That's very different than saying, "My thighs are so fat and disgusting."

**Hillary:** I can hear the difference.

**Therapist:** As much as you wish you could cross your legs, this may be where your body stabilizes. Remember that with this approach, the measure of success is the end of your preoccupation with food and weight. You've definitely accomplished those goals. There's nothing wrong with losing weight — it's just not the main focus.

**Hillary:** I know that my success isn't about weight loss. I could never imagine going on another diet. I've started a yoga class and that's helping me feel more connected to my body.

**Therapist:** And we'll see what happens. It may help you become more flexible and able to cross your legs. Or, you may have to figure out other ways to sit and be comfortable.

## Responding to Others

As your client processes her own reactions to changes, or lack of changes, in her body size, she will inevitably have to deal with the reactions of others. In our thin-obsessed culture, weight and diets are frequent topics of conversations and people often feel free to comment on another person's size. "Oh, you look like you're losing weight," is a comment sometimes made to clients. Although this statement is supposed to make a person feel good, it can create anxiety for clients working on an internal approach to solving their problems. If your client has stopped weighing herself, she may not know if this is a correct observation.

**Gretchen:** My coworker told me I'm losing weight. I found myself having some mouth hunger when I got home from work.

**Therapist:** What do you think happened for you?

**Gretchen:** She took me so off guard. I'm not sure if I really have.

**Therapist:** It's interesting that clients will tell me that sometimes someone will say, "You look great. You've lost weight," when, in fact, they haven't. But, they have made changes in their lives and are feeling much better about themselves and this shows in the way they take care of and carry themselves. In our culture, people often assume that if you are feeling better, you must have lost weight!

**Gretchen:** I have been feeling great. I'm eating when I'm hungry and I feel so normal. I actually feel very comfortable with my body. I wouldn't mind losing weight, but I'm also fine if I stay right here. It's been great to get some new clothes that I really like.

**Therapist:** I can hear that you are feeling really great. So let's look at what you can do when someone makes a comment to you about your weight. What did you do at work?

**Gretchen:** When my coworker said it, I just said thank you. But that doesn't feel right to me. Is she saying I didn't look good before? That bothers me because I don't want anyone judging me based on my size. Also, if I say thank you, it's like I'm agreeing with her that it is good that I lost weight. It totally misses the point that my relationship to food is completely different, and that I just don't focus on weight anymore.

**Therapist:** Can you think of a way to respond that might reflect that feeling?

**Gretchen:** I guess I could say that I don't keep track of my weight anymore, but perhaps what she is noticing is that I've made some changes in my life that make me feel very happy.

Clients vary in their comfort level of responding to comments about weight loss. Even when a client knows that she has lost weight, she is likely to feel that the intended compliment undermines her commitment to accept herself — a commitment that supports her ability to eat in an attuned manner. She may choose to explain in more detail her new views of food and weight with close friends or family, while she develops a stock answer for acquaintances or people with whom she does not wish to reveal her personal struggles. Your stance communicates that her success comes from ending her preoccupation with food and weight rather than the actual amount of weight loss if it occurs will reinforce her ability to move through the world at whatever size her body stabilizes.

Clients who stabilize at a larger size face a different set of comments. They may deal with the constant pressures of new diet plans presented to them because of the assumption that they cannot possibly be satisfied at their current size. Even though they have successfully cured their compulsive eating, clients may find that significant people in their life continue to negate their accomplishments. Again, your client must develop a response to others that reflects her own sense of well-being and creates an acceptable comfort level. One client told her mother, "I know you would like me to be thinner, but it's not in the cards for me. I've tried every diet possible, and I've learned that this made me even fatter than I might have been. I'm very comfortable with my eating, and I'm learning to be more comfortable with my body. I know you worry about me, but I've been exercising regularly, and at my last physical, my doctor said I was in good health. I hope you can learn to accept me the way I am. But if you can't, I would appreciate it if you would keep your comments to yourself. They just don't help me."

Helping clients with body image can feel like a daunting task at times. Yet as your client develops a more accepting view of herself that allows her to participate more fully in the world and decode issues that she has linked to her size, the rewards are immense. The majority of clients find that they can see a significant decrease in their overeating much more quickly than they can improve their body esteem. It is important for you and your client to remember that changing body image is a process that occurs over a long period of time. In fact, as the body changes throughout a person's life cycle, your client will need to repeatedly assess her sense of her body and deal with changes that she may not necessarily perceive as desirable. To the extent that your client can accept and appreciate her body at different stages of development, she will find it easier to cope with the natural transformations that occur at puberty, pregnancy, midlife and, ultimately, aging.

# ENDNOTES

1. Fraiberg, S. (1959). *The magic years.* New York: Charles Scribner's Sons, p. 42.
2. Kater, K. J. (2002, November). An effective model for preventing culturally induced body image, eating, and weight concerns before they start. Feminist Perspectives on Body Image, Trauma & Healing, 12th Annual Renfrew Center Foundation Conference for Professionals. Philadelphia, PA.
3. Pope, H. (2000). *The Adonis complex: The secret crisis of male body obsession.* New York: Free Press.
4. Stice, E., Cameron, R., Killen, J. D., Hayward, C., & Taylor, C. B. (1999). Naturalistic weight-reduction efforts prospectively predict growth in relative

weight and onset of obesity among female adolescents. *Journal of Consulting and Clinical Psychology, 67* (6), 967–974.

5. Field, A. E. et al. (2003). Relation between dieting and weight change among adolescents. *Pediatrics, 112*(4), 900–906.

6. Orbach, S. (1978). *Fat is a feminist issue.* New York: Berkley Books.

7. Bloom, C. & Kogel, L. (1994). Tracing development: The feeding experience and the body. In C. Bloom, A. Glitter, S. Goodwill, L. Kogel, & L. Zaphiropolous (Eds.), *Eating problems.* New York: Basic Books, p. 55.

8. Erdman, C. (1995). *Nothing to lose.* San Francisco: HarperSanFrancisco, p. 75.

9. Hutchinson, M. (1985). *Transforming body image: Learning to love the body you have.* Trumansburg, NY: The Crossing Press.

# CHAPTER 7

# TREATMENT
# CONSIDERATIONS

We have presented a framework for treating compulsive overeating that integrates direct interventions into clients' eating patterns with a psychological understanding of the function of the overeating behavior. This approach also uses research to validate the reality that diets do not work and that people naturally come in different shapes and sizes. We explored the cultural pressures that contribute to body dissatisfaction, which are frequently used by clients to represent internal conflicts. While we will offer more information about health issues and suggestions for prevention in the final chapters, at this time we invite you to consider the practical implications for your work as a therapist in relationship to treating clients with compulsive eating problems. Some of these considerations will raise questions that do not necessarily have a single answer but require you to think about your own treatment philosophy as well as the needs of your clients.

## Reactions to the Non-Diet Paradigm

You may read the pages in this book and be convinced that the non-diet approach provides a valuable treatment strategy for your clients who eat compulsively. In fact, you may have already used these concepts in your work and gained support from the information and case examples presented. However, we recognize that some therapists will continue to feel that weight loss should be a goal and may continue to encourage clients to diet, especially if this is the client's stated wish. If you find that your client eventually struggles with her weight loss plan, you may find some of the concepts presented thus far to be useful in helping her understand her difficulties and allow her to decide about whether to continue to diet.

If a client tells you that she has heard about an approach to help her end her compulsive relationship with food by stopping all diets, the information presented in this book will allow you to support her attempt to solve her compulsive overeating, even if the philosophy differs from your own beliefs. Your understanding of the non-diet approach can alleviate conflicts for your client as illustrated in the following example.

Jen, a businesswoman in her early 30s, joined a group to end her compulsive eating. She reported a strong, positive relationship with her individual therapist with whom she had been in treatment for 4 years. The therapy had focused on a variety of issues including a history of sexual abuse, perfectionist expectations, and continued efforts to lose weight. Jen reported that she struggled with her weight since childhood and considers herself a professional yo-yo dieter. Her therapist had witnessed Jen's dieting attempts that had led to significant weight loss followed by weight gain. Jen had made the decision to end all diets, feeling they led to depression, frustration, added pounds, and physical complications. The last commercial diet program she tried led to severe medical problems, which necessitated the removal of her gall bladder. Jen told her therapist about the non-diet approach to end her compulsive eating. While her therapist agreed that the approach made sense, she suggested that Jen go on one more diet to lose weight and then she could implement these new concepts. Jen refused to try yet another diet. She struggled to balance her individual treatment with the non-diet approach, which her therapist agreed made sense intellectually but was reluctant to embrace.

Other therapists may find that the philosophy of the non-diet approach makes clinical sense, yet may not feel suited to treat clients with this problem. Perhaps you are not particularly interested in this problem as a specialty in your practice. Or you may struggle with your own eating and weight issues and recognize that while you accept the therapeutic efficacy of the non-diet approach, you are not in a position to integrate this work into your practice at this time. With this insight, you may consider referring clients for consultation with another professional who can provide your client with an adjunct service to compliment your treatment, such as a group. At the same time, you can support your client's pursuit of attuned eating and body image acceptance.

Another possible reaction to the previous chapters is that while you accept the idea that diets do not work, and agree that cultural notions of thinness are unreasonable, it still seems difficult to promote the concept to clients that they can eat in an unrestricted manner. Yet clients who legalize food in the service of ending compulsive eating without qualifications are in the strongest position to cure their problem. Keep in mind that these clients stay focused on moving toward attuned eating in which they eat *what* they are hungry for *when* they are hungry; the idea that this approach condones eating whatever a person wants whenever they want is a misperception of the work. As these clients solve their compulsive eating, they become able to make decisions about their nutritional needs and preferences.

If you doubt the validity of this stance, then it is understandable that you would feel irresponsible using these premises in the treatment of your clients. Perhaps you can focus on the aspects of the approach that seem therapeutically sound to you. For example, you may agree that body image problems can express other emotional issues and use that information to help your client understand that process. Or you may agree that identifying the difference between physical and psychological hunger is a useful tool and help your client learn to respond to her stomach hunger even if she is not engaged in the process of legalizing foods. You may have a client who chooses to fully embrace the non-diet approach. If she is able to find the freedom from compulsive eating described in this book, you may alter your clinical point of view.

If you choose to implement the non-diet approach, you will need to consider many aspects of treatment. You must assess the needs of potential clients. You may offer group or individual therapy. As you engage in the treatment process, you must examine transference and countertransference issues that arise in the course of this work.

## Initial Assessment

If a client seeks individual therapy for her compulsive eating, the initial sessions provide an opportunity to evaluate her perceptions and experiences regarding food and weight. If you are offering a group for compulsive eaters, it is still important to conduct an initial evaluation of approximately one to three sessions to decide if this is the optimal treatment setting for a particular client. In either case, the evaluation phase provides an opportunity to explain the non-diet approach to a prospective client who is unfamiliar with this work or answer any questions of a client who is already versed in this method.

If a client has already begun to implement aspects of attuned eating, you can ask her specific questions to determine her progress and begin to offer suggestions to further her work in this area. Some clients may say that this approach makes a lot of sense to them but they are not convinced that they can actually follow this philosophy for themselves. You can reassure these clients that at this point in the process, it is enough for them to accept that diets don't work and have an intellectual understanding of the guidelines. If they pursue individual treatment, you will be in a position to support and guide them. If they join a group, part of their experience will be to gain support from other members that will help them implement strategies for themselves. Of course, some prospective clients may decide that they are not interested in this method of treating compulsive eating at this time.

## PERSONAL HISTORY CONSIDERATIONS

In addition to describing the non-diet approach, you can use these initial sessions to learn about a client's background and current life issues. This information will further your understanding of her history with weight and food and perhaps offer insight into the function of her compulsive eating in the present. Moreover, if she joins a group, your initial understanding of her dynamics can become essential in helping her as she moves into psychological territory. Useful questions may include:

- When did you begin your first diet?
- What triggered your first diet?
- What has happened for you since then in terms of dieting and weight?
- What is your understanding of why diets haven't worked for you?
- Who do you resemble most in your family and extended family in terms of body type?
- What were mealtimes like in your family?
- Does anyone else in your family struggle with eating problems?
- How do you feel about your body at this point in time?
- Can you describe your body to me?
- How do you go about deciding when and what to eat?
- Do you know when you are hungry?
- Do you have any medical problems?
- What do you know about any emotional factors that are related to your overeating?
- How do important people in your life respond to you in terms of your body size?

These questions, along with a social history, will give you an initial understanding of your client's relationship to food and her body, as well as an evaluation of her level of functioning. If your client has not had a recent medical evaluation, this should be advised. If a client suspects that medical issues, such as a thyroid problem, affect her weight, she should seek appropriate treatment for these conditions. However, for the majority of clients who present with compulsive eating problems, the dynamics of deprivation and affect regulation are the root causes of their struggle.

## CULTURAL CONSIDERATIONS

As you consider your client's body image, you may find that her identification with a subgroup in the culture allows her to maintain less stringent attitudes toward thinness. For example, some African American and lesbian women have broader views and higher self-esteem concerning acceptable body size. To the extent that this is true for your client, her more tolerant attitude will ease her difficulties as she normalizes her eating. To the extent that she has integrated the mainstream culture into her body image, she will confront the same problems regarding her dissatisfaction discussed throughout this book.

## DIETARY CONSIDERATIONS

Occasionally, a client will tell you in the initial consultation that she does not eat certain types of food because of a particular philosophy such as being a vegetarian or keeping kosher. In general, these practices are compatible with the non-diet approach to ending compulsive eating as they are based on philosophical beliefs rather than a fear of fat. However, it is important for you to explore your client's views in a respectful manner and help your client make adaptations as warranted. For example, Adrienne stated that she was a vegetarian, but several weeks later acknowledged that she had hoped that avoiding meat would help her lose weight. As Adrienne noticed cravings for red meat, she allowed herself to make the match and chose to let go of her vegetarianism. Conversely, Carmen discovered that as she became an attuned eater, she preferred a vegetarian diet and eliminated beef and chicken from her repertoire of foods. Michael adopted a kosher diet but occasionally craved bacon. To satisfy this hunger, sometimes he substituted grilled salami to attain a smoky flavor and other times he bought a kosher style bacon substitute that tasted to him like "the next best thing."

## THERAPEUTIC CONSIDERATIONS

In the course of an evaluation for group therapy, you and/or your client may conclude a group is not the appropriate treatment for her. Some clients decide that they have too many emotional issues to tackle and therefore prefer to start individual therapy with you, integrating the work on compulsive eating into these sessions. Other clients relate that they do not like groups or have had negative experiences in groups and therefore prefer individual treatment. If, following an evaluation, you assess that the personality of a prospective client would not work well in a particular group, you will need to consider other alternatives with her.

## DIFFERENTIAL DIAGNOSIS

The initial evaluation also requires the differential diagnosis of other eating disorders. The non-diet approach is not indicated for clients who actively present with anorexia nervosa or bulimia. Clients with anorexia nervosa would be unable to make use of concepts such as listening to physical hunger or legalizing foods during the acute phase of their illness. While clients with bulimia may benefit from learning guidelines such as the difference between physical and psychological hunger, stocking foods would be contraindicated for this group who is actively bingeing and purging. At the same time, however, a client may present who has suffered an eating disorder in the past. While she is not actively symptomatic, she still struggles in her relationship with food. She may find that her eating continues to feel disordered and benefit from the principles of the non-diet approach.

---

# THE CASE OF DAWN

Dawn is a 24-year-old graduate student who was hospitalized for anorexia nervosa during her sophomore year of high school. She was able to successfully regain weight so that she was no longer in a life-threatening situation. However, she continued to control her food intake because of her fear of gaining more weight. At the time of her initial consultation, she reported that this ongoing fear of food created great difficulties for her in social situations where she could not predict what food would be offered. She felt so frightened of food that she often cancelled out on these engagements, a behavior that she found troubling. Recently, she had "lost control" over some of her eating, turning to cookies late in the evening. These overeating incidents were so upsetting to her that on two occasions she forced herself to vomit. It was this behavior that caused her to seek treatment.

Dawn was able to agree to stop purging, even if she ate "too many" cookies. The therapist explained the basic tenets of the non-diet approach, focusing on helping Dawn learn to tune into her body's signals for hunger and satiation instead of continuing the measuring and weighing of food that had persisted since adolescence. Dawn was receptive to these concepts, and over an 8-month period she gradually shifted the way in which she decided when, what, and how much to eat. This change in her eating behavior allowed her to attend social gatherings without the fears that she previously experienced. In terms of the cookies, Dawn was willing to use the concept of stocking to help sort out whether the break in her usual restraints stemmed from feelings of deprivation or emotional factors. The therapist offered this strategy only when she was sure that Dawn had given up vomiting as a way of compensating for overeating episodes. As the result of legalizing and stocking cookies, Dawn saw a decrease in her binges over a 1-month period as the cookies no longer glittered for her. When Dawn turned to the cookies due to mouth hunger, she was able to identify feelings triggered by the meaning of completing her dissertation in the next few months. The therapist treated Dawn individually because her eating disorder made her situation different from the typical dynamics of the compulsive eater.

---

Some therapists offer groups that combine eating issues along the continuum, including anorexia nervosa, bulimia, and compulsive eating. Carol Emery Normandi and Laurelee Roark, authors of *It's Not about Food*, write, "In our groups we combine women with all eating disorders together because we believe that although women manifest the symptoms differently, the core issue is still the same: learning to love and respect ourselves and our uniqueness."[1]

We prefer to place compulsive eaters in a separate group because the interventions are different than for those with anorexia nervosa or bulimia. In contrast to compulsive eating, treatment for anorexia and bulimia focuses on the dangerous restricting and purging behaviors that must be monitored closely; as these symptoms abate, these clients can also use the concepts of attuned eating. Clients across the continuum of eating problems represent a disenfranchised group of people in our society who can come together and challenge the status quo. The power of the non-diet group, regardless of how you choose to conceive of it, lies in the shared experience of rejecting diets, implementing attuned eating, ending shame about eating and body size, and embracing a life stance that encourages full participation in the world that stems from the commonalities of participants.

## Group Treatment

The advantage of group treatment for compulsive eaters is that the group setting breaks down the isolation most people experience in terms of their eating problem. While people may constantly talk about their weight and food issues, these exchanges rarely explore the true emotional pain experienced by the compulsive eater. Furthermore, deep feelings of shame are often ameliorated as participants share the details of their overeating experiences and find that their eating behaviors are similar to others struggling with the same problem. Clients who give up diets and work toward greater body acceptance actively go against cultural norms. The support of group members engaged in a similar process is invaluable in helping these clients sustain their confidence in choosing this route; as one member struggles she can often look to other members who feel calm with food and peaceful enough with their bodies to offer hope.

## RESEARCH ON NON-DIET GROUPS

Initial research of the non-diet approach in group settings offers encouraging results. Again, the focus is on variables related to overall well-being rather than using weight loss as the primary criterion. In 1990, Donna Ciliska, author of *Beyond Dieting*, studied the outcome of a 12-week non-diet approach for a group of large women. The results showed improvements in self-esteem and restrained eating along with short-term improvements in body dissatisfaction, drive for thinness, depression, and social adjustment.[2] In that same year, a group of 87 large women participated in a 10-week group that focused on eating in response to hunger, ending restrictive dieting, size-acceptance, and coping skills to deal with emotional stress. The results indicated significant improvements in eating attitudes, body image, self-image, self-esteem, and depression as well as some weight loss. At a 2-year follow-up of 57 of the participants, improvements on psychological measures were maintained or increased, along with a 3.1 kilograms of weight loss compared to baseline.[3] Polivy and Herman designed a program called "Stop Dieting" to promote attuned eating and improved self-acceptance. Their reported findings included increases in self-esteem and decreases in depression and binge eating behavior. These results were largely maintained at a 6-month follow-up.[4] Carrier, Steinhardt, and Bowman reported significant improvements over a 3-year period in areas of self-esteem, self-acceptance, self-nourishment, and restrained eating.[5] Researchers Steinhardt and Nagel investigated the effectiveness of the Overcoming Overeating approach developed by Hirschmann and Munter. While acknowledging the limitations of their study, including a nonrandom sample of readers of *Overcoming Overeating*, they found a decrease in eating preoccupation, body preoccupation, and emotional eating over a 2-year period.[6]

In 2002, Bacon et al. concluded that a non-diet approach offers an effective alternative to traditional diet programs in terms of physical and emotional well-being. Over a 1-year period, this study found that some weight loss occurred within the diet group, but there was a dropout rate of 41% as compared to 8% in the non-diet group. The results revealed that the non-diet group produced similar improvements in metabolic fitness, psychological factors, and eating behavior without the problems associated with a high attrition rate. Self-esteem rose initially for those in the diet group but was not maintained over time. In contrast, the non-diet participants showed a significant improvement in self-esteem 1 year after treatment was initiated. The authors conclude that a non-diet approach, even in the absence of weight loss, produces similar health benefits to traditional weight loss protocols, without the problems of attrition and diet failure.[7]

If you decide to offer a group for compulsive eaters, there are numerous decisions to make. Should the group be time limited or open ended? What is the composition of the group? What are the criteria for entering the group? What is the format of the group? While each therapist will make decisions as to how she will conduct such a group based on her treatment philosophy and skills as well as the needs of her clients and parameters of an agency, we offer a paradigm for a successful group model.

## TIME-LIMITED GROUPS

Time-limited groups can provide an excellent method to present the concepts of the non-diet approach and help clients begin to implement changes into their relationships with food and their bodies. In this model, all attendees receive didactic information each week, usually over a 6- to 12-week period, which teaches the guidelines of the approach in an orderly fashion. During each session, participants can also share their experiences from the past week as they attempt to use techniques such as identifying and responding to hunger, making matches, ending negative self-talk, and the like. (See Appendix C, 6-Week Group, for a sample outline of a program.) The disadvantage of the time-limited group is that while a client receives a solid foundation in understanding the non-diet approach, she will not have ample opportunity to truly integrate new patterns of eating into her life and make use of psychological interventions when she encounters obstacles or tries to face emotional issues without turning to food. At the completion of a psychoeducational group, members may renew for another 6- to 12-week period of time; however, as some group members drop off, the effectiveness of the group support diminishes. Time-limited groups may be viewed as an introductory class that feeds into an ongoing group, thereby providing motivated participants with the opportunity to continue in a treatment situation. While this scenario may work well for some clients, others find the transition to a new set of group members to be unappealing or difficult and do not follow through.

## ONGOING GROUPS

Ongoing groups provide members with a safe place and enough time to solve their compulsive eating problems. In an ongoing group, members can be at different places along the continuum of the treatment process. While one member may work on identifying hunger, another member may explore her conflicted feelings that resulted in mouth hunger. These disparities in the focus of each client's work actually enhance the group process. When someone new joins the group, she benefits from hearing about the experiences of another client who, after 1 year, eats in an attuned manner and has stopped bingeing. Often when a client terminates, a newer member will state, "You have been my role model. I hope I can get to where you are." For the more senior member of the group, the new client offers an opportunity to be reminded of the importance of keeping up with the basics of the approach, such as supplying plenty of food and reflecting on how far she has come. Typically, these clients will state to a newer member, "I remember feeling just the way you do when I first started. But now I rarely . . ." In an ongoing group, clients are invited to participate for as long as they need in order to gain the support and interventions that will help them meet the goal of ending compulsive eating. While the amount of time varies for each client, members typically participate over a 6-month to 2-year period.

A typical framework for a non-diet group would involve 60- to 90-minute sessions on a weekly basis. Groups of approximately four to eight clients offer rich interactions and ensure that each member receives adequate attention. Members are expected to attend each week in order to create a secure environment. Each member will discuss her process and the therapist will respond directly to her needs. The focus of each meeting remains centered on different aspects of ending compulsive eating and negative body image. Although clients may be tempted to describe emotional situations in their lives that create anxiety, clients are gently encouraged to remain centered on their behavioral experiences with food.

## OVERCOMING OVEREATING GROUPS: A MODEL

Our model for this group work derives from the original Overcoming Overeating groups started in the early 1980s. Unlike other therapy groups where the dynamics of clients' interactions within the group are used to process individual reactions and concerns, the compulsive eating group remains concentrated on the work of each member in relation to ending her compulsive eating. Yet the group provides more than support as the therapist guides her clients through complicated psychological issues that emerge throughout the process.

Each week, every group participant takes a turn sharing her experiences during the session. Early in the process, clients focus on the basic tenets of the non-diet guidelines, indicating whether they experienced physical hunger, made any matches, stopped when satisfied, and so on. As they explain any difficulties, the therapist may ask for elaboration, offer suggestions, or ask other group members to share their thoughts about the situation. It is extremely helpful at this juncture to ask clients for very specific details about their eating experiences. Questions such as, "What exactly did you eat?" "What were you really craving?" and "How much did you eat?" help clients begin to analyze their eating more accurately. What was once a shameful occurrence loses its power as words are connected to the experience and shared with a group of compassionate people who can relate to her situation.

The therapist may also point out to the client any positive steps that occurred, such as cooking a meal that provided great satisfaction, and ask her to reflect on how that felt. Or perhaps a client explains that she was at a buffet and surprised herself by eating just a bite or two of dessert. As you ask her to describe why she thinks that happened and how she felt, you can help her understand that ending deprivation allows her to listen to her stomach and reinforce the idea that she can be trusted around all types of food.

If a client who is in the early stages of the approach reports that she felt upset about a situation and engaged in overeating, let her know that you understand that this is upsetting to her and explore the way she responded. Did she yell at herself for her need to reach for food, or was she able to remind herself that she was feeling psychologically uncomfortable and needed the food to soothe herself in the moment? Check in with her to make sure that she is paying attention to her hunger needs as much as possible and that she is keeping enough food in her home to feel secure. Remind her that as she builds her repertoire of attuned eating experiences, she will be in a stronger position to look more carefully at her emotional overeating.

As a client begins to consistently implement the guidelines of the non-diet approach, she will use the group to explore psychological factors that contribute to her compulsive eating. For example, one client may find that after weeks of keeping her kitchen stocked in a way that helped her feel comfortable around food, she suddenly cannot find time to go to the grocery store. After considering any logistical explanations, she must determine the meaning of this change in her behavior so that she can return to her previous level of caretaking. Another client may notice that she eats out of stomach hunger on a regular basis but binges on Sunday evenings and needs to figure out why this occurs. The dynamics of each client's process vary, providing instructive and exciting learning opportunities within the group setting. As you work with each person, you will draw on your clinical skills to further their progress toward ending compulsive eating.

In addition to focusing on their relationships with food, clients may also use their time in group to discuss body image issues. Perhaps a client is going to a party and needs to talk about what to wear so that she will feel comfortable. Or she may struggle with a situation in which she fears a seat will be too small for her. She may also report an example of being out in the world and feeling fine in the body she has. She may bring in her fears about an upcoming doctor's appointment and need support as to how to approach this situation, or she may share a positive experience with a medical professional in terms of her weight and offer this information as a resource for other group members. She may reveal a specific negative body thought that requires your help in analyzing the underlying conflict that fueled the yelling. As with eating experiences, the possible scenarios for discussion are as diverse as the members of the group. The purpose of the group always remains first and foremost to provide a therapeutic environment offering support and consistent guidelines regarding the non-diet approach to treating compulsive eating, and second to provide opportunities to explore psychological factors as they arise in relation to obstacles and mouth hunger. If a client's psychological needs extend beyond the goals of the group, it is important to recommend that she seek treatment outside the group setting.

In order to supplement the goals of the ongoing group, you may choose to use an exercise or visualization that can help clients gain further insight into their relationships with food or their bodies. Some suggestions have appeared in previous chapters; other ideas are included in the appendix. After completing an exercise or visualization, each member can report and reflect on her experience in the group. You may also consider devoting a session to a particular topic related to concerns of the group members such as sexuality, the holiday season, or physical exercise and movement. Another useful group activity involves planning a potluck meal where each person brings plenty of food. This event offers group members an opportunity to process an eating experience as it occurs. Are they hungry? Which foods provide a good match? Can they stop when satisfied? How does it feel to eat in front of other people? Do they have the feeling that if they don't eat something in the moment, they won't be able to get it later? Along these lines, it is important to have bags or containers available that group members can use to take home foods that appeal to them in general but they do not crave in the present. This experience provides practice for other social situations and gives you the opportunity to coach clients through an attuned eating experience. In general, clients should be encouraged to bring their food bags to the group each week so they can meet their hunger needs should they arise.

## GROUP COMPOSITION

The composition of groups may vary based on the needs of the clients you serve. Psychoeducational groups usually do not require any formal screening and often consist of male and female participants. In our experience, women seek groups in much greater numbers than men, and therefore the majority of ongoing groups that we have led have consisted of all female membership. Women's groups can foster a safe environment as participants disclose intimate details, especially those related to body issues. Another example of a group based on commonalities occurred when a therapist led a group on breaking compulsive eating for male religious leaders. Each man struggled with compulsive eating, and they discovered that much of their mouth hunger stemmed from issues related to taking care of others' emotional and spiritual needs and feeling depleted in the process. Though each had made the decision to pursue this path based on deep spiritual beliefs, the demands of their profession often left little time for their own spiritual refueling, and food had become a means of attempting to fill themselves up. In this case, a group of men in general who shared a chosen profession in particular were able to offer each other understanding, support, and a frame of reference to explore their issues with food.

## FORMING A GROUP

If you are considering the possibility of beginning a new group, you will need to find referrals. Other therapists make an excellent source because their clients already have a treatment setting to bring in emotional issues that they uncover in the process of ending compulsive eating. You may also attract clients through workshops, educational programs, and other types of advertising. Drawing clients from your own practice creates the potential for complex transference issues and should be considered extremely carefully. For example, Brenda identified her compulsive eating issues 1 year into her individual treatment. Her therapist referred her to a colleague's non-diet group, but Brenda insisted that she would prefer to join her therapist's group instead. Brenda's therapist felt that this would be a mistake. Brenda had a strong transference reaction in which she saw her therapist as withholding and distant, similar to the way in which she had experienced other important adults in her life. As they continued to explore this issue together, Brenda understood that her wish to participate in her therapist's group was motivated by a desire to learn whether her therapist gave more warmth and attention to other clients. Brenda related this concern to her experience growing up in which her "cuter" younger sister, who was an extremely talented skater, received the bulk of the family's admiration. As Brenda elucidated these concerns, she realized, with the help of her therapist, that these issues needed to be resolved through her individual therapy. She decided to join the non-diet group with a different therapist. As competitive issues were triggered in the group setting, Brenda brought them to her individual therapy for further exploration.

Conversely, clients participating in an ongoing group may decide to pursue individual therapy following the completion of their goals related to ending compulsive eating. Entering into individual treatment with the group leader can work well because of the established relationship and continued support about the non-diet approach. However, this decision is also subject to transference issues, which should be well thought out before entering into a commitment.

Thus far we have described an ongoing group that fully embraces the guidelines of the non-diet approach, including the concepts of legalizing and stocking food. Accepting people into the group who mutually strive toward this level of making peace with food provides the optimal holding environment. In our experience, clients who establish an abundance of food on a consistent basis truly end their compulsive eating. The lack of ambivalence about this method communicated by the group leader and other members provides a reassuring framework to new clients who understandably feel frightened by this guideline, helping them to move toward their goals.

As the non-diet approach gains more acceptance in the therapeutic community, debate will continue as to what it means not to diet. This occurrence will represent a profound shift as clinicians move from questions about whether clients should diet to consideration of techniques that normalize clients' relationships with food without the use of restrictions that repeatedly backfire. At this point, you will have to make a decision based on the material in this book and other information you pursue as to the criteria of your non-diet group. Can a person join who says she wants to stop dieting, but does not want to integrate certain foods into her life because she believes they are "too fattening"? Will you maintain the expectation of stocking as a norm of the group? Will you mix clients who are working to end compulsive eating in different ways? The way in which you formulate your answers to these questions will have a significant impact on the group process and experiences of individual members.

## Individual Treatment

When you choose to work with a person individually, the treatment considerations change significantly. Whether a new client approaches you who presents with compulsive eating issues or you identify overeating as a problem for someone already in your practice, you can focus on where your client currently stands in relation to ending diets and normalizing eating. If a client insists that her new diet is the answer for her, you may accept her belief and then listen carefully for her experiences with a particular method. If she encounters difficulty adhering to a plan, you may use this as an opening to provide information about the failures of diets and offer other solutions. Another client may say that she is willing to end diets but continues to focus on only eating certain types of foods in an attempt to lose weight. Yet another client may fully embrace all elements of the non-diet approach.

When a person chooses to work with you individually on her compulsive eating, it is helpful to check in at some point during each session about her specific behaviors with food, just as you would in the group setting. Although your client will bring in other issues related to her psychological well-being that you will explore, consistency in discussing the mechanics of the non-diet approach establishes a structure that ensures her progress in this area. If she reaches a point where her eating and body issues no longer dominate her concerns because she has generally solved these problems, you may wish to check in with her on a regular basis, such as once a month, to help maintain her integration of attuned eating.

## Termination

How do you decide when a client is ready to stop treatment for compulsive eating? Clients usually terminate treatment when, for the most part, they no longer feel compelled to reach for food unless they are physically hungry. Clients will state that they could never imagine going on a diet again. Food is fully integrated into their kitchens, their lives, and their psyches and the act of eating is equated with self-care rather than self-loathing or anxiety. Clients also experience relief from the constant negative body images that plagued them prior to treatment. Clients will vary about the extent to which they admire their bodies. Some clients will come to love the bodies they inhabit while others will reach an acceptance of their body sizes that allows them to live fully in the world and take good care of their physical selves by moving their bodies, seeking regular medical care, and dressing in ways that feel comfortable and attractive. Another consideration for you at this juncture is whether you will offer some type of continued support following the termination of a client from a group or individual treatment. For example, a monthly group may provide a setting for people to come together and discuss any issues that arise regarding their eating or body image. Or you could offer workshops on a particular topic that would interest former clients who have moved in the direction of attuned eating. A client could arrange a consultation with you as needed or schedule monthly sessions to focus on any issues that occur in the process of sustaining her new way of eating. These options are influenced by your interests, the needs of your clients, and the demands of the institution where you provide your services.

## Promoting a Size-Accepting Environment

Regardless of where you stand on the philosophy of treating compulsive eating and your decision about whether to implement the methods presented in this book into your practice, we would like you to reflect on what messages clients receive when they visit your office or agency. Are there magazines in your waiting room? If so, are they full of articles that foster diets and disordered eating? Are there models on the covers who represent an unrealistic ideal of thinness? Although you may offer these magazines with no thought of promoting these behaviors, they reinforce messages to all of your clients about what is considered normal and acceptable in our culture. Consider replacing these magazines with neutral subjects, or even putting out magazines, newsletters, or books that present alternative images and articles reflecting non-dieting behaviors and size diversity.

Another consideration relevant to all practitioners concerns the size of chairs available to clients visiting your office or agency. Large clients should feel welcome and comfortable and, therefore, the furniture in your office must accommodate different body shapes and sizes. Couches or sturdy chairs without armrests provide adequate support for larger clients, and your sensitivity to this issue conveys the idea that people of all size are acceptable.

## Transference and Countertransference

Treatment considerations presented thus far primarily concern your decisions about what treatment to offer and how to go about integrating this work into your practice. Based on your understanding and implementation of the non-diet paradigm, you are in a unique position to understand the subtleties of transference and countertransference issues that may arise in the process of working with clients who have eating and body image problems. Although these concepts are integral to psychological treatment, relatively little information exists concerning the experience of body size and its impact on clinical work.

### POTENTIAL ISSUES

Therapy takes place within the context of culture, and in chapter 2 we elaborated on the societal influences that lead to the construction of views about being fat and thin. Among the majority of clinicians as well as the general public, fat remains an unacceptable, shameful body size to be ridiculed but not discussed in an open, nonjudgmental manner. While issues of transference and countertransference are typically discussed in supervision, the topic of the therapist's own weight, her reaction to the size of her client, and her client's reactions to her size are, for the most part, taboo. Yet these issues have a strong impact on the treatment and deserve attention. The following list includes some of the themes that may arise in the course of working with compulsive eating clients.

- How do you feel about larger clients?
- How do you feel about your own body size in relation to your clients?
- Do you feel differently about your body with different clients?
- Do you feel differently about your body at different times with the same client?
- If you are a thinner therapist, how do your clients react to your body size?
- If you are a larger therapist, how do your clients react to your body size?
- How do you respond to a client asking about your personal history with weight?
- How do you respond to a client commenting negatively about your body size?

### Case Examples

Each of these themes provides ideas for professional exploration. These questions do not lend themselves to "right" or "wrong" answers, but rather acknowledge complicated and important dynamics that require the therapist's careful consideration. Each therapist will have her own unique responses and experiences that she must identify in order to understand and make use of interactions between herself and the client in the most therapeutic manner. For example, a therapist describes the following countertransference in her work with a very large client named Jodie, whom she has seen in treatment for 6 months regarding her compulsive eating.

> I promise myself that during this session with Jodie, I will be more aware of the boundaries of time constraints. I've noticed that I always allow the sessions to run over, and I struggle with presenting her with limits. It is more difficult for me to manage these boundaries than it is with other clients. The presence of her size feels familiar, and I finally realize she reminds me of the nurturing women in my family who are obese. Their capacity for giving was so huge; they lost themselves in their excessive focus on others. But I was a guilty recipient of that nurture and attention. Their nurture provided me with love and safety but was colored around the edges by the pain of their lack of self-definition. Jodie also gives excessively to her child, husband, parents, and job, with nothing left for her but stolen moments alone with her favorite food. Why do I struggle with maintaining my boundaries when in her presence? I treat her as if she is too fragile to cope with the boundaries of existence. My gut tells me she is starving for attention and regard for her self-hood — so I behave as if giving her a few more minutes will attend to that pain.[8]

In order to work successfully with compulsive eating clients, a therapist must be able to adopt a stance toward larger people that is truly nonjudgmental. This does not mean that a clinician is free from all possible negative thoughts about fat; rather, she accepts that as a member of this culture, she is equally subject to fat-phobic beliefs and ideas. However, it is essential that the therapist examine and articulate her thoughts carefully, perhaps with the help of a supervisor or consultation group. One therapist describes the bind she experiences as her client, Cammie, compares their body sizes.

> She uses my body as another guidepost with which she diminishes her own status, comparing herself to me and finding herself lacking. I freeze up when the process becomes comparative, and I am reminded of how much I

have always avoided competitive situations. I don't like losing or coming in last; that's easy enough to understand. But
I don't like coming in first either. In this case, my average-
size body clearly "wins" by all criteria provided by the culture. And yet buying into or being beholden to these
criteria feels traitorous to the years I've spent professionally decrying the societal pressures that encourage women
to define themselves in terms of weight and appearance.
The struggle for me is to find a stance that allows me to
stay true to myself without freezing up, so that when
Cammie speaks of my body, I can help her keep her own
experience central.[9]

The therapist must also commit herself to seeking sources
that will move her in the direction of size acceptance. A therapist who feels disgusted by her larger clients is likely to communicate this feeling overtly or covertly. This may generate a
variety of reactions on the part of the client. She may view
the therapist as similar to a parent who insisted she was too
fat, or use the therapist's judgment to affirm her notion that
her fat makes her unacceptable, blocking the exploration of
other emotional issues. If a therapist generally feels comfortable around larger clients and then experiences negative
thoughts with a particular client or in a particular session, she
can analyze this reaction to help her understand something
about the course of treatment. Using personal reactions to
assess clients and the progress of treatment is a familiar concept to therapists, as illustrated in the following scenario.

I was working with a client who presented in therapy
around issues related to her contentious divorce. She challenged me as to whether I could understand the difficulties
of her marriage because she observed that I did not have a
wedding ring on my finger. Her question did not create anxiety for me, and I reassured her that I could. After a few
weeks of discussing her children and her ex-husband in detail, it became clear that Rose was unable to talk freely about
her own experience of the divorce and was more comfortable
focusing on other family members. Although I tried to guide
our conversations toward talking about her own feelings,

I left sessions feeling that Rose was keeping me from seeing the more vulnerable parts of her. Rose also began to talk about her dissatisfaction with weight and compulsive eating, and we identified this as another area for work. During this period I noticed that I was starting to "feel fat" during our sessions. Although I am usually very comfortable with my body, I became acutely aware of my own fuller figure and self-conscious about what she may be thinking about it. I imagined that she thought I was too fat to help her, and that a thinner therapist would be a better role model for her. However, after processing this case in supervision, I concluded that my negative body thoughts were actually an expression of my discomfort around the continued disconnection I experienced with Rose. As we ventured into the area of weight-related issues, I became more susceptible to accepting my bad body thoughts at face value. In the supervisory setting, I became able to identify their translation as a symbol of my internal discomfort as Rose repeatedly tried to distance herself from me by challenging my abilities as a therapist.[10]

## SELF-DISCLOSURE

A client may ask the therapist about her personal experiences with food and weight. The degree to which a therapist responds will depend on her treatment philosophy, the therapeutic needs of the client, and her own comfort level. The use of self-disclosure must be considered carefully and always be in the interest of your client. What lies behind her question? Are you a thin therapist, and she wonders if you can possibly understand her concerns and experiences? Are you a large therapist, and she questions whether you can help her? On the one hand, asking your client about her concerns or fantasies may give you useful information; on the other hand, a straightforward answer can allay her fears and promote the establishment of the relationship. Each therapist must develop her own style in the arena of personal sharing. However, as with any psychological treatment, self-disclosure must serve the purpose of furthering the treatment process rather than gratifying the needs of the therapist. Using supervision or consultation to process the use of self-disclosure helps ensure that the treatment goals remain free from unexplored countertransference issues on the part of the therapist.

Clients seeking therapy for their compulsive eating often wonder how you came to do this type of work and whether you have suffered from an eating problem. Your client is entitled to know your qualifications as a therapist and a specialist. Letting your client know the process by which you embarked on a non-diet approach can also serve the function of educating her about dieting, compulsive eating, and body size. For example, if you previously prescribed diets or restrictive methods, you might let her know of the outcome you observed. You might also let her know the results you attain with clients using the non-diet approach, such as ending bingeing or feeling comfortable with their bodies. You may choose to tell her that this method reflects your own personal experiences with food and weight in whatever way this is true for you. If you are currently dieting or hold the belief that thinness should be the ultimate goal, we would steer you away from using a non-diet approach until you have further explored these concepts. As you share your treatment philosophy and personal experience, it is important to stay away from details that encompass the amount of weight lost or gained or the specifics of what you eat. Clients look to their therapist to decide how to make changes in their life, and it is important for them to listen to and respect their own bodies rather than using your experiences as a measure of their success and failure.

### Case Examples

While some clients may ask about the therapist's size or eating history, other clients will never comment on these issues. In a group setting, one therapist was surprised by the fact that none of her clients mentioned her thin body type. She decided to bring up the topic, as she felt sure that they must have some reactions that could be instructive to the group.

**Therapist:** There is something I am curious about. No one has ever mentioned my size, and I have wondered how you reacted when you saw me for the first time.

**Abbey:** I thought, "Who is this person and how could she possibly understand me?" (Laughter among members and nodding in agreement)

**Cloe:** But then when we started talking I found that you knew exactly what I was talking about.

**Therapist:** I've had the sense that maybe it's hard for people to comment on my size when they first meet me, but by the time they feel comfortable enough to do so, it really isn't such an issue because I am able to understand in a way that maybe you haven't experienced before.

**Pat:** Yes.

**Frankie:** I also had the reaction of what could you possibly know about my situation, but you did. Sometimes I think that a therapist who is larger could still understand what it is like to be fat in a way that would be helpful too.

**Therapist:** You're right that I think I understand much about your experience, but it isn't an experience I've had. I can see that working with a larger therapist could give you a different sense of being understood. I've also wondered though if there's anything about my being thin that was reassuring to you when you first came.

**Pat:** What do you mean?

**Therapist:** Well, most people who come for help with their compulsive eating come with the wish that they will lose weight. I wonder if the fact that I'm thin in any way gives a message that I must know what I'm talking about or that this is the size that you end up as the result of this work.

**Pat:** I don't think I had that thought.

**Abbey:** Actually, I still think that's true. I think that you must eat in the way we talk about in here. I don't think I'm at my natural weight yet and it does help me to think that as I stop overeating, my body will become thinner.

**Pat:** Do you think it's better for a therapist doing this work to be thin?

**Therapist:** I think that people of all sizes can do this work.

**Cloe:** I don't think it matters at all what size the therapist is. I just think it's important that she can understand compulsive eating. I've never had another experience like this where I can talk so freely about food. It's been wonderful.

**Therapist:** You're saying that what's important is the connection with the therapist rather than her size.

**Cloe:** Exactly.

**Therapist:** I guess in a way it's like translating negative feelings into negative body thoughts. If you don't connect with the therapist it may be easier to say it's because she's too thin or too fat rather than exploring the real issue in the relationship. I agree that therapists of all sizes can understand these issues, just like therapists of all sizes can fail to understand these issues. At the same time, if you ever have any other feelings on this topic, please feel free to express them.

Another therapist, who is large, brings up the topic of her size as a matter of course early in the treatment with her clients who struggle with eating problems or body size acceptance.

**Therapist:** I'm comfortable as a larger person talking about my size. I'm wondering if you could share how you reacted when you first saw me.

**Joanne:** Well, I was afraid I might offend you if I talked about my size.

**Therapist:** I really want you to know that it's okay. I'm comfortable with you talking about your body and eating, as well as your reactions to me. I want this to be a safe place for you.

**Joanne:** (hesitates) I was also thinking about whether you are the right therapist for me.

**Therapist:** (with humor) You might think that I'm your worst nightmare! Are you wondering if I can help you with your own eating and weight if I'm so fat?

**Joanne:** Yeah (with a nervous laugh). I was sort of thinking that.

**Therapist:** I have a lot of expertise in this area. Part of my comfort in talking with you comes from the work I've done in accepting my own body and exploring my eating. (Uses this as an opportunity to give some educational information about the effects of yo-yo dieting.) It's okay for you to ask me any questions you have about that.

In this scenario, the therapist's own comfort with her body size allowed her to process her client's reactions in an open and therapeutic manner.

The possible representations of transference and countertransference between therapist and client can provide rich and useful material in the treatment process. The possible scenarios in which these themes occur are as numerous as the relationships that exist between therapist and client. It is up to you to use your psychological expertise, knowledge of eating and weight issues, personal reflection, and the support of other professionals to decide how to best understand and use these concepts with your compulsive eating clients.

## ENDNOTES

1. Normandi, C. E., & Roark, L. (1998). *It's not about food.* New York: Grosset/Putnam, p. 9.

2. Ciliska, D. (1990). *Beyond dieting: Psychoeducational interventions for chronically obese women.* New York: Brunner/Mazel.
3. Roughon, P., Seddon, E., & Vernon-Roberts, J. (1990). Long-term effects of a psychologically based programme for women preoccupied with body weight and eating behavior. *International Journal of Obesity, 14,* 135–147.
4. Polivy, J., & Herman, C. P. (1992). Undieting: A program to help people stop dieting. *International Journal of Eating Disorders, 11,* 261–268.
5. Carrier, K. M., Steinhardt, M. A., & Bowman, F. (1994, September). Rethinking traditional weight management programs: A three-year follow-up evaluation of a new approach. *Journal of Psychology, 128* (5), 517–535.
6. Steinhardt, M., & Nagel, L. (1995). Effectiveness of the overcoming overeating approach to the problem of compulsive eating. In J. Hirschmann & C. Munter (Eds.), *When women stop hating their bodies.* New York: Fawcett Columbine, pp. 329–345.
7. Bacon, L., et al. (2002). Evaluation a "non-diet" wellness intervention for improvement of metabolic fitness, psychological well-being, and eating and activity behaviors. *International Journal of Obesity, 26,* 854–865.
8. Morrison, M. (2003, April). Personal communication.
9. Fried, P. (2003, April). Personal communication.
10. Lurie, R. (2003, March). Personal communication.

# CHAPTER 8

# REDEFINING HEALTH

## Evaluating the Research

For the therapist treating compulsive eating, concern for the client's physical health is always a primary consideration. The notion that people of all sizes can be healthy has gained acceptance in recent years, and these findings have significant implications for your clients' goals related to achieving physical well-being. Research in the area of the effect of weight on health is constantly changing and often contradictory. The goal of this chapter is to provide information based on the work of a variety of experts that will help you evaluate what you read or hear about the links between fat and health and provide strategies that you can use with your clients to move them toward greater physical health at any size.

### BIAS

Health concerns top the list as a major reason clients say that they must lose weight, and the idea that a thinner person is a healthier person is supported in culture through the media, attitudes of family and friends, and professionals in a variety of fields, including therapists. Our society tends to operate on a "thinness-bias." Cogan and Ernsberger explain this phenomenon as "the error of seizing upon results that favor thinness or paying selective attention to thinness-promoting behavior. Information or content that does not support thinness as the optimal health and beauty standard is ignored or even attacked."[1] This bias affects our country's health policies and ultimately the emotional and physical health of its citizens.

Frequently, the headline on the evening news or in the morning newspaper concerns yet another finding on the dangers of being "overweight." How can mental health professionals conscientiously ignore this information? The answer lies in the fact that many of these reports are skewed in what data are highlighted, what conclusions are drawn, and whose interests are served by the reported studies. For example, the Harvard Nurses Study (1995) followed 115,196 nurses ages 30 to 55 over a 16-year period. The front page of the *Boston Globe* reported on the study's conclusions with alarm. The caption read: "Risk found in women's weight gain." The article stated that women who are 20 to 30 pounds overweight risk early death. Joann Manson, the lead researcher of the study, is quoted as saying, "Americans can no longer be complacent about the epidemic of obesity. A weight gain of 10 to 15 lbs. in adulthood should serve as a warning." The article concludes, "In other words, you can't be too thin, unless you smoke, drink, or starve yourself to get that way."[2] When the article continues on another page, it is replete with graphs and charts and highlights dire predictions.

Twelve days later, in a short article on page two that did not contain charts, graphs, or bold headlines, the *Boston Herald* ran an article contradicting the conclusions drawn from the Nurse's Study. The article stated, "Being moderately underweight may be a greater health risk than most people suspect, according to a new study. . . . We found that people who were 20 to 30 pounds overweight were not more likely to die over a 30-year period than average weight persons, said study author David Levitsky of Cornell University. However, the health risks of being moderately underweight are comparable to that of being quite overweight and look more serious than people realize."[3]

The therapist is left to ponder the contradictions. However, the playing field is already uneven. The reports announcing alarming conclusions that fat is unhealthy and weight loss is desirable receive top coverage and repeated exposure. It fits with our thin-bias glasses. The many studies challenging these notions obtain little media attention. This bias is compounded by commercial breaks on television and advertisements in the print media promoting diet products and weight loss programs, adding to the belief that fearing fat and engaging in diet behaviors are both desirable and normative.

## CONFLICT OF INTEREST

Therapists must question whether concern for the public's health is the driving force in the studies touting fat as a killer. In fact, other factors are often at play. Consider the Harvard Nurse's Study, noted above, where a researcher's agenda and conflict of interest muddied the waters. In a press release, the head researcher, Joann Manson of Harvard Medical School and Brigham and Women's Hospital, sounded the alarm on the epidemic of obesity. "Even mild to moderate overweight is associated with substantial increase in risk of premature death."[4] Laura Fraser, author of *Losing It: America's Obsession with Weight and the Industry That Feeds on It,* analyzes the study. She reports that, "When Manson warned of increased risks at a BMI of less than 27, she was actually talking about a statistical 'trend,' as she told me. In other words, when you draw a line on a graph showing how the risk of early death increases with weight, the line starts going up — just barely — at that point. But the increased risk was so small that statisticians say they're not confident it's even there. It's insignificant, which Manson admitted to me."[5] Fraser delves further into this study and its spurious conclusions.

> The results of the study, then, were essentially the opposite of what was being reported: Being twenty to forty pounds over

the ideal makes little difference to your health. Why were the results interpreted the way they were? Perhaps it was a matter of cultural bias and genuine concern about the increasing amount of obesity in the country. And maybe financial interests played a role. Manson, the leading author, is a paid consultant to Interneuron Pharmaceuticals, Inc., the company that developed the diet drug dexfenfluramine. In September 1995, at Food and Drug Administration (FDA) hearings on whether this drug should be approved, Manson used her study to testify about the health risks of obesity in order to justify the use of a drug that is rarely, but sometimes, quite harmful. Telling women who are mild to moderately overweight that they are at a substantial increased risk of dying early because of their size might well give their doctors a rationale for prescribing such a diet drug, which would, of course, boost sales considerably.[6]

Manson, along with Gerry Faich, coauthored an editorial in *The New England Journal of Medicine* promoting the benefits and minimizing the risks of the use of diet drugs — without disclosing that they were paid consultants to the drug company. "It took the *Wall Street Journal* to divulge that information. The revelation infuriated editors at *The New England Journal of Medicine*, who had not been told of the conflict of interest."[7]

Manson is not alone. Obesity researchers often have their work funded by those in the diet industry. The thinness bias gets refueled in many ways. Researchers who challenge the use of weight loss strategies will not receive funding from those in the diet industry who know that such anti-diet results will render their endeavors less profitable. As Fraser points out so eloquently,

> Diet and pharmaceutical companies influence every step along the way of scientific process. They pay for the ads that keep obesity journals publishing. They underwrite medical conferences, flying physicians around the country expense free and paying large lecture fees to attend. Some obesity researchers have clear conflict of interest, promoting or investing in products or programs based on their research. Others are paid to be consultants to diet companies, and sit on the scientific advisory boards of Weight Watchers™, Jenny

Craig™, or other commercial programs — while they also sit on the boards of the medical journals that determine which studies get printed. What it comes down to is that most obesity researchers would stand to lose a lot of money if they stopped telling Americans they had to lose a lot of weight.[8]

A clear example of this conflict is the National Task Force on the Prevention and Treatment of Obesity, funded by the federal government and in charge of setting national health policy. In 1996, *The Journal of the American Medical Association* disclosed that eight out of the nine board members were university-affiliated professors and researchers with financial ties to a minimum of two, and up to eight, commercial weight loss and pharmaceutical companies apiece.[9]

The diet industry, like the advertising world in general, is founded on the premise that something is wrong with the person (consumer) or in her life, which a particular product will correct. The non-diet approach emphasizes attuned eating and self-acceptance, behaviors and attitudes that do not translate into a product line. New diets are constantly falling in and out of fashion, supporting a $50 billion industry. It is the constant messages communicated to the public that diets and weight loss are healthy activities to pursue that keep the diet industry booming. Jon Robison, coeditor of the journal *Health at Every Size*, states, "In the name of improving health, millions of people in this country are continually being pressured to engage in traditional weight loss practices that have no demonstrated efficacy and are often harmful to one's health. This is contrary to the primary directive for health professionals — to do no harm — and is ethically unacceptable."[10]

## STATISTICAL SCARE

Along with biases in reporting and conflicts of interest is the problem of statistical scares based on misrepresentation of the data. You may have heard the often cited claim that "Obesity kills 300,000 people a year." This popularized figure is based on a 1993 study by Michael McGinnis and William

Foege, which appeared in *The Journal of the American Medical Association* (*JAMA*). What they actually reported was that, "dietary factors and activity patterns that are too sedentary" contributed to 300,000 deaths per year.[11] *The New England Journal of Medicine*, along with other media sources, misreported these findings by stating that 300,000 deaths a year were caused by obesity. This inaccurate reporting and its use to validate health policies led McGinnis and Foege to publish a letter in *The New England Journal of Medicine* explaining that the results of their study had been misrepresented by the *Journal* and other media sources. The researchers explained that obesity, high blood pressure, heart disease, and cancer were some of the side effects of dietary and activity patterns, but they *had not* concluded how many deaths were actually causal results of each single factor.[12]

The fact remains, however, that this statistic was and is used repeatedly to justify sounding the alarm on obesity. It has influenced health policy and reinforced the thin bias pervading our culture. For example, two prominent obesity researchers highlighted this misrepresented statistic when they formed the American Obesity Association (AOA). Fraser reports that the AOA's brochure states "Each year obesity causes at least 300,000 excess deaths in the US and costs the country more that $100 billion. Obesity is the second leading cause of unnecessary deaths."[13] The researchers describe obesity as increasing the risks of high blood pressure, diabetes, heart disease, stroke, gall bladder disease, and cancer of the breast, prostate, and colon. Fraser notes, "These very same statistics and lists show up frequently in the literature on obesity, as well as in books promoting dieting, at FDA hearings on new diet drugs, in patient brochures, in diet doctors' clinics, in medical weight loss product sales packets sent to physicians and in ads for commercial weight loss centers."[14] As noted in chapter 2, the risk for many of the diseases cited above stems from factors such as yo-yo dieting and a sedentary lifestyle, not from the fat itself. An increase in mortality attributed to weight appears to follow a U-shaped pattern where the extremely thin and the extremely fat are both at risk. Despite this research, the fear of fat has made its way into national health policy based on inaccurate information. Cogan and Ernsberger make the point that while this pattern is widely recognized by epidemiologists, it is little known by most of the public, including health professionals. Cogan states, "Extreme obesity may be dangerous, whereas moderate obesity may actually serve as a health buffer. This important fact has consistently gone unrecognized by obesity researchers and federal agencies responsible for determining federal policy. Additionally, extreme thinness is associated with mortality . . . yet there is no public health campaign to combat this health threat aggressively."[15]

As this book is going to press, a new study published in the *Journal of the American Medical Association* reports that 400,000 deaths in the year 2000 were attributable to poor diet and inactivity.[16] Immediately, the Department of Health and Human Services issued a press release stating, "With poor diet and physical inactivity poised to become the leading preventable cause of death in America, HHS Secretary Tommy G. Thompson today renewed efforts against obesity and overweight, announcing a new national education campaign . . . 'Americans need to understand that overweight and obesity are literally killing us,' Secretary Thompson said. 'To know that poor eating habits and inactivity are on the verge of surpassing tobacco use as the leading cause of preventable death in America should motivate all Americans to take action to protect their health. We need to tackle America's weight issues as aggressively as we are addressing smoking and tobacco.'"[17]

The idea that thinness, rather than a change in diet and activity, is the solution to preventing deaths is a problem in understanding association versus causation. The problem with the HHS statement is that while it accurately reports that poor diet and inactivity are preventable causes of death, it repeatedly concludes that weight loss is the solution. This is a misrepresentation of the findings. A useful analogy to consider is that baldness is a risk factor for heart disease in men. Yet risk is not lowered by giving these men a toupee, because the baldness is not causally related to the heart disease. Rather, elevated levels of testosterone in men increase heart disease and promote balding as well.[18] Likewise, poor diet and inactivity may lead to a higher death rate and cause weight gain as well. This does not mean becoming thin automatically reduces the risk, as Tommy Thompson's press release leads people to believe.

The manner of presentation regarding the new 400,000 statistic is likely to be used by many organizations, some with a profit motive, to raise the alarm on 'obesity' and to lead to increased discrimination against fat people. Ironically, as people heed the call to lose weight in the name of health, they are likely to become caught in the diet/binge cycle, ultimately leading to higher weights and the increased health risks that accompany yo-yo dieting. Americans of all sizes should be educated about the benefits of healthful eating and physical activity, regardless of whether any weight is lost as a side effect of these lifestyle changes. Otherwise, people are bound to feel discouraged and stop these behaviors if they remain large or to believe that if they are already thin that the important effects of these behaviors do not apply to them.

Fraser examines how, under the direction of former Surgeon General C. Everett Koop, the 1994 "Shape-Up America" campaign used the 300,000 deaths per year statistic, calling obesity "one of the most pervasive health risks affecting Americans today." The message was that increasing numbers of people should embark on a weight loss plan. Both Jenny Craig and Weight Watchers contributed $1 million to "Shape Up America."[19] Berg notes that "Former Surgeon General C. Everett Koop has aligned himself with the commercial weight loss industry in a well-financed anti-obesity campaign. Perhaps he is unaware of the irony that a man long identified with the fight against smoking is now so pressuring teenage girls to be thin that they are turning to smoking as never before."[20]

In her riveting book *Dispensing with the Truth*, Alicia Mundy explains the marketing of the obesity scare. She writes,

Spokespeople for new organizations — groups such as the American Association for the Study of Obesity — with heavy funding from the drug industry and frequently companies selling fat-free products, upped the ante. Get people to perceive obesity as a disease itself, and you've laid the groundwork for selling pills and other medical aids, surgical procedures, and the like to cure it. People know cancer and diabetes are diseases and they require medicine. Get them to call obesity a disease, and you've changed the paradigm. And so the various researchers, experts, and pharmacy representatives became an industry unto themselves. Think of it as "Obesity, Inc." To be sure, doctors at hospitals and research institutions took the obesity threat seriously. But it was the market researchers who turned it into an expensive trend. . . . Obesity was a killer, said the paid experts. It kills 300,000 people a year. . . . [I]t became the mantra of "Obesity, Inc."[21]

While the 300,000 deaths per year due to obesity is popular misinformation that continues to be misused, the actual information presented by McGinnis and Foege supports the current research noted earlier by Steven Blair at the Cooper Institute. His extensive studies demonstrate that fitness level and extent of exercise determine mortality rates regardless of what people actually weigh. Gaesser writes, "The thinner is better studies frequently cited by health professionals are far outnumbered by studies showing that aside from the very extreme, body weight is fairly unrelated to health status and death rates or that weights above the recommended height/weight tables are actually better for health and longevity. . . . The truth is that weight has little, if anything, to do with fitness or health. But that is not the story that has been drummed into us over the years."[22] This type of research challenges commonly held beliefs about the importance of weight loss and may be difficult to integrate at a professional or personal level. However, as a therapist it is important for you to be cognizant of this body of research.

The information presented thus far should help you become a more critical reader of the research. While you may not have the time or interest to pursue the complete facts behind every study, understanding the possibility that research is skewed may prevent you from accepting the results at face value, which, in turn, will affect the way you process your client's concerns.

## Lifestyle

Healthful eating and exercise are important factors in your client's move toward good health. Yet for the compulsive eater who is likely to have a history of trying to implement these lifestyle changes, such recommendations have the potential to backfire. When exercise equals punishment, your client is unlikely to sustain physical activity. When healthy eating equals deprivation, your client is likely to overeat. When the promotion of lifestyle changes emanates from a fear of fat, they have the same dynamics and consequences for the compulsive eater as a diet. Of course, no professional would discourage your client from integrating healthful behaviors into her life. The key is a shift in attitude and understanding on the part of both professionals and clients that emphasizes physical and emotional health at every size rather than a focus on weight loss.

### EXERCISE

As you begin to question the accuracy of what you hear, it is important to understand that there is agreement among researchers and professionals that exercise contributes to the health of everyone, including clients who have specific medical problems. Frequently, there is an assumption that large people do not exercise because they are lazy, and that if they did exercise, they would not be fat. However, there are people of all sizes who exercise, and people of all sizes who do not. We take the stance that exercise benefits everyone and that doctors should advise all patients, not just those of larger sizes, to exercise on a regular basis. For your clients who have concerns about their health, exercise is a proven means to improve their physical condition, even when no weight is lost through the process. There is abundant research suggesting that exercise can reduce the risk or improve the symptoms of cardiovascular disease, hypertension, hyperlipi-demias, diabetes, and other diseases, even when a person remains at a high weight.[23]

We chose to include information about exercise in this chapter because it is essential in the move toward good health at any size. While exercise is not a precondition to solving compulsive eating problems, this topic frequently emerges among clients who struggle with food and weight issues. It is important for you to have knowledge of the benefits and types of exercise, as well as an understanding of the psychological resistances that often occur.

### Resistance to Exercise

Most clients know that exercise is "good" for them and have some experience with physical activity in the past. Sometimes a client will already be involved in an exercise regime that she enjoys and plans to continue at the time she begins treatment. Occasionally, a client will present with a compulsive exercise problem in which she must exercise daily for long periods of time in order to "feel okay." Most often, clients will discuss the idea that they "should" move their bodies, and then present a variety of reasons to explain their inactivity such as not having time, feeling "too fat" to be seen in public, or not knowing what to do.

For the majority of clients, the concept of exercise is similar to being on a diet. Exercise machines calculate the number of calories burned while exercise instructors comment, "Work harder! You have to make up for those cookies you ate last night." When clients decide to join health clubs, the salesperson often asks, "How much weight do you want to lose?" The message to clients is that exercise will result in weight loss, she must want to lose weight or she wouldn't bother to exercise, and, perhaps most harmful of all, is the idea that exercise is punishment for her transgressions with food. As the result of these overt and covert communications, clients respond to exercise as if it were another diet. Frequently, a client will report that she was "good" for several weeks or several months. However, once she missed a day of exercise, she felt as if she had "blown it" and stopped completely. At some level, she rebels against exercise as she does against the diet; she is being told that she does not fit into society's vision of the right body and this angers her. Just as she loses pleasure in eating foods such as salad or fruit because they have become associated with the deprivation of diets, she loses the joyful feelings of movement because exercise is transformed into punishment.

The solution to this unfortunate set of circumstances for the compulsive eater is to unhook exercise from weight loss. This is a process that requires the client to let go of her internalized belief that exercise will result in weight loss and replace her assumption with a new set of reasons to move her body. This transformation can take a long period of time. Because the word "exercise" has such an ingrained meaning in our culture, the word "movement" can be substituted for those clients particularly sensitive to the negative connotations described above.

As you explore ideas about movement with your clients, the following activity can help them learn more about their current attitudes toward exercise. Based on an application of the concepts of Edward De Bono, author of *Serious Creativity: Using the Power of Lateral Thinking to Create New Ideas*, clients are directed to take their assumption that exercise leads to weight loss and undo it.[24] The therapist states, "Exercise does not lead to weight loss. Then what?" Clients answer with whatever thoughts come to mind. Typical responses include "I would do it for my health"; "I want to be fit and strong"; "I want to be more flexible and build my endurance"; "I would do it anyway because I like the way I feel when I move my body"; and, of course, "I wouldn't do it."

If your client offers reasons to engage in physical activity unrelated to weight loss, encourage her to focus on these factors as sufficient reasons to move her body. In this manner, she can begin the process of discovering internal cues that lead her toward movement and the satisfaction that can occur physically and psychologically from exercise. These experiences are reinforcing to her in the same way that stomach hunger experiences move her away from compulsive eating. Each time she moves her body in an attuned manner, there is an incentive to repeat the experience. Over time, she will find that exercise becomes integrated into her life as a caretaking activity rather than as a form of punishment.

For the client who states that she has no motivation to exercise without weight loss as a goal, the chances are she will be unable to sustain an exercise program without further examination. While some people in her life may view her as intentionally hurting herself by not exercising, there is a high probability that there are psychological obstacles that interfere with her ability to incorporate movement in her life, and these obstacles are worthy of exploration in the treatment. In this situation, "legalizing" the option of not exercising often helps the client end the guilt that plagues her when she is inactive. In the same way that yelling about her body size does not lead to weight loss, yelling at herself for not exercising does not work. In fact, she increases her anxiety and puts herself at higher risk for overeating.

Rita expressed a desire to exercise but found herself unable to follow through on any plans she discussed with her therapist.

> **Therapist:** When you think about exercise, what happens for you?
>
> **Rita:** I imagine that I will lose weight. Last time I exercised on a regular basis I was on a weight loss program and I was very thin.
>
> **Therapist:** Let's say that you begin to exercise and you do happen to lose weight. What about that scenario creates a problem for you?
>
> **Rita:** I hear my parents' voices. They've always pressured me to exercise so I will lose weight. If that happens, I will feel like they've won. (Rita has worked hard to separate from her family who was very controlling of her life into her early adulthood.)

**Therapist:** In a way it gives your parents as much power if you don't exercise because they want you to, as if you choose to exercise because they do want you to. It seems to me that one of the goals in our work together is to help you continue to feel separate enough so that you can decide whether to exercise based on your needs, and not in reaction to your parents.

Yasmine always enjoyed exercise, but could not seem to sustain her workout in the consistent manner she preferred. She would exercise several times per week for a couple of months, and then find herself inactive for the next month. After an exercise session, Yasmine reported feeling very good and could think of no reason that she would resist movement. Yasmine had made great strides in ending her compulsive eating and accepting her larger body size, and she was in excellent health. Finally, in a group session, Yasmine was able to pinpoint her difficulty with exercise. She explained that she always assumed that exercise would lead to weight loss, but that was not the case for her. Although she had been previously unaware of these feelings, part of her wondered why she should bother with an exercise routine if no one could see the results. Yasmine was able to answer her own question by reaffirming that she knew she felt better when she exercised; she felt stronger and believed it supported her good health.

For 2 years, Constance talked about her belief that exercise would be good but never followed through with any plans to join the local YMCA or use her exercise videotapes at home. As her physical health deteriorated, the therapist urged Constance to examine her resistance to exercise, as it could potentially alleviate some of her problems. Again, Constance stated that she would sign up for a program, but did not. Although Constance was monitored carefully by her doctor, the therapist felt that exercise was, in this case, of the utmost importance to Constance's physical well-being.

**Therapist:** I know we've talked in here before about the importance of movement and how hard it is for you to implement. But you're also telling me how worried you are about your health. I know you've also told me that when you move your body, you enjoy it and you feel better.

**Constance:** I know and I really want to. But I just never seem to do it.

**Therapist:** I wonder if there are some strategies that could help you to get going. You might want to remind yourself that once you get started, the exercise feels good to you. Or it might help to think of exercise as something you nudge yourself to do because in the end, it feels worth it.

**Constance:** I guess that's what I've learned about grocery shopping.

**Therapist:** I wonder what it would feel like to think about exercise in that way – it's just something that needs to become part of your life. But not because I'm telling you or someone else is telling you, but because *you've* said it's important to you.

**Constance:** Actually, that makes sense. You know, I keep thinking I shouldn't have to join a club or go anywhere special to get exercise. It should just happen naturally.

**Therapist:** Can you explain that more to me?

**Constance:** My parents never joined a health club. We were too poor. And besides, living in a rural area, you got plenty of exercise just being outside and working in the fields. No one got a personal trainer or used a special machine.

**Therapist:** This is something new you are telling me, and I'm glad you were able to put this feeling into words. You're saying that you feel exercise should happen naturally in the course of your day.

**Constance:** Yes.

**Therapist:** You know, I agree with you that human beings prefer to move, and historically they had to move. After all, cars and televisions are fairly new inventions. But the reality is that it is now pretty easy to get through a day without moving much at all.

**Constance:** You're right. But I think that joining a club still doesn't seem right. At least going for a walk seems more natural.

One month later, Constance reported that she connected with the idea that exercise was something she must do whether she liked it or not, and had begun to walk once a week. She understood that beginning this activity was a significant accomplishment for her and planned to try to increase the frequency.

These examples underscore the way in which issues related to exercise can emerge and be processed in the treatment of clients with compulsive eating. Again, there are as many variations as there are clients, although common themes emerge. Discussion of exercise should relate to the client's perceptions of the importance and meaning of activity in her life, and can be explored therapeutically in the same manner as other significant issues that are brought to treatment.

### Types of Exercise

Knowledge about exercise will vary from therapist to therapist, and similar to information about eating, may be based on the clinician's personal experience. While in-depth coverage of this topic is beyond the scope of this book, there are some concepts that may be useful when discussing movement or exercise with your clients.

Different people like to move in different ways. It is important for clients to identify activities that feel pleasurable. Clients may consider "stocking" on their exercise options, just as they do with food options. This places your client in a position to listen to herself when she recognizes that her body craves movement. For example, she may keep a pair of walking shoes in her car, a set of weights at home, and belong to a YMCA that has a swimming pool. She may purchase a yoga videotape, sign up for a Pilates class, or get her bike tuned up. Your client must own the proper clothes and shoes to ensure that she can move her body in a comfortable and safe manner. Making exercise easily accessible is an important step in the process of beginning to make her body more fit.

There are many types of exercises available for clients, and these different types of movement lead to different types of results. For example, aerobic exercise such as walking, running, and biking improves the cardiovascular system leading to lowered heart rate response and blood pressure. Anaerobic exercise such as weight lifting increases strength, endurance, muscle mass, and bone density, which can help decrease the chances of developing osteoporosis and help improve arthritic symptoms. In a sense, the combination of these two types of exercise is like an English class comprised of reading and writing; each one is important for a person to learn in order to increase competency. Other types of movement such as yoga and Pilates improve flexibility, balance, and strength. As your client considers how to move her body, you must be sensitive to both her needs and limitations. She must start at a place that feels comfortable to her and build her exercise regime in a manner that does not lead to rebellion. As she collects positive movement experiences, she will move away from the use of exercise as punishment toward a more positive and sustaining attitude that will allow her to integrate exercise into her life.

Large people often feel ashamed of their bodies, and therefore may find it difficult to exercise in public. Your knowledge of programs in your area that are size friendly may help your client find a way to exercise that feels nonthreatening. For clients who are able to afford some personal training sessions, this service can provide an entrée into the world of exercise that feels safe and supportive. It is important to identify personal trainers who will focus on fitness rather than weight loss. *Great Shape: The First Fitness Guide for Large Women* by Pat Lyons and Debby Burgard also offers useful information about exercise at a larger size.[25]

## HEALTHFUL EATING

Moving from a new attitude toward exercise to a new attitude toward food, we ask the question: What comprises "healthy" eating? We would probably all agree that eating some fruits and vegetables is a good idea. We might also consider getting enough protein and eating a wide range of foods. Beyond this simple advice, healthy eating becomes more complicated.

In an attempt to provide Americans with guidelines regarding healthy eating, the government released the Food Pyramid in 1992. This diagram shows the bulk of food servings coming from the grain category, followed by the fruit and vegetable group, and then the dairy, meat, fish, poultry, eggs, beans, and nuts category. The smallest daily allowance of food comes from the fat category, which is displayed in the narrow point at the top of the pyramid. Low fat eating became the buzzword for health and fat free products proliferated at local grocery stores.

Now there is talk of revamping the Food Pyramid. Walter Willet, an epidemiologist and health researcher at the Harvard School of Public Health who has conducted hundreds of studies, was asked what he believes to be the most recent, damaging nutritional advice. He replied that it is the "all fats are bad" messages. Willet explains that when people switched to low fat products such as Snackwell cookies, they did not achieve the weight loss expected. "And a lot of them found it hard to stay on a low-fat diet because it's not satisfying. They overate, and the result was an explosion of obesity."[26] Willet suggests that people must include unsaturated fats in their diet, which can actually reduce fatal heart arrhythmias. "One of the best sources of omega-3 fatty acids in our diet was full-fat salad dressing because it's almost always made from soybean oil. . . . When they switched to fat-free salad dressing, people eliminated a healthy source of omega-3 fatty acids. It's troublesome. Salad dressing on the side is a bad idea."[27] Yet chances are that you know people who continue to skip the dressing on their salad or insist on fat-free dressings in the name of health, and probably with a hope for weight loss.

Willet proposes a new Food Pyramid that looks very different from the one developed by the USDA. For example, while he encourages people to eat more nuts and legumes, he discourages the consumption of foods such as potatoes.[28] The question remains whether Willet's suggestions will provide the healthiest eating regime for Americans, or whether new research in the next year, decade, or century will render his eating advice to be incorrect as the science of nutrition continues to develop. The bind for clients at this point is that one expert's "good" food is another expert's "bad" food.

Another example of changing dietary recommendations relates to eggs. Due to cholesterol concerns, eggs became a "bad" food to be avoided as much as possible by the general population. Yet we know now that the cholesterol contained in eggs does not increase blood cholesterol. When people categorically eliminated eggs from their diet, they unknowingly sacrificed an excellent nutritional food source. For example, eggs contain lecithin, an essential nutrient linked to benefits in liver function, heart function, memory, and brain development.

## Orthorexia Nervosa

In the quest to eat healthfully, some people have developed an obsession with foods that they consider to be extremely healthy, such as non-fat, organic, and vegan diets. Steven Bratman, M.D., author of the book *Health Food Junkies*, has coined the term "orthorexia nervosa" to describe cases in which the quest for healthy food . . . "become[s] a disease in its own right, as bad in a way as the diseases it is meant to forestall or cure."[29] He provides a self-test for readers ("yes to two or three of these questions means a touch of orthorexia; four or more means, you're in it pretty thick.")

- Do you spend more than 3 hours a day thinking about healthful food?
- Does your diet socially isolate you?
- Do you care more about the virtue of what you eat than the pleasure you receive from eating it?
- Do you plan tomorrow's food today?
- Do you feel guilt or self-loathing when you stray from your diet?
- Have you found that as the quality of your diet has increased, the quality of your life has correspondingly diminished?
- Do you keep getting stricter with yourself?
- Do you feel an increased sense of self-esteem when you are eating healthy food?
- Do you look down on people who don't eat healthy food?
- Do you sacrifice experiences you once enjoyed to eat the food you believe is right?
- When you are eating the way you are supposed to, do you feel a peaceful sense of total control?[30]

## Integrating Healthful Eating

When dietary recommendations change constantly, how should people decide what to eat? After all, what is considered healthy today may be found to be detrimental tomorrow. Furthermore, it would be impossible for you or your client to keep up with all of the latest nutritional information, let alone research all points of view on each new idea. In the end, listening to one's own body and eating a wide variety of foods provide the most reliable means of making food choices.

As your client solves her compulsive eating problem and becomes an attuned eater, she may find that she is now in a strong position to adjust her diet in ways that promote her health. Now that she no longer chooses foods based on deprivation and a fear of fat, she can consider both the types of foods she enjoys as well as foods that she believes have a positive effect on her body. For example, Tom had successfully ended his compulsive eating. After a medical check-up in which he learned that his cholesterol was high, he decided to consult a dietitian referred by his therapist. She explained nutritional information to him related to fat, sugar, and fiber. Tom decided to increase the amount of beans and fruit in his diet, two types of foods he liked but consumed in small amounts. He also decided to buy some fat-free ice cream to provide an alternative when he desired something soft and creamy. At the same time, Tom continued to purchase regular ice cream for occasions when this was exactly what his body craved. Tom viewed these changes in his diet as caretaking his health rather than as a means of weight loss, an attitude that did not create feelings of deprivation. He continued to keep all foods legal and asked himself each and every time he was hungry what made the best match for him in every way. The information garnered from the dietitian was not actually new to Tom. In the past, he had attended several programs and had met with dietitians who had offered similar information. He reported that he could make use of what he heard in a different way at this point in his life because he was now convinced that he would never need to feel deprived again.

Pam believed that putting soy in her diet would contribute to her physical well-being. As the result of feeling in tune with her hunger, she decided that a glass of soy milk in the afternoon would coincide with her body's need to have some protein. Like Tom, Pam focused on adding nutritional quality to her diet without worrying about eliminating her formerly forbidden foods. While it may be tempting to instruct clients to pick certain foods for health reasons from the start, *it is only when all foods are truly permissible that the compulsive eater can sustain health-related choices.* In other words, the process of curing compulsive eating must take place first and cannot be sidestepped. As a therapist, it is important for you to maintain a nonjudgmental stance toward your client's food choices so that she remains free of external pressure and can make her own decisions. Rather than telling Pam that she is "good" for adding soy milk on a regular basis, you can acknowledge that her decision seems to work well for her and seems to help her feel that she is taking good care of herself. This statement promotes her internal structure about attuned eating without any hint of deprivation.

## Health Considerations

Exercise and dietary changes can improve the overall health of your compulsive eating clients. However, clients may present with or develop specific problems that create a risk for them, such as high blood pressure, high cholesterol, or diabetes. In your role as therapist, it is important to confirm with your client that she is seeking appropriate medical care. If your client receives advice from her doctor to make dietary changes in order to treat a health issue and she is able to follow these recommendations, no problem exists. Unfortunately, many clients report that following a visit to their doctor in which they were instructed to restrict food, they immediately had an overeating experience. To the extent that the diet offered by a doctor increases overeating, these recommendations have an unintended negative effect. It is important for you to understand that the majority of these clients are not self-destructive or unmotivated to become healthy. Rather, the dynamics of compulsive eating render them extremely sensitive to perceived deprivation. Additionally, clients who are compulsive eaters frequently turn to food for comfort when they experience anxiety. While a doctor may hope scare tactics or dire warnings will convince patients to restrict their diets, the fear that ensues actually puts patients at greater risk of overeating. Furthermore, information about the effect of food on various disease processes can be complicated and frequently changes. With high-risk clients where food intake clearly plays a role in medical symptoms, we suggest including a dietitian as part of the treatment team.

Too often, the assumption that weight loss will improve overall health in general, and diseases such as Type 2 diabetes, high blood pressure, and high cholesterol in particular, has perpetuated the myth that dieting is healthful and should be recommended. According to Ernsberger and Cogan, research has shown that improvements in the conditions listed above following weight loss are "transitory and evaporate in the long-term, even when weight loss is maintained. . . . If dieting does not improve long-term health, why is it still enthusiastically endorsed as a prioritized health improvement strategy?"[31] Ernsberger offers a thought-provoking view of the way in which the medical industry embraces the notion of weight loss as a cure for disease.

> The position of weight loss in medicine today can be compared to the role of bloodletting 150 years ago. Bloodletting became popular because doctors found that if feverish patients were bled, their fever would break and their skin would become cool and clammy. Thus, bloodletting improved the symptoms of sick patients. Of course, we now know that blood loss created a state of shock that lowers body temperature but ultimately increases the risk of death. Similarly, weight loss provides short-term improvements in symptoms, but may not be ultimately beneficial. Before weight loss can be removed from its exalted status as a therapy, a revolution in medicine may be required comparable to the one that brought on the end to the practice of bloodletting.[32]

The following section illustrates new ways in which medical concerns may be understood based on the expertise of professionals outside of the field of mental health. These ideas are by no means exhaustive but offer a shift in thinking about the physical problems of large people. The goal of this new paradigm is to ensure that clients receive proper medical care without the shame and blame that often result from their experiences with health professionals.

As we explore this complicated topic, it is important to realize that people can be fat for many reasons. We've already discussed three important factors that can contribute to a higher weight: genetics, yo-yo dieting, and the use of food for emotional reasons. Certain medications also have the side effect of increased appetite and weight gain. As researchers learn more about the human body, there is evidence of specific conditions that actually cause a person to gain weight as a result.

For example, polycystic ovary syndrome (PCOS) is a disease in which women have cysts on their ovaries and irregular menstrual cycles. Another *symptom* of this illness is weight gain. In Metabolic Syndrome, also know as Syndrome X, obesity is part of the overall picture. Again, weight loss is often recommended, but new findings indicate that weight gain is not the cause of the problem but rather a *part* of the disease process. People who suffer from a hypothyroidism have an imbalance of thyroid hormones and will gain weight as a *result* of the illness. People who have any of the aforementioned conditions cannot successfully lose the weight that is a characteristic of the disease, nor will weight loss cure the underlying disease. Yet because of the assumptions made about people's responsibility for their fatness, true physical problems may go undiagnosed as patients are advised to diet.

## BLOOD PRESSURE

While conducting workshops on the treatment of eating problems, two therapists, one fat and the other thin, asked the audience, "Which one of us do you think has high blood pressure?" Not surprisingly, the respondents chose the fat presenter. Yet the reality was that the thin therapist, who also exercised and meditated regularly, had elevated blood pressure (as did both of her parents) that required medication to control. The fat presenter, on the other hand, had stable, low blood pressure at 110/70. The assumption that "overweight" and medical problems go together is so ingrained in our culture that we often view this as fact.

Are these assumptions completely unfounded? The audience's supposition that the fat presenter had high blood pressure is consistent with the fact that hypertension in obese men and women is two to three times more common than in the thinnest of the population.[33] Yet, as noted in chapter 2, over 85% of the variation in blood pressure across the population has nothing to do with body fat. One hypothesis is that high blood pressure may be the result of weight cycling, which typically leads to increased weight as well. For example, obese animals have normal blood pressure, maintaining a steady weight and consuming a constant amount of food on a daily basis. However, when animals are forced to lose and regain weight, mirroring the behavior of yo-yo dieters, they develop hypertension in similar fashion to their human counterparts.[34]

Gaesser discusses a well-documented but rarely publicized observation that high blood pressure in obese people only slightly increases the risk of premature death.

> The reverse applies to both non-obese and thin people, for whom hypertension more than doubles the risk of premature mortality. . . . So if a hypertensive obese person follows the advice to lose weight in order to lower blood pressure and the remedy doesn't work, then what you have is a weight-reduced hypertensive who is now statistically more likely to die from cardiovascular disease than before. This may help explain the seemingly inexplicable finding in so many studies that men and women who have undergone sustained weight loss are at greater risk of cardiovascular disease mortality than others.[35]

If your client suffers from high blood pressure, she may consider several alternatives to weight loss. In addition to exercise, she may adjust her diet. She may experiment with the reduction or elimination of salt in her food intake to learn if she is salt sensitive. A reduction in blood pressure has been demonstrated in the Dietary Approaches to Stop Hypertension (DASH). Results revealed that an individual could lower blood pressure in just 2 weeks by adding more fruits and vegetables and eating less saturated fat, independent of weight loss. She may also focus on stress-reducing measures such as meditation or massage. She may require medication to control her blood pressure, as was the case for the thin, exercising, meditating presenter who had a genetic predisposition for high blood pressure.

## CHOLESTEROL

Clients may also tell you that they have a high cholesterol level. Although this problem is frequently associated with higher weights, the two are only weakly correlated. In other words, the assumption that obesity causes high cholesterol may be a spurious connection. Ernsberger and Koletsky explain that this weak link is likely due to dietary and activity patterns. Factors such as a diet high in fat and low in fiber and vegetables and a sedentary lifestyle may separately promote increased cholesterol levels. These factors may also produce increased body weight, leading to the assumption that it is the weight that causes the medical symptom. They advocate intervention at the dietary and activity levels, as opposed to weight loss, for favorable and long-term results, along with effective medications when needed. Gaesser concurs with the idea of eliminating weight loss as a useful treatment, noting studies that show 99.5% of decreases in cholesterol were attributable to factors other than weight loss. He states, "Diet and exercise, alone or in combination, are far more important than weight, or weight loss, in improving the health of persons either with diabetes or heart disease, or of those who have risk factors for these diseases."[36] It is important to note that focusing on dietary changes and increased physical activity for health is not the same as promoting weight loss, even if your client sees a change in body size as a side effect of these behaviors. Learning to accept her body at any size, eating in an attuned manner, and engaging in self-care promote health and create a path for your client where she can avoid the pitfalls of deprivation and self-hatred fueled by diets and a fear of fat.

## DIABETES

If your client reports that she has diabetes, it is essential that she work conjointly with a dietitian, preferably one who is familiar with the non-diet approach. Dana Armstrong, RD and certified diabetes educator, and Dr. Allen King have gained attention for their groundbreaking work in using attuned eating to treat diabetes. As they became discouraged with the lack of success when using traditional approaches focusing on weight loss and dietary restrictions, the team applied the concepts of attuned eating to their patients with diabetes. These newly diagnosed patients are instructed to eat as usual, and then test their blood glucose values so that they can receive constant feedback about the effect of various foods on their body. King and Armstrong emphasize the importance of people discovering for themselves how their bodies reacts to food intake, rather than allowing patients to accept the idea that "sugar is bad" without ever learning the physiology of the body. Armstrong explains that as the body breaks carbohydrates into glucose molecules that require insulin, there is no differentiation between the amounts of insulin required for 45 grams of glucose from a Snickers® bar as opposed to 45 grams of starch from a baked potato. By paying attention to how her body feels, as well as frequently testing blood sugar levels, a patient can stay in charge of her own eating regime and decrease the sense of deprivation that places her at risk of overeating.

Steven reported that he loved to eat chicken fried steak. However, when he tested his blood sugar level after eating this meal, he had a reading above 300, well over the preferred range of less than 180 after a meal. Rather than telling Steven that he must eliminate this favorite food, his dietitian asked him for more information. She learned that he also had mashed potatoes, gravy, and creamed corn because it was included with the meal rather than because he really desired them. The dietitian asked Steven to consider tuning in to what he truly craved and make adjustments as needed. In a later meeting, Steven reported to the dietitian that he once again had the chicken fried steak. This time, however, he chose broccoli and a baked potato as side dishes. His blood glucose level following this meal was 168. Through this process, Steven was able to learn how his body reacts to various foods, continue to eat the foods that he loves, and successfully manage his diabetes.

Steven, like many patients who have diabetes, is fat. Given the statistic that as many as 80% of people who suffer from Type 2 diabetes are "overweight," how can health professionals justify loosening up on the standard of weight loss as a necessary part of the treatment of diabetes? In controlled trials of weight reduction for adults with Type 2 diabetes, improvements, as measured by monitoring glycosylated hemoglobin that provides the prevailing glucose level over a period of several weeks, were short lived. Despite immediate improvements, by the 6- to 18-month follow-up participants returned to initial values, regardless if weight loss was maintained. In a prospective study of the relationship between weight change and mortality in Type 2 diabetes, those who had lost weight had a *higher* risk of death, although the reasons remain unclear.[37] Gaesser notes that most people with Type 2 non-insulin-dependent diabetes can significantly improve their condition through changes in diet and exercise without weight loss. While remaining clinically obese, they may also be able to discontinue medications.

According to Ernsberger and Koletsky, "Given that diabetes type-2 is a genetic disease and that most of its victims are obese, it follows that the genes causing diabetes must also facilitate weight gain. There is now excellent evidence that this is the case."[38] In the development of diabetes, an increased level of insulin is the first red flag, followed by an increase in weight. Peter Bennett, an epidemiologist, proposes that insulin resistance, not obesity, may be the contributing factor to the development of diabetes. He explains, "Genetic factors initiate the disease process, leading to insulin resistance and a compensatory increase in insulin production by the pancreas. High levels of insulin lead to weight gain, which can further exacerbate insulin resistance. After many years, the system decompensates and blood glucose rises. Dietary factors may also contribute to the development of diabetes. . . . Future diabetics ate more saturated fat and took in few vegetables and vitamin C. Thus, although genetic factors predominate, life long dietary habits can modify genetically determined risk."[39]

This information fits in with a cluster of diseases experienced by many diabetics known as metabolic syndrome X, and often referred to as metabolic syndrome or syndrome X. Along with fat concentrated in the abdominal area, patients with syndrome X may have high blood pressure, abnormal levels of cholesterol and triglycerides, and glucose intolerance. These conditions are associated with insulin resistance and, consequently, high insulin levels, which further promote weight gain. In their book, King and Armstrong explain to their readers who have syndrome X that, "Changing your level of activity and changing your relationship with food are great places to start. These changes are usually not expensive and generally quite safe and are the cornerstone of treatment for both syndrome X and diabetes. For some people, these changes are enough to decrease the levels of insulin resistance and diminish the signs of the syndrome. In addition there are also medications available for the treatment of the various components of syndrome X."[40] It is important to view the use of medications as a valid option for people of all sizes who have these medical issues, rather than as a failure. People can see positive changes in their medical conditions using this variety of interventions, without losing weight.

In addition to high blood pressure, high cholesterol, and diabetes, numerous other conditions are frequently associated with weight and may be of concern to your client. For example, gallstones are typically noted as a consequence of being fat. While it is true that gallstones are more frequently seen in large people, research shows that body weight itself is not the direct culprit. Rather, large and quick weight losses are a proven, direct cause of gallbladder disease. This fact puts fatter people at a higher risk as a group because of their greater likelihood to engage in crash dieting.[41] This example demonstrates once again that yo-yo dieting, rather than a sustained larger weight, creates medical risks for clients.

## RECONSIDERING WEIGHT LOSS

Complete consideration of all the medical risks attributed to weight is beyond the scope of this book, and your client must make decisions about her health in conjunction with her doctor.

Yet certain ideas will help challenge the assumptions that you and your client may both have about the necessity of weight loss to solve medical problems. This ability to question the prescription to lose weight can facilitate your client in the process of receiving a correct diagnosis of her health issues, responding to her problems in a manner that does not promote the diet–binge cycle, and making peace with the body she has while engaging in healthful behaviors. In summary:

- Yo-yo dieting causes and exacerbates medical problems.
- There are medical conditions in which weight gain is a symptom rather than a causal factor.
- Research is often contradictory at best as to how weight loss improves medical problems. (This is partly because no one has success in keeping weight off long enough to measure any benefits due to the fact that diets don't work!)
- Dietary changes (not dieting) and/or physical activity can improve or resolve medical problems for people of all sizes, even when no weight is lost.
- People with compulsive eating issues generally must solve this problem first in order to integrate dietary interventions.

This type of information is extremely important to clients who are in the process of ending compulsive eating patterns. If a client believes that the only way she can make her body healthy is to lose weight, she will become vulnerable once again to the diet–binge cycle. By the time she has come to see you, she has made numerous attempts to lose weight and keep it off, but cannot do so. She is already sensitive to the deprivation that results from being told to diet. Rather than facilitating her physical health, a prescription to lose weight, even for medical issues, is likely to trigger overeating behaviors that ultimately compromise her well-being.

Instead, as your client moves through the process of becoming an attuned eater, she may now attempt to adjust her eating behaviors in ways that feel caretaking to her, regardless of her size. Additionally, her ability to tune into the effect of food on her body will enhance her ability to use food in ways that promote her health. For example, Ronald Krauss, head of the American Heart Association's nutritional committee, reported on the effect of a low-fat diet on lowering the risk of heart disease. He found that one third of the people following a low-fat diet *increased* their risk of heart disease, another third were unaffected, and a final third reduced their risk. Berg also notes a study that found that 67% of men following a very low-fat diet had adverse changes to their blood lipids, potentially increasing their risk of heart disease.[42] Just as we are learning that all medications do not affect people in the same way, following medical advice strictly in a "one size fits all" fashion may prove detrimental. It is important for each person to determine her own response to a particular intervention. Removing the pressure to lose weight will help your client focus on other steps toward health.

A client named Felicia stopped eating eggs many years ago because of a high cholesterol reading at the time of her annual physical exam. To her surprise, when she was rechecked 6 months later, her cholesterol level had actually increased. Felicia decided to consult with a dietitian to see if she could learn more about why her sacrifice of eggs had not led to the expected results. The dietitian explained that the cholesterol contained in eggs does not necessarily turn into blood cholesterol. Rather, foods high in saturated fat lead to increased blood cholesterol. Furthermore, Felicia was already aware that the foods she chose to substitute for eggs did not satisfy her in the same way. As Felicia reflected on her eating behavior over the past 6 months, she suspected that she was eating more than she needed at times to make up for the lack of satisfaction, often with foods that were high in saturated fat. Felicia returned to having eggs when she craved them, and her cholesterol returned to its previous, lower level. She decided to add regular exercise into her routine and further improved her cholesterol readings.

Fred reported that he attended a county fair where he had two hot dogs and shared some cotton candy with his son. Yet when he tested his blood glucose level, it was lower than when he ate the conventional foods on a diabetic diet. He asked his dietitian about this unexpected result. She explained that the hot dogs were protein as opposed to carbohydrates. Even though he had two hot dog buns and some cotton candy, he engaged in 7 hours of walking, which had a positive effect on carbohydrate utilization. Fred's willingness to test his glucose level even when he believed he was "bad" allowed him access to important information about his body.

These examples illustrate how important it is for your client to get to know her own body and its reaction to particular foods. These scenarios also underscore the concept that honoring the wisdom of the body can make good nutritional sense in the face of changing, and often contradictory, nutritional advice.

## Building a Network of Health Professionals

The non-diet, size-acceptance movement spans across all professions, and there is increasing awareness among doctors and dietitians that health, rather than weight loss, is the important focus of treatment. Some of these professionals have developed a paradigm called Health At Every Size (HAES) that offers a definition of health that is not contingent on weight (see Appendix H, The Tenets of Health at Every Size). As you help your clients find freedom from compulsive eating, it is useful to build a network of service providers in related fields whose treatment will compliment, rather than contradict, your work.

### CHOOSING A DIETITIAN

When a client presents with  high-risk health issues, a dietitian can help her use a non-diet approach in relation to her physiological needs. A dietitian who understands the non-diet approach will focus on health rather than size. She will provide your client with accurate information regarding nutrition and the effect of food in her body. She will support your client in learning to listen to the feedback that her own body gives her, without judgment. She will steer away from recommending that your client count calories or fat grams and will reinforce the value of attuned eating. If she asks your client to keep a log of her food consumption, the purpose will be to keep track of her hunger, matching, satisfaction, and its effect on her body and mood rather than to control her eating.

Work with a dietitian can also be helpful to clients who want a better understanding of how their bodies react to certain foods. For example, it is common for female clients to report an increase in chocolate cravings prior to menstruation. In her book *Why Women Need Chocolate*, Debra Waterhouse emphasizes that female food cravings are "a normal, biological need for a specific food that will balance a woman's body and mind and revitalize her well-being."[43] She explains the brain chemistry of food cravings, noting that the sugar and fat from chocolate boost serotonin and endorphin levels, resulting in positive mood and renewed energy. "No study has ever found that women frequently crave tofu, Spam, or nonfat cottage cheese, and no study has ever found that men frequently crave chocolate. . . . Only women crave these foods consistently."[44] On the one hand, if your client can trust her body and listen to its messages, she will automatically honor her chocolate cravings and achieve the desired physical and psychological effects. She will notice that these cravings naturally decrease as she continues in her cycle and returns to her usual level of chocolate consumption. However, the physiological explanation from a trained professional may help reassure your client that her cravings are natural, thereby building her confidence in listening to her body's signals. Men may also be reassured to learn that strong cravings for meat, for example, are in sync with their natural need for a greater supply of protein to support their higher muscle mass.

If your client is one of the many people who believes she has a "carbohydrate addiction," she may want to seek the advice of a dietitian to help her understand her experience. Although there is no hard evidence to support this claim, your client may find that when she eats carbohydrates, she frequently binges. If your client routinely restricts foods high in carbohydrates because she considers them to be "bad" foods, it is not surprising that she will eat more than her body needs, and she is likely to find that the processes described in this book will solve this issue. Occasionally a client will report that when she consumes foods high in this substance, she continues to experience cravings and excessive consumption, even once carbohydrates are legalized.

According to Elisa D'Urso Fischer, RD, a dietitian using the non-diet approach, people have wide fluctuations in blood sugar; some clients may be more sensitive to these fluctuations because of a genetic predisposition. In general, when a person experiences low blood sugar, a food high in carbohydrates, such as a bagel or a piece of cake, will give her a peak in blood sugar followed by a corresponding drop. This occurs because all of the carbohydrates turn into blood sugar, causing the body to release insulin. The insulin brings down the blood sugar and then triggers more carbohydrate craving. Therefore, a person eating a bagel and coffee for breakfast may be surprised to find herself hungry again a short time later. D'Urso Fischer explains that pairing a protein with a carbohydrate can help this effect because protein, unlike carbohydrates, stabilizes blood sugar so that fullness lasts longer. The protein remains available to the body for blood sugar as needed, but does not create the peaks associated with carbohydrates. She elaborates that because of the popular low-fat message, people eliminate foods from their diet that can help prevent this situation, such as cream cheese or peanut butter on a bagel. D'Urso Fischer adds that the compulsive eating client's mistrust of her body's cues fuels the problem as she tries to avoid eating when she is truly hungry, or ignores a craving for cheese with her crackers. In these situations, a dietitian can again provide the physiological explanations. She can give your client information that will allow her to experiment with foods so that she can decide how her own body responds.

## CHOOSING A DOCTOR

It is important for your client to find a doctor with whom she feels comfortable. Health problems can exist for clients at any size. As discussed earlier, weight is often blamed as the culprit for a range of physical conditions. Unfortunately, when a larger person seeks treatment for any number of complaints, a doctor may advise her to lose weight rather than considering other possible treatments. According to Ernsberger, "Many people have told me that their worst experiences of discrimination have taken place in the doctor's office. Indeed, a particularly virulent form of fat bigotry seems to be endemic among physicians. . . . One third of family practice doctors admit to feelings of discomfort, distaste or hostility when treating obese patients. . . . Nine out of ten health professionals identify emotional problems as the major cause of obesity, despite overwhelming evidence that a person's genes are responsible for a tendency to gain weight easily."[45]

There are several ideas that your client may find useful as she works with her existing doctor or chooses a new doctor. First, when a client is told to lose weight before receiving treatment of any other kind, she can ask whether thin people ever have the same condition. As the answer will inevitably be yes, she can then ask why she is not receiving the same treatment. If a doctor focuses on weight loss and dieting, a client may respond, "I understand how you feel. But I'm not here about my weight. I'm here about these symptoms. Can you help me?"[46] Maggie, a client using the non-diet approach, saw her doctor for a routine physical exam. On the way out the door, he turned and said, "You should lose some weight." Maggie asked him why he was making this recommendation when he had just concluded that her physical health was excellent. The doctor apologized to her and withdrew his recommendation.

If your client is unable to attain an acceptable outcome, she may consider finding a new doctor. Some clients choose to learn more about a doctor's attitudes toward fat before making an appointment by asking if the doctor is comfortable treating larger people. Your client may also want to choose a doctor who is sensitive to the needs of very large patients, such as having gowns that are adequate in size and using blood pressure cuffs that will fit around the arm. Appendix E contains a sample letter that a client may consider as she chooses a doctor who can meet her needs.

Routinely, doctors weigh patients who come to their offices. Yet part of the body acceptance work discussed in chapter 6 was to help clients end their obsession with the scale. Doctors may need to know a patient's weight when it comes to prescribing medications or performing surgery. They will also want to be aware of any major changes in weight in either direction. However, there is no medical necessity for weighing patients each and every time they come for a visit. Some clients using the non-diet approach let the nurse or doctor know of their wish not to be weighed, and this request is often honored. Other clients choose to step on the scale backward so that they will not be subject to the triggers that accompany reading the number on the scale. Of course, some clients will use this as an opportunity to find out what they really do weigh. If this action results in consequences such as an increase in mouth hunger, you and your client can explore this situation further.

## Wellness

Up until now, your client may have focused primarily on weight loss as the primary means of improving her health. As her compulsive eating diminishes, she may become interested in other ways to improve her total well-being. In addition to the considerations of eating and physical activity already described, we would like to emphasize other aspects of wellness that can contribute to the overall physical and emotional health of your clients.

## MEDITATION

Contemporary lifestyles are often fast paced and pressured, resulting in the feeling of being "stressed out." This stress takes its toll physically and mentally. Meditation, an ancient art where the practitioner relaxes the body and quiets the mind, has been shown to alleviate the negative effects of stress. Some schools of meditation focus on a thought, such as peace, or on a particular object. Other meditation practices use the breath as the focal point, and still others use a mantra, which involves the repetition of a word, phrase, or sound.

While people frequently embrace meditation for spiritual reasons, its physical and emotional benefits have long been recognized. Meditation, which became popular in the United States during the counterculture revolution of the 1960s, has now become mainstream and has been studied scientifically to uncover its benefits. The two most researched types of meditation are Transcendental Meditation (TM), founded by Maharishi Mahesh Yogi, and the Relaxation Response, developed by cardiologist Herbert Benson. Practitioners of these techniques meditate twice a day for 20 minutes. Studies of TM show that this technique is associated with reduced health care use, increased longevity and quality of life, reduction of chronic pain, reduced anxiety, reduction of high blood pressure, and reduction of serum cholesterol level.[47] Benson became convinced that meditation was a treatment for high blood pressure and conducted research to this end at the Harvard Medical School. He identified the Relaxation Response as a group of physiological and psychological effects that are common to a variety of meditation and relaxation practices. Other identifiable physical benefits include deep rest as measured by decreased metabolic rate, lower heart rate, and reduced work load on the heart; lowered levels of lactate as well as cortisol, both chemicals associated with stress; reduction of free radicals, which are unstable oxygen molecules that can cause tissue damage and are thought to be a major factor in aging and in many diseases; and improved flow of air to lungs resulting in easier breathing, which has been helpful to people with asthma.[48] Meditation has been found to increase mental clarity and emotional stability, enhance creativity, alleviate anxiety, and reduce depression.[49] Some corporations have incorporated the teaching of Transcendental Meditation into their employee wellness programs because of the proven benefits.

Scientific studies indicate Buddhist meditation and its core practice of mindfulness offer similar positive benefits. The Dalai Lama, observing the relationship between Buddhist mediation and Western science, commented that Buddhist philosophy and Western science now inform each other in a reciprocal fashion. According to Richard Davidson, a neuroscientist at the University of Wisconsin, "Mindfulness meditation strengthens the neurological circuits that calm a part of the brain that acts as the trigger for fear and anger."[50] John Kabat-Zinn, Ph.D., author of numerous books on mindfulness meditation, is the founder and director of the Stress Reduction Clinic at the University of Massachusetts Medical Center, which serves as a model for hospitals across the country. The mindfulness approach incorporates formal sitting meditation with the focus on awareness of the breath, an informal practice that focuses on bringing full attention and awareness into the present moment without judgment. Physicians are referring their patients to mindfulness programs for many reasons including heart disease, anxiety, stress, chronic pain, sleep disorders, GI distress, anger management, and skin disorders. Insurance companies are increasingly looking at the benefits of meditation and are paying for all or part of these programs.[51]

## HUMOR

There is also an increasing amount of research showing that thoughts, moods, and emotions have a significant impact on the body's health and healing abilities. Building humor and laughter into her life can contribute to the physical, emotional, and spiritual health of your client. In the eighteenth century, Voltaire believed that the art of medicine entailed keeping the patient amused while nature healed the illness. In 1964, Norman Cousins, editor of *The Saturday Evening Post*, echoed this sentiment as he helped make the public aware of the effects of humor. Cousins was diagnosed with an extremely painful and crippling form of arthritis and his doctors forecasted a poor prognosis for a full recovery. Intrigued by the notion that negative thoughts could lead to disease states, Cousins decided to explore whether positive emotional states could produce the opposite effect. Cousins looked for humor and laughter every chance he could and discovered, for example, that a half hour of a funny movie offered him 2 hours of pain-free and comfortable sleep. Cousins reported a full recovery 6 months later and went on to write the book *Anatomy of an Illness.*

Laughter triggers the release of endorphins, which act as natural painkillers, confirming Cousin's experience. Endorphins help by blocking pain and by producing a general sense of well-being. Other research points toward a significant drop in cortisol and adrenalin, the stress hormones, as the result of laughter. Reducing the level of stress hormones is important because high levels can weaken the immune system.[52] Moreover, laughter can improve the functioning of the immune system by raising levels of infection-fighting Y-cells, disease-fighting proteins called gamma-interferon, and B-cells that produce disease-destroying antibodies. Also, because laughter increases breathing, use of oxygen, and heart rate, it can stimulate the circulatory system, bringing healthful lymphatic fluids to diseased areas and temporarily reducing blood pressure.[53] A good belly laugh results in muscle relaxation and is also a cardiac exercise. Frequent belly laughter empties the lungs of more air than they take in, resulting in a cleansing effect similar to deep breathing. Relax and laugh — what a wonderful prescription for health!

Meditation and laughter are two aspects of wellness scientifically proven to promote better health. There are numerous other behaviors shown to improve health, ranging from a good night's sleep, to drinking plenty of water daily, to flossing one's teeth on a regular basis because excess plaque can enter the bloodstream and contribute to heart disease. The extent to which you focus on these various behaviors with your client will depend on the goals of therapy and your own treatment philosophy. However, as your client recognizes the multiple factors that contribute to physical and emotional well-being, the focus on weight loss as the only means to health will diminish.

## The Rise in "Obesity"

Up until now, we have discussed the idea that people naturally come in different shapes and sizes, and that people can be healthy at all sizes. Yet we must also address the fact that there has been a reported increase in body weights that cannot be explained by genetics alone. First, the way BMI is categorized leads to a skewed picture of the incidence of obesity. Since 1991, the actual increase in weight for the typical American is only an average of 7 to 10 pounds, yet this translates into a marked increase in the number of people with a BMI that is greater than 30 (the number designated as the indicator of obesity). Since obesity is defined as a threshold, a fairly small rise in average weight has a disproportionate effect on obesity rates.[54] Furthermore, in recent years there has been a disproportionate increase in the number of extremely large people. In chapter 1, we discussed the adaptive nature of the human body from an evolutionary standpoint. Some experts posit the idea that extremely fat people carry genes that were adaptive within a hunting-gathering environment. Observations show that members of populations most prone to starvation become the fattest after exposure to a sedentary lifestyle and a Western diet.[55] As our environment changes, resulting in a more sedentary lifestyle and an increased abundance of food, what was once an adaptive physical trait, the ability to store fat, no longer serves a survival function.

The majority of large people have "dieted up" to their current size. Yo-yo dieting typically leads to weight gain, so a person who may have been designed to be larger than the cultural norm ultimately ends up at a much higher weight. It is also the case that people live a much more sedentary lifestyle than ever before, a situation that is not conducive to the evolutionary preferences of the human body. People forgo natural levels of activity when they watch TV, use computers and video games, drive, and rely on high-tech conveniences such as the remote control and automatic garage door opener. These changes are affecting the physiology of the body and contribute to the disease process. Stressful lives mean that people turn frequently to fast foods, even when their bodies crave other types of nourishment. As portions become "super sized" and people are caught in the diet–binge cycle, they consume amounts and types of foods not necessarily in tune with what their body naturally desires. In combination, these factors lead to higher weights. Developing a stance in which a person eats in an attuned manner, honors her body's desire for movement, and finds healthy ways to manage stress may alleviate current trends.

Additionally, increasing weights among poorer Americans reflect factors such as the lack of availability and/or the high cost of fresh foods as compared to cheaper items that tend to be high in fat and sugar. This reality limits choices and makes attuned eating more challenging. Fewer opportunities exist as well for physical activity in lower socioeconomic strata. These issues must be explored and addressed at the macro level so that policies that foster improved quality of living will become a national priority.

## DIET DRUGS

In chapter 2, we presented the idea that there is a bell-shaped curve for weight, and that what Americans consider to be "normal" actually falls far to the left of what is average. We also discussed the idea that people at either end of the curve, those extremely thin and extremely fat, are at high risk for medical problems and premature death. If you have a client who falls into the "extremely fat" category, she may receive advice from a doctor to take some type of action. "Diet drugs," both over-the-counter and prescription, have been used for decades, often with dangerous results.

In the 1990s, a series of drugs were introduced that were designed to help people lose and maintain weight. Results were unimpressive and the risks were great. Research indicated that an average loss of 5.5 pounds could be expected at the end of 1 year for the drug fenfluramine as compared to a placebo, 7 to 11 pounds for Meridia®, and 8 pounds for Xenical®. Once the drug is stopped, the pounds return.[56] Most diet pills are approved for safety for 1 year, yet a person would have to continue taking the pills indefinitely to maintain this modest weight loss. Risks are associated with each diet pill. While such pills are supposedly prescribed to induce weight loss with the assumption that the person will thereby enjoy greater health, the reverse is often true. Berg notes some of the adverse effects of popular prescription diet pills. Meridia, for example, can cause high blood pressure and increased heart rate. Interestingly, the drug is intended for the severely obese but not if they suffer from high blood pressure, heart disease, an irregular heart beat, or have survived a stroke, problems often blamed on obesity. Xenical has the side effects of oil leakages and soft stools as it releases undigested fats.

In 1994, two diet drugs, fenfluramine and phenteramine, became widely prescribed in a combination commonly referred to as fen-phen. Two years later, dexfenfluramine, marketed as Redux®, gained FDA approval. In 1997, 6 million people were using these pills when the drugs were withdrawn from the market due to safety concerns. Serious complications, including death, were attributed to the diet drugs. The FDA stated that up to one third of users might have developed leaky heart valves and reports show that at five medical centers, 25 to 30% of patients taking the drugs had abnormal echocardiograms although they were asymptomatic. When the pills were pulled from the market, the FDA had reports that at least 100 patients suffered from heart valve disease, including three who died as a result. There were also numerous confirmed reports of primary pulmonary hypertension related to the use of fen-phen. In this rare disease, which increased dramatically as the result of the diet drug, there is a thickening of the capillaries that send oxygen to the lungs, resulting in death by slow suffocation. Most of the victims who died were healthy young women, some of whom had used the pills for less than a month.[57] The actual total number of complications and/or deaths from fen-phen use far exceeded these numbers. "Around 45,000 women — an epidemic by any person's standards — were believed to have developed one of two different diseases linked to their lungs or to their heart from taking the drugs."[58]

Over-the-counter diet pills can also cause serious damage. Practically all of these weight loss pills contain amphetamine-like ingredients that increase heart rate, speed up nervous system functioning, and raise blood pressure, and/or laxatives that can cause dehydration and affect electrolyte balance. These substances can be addictive or habit-forming. Other side effects may include nervousness, tremors, diarrhea, heart failure, and even death. Because over-the-counter diet pills are classified as food supplements rather than drugs, these products are relatively unregulated, and there is no mandatory reporting procedure for these side effects. Dieters' tea contains strong botanical laxatives and diuretics. These teas can cause diarrhea and significant fluid loss. Senna, a common herbal laxative used in such preparations, can lead to arrhythmia and heart failure. In recent years, the FDA has received reports of health-related problems, including the deaths of four young women where dieters' tea was the likely cause. The American Association of Poison Control Centers reports that in 1989, 47,000 calls were received concerning adverse reactions to these diet products that necessitated medical care[59] or hospitalization. Since 1997, sales of diet pills and related supplements have increased 10 to 20% annually.[60]

One of the most serious ingredients found in more than 200 weight-loss products and energy boosters is ephedra. This herb contains ephedrine, which is derived from an Asiatic shrub and also referred to as Ma Haung. This herb acts as a stimulant on the nervous system in a way similar to amphetamines. One of the best-selling over-the-counter diet products containing ephedra is Metabolife®. For years, the company denied that the preparation caused any adverse side effects. However, in 2002, under threat of federal investigation and criminal charges, the president of Metabolife acknowledged that between 1997 and September 2001, the company received approximately 13,000 complaints of "certain health related issues," including seizures, stroke, heart attack, and death.[61] As of 2003, the FDA reports that 12 million Americans use ephedrine and that it has been linked to 120 deaths.[62] However, many ephedra deaths go unreported and therefore are not represented in this figure.

## GASTRIC BYPASS SURGERY

The most current popular intervention for people who are said to be at least 100 pounds over "ideal" body weight is the gastric bypass surgery. Gastric bypass surgery involves a procedure where part of the stomach is removed to necessitate the restriction of caloric intake. As the stomach is reduced from about the size of a football to the size of an egg, there is room for only about 2 to 3 tablespoons of food at a time. Eating more than this amount at a meal can cause pain, nausea, and vomiting.

If your client considers having gastric bypass surgery, she must be made aware of the risks. The death rate from the procedure is 1 in 100 to 200 patients, usually from a blood clot that floats to the lungs or because stomach juices leak out into the blood and cause serious infection.[63] It has been reported that 10 to 20% of surgical patients have been rehospitalized at least once as the result of surgical complications such as infection at the incision site, hernia at the incision, a hole in the stomach or intestine causing bleeding and infection, or popping staples or bands (depending on the type of procedure used); one third of patients develop gallstones. Other long-term complications affecting about 30% of surgical patients include nutritional deficiencies such as anemia and osteoporosis.[64] As the result of weight loss surgery, patients can only process tiny amounts of sugar and develop "dumping syndrome" in which they experience nausea, vomiting, bloating, diarrhea, shortness of breath, weakness, sweating, or dizziness. Due to the fact that the body no longer absorbs all substances that pass through it, it is unclear what the long-term effects may be regarding nutritional deficiencies and adequate absorption of medications.

According to centers providing gastric bypass surgery, patients typically lose 50% of their excess body weight. Proponents of gastric bypass surgery claim that benefits include improved self-esteem, relationships, and quality of life, and a reduction in problems commonly associated with obesity such as blood pressure, cholesterol, Type 2 diabetes, and sleep apnea. Other conditions that may improve include congestive heart failure, urinary incontinence, menstrual irregularities, and fertility. Conditions unlikely to change after surgery are arthritis, vascular disease, and depression.[65] These centers emphasize that in order to keep their weight off, patients must eat a low calorie diet and exercise regularly.

Weight loss peaks approximately 2 years after the surgery, often followed by a gradual but accelerating regain of weight. In fact, most people who have the surgery begin regaining weight after 2 years, with some regaining all of the weight back. While the weight is often regained, the physical side effects and altered digestive tract are permanent.[66]

There is a growing demand for the surgery, which was given limited endorsement in 1991 by an NIH panel consisting mainly of surgeons and weight loss experts. The following year, 16,200 people in the United States underwent the surgery. By 1997, that number increased to 23,100, and in the year 2000, that figure was up to 63,100.[67] Hospitals are scurrying to meet this demand. At an average cost of $15,000 to $30,000, gastric bypass surgery ranks high in profitability for hospitals and free-standing centers. This cost does not reflect ancillary or follow-up care. As hospitals expand their weight-loss surgery clinics, there is concern that some doctors are performing this risky procedure with insufficient training, or may be taking patients who fall below the "morbidly obese" category in an effort to boost their incomes. Another concern is that the procedure has gained popularity so rapidly, especially as celebrities undergo the operation, yet "there are no national standards for training surgeons and no comprehensive database to monitor deaths and complications."[68]

While the long-term risks of adults undergoing gastric bypass surgery are assessed, a new trend raises additional concern. This procedure is gaining acceptance among some surgeons as a treatment for very large children, some as young as 13 years of age. The fact that adults undergoing this surgery are at risk for nutritional deficiencies raises great concerns for children who are still growing. Gastric bypass could interfere with a child's use of calcium, for example, which is necessary for building strong bones. Dr. Timothy Sentongo, a gastrointestinal specialist at Chicago's Children's Memorial Hospital, states, "Doing something in the first 20 years that can affect you for the next 50 years . . . ethically, it's very hard to justify."[69] There is also concern that children want to undergo this procedure because of the prejudice against fat that they experience. This notion raises the question as to whether a risky surgical procedure should be the solution for victims of social prejudice.

It remains to be seen what the long-term results of gastric bypass surgery will be. Yet it is clear that obesity surgery is not the solution to the epidemic of compulsive eating and body dissatisfaction. If you have a client who has already had the surgery, or plans to, the principles of attuned eating can only enhance her postsurgery adjustment. In addition, you can help her focus on bodies image concerns, the use of exercise, and the management of affective states without reliance on food as important parts of her therapy.

## A Final Thought

New ideas, research, and treatments are developing at such a rapid pace that by the time this book is on the market, there are likely to be subjects and ideas that we have not addressed. Yet certain truths remain. People come in different shapes and sizes. People feel better, both physically and psychologically, when they listen to their bodies to tell them when, what, and how much to eat. A multidimensional approach that considers a person's total well-being, rather than a narrow focus on weight loss, promotes health. As you evaluate new data, these principles will help you decide how to integrate this information into your personal and professional life.

## ENDNOTES

1. Cogan, J. C., & Ernsberger, P. (1999). Dieting, weight, and health: Reconceptualizing research and policy. *Journal of Social Issues, 55* (2), 189.
2. Bass, A. (1995, September 14). Risk found in women's weight gain. *The Boston Globe*, A1.
3. Scripps, H. (1995, September 26). Here's the skinny: Thin is in but fat's where it's at. *The Boston Herald*, p. 2.
4. Fraser, L. (1997). *Losing it: America's obsession with weight and the industry that feeds on it*. New York: Dutton, p. 12.
5. Fraser, L. (1997). *Losing it: America's obsession with weight and the industry that feeds on it*. New York: Dutton, p. 13.
6. Fraser, L. (1997). *Losing it: America's obsession with weight and the industry that feeds on it*. New York: Dutton, p. 14.
7. Mundy, A. (2001). *Dispensing with the truth*. New York: St. Martin's Press, pp. 81–82.
8. Fraser, L. (1997). *Losing it: America's obsession with weight and the industry that feeds on it*. New York: Dutton, p. 212.
9. Berg, F. M. (2000). *Children and teens afraid to eat: Breaking free in today's weight-obsessed world*. Hettinger, ND: Healthy Weight Network, p. 29.
10. Robison, J. (2001, Spring). What are the basic assumptions of the old or traditional approach to weight and weight management? What empirical data support or challenge these assumptions? *Perspective: A Professional Journal of the Renfrew Center Foundation, 7* (1), 8.
11. McGinnis, M. J., & Foege, W. H. (1993, November 10). Actual causes of death in the United States. *The Journal of the American Medical Association, 270* (18), 2207–2212.
12. McGinnis, M. J., & Foege, W. H. (1998, April 16). Letters to the editor. *The New England Journal of Medicine, 338*, 1157.
13. Fraser, L. (1997). *Losing it: America's obsession with weight and the industry that feeds on it*. New York: Dutton, 1997, p. 172.
14. Fraser, L. (1997). *Losing it: America's obsession with weight and the industry that feeds on it*. New York: Dutton, 1997, p. 172.

15. Cogan, J. (1999). A new national health agenda: Providing the public with accurate information. *Journal of Social Issues, 55* (2), 384.

16. Mokdad, A.H., Marks, J.S., Stroup, D.F., & Gerberding, J.L. (2004). Actual causes of death in the United States, 2000. *Journal of the American Medical Association, 291* (10), 1238–1245.

17. United States Department of Health & Human Services (2004, March 9). Citing "dangerous increase" in deaths, HHS launches new strategies against overweight epidemic. [Online]. http://www.hhs.gov/news/press/2004pres/20040309.html [2004, March 19]

18. Lotutu, P.A., Chae, C.U., Ajani, V.A., Hennekens, C.H., & Manson, J.E. (2000). Male pattern baldness and coronary heart disease. *Archives of Internal Medicine, 160,* 165–171.

19. Fraser, L. (1997). *Losing it: America's obsession with weight and the industry that feeds on it.* New York: Dutton, 1997, p. 143.

20. Berg, F. M. (2000). *Women afraid to eat: Breaking free in today's weight-obsessed world.* Hettinger, ND: Healthy Weight Network, p. 159.

21. Mundy, A. (2001). *Dispensing with the truth.* New York: St. Martin's Press, p. 42.

22. Gaesser, G. (2002). *Big fat lies: The truth about your weight and your health.* Carlsbad, CA: Gurze Books, pp. xix–xx.

23. Miller, W. C. (1999). Fitness and fatness in relation to health: Implications for a paradigm shift. *Journal of Social Issues, 55* (2), 207–219.

24. DeBono, E. (1992). *Serious creativity: Using the power of lateral thinking to create new ideas.* New York: HarperBusiness.

25. Lyons, P., & Burgard, D. (1990). *Great shape: The first fitness guide for large women.* Palo Alto, CA: Bull Publishing.

26. Cleary, A. J. (2003, Winter). Razing the pyramid. *Eating Well,* p. 20.

27. Cleary, A. J. (2003, Winter). Razing the pyramid. *Eating Well,* p. 19.

28. Cleary, A. J. (2003, Winter). Razing the pyramid. *Eating Well,* p. 23.

29. Bratman, S. (2000). *Health food junkies.* Broadway Books: New York, p. 19.

30. Have Your Good Dietary Intentions Overshot the Mark? Tufts University Health and Nutrition Letter: April 2001.

31. Cogan, J. C., & Ernsberger, P. (1999). Dieting, weight, and health: Reconceptualizing research and policy. *Journal of Social Issues, 55* (2), 192.

32. Ernsberger, P., & Koletsky, R. J. (1999). Biomedical rationale for a wellness approach to obesity: An alternative to a focus on weight loss. *Journal of Social Issues, 55* (2), 233.

33. Ernsberger, P., & Koletsky, R. (1999). Biomedical rationale for a wellness approach to obesity: An alternative to a focus on weight loss. *Journal of Social Issues, 55* (2), 228.

34. Ernsberger, P., & Koletsky, R. (1999). Biomedical rationale for a wellness approach to obesity: An alternative to a focus on weight loss. *Journal of Social Issues, 55* (2), 229.

35. Gaesser, G. (2002). *Big fat lies: The truth about your weight and your health.* Carlsbad, CA: Gurze Books, p. 62.

36. Gaesser, G. (2002). *Big fat lies: The truth about your weight and your health.* Carlsbad, CA: Gurze Books, p. 72.

37. Ernsberger, P., & Koletksy, R. J. (1999). Biomedical rationale for a wellness approach to obesity: An alternative to a focus on weight loss. *Journal of Social Issues, 55* (2), 226–227.

38. Ernsberger, P., & Koletksy, R. J. (1999). Biomedical rationale for a wellness approach to obesity: An alternative to a focus on weight loss. *Journal of Social Issues, 55* (2), 226.

39. Ernsberger, P., & Koletksy, R. J. (1999). Biomedical rationale for a wellness approach to obesity: An alternative to a focus on weight loss. *Journal of Social Issues, 55* (2), 226–227.

40. Armstrong, D., & King, A. (2001). *New drug treatments for diabetes.* Lincolnwood: Publications International, Ltd., p. 70.

41. Armstrong, D., & King, A. (2001). *New drug treatments for diabetes.* Lincolnwood: Publications International, Ltd., p. 231.

42. Berg, F. (2000). *Women afraid to eat: Breaking free in today's weight-obsessed world.* Hettinger, ND: Healthy Weight Network, p. 179.

43. Waterhouse, D. (1995). *Why women need chocolate.* New York: Hyperion, p. 14.

44. Waterhouse, D. (1995). *Why women need chocolate.* New York: Hyperion, p. 20.

45. Ernsberger, P. (1988, Fall). The discriminating doctor. *Radiance,* p. 53.

46. Ernsberger, P. (1988, Fall). The discriminating doctor. *Radiance,* p. 53.

47. Orme-Johnson, D. W., Alexander, C. N., & Hawkins, M. A. (in press). Critique of the National Research Council's report on meditation. *Journal of Social Behavior and Personality.*

48. Benefits of meditation. [Online]. (2003, January 1). Holistic-Online.com. Available: http://www.1stholistic.com/meditation/hol_meditation_benefits_physical.htm [2003, August 7].

49. Meditation. [Online]. (2003, September 28). Focal Point Yoga. Available: http//www.focalpointyoga.com/meditation.htm [2003, August 7].

50. Gyatso, Tenzin, the 14th Dalai Lama (2003, April 26). A monk in the lab: A *New York Times* editorial. *The New York Times,* A19.

51. Livni, E. (2000, July 5). Mindfulness medication: Modern medicine turns to an ancient practice. [Online]. abcNEWS.com. Available: http://www.newyorkcityvoices.org/jul00p.html.go.com/sections/living/DailyNews/mindfulness0705.html [2003, July 14].

52. Wooten, P. (1996). Humor: an antidote for stress. *Holistic Nursing Practice, 10* (2), 49–55.

53. Humor therapy. [Online]. (2000). Wholehealthmd.com. Available: http://www.wholehealthmd.com/refshelf/substances_view/1,1525,10152, 00.html

54. Friedman, J. M. (2003, February 7). A war on obesity, not the obese. *Science, 299*, 856–858.

55. Friedman, J. M. (2003, February 7). A war on obesity, not the obese. *Science, 299*, 856–858.

56. Berg, F. M. (2002) *Women afraid to eat: Breaking free in today's weight-obsessed world.* Hettinger, ND: Healthy Weight Network, p. 151.

57. Berg, F. M. (2002) *Women afraid to eat: Breaking free in today's weight-obsessed world.* Hettinger, ND: Healthy Weight Network, p. 152.

58. Mundy, A. (2001). *Dispensing with the truth.* New York: St. Martin's Press, p. 8.

59. Berg, F.M. (2001). Children and teens afraid to eat: Helping youth in today's weight-obsessed world. Hettinger, ND: Healthy Weight Network, p. 100.

60. Raloff, J. (2002, August 10). Diet pills: It's still buyer beware. [Online] Science News. Available: http://www.science news.org/20020810/food.asp [2003, July 10].

61. Katz, D. (2003, August). One can make you small. *Oprah Magazine*, p. 146.

62. Brokaw, T. (2003, July 23). *NBC Evening News with Tom Brokaw.*

63. Kowalczyk, L. (2003, January 12). Thousands seek obesity surgery. *The Boston Globe*, A6.

64. Gastrointestinal surgery for severe obesity. [Online]. National Institute of Diabetes & Digestive & Kidney Diseases of the National Institutes of Health. Available: http://www.niddk.nih.gov/health/nutrit/pubs/gastsurg.htm#explore [2003, May 25].

65. Sweet, W. A. (2000, November 7). The Surgical Weight Loss Center. [Online]. Available: http://www.swlc.net/bariatric_surgery/gastric_by-pass_outcomes.htm [2003, July 10].

66. Ernsberger. P. (2000) Weight loss surgery. [Online]. Council on Size and Weight Discrimination. Available: http://www.cswd.org/medwls.html [2003, May 23].

67. Kowalczyk, L. (2003, January 12). Thousands seek obesity surgery. *The Boston Globe*, A1.

68. Kowalczyk, L. (2003, January 12). Thousands seek obesity surgery. *The Boston Globe*, A6.

69. Tanner, L. (2002, November 4). Surgery gains acceptance as option for obese youth. *The Boston Globe*, A2.

# CHAPTER 9

# CHANGING THE WORLD . . . A LITTLE BIT AT A TIME

Once upon a time there was a wise man who used to go to the ocean to do his writing. He had a habit of walking on the beach before he began his work.

One day he was walking along the shore. As he looked down the beach, he saw a human figure moving like a dancer. He smiled to himself to think of someone who would dance to the day. So he began to walk faster to catch up. As he got closer, he saw that it was a young man and the young man wasn't dancing, but instead he was reaching down to the shore, picking up something, and very gently throwing it into the ocean.

As he got closer he called out, "Good morning! What are you doing?" The young man paused, looked up and replied, "Throwing starfish in the ocean."

"I guess I should have asked, why are you throwing starfish in the ocean?"

"The sun is up and the tide is going out. And if I don't throw them in they'll die."

"But, young man, don't you realize that there are miles and miles of beach and starfish all along it. You can't possibly make a difference!"

The young man listened politely. Then bent down, picked up another starfish and threw it into the sea, past the breaking waves and said, "It made a difference for that one."[1]

As a therapist, you have the power to help your clients, one at a time, end the unrealistic expectations about thinness that lead to dieting and compulsive eating. There is an interactive effect between individuals and culture; people take in ideas from culture about what is desirable, but as personal ideas are transformed, so too is our society. It is with great hope that future generations will be free from the obsession with food and weight that we offer ideas to be used by therapists in private practice, social service agencies, schools, and hospitals that can convey healthier messages about eating behavior and body size to specific clients and society at large.

## Prevention

Raising children who feel comfortable with their bodies and eat in an attuned manner is an essential step toward preventing the problems of body dissatisfaction and compulsive eating. Clients may seek treatment because of concerns about a child's weight or eating patterns, or this topic may arise in the course of therapy for other issues. You may also work in a setting, such as a school, where there is high parental interest in learning how to develop healthy feeding patterns for children. Helping parents reconsider their ideas as to what constitutes a healthy relationship with food provides an important opportunity to reduce eating problems for future generations.

Throughout this book, we emphasized the importance for clients who are working their way out of compulsive eating patterns to be meticulous in responding to their bodies' cues as they consider when, what, and how much to eat. For the general population, as well as the client who has cured her compulsive eating, the definition of attuned eating may become somewhat more flexible. In other words, a healthy relationship with food means eating in response to physical hunger *most* of the time. However, normal eating can also include experiences such as eating occasionally because something looks good, eating past fullness at a special meal, eating in response to an emotion once in awhile, or choosing foods based on nutritional content because this feels caretaking. Attuned eating means that eating for satisfaction is predominant, and experiencing deprivation is virtually nonexistent. Attuned eating is a natural skill. It can be relearned by people who have lost touch with their hunger and can be reinforced and nurtured with children so that they maintain this healthy relationship with food throughout their lives.

## FEEDING CHILDREN

Catherine told her therapist that she was concerned about her daughter Hannah, age 9, whose was beginning to develop a rounder stomach. Catherine explained that she does not want Hannah to become fat and feel bad about herself. To that end, Catherine began to cut out dessert and sugary snacks from her daughter's diet. Catherine also told Hannah that they could go on a diet together because Catherine had become worried about her own weight as well. As the therapist questioned Catherine about the family's lifestyle, she discovered that the family was relatively inactive and for their convenience relied on take-out foods most evenings. In this scenario, Catherine's genuine concern for her daughter's well-being had the unfortunate effect of setting the stage for future problems for her daughter. As the result of eating restrictions, Hannah is likely to overeat these foods when they are available, or perhaps even sneak them. She will lose the ability to connect with her own signals to tell her what she craves — a problem compounded by the lack of variety provided to her at meal times. Hannah also learns that she must be thin to feel good about herself, or like her mother, will need to focus on weight loss throughout her life in order to feel okay.

In her insightful book *Like Mother, Like Daughter: How Women Are Influenced by Their Mothers' Relationship with Food — and How to Break the Pattern,* Debra Waterhouse explains how mothers, often unknowingly, pass a legacy of eating problems to their children. She writes,

> Your good food intentions can have unexpected outcomes and . . . your own relationship with food can negatively affect your daughter's. For example, if you:
>
> —enforce strict eating rules
>
> —restrict your daughter's fat and sugar intake
>
> —restrict your own fat and sugar intake
>
> —exercise control over your daughter's eating habits
>
> —encourage your daughter to diet
>
> —diet
>
> —weigh yourself and feel uncomfortable with your body
>
> then you are in some way passing the torch of dieting, disordered eating, and body dissatisfaction on to your daughter. If your mother practiced any of these behaviors, then she passed the legacy on to you.[2]

For many clients like Catherine, the behaviors listed above are viewed as promoting healthy eating without awareness of the havoc they wreak on a child's relationship with food and her body.

You have already learned about the research that supports the idea that children are naturally able to listen to their physical hunger and regulate their caloric and nutritional intake when a variety of foods are offered. When parents interfere with this regulatory ability by trying to restrict food intake or by forcing the consumption of particular foods, the typical result is a loss of this attunement and an increase in power struggles between parent and child during meals. Instead, you can teach parents how to support their children's physical hunger and keep the feeding process as an act of nurturance rather than control. According to Jane Hirschmann and Lela Zaphiropoulos, authors of *Preventing Childhood Eating Problems*, encouraging self-demand feeding ultimately leaves children more open to learning information about food because parental advice does not turn into a power struggle. They emphasize that children who stay in close touch with their bodies' cues for hunger and satiation will eat nutritiously because "their natural appetites will call for the full range of food elements that are necessary for healthy growth and development."[3]

Parents must make many decisions each and every day about when, what, and how much food to provide for their children. By following the principles outlined in chapter 3, parents can organize their ways of feeding children without the anxiety or power struggles that can often occur between parent and child.

## Reinforcing the Stomach–Hunger Connection

As the young child transitions from the breast or bottle to solid food, she increasingly exerts control over her feeding experience. She may utter a sound that indicates she is hungry, push away a food that she dislikes, or eat with pleasure at the discovery of a new taste. Parents can help her connect these actions with her body by making statements such as, "Your tummy must be hungry," or "Your tummy has had enough." These words help the toddler understand that her eating and stomach go together and sustain behaviors that were present since birth; when she is hungry, she must eat, and when she is satisfied, it is time to stop. As language develops and she becomes able to assert herself, the child will ask for specific foods such as an apple, cookie, cereal, or a piece of cheese. Again, parents can reinforce the stomach–hunger connection by saying, "Your body wants some protein," or by asking "Does that feel good in your stomach?" In this manner, the parent conveys to the child that she is in charge of her eating and is capable of making her own choices by listening to her body's physical cues.

## Family Mealtimes

The concept of mealtimes provides structure to a family both in terms of organizing the preparation of food and providing an opportunity for connection among family members. This structure also offers security to a child who knows that food will be easily available at certain times of the day. Yet at the same time, children may become hungry at other times of the day, or may not be particularly hungry when it is "time for dinner." Perhaps after a long day at school, a child experiences hunger that requires more than a small snack. When she eats what could be labeled a "meal," she becomes able to focus on her homework or return to playing with a friend. If she does not respond to her hunger at a physical level, she may feel uncomfortable, become irritable, and find herself unable to concentrate on school work. On a psychological level, she may feel that her needs are "wrong" or "bad," believe that she is a burden for requiring more care than she is supposed to, or experience the need to sneak food in order to meet her needs. Or a preschooler may become hungry at 5:30 P.M. even though her father will not arrive home to eat with the family until 7:00. Rather than creating stress for everyone by telling her to wait, feeding her at 5:30 alleviates her hunger. Perhaps she will eat only a small amount and still find herself hungry for dinner. Or she may sit with her family and converse about her day, even though she is not hungry and therefore does not eat. Finally, her parents may allow her to leave the table if she is antsy, providing an opportunity for a calmer experience for the rest of the family. As she grows older, she will know that she is always welcome at the table, and this structure will be reassuring.

## Role of the Parents

Ellyn Satter, a specialist in the field of children's eating, provides a useful description of the roles of parents and children in the feeding interaction. She explains that it is the parents' responsibility to provide a wide variety of food at mealtimes, and it is up to the child to decide what and how much to eat.[4] In other words, parents must give their children numerous choices at the table, such as bread, fruit, vegetables, protein, starch, and dessert. The child may choose from all of the options, or may pick just one of the foods at a particular meal. Parents do not become involved in monitoring or commenting on their children's choices, allowing for conversation that is free of the conflicts often engaged in between parents and children over food. Satter emphasizes that children will naturally regulate their food intake so that they ultimately balance their nutritional needs.

In order for this process to occur, parents must go to the trouble of providing a wide range of food for their children. There is no question that feeding a family requires much time and energy; the payoff is the avoidance of control struggles over food and the development of children who feel good about eating and their bodies. In order to build this method of feeding into the family structure, many issues may need to be addressed.

First and foremost, the ability and willingness of parents to adopt a style of feeding children that is based on trusting the body is related to their own relationship with food. For the parent who already eats in an attuned manner, passing this attitude to children will come naturally. In this situation, it is helpful for you to reinforce this behavior because parents often feel external pressure from other parents, family members, and the media to limit or alter their child's diet. For the parent who diets, overeats, or controls her eating, the idea of allowing her child to naturally regulate her food intake will feel frightening. Yet these parents often observe that, in fact, their child seems to know when she is finished eating; perhaps she eats three fourths of a brownie and leaves the other piece on her plate because she has had enough. By reassuring the parent that this concept really works, and asking her to observe her child's natural relationship with food, she may become convinced that her child can make choices without parental interference. If parents' messages to restrict foods have been integrated into the eating behavior of the child or adolescent so that she has already lost touch with her body's signals, the family will need to make an active effort to help her relearn how to eat in an attuned matter. Books such as *Like Mother, Like Daughter* and *Preventing Childhood Eating Problems* offer excellent information for clients and families who are interested in learning more about how to help their daughters (and sons!) become instinctive eaters.

## Meal Preparation

As more families have two parents working outside the home, the preparation of meals has become an increasingly stressful and less frequent occurrence. On the one hand, many parents, especially mothers, find themselves feeling guilty when they are unable to prepare home-cooked meals on a regular basis. However, the reality is that many families do not have the time (or perhaps the desire) to spend preparing meals. Yet the family must eat! If fast food is the only option, children will develop a diet that consists of fast food. You can help parents figure out creative solutions that will help them provide a variety of choices for their family. For example, a family that has children involved in sports practices at dinnertime may prepare a pot of chili, which can easily be reheated as people arrive home. Keeping pasta and a jar of sauce on hand allows for quick preparation of a hot entrée after a long day at work. Stopping at the grocery store to buy prepared fruit or use a salad bar can ease the time involved in offering these choices. Cooking on the weekend may provide a helpful strategy for some parents. By keeping groceries well stocked with a variety of food choices, parents will find that they can put a meal on the table that will satisfy the entire family. Sometimes, fast food may be a great option. The key is for you to help families understand the importance of providing their children with a wide range of food choices, while at the same time developing a flexible attitude so that they do not excessively worry about their role.

Parents may express concern that they will feel like short-order cooks if they must cater to every whim of their child. Respecting a child's hunger needs does not mean that a parent remains at the child's beck and call. Nor does it mean that a parent will buy every single item a child wants. Budgetary issues impact food quantity and selection. A craving for a particular type of cheese that is not in the house does not mean that a parent must drop everything and run to the grocery store. What is important is that overall, the child is able to have foods available to her that she desires, and that an inability to provide certain options stems from issues of budget or convenience rather than an attempt to control the child.

Parents should get to know their child's eating preferences so that there will be something on the table she enjoys. If the dinner is meatloaf and the child dislikes it, a parent can provide other options. She may put bread, fruit, and deli turkey on the table as well. She may check with the child before dinner to ask what she would like. Children usually prefer simple foods, and if a parent accepts the notion that a child may like different items, preparing a package of macaroni and cheese, cooking a frozen pizza, or pouring a bowl of cereal with milk is less likely to feel like a burden. Some children can easily tell their parents what they are hungry for; other children respond better to having a variety placed before them and choosing. With younger children, a parent might say, "I am about to sit down for dinner. If you need anything else, please let me know now." Older children are able to get and/or prepare a special food they may desire.

Children frequently become hungry before bedtime. This can be a natural expression of physiological hunger, satisfied by making a match. However, children who know that their parents will feed them when they say they are hungry can also use this statement as a way to manipulate bedtime. Therefore, parents may choose to have a cut-off time for eating, reminding the child that if she is hungry, this is her last opportunity to eat for the day.

## The Selective Eater

Many children are described as "picky eaters." This term has negative connotations so we prefer to use the term "selective eaters." It is natural for children to go through stages where there are only a few foods that they want frequently. If a child is growing properly, this phase is nothing to worry about. The less anxiety a parent communicates to the child about her eating habits, the more likely she is to expand her eating repertoire when she becomes ready to do so. However, when parents become very involved in their child's intake, control struggles often ensue, which become integrated into the feeding relationship and interfere with the child's natural expansion of her food preferences. Adults who consider their own eating habits as children are likely to notice that their food preferences shifted significantly over time. Parents who remain concerned about nutrition may consider supplementing their children's diets with a multivitamin.

Some parents may feel strongly that their child should try foods that are on the table. Tastes do change, and repeated exposure to a particular food can result in a child accepting that food. However, forcing a child to eat something she does not want can set the stage for major battles. A parent may approach this situation by saying, "I'd like you to try a bite, but if you don't like it, you don't have to eat it. In fact, you can spit it out." If a child still refuses to take a taste, it is better for the parent to let the issue go for the time being rather than create tension and power dynamics at the table.

## Misuses of Food

Some parents may already engage in the use of food with their children for purposes other than nourishment. Parents may use food as a reward — if you clean your plate, you can have dessert; as punishment — if you don't clean your room, you can't have dessert; for psychological soothing — if you stop crying, you can have a piece of candy; or as an interpretation of love or rejection — I made these cookies just for you; you have to eat them. These actions interfere with the child's attunement to her own eating behaviors and foster the use of food for self-soothing. Children naturally want to express their autonomy. A child who is able to stay in charge of her eating will feel secure in her independence and remain able to feed herself according to her body's needs. A child who learns that eating — or not eating — certain foods can upset or please her parents develops a powerful means by which to express herself that ultimately creates struggles within her family and herself. She becomes at high risk for turning to food to manage emotions, as described in chapter 5.

### Examples of Attuned Feeding with Children

The concept of feeding children in a relaxed, nonrestrictive manner in order to promote healthy eating behaviors will surprise many of the people you work with. You may also question the efficacy of this model. Here are some examples of situations that may help your clients — and even yourself — become more convinced of the value of this paradigm.

A PBS television show that illustrated the work of researcher Leann Birch observed the behavior of children who were fed in both restrictive and nonrestrictive environments. Following a meal that should have left them full, a plate of "treats" was available to children in a room full of interesting toys. Elizabeth, a child who was allowed to eat what she wants at home, played with the toys until she became bored and then had a few bites of popcorn. Morgan, who was restricted from sweets by his family, focused on the food rather than the toys and ate large amounts of the various offerings, despite his lack of hunger. Birch reiterates that restriction fosters consumption in the absence of hunger and that conversely, pressuring children to eat healthy food actually turns them off to those foods.[5]

This phenomenon — that children (and for that matter, all of us) want what they cannot have and don't want what they are pressured to eat — was again made very clear in the interesting example of a colleague's son who had some complications at birth. As a result of continued problems, he could process some types of foods but not others. His mother served carrots as snacks to his siblings and friends as a healthful snack, but raw vegetables upset his stomach. Instead, he was offered potato chips that he could easily digest. He lost interest in the chips very quickly but experienced deprivation regarding the carrots, which he could not have. This reversal of food interests illustrates the sensitivity of children to parental messages about what they "should" and "shouldn't" eat.

Children who are allowed to stay in charge of their eating may choose foods that do not conform to typical meal patterns. Yet they are driven by an attunement to their bodies' needs rather than by a reaction to external pushes and pressures. If your client can tolerate the anxiety she is likely to experience when she first lets go of parental control over her child's eating, she is likely to attain positive results, as illustrated in the following examples.

> Three-year-old Lily ate a brownie for lunch and then took a nap. When she woke up, she pointed to a can of stewed tomatoes in the pantry. Her mother warmed them for her and she consumed most of the can.

> Seven-year-old Andrew walked into his house after school to the smell of chocolate chip cookies baking in the oven. "Those smell good," Andrew said to his mother. "Can I have some cantaloupe?" Later in the evening, Andrew wanted a cookie. He ate one and started on a second, but after one bite announced that he was full.

> Susie had a recent food jag in which she wanted chocolate ice cream for breakfast. Although her mother sometimes felt a twinge of doubt as she served her this nonbreakfast food, she found that Susie preferred fruit and cereal for dinner. Susie's mother relaxed as she saw that her daughter ate many types of foods throughout the day and decided that the order in which she ate them was not important. Several months later, Susie's eating patterns changed once again as she tended to select eggs and toast for breakfast.

After collecting large bags of candy on Halloween, several demand-fed children poured out their treats and had fun trading with each other. They each had a couple of pieces of candy and then stored their bags in a special place. Although they may not have eaten less candy than some of their friends who were only allowed one or two candies per day, they did not eat large amounts. In fact, after several months, much of the trick or treat candy was thrown away because it became stale. There were never battles between parent and child over eating the Halloween candy, and candy was available in the home throughout the year.

Eleven-year-old Seth was frustrated because when a couple of his friends came to his house after school, they spent a lot of time eating rather than wanting to go outside to play. Seth noticed that Josh actually put some candy in his pocket before he went home.

The reality is that children are constantly exposed to all types of foods at school, camp, parties, and friends' homes, and all children will eat some high-fat, high-sugar foods. A child who is not restricted will eat as much as she needs for her body, knowing that she can have it again when she likes, or may even save it for later. A child who judges these foods as "bad" or restricted will eat them whenever she can because she does not know if and when she will be able to eat them again.

## Examples of Modeling Size Diversity

As we were writing this chapter, several of our children returned home from different overnight camp experiences. One child reported that when a fat child exhibited "annoying behaviors," other campers responded, "Go eat a cookie." This child identified the unfairness of this response and confronted his cabinmates by asking, "How would that make *you* feel?"

At another camp, two female cousins described a situation in which a counselor told the campers to sit three to a seat as they boarded a bus for a field trip. He then smirked and added in a belittling tone that Pat, a fat boy, would need his own seat. These teenage girls recognized the humiliation contained in these words and suggested to their parents that they contact the camp director. They also reported a different incident in which a counselor-in-training berated Pat for his weight and stated that he should stop eating so much. The girls proceeded to explain that body size is partly genetic and that it is what is on the inside that counts. As more and more children are raised in an atmosphere of attuned eating and size acceptance, their attitudes will help shape culture.

## The Larger Child

If a child is encouraged to eat in an attuned manner without the restrictions that lead to overeating or the use of food to solve emotional problems, she will grow into the weight she was meant to be. Assuming that she does not have any medical problems that need to be addressed, much of her size will be genetically determined. This can create a difficult situation for the child who is larger than the cultural norm, and she is likely to suffer some of the pain fostered by anti-fat attitudes in society. Yet parents can help her build a positive body image by not colluding with messages that she must lose weight to be happy. Instead, parents can work toward accepting her larger size and helping her confront the prejudices she is likely to face.

In order to help a fat child develop a positive body image, parents can take many steps. For example, they can:

- Make sure their child has attractive clothes that fit properly
- Encourage physical activity for pleasure rather than weight loss, especially by being active together as a family
- Stop criticizing their own bodies in front of their children
- Stop criticizing the bodies of friends, relatives, and public figures that are larger than the norm
- Stop praising friends, relatives, and public figures based on body size

- Stop engaging in diet talk in front of children
- Advocate for children if they are teased or treated poorly by teachers and other people in authority
- Teach children to speak up for themselves when teased by peers, and to understand that bullying behavior is unacceptable
- Provide positive examples of fat people who are successful and reading material that offers diversity in size
- Talk openly about feelings

As a therapist, you may work with one or both parents to examine how the family dynamics and attitudes contribute to a child's problems with food and weight. Or you may see the child as your client and help her develop a stance of attuned eating for herself and work on her body image. If you find that a child's eating behaviors are symptomatic of deeper family conflicts, you may treat the family system. As with your adult clients who eat compulsively, your stance that people naturally come in different shapes and sizes combined with a philosophy that deprivation leads to overeating will facilitate the prevention of eating problems for the children you come in contact with in your work.

## SCHOOL STAFF

You may also promote the prevention of eating problems for children and adolescents by providing education to school staff members. If you already work in a school setting, nurses, classroom teachers, and physical education teachers can benefit from your expertise. If you are not in a school setting, you may find that the counseling staff will also welcome your understanding of eating problems and body issues if these are areas in which they are not well versed.

In 1993, the National Educational Association conducted a study on the pervasiveness of size discrimination and human rights violations within school systems. The organization published its findings in "Report on Size Discrimination," which concluded that this problem exists at every level within these institutions. Large students experienced "ongoing prejudice, unnoticed discrimination and almost constant harassment," and teachers experienced "socially acceptable yet outrageous insensitivity and rudeness."[6]

Your task will depend on the attitudes you confront as you work within the school. You may find that a teacher treats a large student unfairly because of her ingrained bias against fat. Or you may learn that a large teacher continually feels inferior to her colleagues and needs to develop ways to empower herself. Problems may erupt between students as a child is teased because of her weight and harassed on a regular basis. All of these situations lend themselves to your expertise as you select the appropriate intervention based on the non-diet, size-acceptance paradigm.

One of the most important functions you can serve as a consultant to a school is to raise the consciousness of the staff about their impact on the attitudes and behaviors of children. For example, a therapist visited a school and discovered that an elementary-level teacher displayed a poster that taught kids to label feelings. Included in the picture was a child stating, "I feel fat." However, fat is not a feeling, but rather a description of size. This teaching tool promotes the cultural idea, albeit unintentionally, that the label of fat represents a host of affective states, while discouraging the exploration of the true feelings masked by the idea of "fat."

School nurses, operating as health professionals, may comment to a larger child about her eating habits or weight. There may be times when it is appropriate for a nurse to make a referral to another professional, such as a dietician or social worker, if she detects a specific issue. However, it is also important for the nurse not to assume that a larger child has an eating problem or underlying emotional issues. Conversely, she cannot assume that a thin or average-weight student is a healthy eater with no psychological problems. The key is to teach other health professionals to evaluate children based on a range of factors other than body weight.

Physical education programs have the potential to help children learn the joy and benefits of movement or to provide a negative, shameful experience. Traditionally, gym classes favor lean, athletic children who perform well and receive high marks for their abilities. The less athletically endowed child, especially if she is large, is subject to feeling humiliated and excluded from the activities offered. This experience is intensified by procedures such as weighing students and letting children choose who they want to be on their teams, which inevitability means that some student will be the last child picked. However, gym time at school, which is meant to encourage physical activity for health and pleasure, often has the reverse effect for the child who does not meet ideal standards.

Ironically, those children and teens that seem to be immune from these problems may also suffer consequences. For example, a therapist spoke with an eighth grade class about their experience of being weighed in gym. Many of the girls, despite their "normal" size, acknowledged either restricting their food intake or using vomiting, laxatives, diet pills, or excessive exercise prior to a scheduled weigh-in. The therapist learned that the gym teacher did not realize that some of his thinner, more athletic students suffered from eating disorders. In fact, she discovered that he often praised his star student, who was actually bulimic, and used her as a role model for the class because she typically stayed after school to run an additional 2 miles. After consulting with the therapist on several occasions, the gym teacher decided to stop weighing students and focus on each child reaching optimal fitness goals regardless of size.

A disturbing trend in gym classes across several states is the creation of a BMI report card that is sent home for all children. The stated purpose of these report cards is to alert parents that their children are "overweight" or "obese" so that they will intervene before the so-called problem worsens. Unfortunately, a single number is a poor indicator of the state of a child's health. For example, a child falling in the "normal" weight category of 18.5 to 24.9 may be vomiting every day or abusing diet drugs to keep her weight low. Another child with a BMI of 27, also falling into the "overweight" category may exercise regularly and eat a healthful diet but come from a family where a larger body type is inherited. Yet another child may be very muscular due to extensive sports activities and therefore fall into a higher BMI category, while another child may truly have a problem with binge eating. To make matters worse, larger children already suffer from external and internal pressures to become thinner. They, and their parents, already know they are fat. Eliciting greater shame as the school officially denounces their body sizes will lower self-esteem and confidence.

Receiving the BMI report card reinforces behaviors of teasing and competition among peers. For example, one of our children reported that when a larger boy at his middle school received the report card, other students repeatedly asked his number and then laughed. This is typical junior high school behavior that is not likely to stop even if children are told that this information is private.

Since there is no proven treatment to lose weight, what should these families do? Most likely, these children will be placed on diets, initiating the yo-yo diet cycle and resulting in higher than natural adult weights as well as disordered relationships with food. If the message that the school intends to give parents is that it is healthy for children to be physically active and eat a varied diet including fruits and vegetables, then this message should be applied to the entire student body, regardless of BMI.

In an attempt to maximize the positive benefits of physical activity, there is a movement within physical education departments to refocus on fitness, inclusiveness, and participation rather than a sports model that favors natural ability and often leaves the less athletic student with a negative experience. These changes range from creating smaller teams so that all students increase the amount of time they are active to grading based on fitness goals rather than athletic skill so that all children can succeed. According to Phil Lawler, director of the P.E. Institute 4 Life, the goal of this model is "physical education without humiliation and a focus on health and wellness."[7] It is also important for gym classes to offer fun and pleasurable activities that will facilitate the joy of movement.

In your role as a therapist, you can bring this philosophy to the attention of school staff who may be unaware of such programs that facilitate the positive aspects of physical activity for students of all sizes.

## SCHOOL PROGRAMS

Schools have a strong influence on the development of children's belief systems and attitudes. Increasingly, school social workers, psychologists, and other outside experts are presenting information on a variety of social issues including alcohol and drug use, violence, and sex education. As the number of students struggling with food and weight issues continues to rise, schools are implementing programs that have been developed for varying grade levels.

Any program that focuses on sounding the alarm on obesity and scare tactics that encourage caloric restriction for weight loss or that stress the need to be thin for health and happiness will foster the same destructive outcomes explored throughout this book. On the other hand, programs that emphasize attuned eating, health at any size, and body/self-acceptance contribute to the overall health and well-being of the students and the school environment.

You may choose to develop your own program or workshop or you may choose from one of the many curriculums available from various organizations and experts in the field. Depending on your role as therapist, you may have access to the classroom or offer these ideas to school staff. The following are examples of school programs used across the country to prevent eating disorders and poor body image among students and promote healthy and accepting attitudes toward food, their bodies, and each other.

### Elementary Schools

Early prevention programs are important in helping young children learn about nutrition, body acceptance, and positive body image. As reported in chapter 2, 42% of first- through third-grade girls want to be thinner and 51% of 9- and 10-year-old girls feel better about themselves if they are dieting.[8] Body dissatisfaction leads to dieting behavior, which is a significant precursor to the development of an eating disorder. In 1995, Eating Disorder Awareness and Prevention (EDAP), now part of NEDA, formed a partnership with an organization called Next Door Neighbors Puppets to develop The Prevention Puppet Program for early elementary school children. The project teaches young girls and boys about healthy eating, developing a positive body image, and the harmful effects of teasing someone because of their size. The puppets encourage kindness, promote a positive sense of self, and teach children to seek out friends and adults to talk with when they are feeling sad or troubled. These themes are demonstrated in stories that include specific references to eating and body image issues. Currently, there are fourteen puppet troops performing in schools in the United States and Canada. In 2001, The Prevention Puppet Program video and discussion guide were introduced and are available for use in the classroom.[9]

Kathy Kater, LICSW, specializes in the treatment of body image, disordered eating, and eating disorders. Responding to the need for prevention programs, Kater developed Healthy Body Image: Teaching Kids to Eat and Love their Bodies Too! for students in grades four through six. This program aids teachers in ways to empower students and promote healthy body images. Using a variety of stories and activities, students are offered ways to resist unhealthy and unrealistic cultural images while they are encouraged to develop an understanding of healthy eating and the dangers of dieting. In one sample lesson plan, students are invited to participate in a learning activity showing why dieting is both ineffective for long-term weight loss and counterproductive. The teacher takes the students through the predictable results when any of the five basic needs — sleep, water, warmth, air, and food — are not satisfied. Explaining to the children that these are strong needs that must be met if we are to live, the students become actively involved with the consequences of not having enough sleep. For example, students are asked to imagine that night after night they were allowed less and less sleep until finally they only slept about 3 hours per night. The teacher asks how they would feel, and the students respond that they would be cranky, unable to concentrate, and that, when given the opportunity to finally sleep, agree that they would sleep many extra hours to make up for all the nights of sleep deprivation. The same question is posed regarding inadequate liquids to satisfy thirst, with the same conclusion. In another example, the teacher puts the students on an "air diet" reading from a prepared script: "Actually, I think all of you could stand to go on a little 'air diet.' I think you have been breathing entirely too much, and your cheeks are just too rosy. You know the latest style is to have a bluish-gray tone to your skin, and oxygen is what gives your cheeks that rosy glow. I think you'd all be better looking if you cut back on your oxygen so your face will be more drab. Of course, you will need some air to live. But surely you could cut back. Won't it be worth it to have the "right look." Each student then receives a thin straw. Students plug their noses and breathe entirely through the straw. The teacher playfully tells those kids who drop out of the experiment that they must have no willpower! Eventually, the students are allowed to stop the experiment and observe themselves "gulping" air.[10] This experience of imposed deprivation and the inevitable consequences of that restriction flows into the physical need for food, and why diets are detrimental, interfering with a basic need for survival, and bringing with it a host of negative problems.

*Middle School Programs*

A program that teaches students in grades five through nine about fat prejudice and size bias was developed by the Council on Size and Weight Discrimination and led by Nancy Summer and Cathi Rodgveller, both leaders in the size-acceptance movement. The presentations are offered as 2- and 3-hour workshops called Kids Come in All Sizes. The workshop leaders emphasize that size discrimination must be placed in the context of other forms of discrimination, and encourages students to experience the personal and political benefit of fighting prejudice. What makes these workshops unique is that they are designed to be presented by two leaders; one being a teacher or school counselor, and the other being a school "visitor" who is a woman of size. Having a large person as presenter offers an example of the concepts presented and serves as a role model.[11]

Rebecca Manley, M.S., founder and president of the Massachusetts Eating Disorders Association (MEDA), developed a program for middle school girls called Body Confidence. This 10-week curriculum focuses on developing assertiveness, media literacy, self-acceptance, and an awareness of feelings. Manley has put her years of experience into an easy-to-follow curriculum titled Teaching Body Confidence that includes over 30 activities to be used with girls.[12] One sample lesson focusing on enhancing self-esteem is called The Self-Esteem Tree. The teacher invites the students to imagine themselves as a tree. They are asked to assign positive qualities to the trunk, root, branches, and leaves that describe themselves. Then the teacher asks the students to picture the following. "Every time you criticize yourself or put yourself down, you are knocking a branch off your self-esteem tree. What would happen if you continually gave yourself 'put-downs?' What happens to a tree that loses all its braches and roots?"[13] Along with prevention strategies, Teaching Body Confidence includes a video showing advertisements to introduce the concept of media literacy and an outline on "How to Organize a Parent's Night." Her nonprofit organization has also produced a Safe School Survey to assess whether the school is doing all it can to prevent eating disorders and encourage the health of all its members.[14]

Another program for girls in middle school is called "Full of Ourselves: Advancing Girl Power, Health, and Leadership," developed by Catherine Steiner-Adair in her position as director of education, prevention, and outreach at the Harvard Eating Disorders Center (a division of Harvard Medical School), along with Lisa Sjostrom, an educator who has coauthored innovative curricula for high schools. This program teaches seventh-grade girls media literacy and assertiveness skills.

Girls are encouraged to find and use their voices and become aware of the world around them. Conscious-raising issues such as the concept of "weightism" are explored as a social justice concern. Two female leaders in a series of 10 group sessions lead the program with topics such as the "Dieting Dilemma," "Claiming Our Strength," and "The Power of Positive Action." Group leaders are trained and encouraged to look at their own weight and body issues. The girls in the group are trained to serve as peer counselors to fourth-grade girls making their own lesson plans from an activity guide called "Throw Your Weight Around."[15]

Another pilot program from EDAP is GoGirls! for students in middle and high school. The name stands for Giving Our Girls Inspiration and Resources for Lasting Self-Esteem. The curriculum was developed to encourage teens to become media savvy and to use their voices to let advertisers know what is harmful for healthy development. Students in the program examine their own body images, learn about eating disorders and how to prevent them, and become aware of the strong relationship between media and body dissatisfaction, all as part of a marketing class. In the semester-long course, students are offered the chance to make presentations to executives at retail corporations, write letters to advertisers, participate in radio and television interviews, and create awareness campaigns for peers in local high schools.[16]

### High School Programs

Linda Omichinski, RD, has developed a program for students ages 12 to 17 called Teens and Diets: No Weigh. The curriculum focuses on encouraging teens to trust in themselves to make their own decisions on personal health, energy, and emotional needs. One example of an activity used in this program invites students to come to their own conclusions regarding dieting myths. Students are told that they are going to decide whether some common beliefs about diets are correct or incorrect. Ten colorful, plastic balls are each labeled with dieting statements. The teacher throws a ball and the student who catches it reads the statement aloud and then gives her opinion about the statement: right, wrong, and why. If a student is unsure how to respond, she can toss the ball to a classmate until someone responds with an explanation. The balls with false statements are tossed into a wastebasket. The statements include: "Diets make you happier and healthier," "Diets give you energy," "Diets make eating fun," "Diets never become eating disorders," "Diets are sexy," "Diets make you beautiful," "Diets improve your health," "Diets are exciting," "Diets are inexpensive," "Diets work."[17]

*College Programs*

While these programs address the needs of students from the elementary through high school level, focused attention at the university level is crucial. Eating disorders and disordered eating are rampant on college campuses. According to one study, 91% of women on a college campus had attempted to control their weight through dieting, and 22% dieted often or always.[18] As a therapist, you may already be working with college students dealing with a variety of emotional issues. If you suspect a client is struggling with compulsive eating or if she tells you that eating, diet, and weight concerns are problems for her, together you can explore what programs are offered at her college to serve as an additional support.

According to the president of the New York City-based American Anorexia Bulimia Association, Charles Murfosky, "Virtually every college has some kind of program, either a student-run group or treatment options through health services."[19] However, many programs focus predominately on anorexia nervosa and bulimia, with fewer supports for those struggling with compulsive eating. If this is the case, you may decide to meet with staff from an existing program and strategize ways to offer campus-based support for the many students struggling with compulsive eating and yo-yo dieting. Staff at student health centers and resident hall supervisors offer important networking opportunities to begin dialoging about expanding services for the many students who struggle with eating and weight issues along a continuum. If you are in the process of putting together your own group for compulsive eaters, college campuses are a great place to put up posters advertising help and support for those in need.

Educational institutions, from the elementary level through the college years, offer settings in which students learn to challenge and embrace lessons contributing to the formation of an identity and sense of self. To the extent that the atmosphere in the school is accepting and supporting, students have an opportunity to grow fully into their potential.

## Social Change

Therapists work in numerous settings to improve the lives of their clients. From the individual, to the community, to the national level, your skills and perspective have the potential to shape the ways in which people think about and develop their relationships with food and their bodies.

Although you may treat clients for many issues that do not directly affect you, eating and body image impact each and every one of us, without exception. As you move toward or embrace the non-diet approach and size diversity philosophy, consider your own power to bring about social change. Imagine throwing a pebble into a pond. Ripples form into concentric circles, each one branching out and affecting the next one. Think of yourself as that pebble, with the circles representing your personal life, professional life, community activities, the nation, and finally, the world. Actions that begin at the personal level may have far-reaching effects.

Depending on your interests, you can choose where you prefer to direct your energy. Perhaps you enjoy political activism and want to join an organization that seeks to prevent discrimination based on size. Perhaps you enjoy writing and will submit an article to your local paper. Perhaps you will start a group for clients struggling with compulsive eating using a non-diet approach. Or perhaps you will integrate the principles of this book into your own life and teach them to your children. The choice is yours. The impact is immeasurable.

## OURSELVES

Because the professional issues of eating and body image are personal ones as well, the ways in which you think about and act toward yourself, family members, friends, and colleagues is already the start of where this potential to shift ideas and attitudes begins. This concept was articulated by Mahatma Ghandi, who believed that we have to *be* the change we want to see in the world.

In her book *Making Peace with Food*, Susan Kano offers an inventory to assess whether your own behaviors support health and well-being instead of diet, food, and weight conflicts (see Appendix F, Assessing Your Size Attitudes). Statements such as "I encourage someone to pursue slenderness," "I say (or assume) that someone is 'doing well' because she has lost weight," or "I refer to 'good' and 'bad' food" can help you reflect on your own attitudes and consider ideas for change.[20]

### Diet Conversations

As mentioned in chapter 2, conversations about food and weight loss take place constantly in our personal lives as well as in staff lounges with colleagues. As you adopt a new stance toward food and weight, these discussions are likely to strike you as boring at best and destructive at worst. You will need to make decisions about how to handle these situations based on your comfort level with this paradigm and with the other people engaging in the diet talk. Like our clients who also confront this situation, you may choose to remain silent so that you do not actively support these behaviors, you may figure out a way to diplomatically leave the room, or you may choose to speak up about your perspective.

Of the utmost importance is to consider the idea that "connecting" through diet and body hatred is a female phenomenon that leaves women feeling negatively about themselves and each other and fosters competition. Finding new ways to connect with friends, family, and colleagues offers the possibility of richer and more satisfying conversations and relationships for our clients and ourselves. You can foster this positive shift through the ways in which you interact with those around you.

## OUR PROFESSION

The bulk of this book is devoted to treatment techniques that you can use with your clients individually, in groups, or within a family setting. In addition, you may decide to reach greater numbers of people through activities such as workshops, consultation, wellness programs, or the classroom.

Workshops may be offered through institutions including hospitals, mental health centers, community centers, religious organizations, school programs, women's health clinics, and corporate wellness offerings. You might present on topics such as why diets don't work, the principles of attuned eating, body image issues, or feeding children without control issues. You may offer a one-time session or a series of meetings to cover your topic. The use of visualizations, writing exercises, or videos can become the springboard for your workshop. Depending on the needs you identify in the population, as well as your own interests and skills, there are numerous effective and creative ways to communicate the various aspects of building a healthy relationship with food and one's body to your audience.

The setting in which you work may place you in a strong position to educate other professionals about the treatment of compulsive eating. For example, you may offer an in-service to other staff members, including doctors, psychiatrists, therapists, and dieticians, describing the non-diet approach. If you serve in a supervisory role, you can train other staff or interns about how to deal with eating problems. Earlier in the chapter, we suggested ways in which you can promote size diversity and healthful attitudes within schools. If you are in private practice, you may opt to meet one-on-one with other professionals to teach them about what you do and learn more about their philosophies. In addition to helping spread these concepts to other professionals, this activity will give you the opportunity to build your professional network.

If you are a professor or teacher in the field of mental health, you are in a unique position to educate future therapists about the problem and treatment of compulsive eating. These issues may also be addressed under the headings of disordered eating or binge eating disorder. As discussed in chapter 1, while the level of intensity can vary between a person who presents with compulsive eating problems compared to a client with binge eating disorder, each experiences the same dynamics and outcomes described throughout this book. While eating disorder courses often focus on bulimia and anorexia nervosa, adding a section on compulsive eating and the consequences of dieting can further students' professional growth and awareness. Courses on culture or diversity could also include a segment that addresses weightism as a significant form of oppression in our society. Training students to understand the causes, treatment, and social issues related to compulsive eating and body dissatisfaction ensures that future clients will receive the support and therapy they deserve. If you are interested in research, the non-diet and size-acceptance principles offer exciting areas for further study.

## OUR COMMUNITY

In addition to offering workshops through local organizations, you might consider teaching a course at a community college or other institution that offers programs or training in the field of mental health. You can contact local newspapers and magazines to learn if they would be interested in an article related to the topics of reconsidering diets and weight issues. You may also write a letter to the editor to dispute an article that promotes dieting or weight prejudice. If an organization exists in your community that promotes size diversity or attuned eating, you may display their brochures in your waiting room. Conversely, if services are missing in your community that you believe would benefit your clients, you may facilitate the development of these offerings. For example, one therapist worked with a local yoga studio to provide a class specifically for larger women.

## OUR NATION

The majority of us consider our therapeutic interventions to take place at a local level. However, as your awareness of national media and policies related to eating and size issues increases, you will find that many of these matters have a direct effect on your clients. As these national issues trickle down to you and your clients, they invariably affect the context in which you work with her toward change. In the section that follows we highlight some of the different topics at the national level that have implications for all of our lives in terms of attitudes and behavior related to eating and body image. In your roles as a professional and as a private citizen, you may become aware of ideas that will promote a more accepting culture; you may choose to become an advocate yourself.

### Media

Messages from the media, including magazine articles, commercials, and product ads, are pervasive sources of information in our country that frequently promote diets and thinness. You do not have to look far at the check-out line of your grocery store to notice front cover stories plastered on women's magazines offering the newest way to lose weight — often right next to a recipe for a double chocolate layer cake. Never mind that if any of these plans actually worked, they would not need to provide a new diet guaranteed to wash away pounds month after month. Even if we, or our clients, do not choose to buy these magazines, our psyche takes in the information that weight loss promises us the key to happiness, love, and success.

A major women's magazine contacted one of the authors about interviewing someone who had successfully worked with the non-diet approach. One of her clients relayed her story to the writer, who stated that this was exactly the scenario she had in mind. She then asked the client to submit a picture; the client was subsequently eliminated from the story. When the author expressed her concern to the journalist that her client's weight, which was larger than the accepted model size, was the main reason for her rejection, she received the following, honest reply: "I'm glad you asked that because you are absolutely right: even though editors pretend they are pro-size acceptance, I know darn well that what they want for this piece are a few slightly overweight women who have been made to feel that they are fat. I'm sure they'd reject extremely large women, so don't even bother to ask them. And they won't want anyone over age 45 either; they prefer women in their 20's and 30's because they're trying to get the age of our readership down for advertising purposes."[21]

It is not only the average woman whose picture may be rejected because she does not fit into the strict requirements for thinness. In a 2002 *New York Times* article, Kate Betts writes, "I owe Renee Zellweger an apology. Over a year ago, as the editor of a fashion magazine, I pulled her picture off the cover of an issue at the last minute, swapping it for a photo of a lanky swan in a whiff of Dior chiffon. The problem wasn't the usual one that kills covers. The lighting was impeccable. Her dress was a glamorous Galliano, and there was a lot of talk about her new movie, 'Bridget Jones's Diary' and a starring performance that would be hailed with an Oscar nomination. No, the problem was much more primal, born of one of the not-so-secret obsessions of the fashion world: she was too fat."[22]

In the September 2002 issue of *More* magazine, Jamie Lee Curtis decided to be photographed in a way that showed the true shape of her body, without the usual editing. She states, "There's a reality to the way I look without my clothes on. . . . I don't have great thighs. I have very big breasts and a soft, fatty little tummy. And I've got back fat. People assume that I'm walking around in the little spaghetti-strap dresses. It's insidious-Glam Jamie, the Perfect Jamie, the great figure, blah, blah, blah. And I don't want the unsuspecting forty-year-old women of the world to think that I've got it going on. It's such a fraud. And I'm the one perpetuating it."[23]

It is not only the photographs in the articles that send messages about thinness that increase the vulnerability of its readers. The content of the articles often contains information that promotes unrealistic, and often unhealthy, advice based on a fat-phobic stance in the guise of science. For example, an article reports, "There is some evidence that breastfeeding can speed up the weight loss process. The process of milk production actually requires 500 extra calories a day. Even after accounting for the calories that come from fat deposits that women build up during pregnancy, you can still create a 300-calorie daily deficit through breastfeeding. In 17 days you could lose one pound." On the same page, another note of advice reads, "Obviously, women must gain weight in order to carry a healthy child. Because of that, pregnancy can be a stumbling block for those who are trying to stay in shape." These insidious messages diminish the natural wonders of the female body with a one-dimensional attitude that prizes thinness over complex physical and emotional processes.

Scattered between these articles and photographs are the numerous ads that magazines depend on to stay afloat. Targeting women, these advertisements often promote thinness through diet products or use the promise of thinness as a way to sell products. For example, brands of cigarettes aimed at female consumers use words such as "ultra-slim" to increase the appeal of their products. Ads frequently display a glamorous, thin woman with the cigarette, indicating that smoking, thinness, and success are all interrelated. Not only is this ideal unachievable, but an unhealthy woman is what is being promoted.

Television commercials communicate similar types of messages. In a particularly offensive commercial, a diet program was promoted by playing on the tragedy of the September 11, 2001 terrorist attacks in New York City. The ad focused on a teacher in a classroom of children saying that if something like this ever happened again, she would now be able to rescue the students because of the weight loss from this particular product. Not only do we now need to be thin to fit in, but we need to be thin to be patriotic!

Jean Kilbourne, a nationally known writer and speaker, has devoted her career to examining the effect of advertisements on cultural image and has created several videotapes that increase people's awareness of how ads manipulate our point of view to feel inferior. Increasingly, people are banding together to voice both their approval and disapproval of particular ads. For example, an advertisement campaign put out by a major soft drink company featured an ultrathin girl meekly drinking the diet soda and announcing with pride that her nickname at school was "skeleton." A Boston consumer group called Boycott Anorexic Marketing (BAM) successfully protested the ad.

Programs such as The Media Watchdog created by the National Eating Disorder Association (NEDA) brings students, health professionals, parents, concerned consumers, and those struggling with eating disorders together in order to encourage advertisers and companies to promote healthy media messages about food and body image. Over 1,000 volunteer "watchdogs" are working with NEDA and its board of directors via the Internet to monitor advertisements that impact positively or negatively on body satisfaction. Watchdogs look to TV, radio, and magazines for positive or negative ads that merit attention of praise or protest. NEDA staff reviews the submissions and writes at least one letter of praise and/or protest each quarter. Watchdog members have the option of adding their names to the letter along with the NEDA staff and board of directors. In turn, these letters are posted on the Watchdog website. The NEDA staff work continuously with the advertisers they are protesting until they get a response regarding the strategies and messages used by the company. Since The Media Watchdog's inception in 1997, over 50% of the protested advertisements have been discontinued.[24]

The website offers ideas of what to look for in order to identify positive and negative ads. To evaluate positive ones, look for ads that:

—Display a variety of natural body shapes
—Attribute similar positive characteristics to heavy and thin people
—Incorporate images of people eating balanced meals, including desserts, to fuel one's body as part of a healthy lifestyle
—Include women in situations which imply equal social power and an understanding that women are more than objects of beauty

Here are some elements to watch for in offensive ads:

—Inclusion of an emaciated model or a model whose features have been computer enhanced
—Inclusion of a large person whose attributes or character are portrayed negatively
—Glamorization of people on diets, or ads that present people relying on food as a way to respond to stress, frustration or loneliness[25]

The Renfrew Center Foundation, a nonprofit organization working toward education, prevention, treatment, and research for eating disorders, has launched a campaign called Stick to a Healthy Body Image. This campaign applauds magazine articles and advertisements that feature healthy body images and protests those that send negative food and weight messages. This effort involves purchasing a roll of stickers that say either "This Promotes Eating Disorders!" or "This Promotes Healthy Body Image!" Consumers put the appropriate sticker on the article or ad and then mail it to the magazine editor. The goal is to take action and promote awareness that eating and body image problems are public health issues.[26]

## PUBLIC POLICY

Legislation and the direction of the national agenda also have significant power over our lives and the lives of our clients. These topics are worthy of noticing and often emerge as topics for group discussion as clients bring these issues into treatment.

## Civil Rights Legislation

Prejudice against fat people is a political issue. Commonly held myths and stereotypes are often used to justify discriminatory practices against people of size in a number of areas including employment, education, housing, access to quality medical care, and public accommodations. Along with these civil rights violations is the ongoing social stigma associated with being fat and the culturally sanctioned ridicule and harassment to which fat people are subjected.

Despite the pervasive size discrimination in our nation, there is little statutory protection for fat people. There are no federal laws that prohibit discrimination because of weight. Michigan is the only state with legislation making it illegal to discriminate on the basis of height and weight; this is known as the Elliot-Larsen Civil Rights Act. The District of Columbia Human Rights Law forbids discrimination on the basis of appearance, putting weight in this category, and in Santa Cruz, California, a local ordinance prohibits discrimination in employment, housing, and public accommodations on the basis of height and weight.

In 2000 San Francisco passed a law making it illegal to discriminate on the basis of height and weight, falling under legislation that already protected against discrimination on the basis of gender, ethnicity, age, and sexual orientation. Marilyn Wann, an activist and author of the book *Fat!So?*, noted that the push to include legal protection for fat people in the city's anti-bias laws was prompted in 1999 following a billboard advertisement from a health club chain that featured an alien who predicted, "When they come they will eat the fat ones first."[27] Organizations such as NAAFA and the Council on Size and Weight Discrimination continuously work at promoting legislation to ensure that the rights of people of size are protected.

## "Anti-Obesity" Campaigns

People who are in the position to influence public health policy naturally have an interest in promoting the health of all

Americans. Much of the focus, however, stems from a fear of fat that facilitates the idea that weight loss, at all costs, is necessary. Rather than publicizing anti-obesity campaigns, which further stigmatize fat people in our country, effort should be spent on activities that foster health and well-being, as suggested in chapter 8. In particular, time and energy could be redirected toward policy and practice that teaches the hazards of dieting, the benefits of sustained physical activity, the problems of eating disorders, the connection between smoking and the pursuit of thinness for young women, the connection between poverty and weight, and the importance of eating a variety of foods in accordance with one's hunger.

## Work Incentives

A trend in work settings across the country is to offer weight loss contests and weigh-ins, with "winners" receiving rewards ranging from cash to additional time off. These businesses hope to offset expenses, which they attribute to obesity, including health insurance costs and missed days of work. Unfortunately, this institutionalization of dieting behavior carries all of the consequences discussed throughout this book, such as increasing overeating in the long run, lowering self-esteem when pounds return, and promoting weight cycling, which increases the risk of medical problems.

Perhaps even more insidious in these policies is the promotion of competition in the workplace based on body size. Due to genetic factors, not everyone can achieve a particular weight. Due to emotional factors, some employees may not be in the position to end their overeating. How will an employee feel when she commits herself to following the contest or incentive offered through the workplace, only to fail for reasons beyond her control? How will coworkers judge each other, as they are encouraged to go to all sorts of lengths to become thin for the sake of the office?

Understandably, companies have an investment in the wellness of their employees, which, in the best of circumstances, proves to be mutually beneficial. Rather than focusing on weight loss, the workplace can become a setting where employees can learn and integrate behaviors known to promote health at every size. For example, exercise programs focusing on fitness instead of weight loss offer an important resource to employees, especially if they are on the premises with time given to make use of these facilities. Lectures about the concepts of attuned eating, in addition to nutritional information, give workers invaluable skills with which to take charge of their relationships with food. Stress reduction techniques, such as teaching meditation, help employees learn lifelong strategies that will improve their overall health. Employee Assistance Programs with counselors who are trained in the treatment of compulsive eating can provide workers with a means to examine psychological issues that may be connected to overeating. In their book *The Spirit and Science of Holistic Health*, Jon Robison and Karen Carrier, experts in health promotion, suggest more productive strategies for companies that seek to improve the health of its employees.[28]

*Food Taxes*

An interesting debate is currently raging related to the responsibility of food manufacturers in contributing to the increasing size of Americans. Some policy makers are proposing that a "junk food" tax be charged on certain high-sugar, high-fat foods for consumers purchasing these products at grocery stores. Others have sought to hold food makers and fast food chains accountable in a court of law. At the center of this controversy is the question as to who is ultimately responsible for the harmful effects a product can cause, similar to the way that cigarette companies are now punished for the damaging effects of nicotine.

We take the stance that if a particular product is known to have dangerous effects for the entire population, regardless of body size, that product should be eliminated or carry warning labels. An example of this issue regards trans-fats, which are a by-product of turning cooking oils into room temperature solids, and which appear to be linked to disease.

Trans-fats can be found in items such as the oil used to cook French fries, certain cookies, and, most abundantly, in margarine; ironically, margarine has been promoted for decades as a healthy substitute for butter. Even though trans-fats are found in foods high in fat, the issue is not one of targeting people to lose weight, but rather a legitimate concern about a substance.

"Junk food taxes," on the other hand, seek to control people's eating behavior by adding costs to specific foods. These policies are fueled by a fear of fat. While proponents of these taxes may claim that the food content can contribute to disease, eating a Twinkie or potato chip does not, in and of itself, lead to medical problems. Furthermore, many items on the market are known to have possible negative consequences, yet they are not taxed for their possible misuse or required to fund the treatment for people who suffer consequences. The over-the-counter diet products described in chapter 8 are such examples.

The major issue to consider as a therapist interested in helping clients end compulsive eating is that junk food taxes imply that there are "good" and "bad" foods. For the client who is legalizing foods, being penalized for choosing a food high in sugar or fat reinforces her sense of deprivation and may actually trigger overeating. As she judges herself and her food options negatively, she punishes herself through her internalized yelling, and these self-recriminations are now concretized by government policy.

An article appearing in *The New Yorker*, which considers American's reliance on fast food, uses Leann Birch's research to understand the dilemma. "Because children on restricted diets had been told that junk food was bad for them, they clearly thought that it had to taste good. When it comes to junk food, we seem to follow an implicit script that powerfully biases the way we feel about food. We like fries not in spite of the fact that they're unhealthy but because of it."[29] People tend to want what they cannot have, not because they are bad or undisciplined, but because this is human nature. In the attempt to get Americans to eat healthier food, the possibility exists that we will create a nation of people increasingly driven toward the very products they are meant to avoid.

## A New Direction

While rethinking our own attitudes toward health, as well as our nation's, it is worthwhile to consider the national policy of our neighbor, Canada.

> Health Canada promotes healthy eating, active living and positive self and body image through the nation-wide Vitality program. Vitality challenges the idealized image of bodies as acceptable only if they're thin. It tells us to relax and enjoy life. The Vitality approach calls for a shift from negative to positive thinking: from restrictive eating to taking pleasure in eating a variety of foods; from exercise to burn calories to being active your way, every day; from obsession and preoccupation with weight to accepting and recognizing that healthy bodies come in a range of weights, shapes, and sizes. It assures us that health and well-being are linked to self-esteem and positive body image. People who feel good about themselves and their bodies are more likely to live healthy and happy lives. Vitality urges social acceptance of a wider range of healthy weight and body sizes. It says that overweight and thin need to be viewed not as opposites but as points on a continuum without value judgments at either end. People who are healthy and accept themselves on their own terms are in a stronger position to withstand the oppressive thinness message.[30]

In recommending policy for our nation, Jeanine Cogan, a social psychologist who wrote the findings for the Eating Disorders Information and Education Act of 1997, suggests the following changes:

Recognizing and addressing the health threat imposed by the thinness pursuit and eating disorders
Promoting weight stability rather than weight loss
Ensuring that the conclusions of federal agencies are neutral rather than serving special interest groups

Protecting the consumer from harmful diet programs and
drugs
Providing public education campaigns emphasizing physical and psychological health rather than body weight[31]

## OUR WORLD

There are many reasons to celebrate the culture in which we
live. However, it is necessary to reflect on where, as a nation,
our weaknesses lie so that we can develop alternative ways
to foster positive growth. While our own citizens and people
abroad have found pleasure in many aspects of our Western
lifestyle, we have also exported to many parts of the world a
pervasive sense of body dissatisfaction that goes along with
our relentless pursuit of extreme thinness. Eating disorders
now affect people of every nation except for developing countries where food is scarce. It is our obligation to ourselves and
our neighbors, both near and far, to promote body acceptance
and model non-diet behavior.

The familiar notion to "think globally and act locally"
applies to this process of making peace with food and our
bodies. To be at peace with oneself allows for being at peace
with others. As each individual makes the decision to act
locally, starting with her own practice of body acceptance,
she will bring that openness to those in her life, which, like
the concentric ripples of the pond, will continue to spread
outward. As she begins to trust and respond to her physical
hunger, she will be locally refueling her body, mind, and spirit,
and the fullness of that energy will be felt by others.

There are already waves of change as people begin to
share new ways of being with themselves and the world
in which they live. There are books for young children that
promote size acceptance and a positive sense of self-esteem.
*I Like Me!* by Nancy Carlson uses a pink pig that celebrates herself in her wholeness, whether she has moments of success or
failure. Standing in front of the mirror in the morning when she
wakes up she says, "Hi, good-looking!" She enjoys the curl of

her tail, finds pleasure in her ample belly, and admires her small feet."[32]

We need to send our children out into the world knowing that they are loved in the fullness of who they are and not by the number on a scale. Maya Angelou writes of this acceptance in her poem, *Phenomenal Woman*. One version of this work pairs her beautiful lyrics to the paintings by the French post-impressionist painter Paul Gauguin. The poem begins, "Pretty women wonder where my secret lies. I'm not cute or built to suit a fashion model's size."[33] The paintings depict women of strength and power who emit rays of joy and mystery.

It is through these personal revelations and in the embracing of the self that each individual has the power to "act globally" by the revolution that they create within. The power of these actions feeds the momentum to effect positive change for the benefit of others. There are many opportunities in our everyday life to take a stand. It might be through the act of ordering exactly what you are hungry for at a restaurant without any apology, or stocking your home with the foods you love. You may find opportunities in your professional life as well. Living your own life fully flows naturally into living life to the fullest. New energy and ideas manifest themselves in a variety of ways that benefit others. Living your passion and your truth opens doors for others as well as for yourself. Embracing the attitude that we all deserve to be happy and enjoy life today rather than putting our lives on hold until some magic weight is reached is quite profound.

Increasingly, people are working in a variety of settings to promote this message. For example, in her position as editor for the teen magazine *YM*, Christine Kelly made a difference. In 2002, she announced that she would no longer run articles on dieting and would include large size models in her magazine. Kelly stated, "We thought it was really important to take a stand."[34] Jody Abrams, activism chairwoman for NAAFA and a social worker, entered the new market of size-friendly retail stores. In 1999 she opened a clothing boutique called Bodacious Babes, explaining that the goal is to promote body diversity and size acceptance. Mary Evans Young established International

No Diet Day in 1992. Having recovered from her own eating disorder and wanting to prevent dieting behavior and promote size acceptance, this British woman began a yearly campaign that has been celebrated in Australia, Canada, England, Germany, New Zealand, Norway, Russia, South Africa, and across the United States, among other locations around the world. In all of these instances, personal conviction led to opportunity for promoting change.

The movement toward size-friendly services and environments has even reached the travel industry. In Mexico, a resort south of Cancun caters to people of size. The Freedom Paradise Resort offers a vacation spot to people afraid to go to the beach for fear of ridicule. From beach chairs to accommodate girth to a trained staff that understands the prejudice to which fat people are subjected, this setting invites people to live their motto: "Live Large, Live Free!"

These are but a few of the ways that people are working toward healing the scars of body hatred and discrimination. Through connection to ourselves and each other, the sweeping tide cannot help but carry us across the oceans to a shore of hope and acceptance. Through your expertise as a therapist, combined with the knowledge and tools of the non-diet paradigm, your potential to help clients end their compulsive eating is immense.

## A Look toward the Future

As several members of a group contemplated their newly found freedom from compulsive eating, a client wondered out loud why people were not flocking to the non-diet approach of ending overeating. A conversation ensued in which these women discussed the power of the diet industry, the difficulty people experience in giving up weight loss as an overriding goal, especially because of the magic promised by becoming thin, and the fact that this method of making peace with food is a complicated process addressing so many different levels of one's life. There was consensus among participants that they needed the support of the group to understand and integrate the varying aspects of the approach, and each stated that although they were aware of the non-diet concepts for some time, they had to be "ready" to embark on this journey. All were grateful for the calmness they now experienced around food, the stronger connection they had to their bodies, and the emotional doors that opened for them as they looked to themselves, rather than food, to face life's challenges.

As you work in the area of compulsive eating, we hope you will experience the excitement that occurs when your clients discover a freedom from food that they never dreamed was possible. As your clients become empowered, you will achieve professional satisfaction in knowing that you contributed to the end of dieting behavior and negative body image, and instead helped them build a healthy relationship with food and their bodies.

At the same time, you may encounter strong resistance from some clients, colleagues, professionals, family, and friends who view you as irresponsible, or even irrational, as you try to implement a non-diet, size-accepting approach. Although you have the tools to understand the intensity of their reactions, it can be difficult to stand alone at times, and therefore networking with others who share your point of view is very important.

Although we have presented a clinical intervention for the treatment of compulsive eating, this approach requires change in the culture every step of the way. Being a change agent carries its consequences, as elaborated by the German philosopher Schopenhauer who elucidated the following process: "All truth passes through three stages. First it is ridiculed. Second it is violently opposed. Third it is accepted as being self-evident."[35]

The moment when an idea, trend, or social behavior crosses a threshold, tips, and spreads throughout society has been labeled as the "tipping point." It is through our professional knowledge and personal energies that each and every one of us can contribute to that moment when attuned eating and size diversity find their place as accepted and desirable norms and behaviors in our culture.

*If this book has touched your professional and/or personal life, please consider recommending it to someone you know so that it can become part of the tipping point.*

# ENDNOTES

1. Author Unknown. The young man and the star fish. [Online]. Ask Alana. Available: www.askalana.com/stirues/starfish.shtml [2003, June 20].
2. Waterhouse, D. (1997). *Like mother, like daughter: How women are influenced by their mothers' relationship with food — and how to break the pattern.* New York: Hyperion, 1997, pp. 19–20.
3. Hirschmann, J., & Zaphiropoulos, L. (1993). *Preventing childhood eating problems.* Carlsbad: Gurze Books, p. 5.
4. Sattler, E. (1987). *How to get your kid to eat — but not so much.* Palo Alto, CA: Bull Publishing Co.
5. (2001, May 1). Scientific American Frontiers: Fat and Happy. *PBS.*
6. National Education Association Board of Directors. (1994, October 7). Report on Size Discrimination. [Online]. Lectric Law Library's Stacks. Available: http://www.lectlaw.com/files/con28.htm [2003, January 20].
7. Lawler, P. (2003, August 7). Personal interview.
8. The prevention puppet program. [Online]. (2002). The National Eating Disorders Association. Available: http://www.nationaleatingdisorders.org/p.asp?WebPage_ID=301 [2003, June 5].
9. The prevention puppet program. [Online]. (2002). The National Eating Disorders Association. Available: http://www.nationaleatingdisorders.org/p.asp?WebPage_ID=301 [2003, June 5].
10. Kater, K. Healthy body image: Teaching kids to eat and love their bodies too! [Online]. The National Eating Disorders Association. Available: http://www.nationaleatingdisorders.org/p.asp?WebPage_ID=302 [2003, June 5].
11. Summer, N., & Rodgveller, C. (1996, November/December). "Kids come in all sizes" workshops. *Healthy Weight Journal, 10* (6), 112.
12. Manley, R. (2001). *Teaching body confidence: A comprehensive curriculum for girls.* Newton, MA: MEDA, Inc.
13. Manley, R. (2001). *Teaching body confidence: A comprehensive curriculum for girls.* Newton, MA: MEDA, Inc. A14.
14. Safe school survey: Do you have a safe school environment? [Online]. (2003). Massachusetts Eating Disorder Association. Available: http://www.medainc.org/promotingasafeschool.htm [2003, August 4].
15. Giedrys, S. A. (1999, February 11). Creating a curriculum to help girls battle eating disorders. [Online]. *The Harvard University Gazette.*

Available: http://www.news.harvard.edu/gazette/1999/02.11/eating.html [2003, July 17].

16. What is go girls? [Online]. (1998). Eating Disorder & Prevention Awareness. Available: http://www.goldinc.com/gogirls/summary.htm [2003, August 12].

17. Omichinski, L. Teens & diets: No weigh. [Online]. HUGS for Better Health. Available: http://www.hugs.com/01facilitator/corp/teenanddiet-noweigh.htm [2003, July 15].

18. James, E. P. (2000, Fall). Eating disorders on campus. [Online]. *News Outreach Making Life Better.* Available: http://www.outreach.psu.edu/News/Magazine/Vol_3.1/eating.html [2003, August 4].

19. Hubbard, K., O'Neill, A., and Cheakalos, C. (1999). Out of control. *People Weekly, 51,* 53.

20. Kano, S. (1989). *Making peace with food.* New York: Harper & Row, pp. 222–223.

21. Anonymous. (2001, March 4). Personal communication.

22. Betts, K. (2002, March 31). The tyranny of skinny, fashion's insider secret. *The New York Times,* sec. 9, p. 1.

23. Wallace, A. (2002, September). Jamie Lee Curtis: True thighs. *More Magazine,* 92.

24. Media watchdog program. [Online]. (2002). National Eating Disorders Association. Available: http://www.nationaleatingdisorders.org/p.asp?WebPage_ID=300 [2003, June 5].

25. Media watchdog program. [Online]. (2002). National Eating Disorders Association. Available: http://www.nationaleatingdisorders.org/p.asp?WebPage_ID=300 [2003, June 5].

26. Stick to supporting healthy body image: The Renfrew sticker campaign. [Online]. The Renfrew Center Foundation. Available: http://www.renfrew.org [2003, August 2].

27. Quinn, A. (2003). A weighty victory. [Online]. Available: http://www.stanfordalumni.org/news/magazine/2003/julaug/features/wann.html.

28. Robison, J., & Carrier, K. (In press). *The science and spirit of holistic medicine.* Bloomington, IN: 1st Books Library.

29. Gladwell, M. (2001, March 5). The trouble with fries. *The New Yorker,* p. 57.

30. Berg, F. Vitality, Health Canada. [Online]. The Healthy Weight Network. Available: http://www.healthyweightnetwork.com/assoc.htm [2003, July 15].

31. Cogan, J. C. (1999). A new national health agenda: Providing the public with accurate information. *Journal of Social Issues, 55* (2), 384.

32. Carlson, N. (1990). *I like me.* New York: Puffin Books.

33. Angelou, M. (2000). *Phenomenal woman.* New York: Random House.

34. Kelly, C. (2002, April). Editor's page. *YM,* 42.

35. Schopenhauer, A. (2002). [Online]. Quotable Quotes. Available: http://www.quotablequotes.net [2003, August 12].

# FOOD HOUSE FANTASY

This visualization can be used with clients who are trying to determine what types of foods to bring into their homes. Instruct them to sit in a comfortable position, close their eyes, and take several deep breaths. Then, read as follows:

> Imagine yourself alone in a beautiful meadow filled with wildflowers and the sound of birds singing. The sun warms your skin, and you are struck by the beauty of all that surrounds you. You see a path leading from the meadow into a wooded area and you decide to follow it. The woods are damp, plush, and green, redolent of pine. The path narrows, but you continue to follow it. Up ahead, in a clearing lit by streaks of sunlight, you see a house. As you approach, you notice a sign over the front door. On the sign is your name and the words FOOD HOUSE.
>
> You open the front door and walk in. Inside you find a house filled with all the food you have ever wanted. You feel the accumulation of years of tension leave your body as you realize that you have found a treasure. Look around. Take your time. You have as long as you need.

When you decide to leave, remember that you can return whenever you want. You know where this house is. You know how to find it. Now, go to the meadow and rest for a while. Then open your eyes.[1]

Use the results of this visualization to help your client explore her needs at this time:

- A client who sees her food house as a gingerbread house may be ready to bring in sweets as part of her process of legalizing foods.
- A client who sees her food house empty may not be ready to bring in "illegal" foods.
- A client who sees her house full of foods from her childhood may want to prepare these foods for herself in the present.
- A client who sees her food on beautiful dishes in a well-organized kitchen may need to rearrange her own kitchen.
- A client who sees foods that she does not typically buy for herself, such as steaks, seafood, cakes, candy, fresh fruits, casseroles, or vegetables, may consider experimenting with these items.
- A client who feels calm as she looks around her food house may feel reassured that she is ready to surround herself with food.

# ENDNOTE

1.  Hirschmann, J., & Munter, C. (1995). When women stop hating their bodies. New York: Fawcett Columbine, pp. 144–145.

# BUILDING A POSITIVE BODY IMAGE

In our culture, women typically focus on the negative aspects of their body images. This exercise offers adjectives to help your clients describe their perceptions of their bodies.

Ask your clients to circle all of the words that describe their bodies. As they reflect on their choices, they may be surprised to realize that all of the words offered have positive connotations.

| | | |
|---|---|---|
| healthy | graceful | agile |
| strong | dependable | soft |
| flexible | poised | cuddly |
| coordinated | balanced | sensual |
| quick | muscular | fit |
| curvaceous | playful | mobile |
| commanding | capable | sexy |

(From *Outsmarting the midlife fat cell* by Debra Waterhouse, p. 89. Copyright 1998. Reprinted with permission from Hyperion Books New York, NY.)

# 6-WEEK GROUP

The following outline can serve as the basis for a 6-week group to teach the basic tenets of the non-diet philosophy. All of the topics draw from the concepts presented in this book. For specific exercises, page numbers are given.

## Week 1

A. Introduction
   1. Your background
   2. Brief summary of the causes of overeating
      a. Deprivation
      b. Use of food to manage feelings
B. Why Diets Don't Work
   1. Feast or famine
   2. The diet–binge cycle
   3. Concept of using attuned eating, rather than dieting, to determine when, what, and how much to eat
   4. Concept of weight loss as possible "side effect" rather than goal

C. Identifying Stomach Hunger
 1. Stomach hunger versus mouth hunger
 2. The Hunger Scale (p. 83)
 3. Participants' examples of knowing when they are physically hungry
D. Introduction to the concepts of legalizing and stocking

## Week 2

A. Check-In
 1. Participants' experiences with physiological/stomach hunger
 2. Participants' reactions to the concepts of legalizing and stocking
B. Legalizing and Stocking (continued)
 1. How to get started
 2. The pitfalls of stocking
C. Moving toward Body Acceptance: Guidelines
 1. Closets
 2. Scales
 3. Mirrors

## Week 3

A. Check-In
 1. Participants' experiences with physiological/stomach hunger
 2. Participants' experiences/concerns with legalizing and stocking
 3. Participants' experiences with body acceptance guidelines
B. Making the Match
 1. Ways to identify what food will satisfy hunger
 2. Participants' examples of knowing what they are hungry for
C. The Food Bag
 1. Why it is important
 2. What to put in it
D. Living in the Present: Challenging the Magic of Thinness

# Week 4

A. Check-In
  1. Participants' experiences with physiological/stomach hunger
  2. Participants' experiences with making the match
  3. Participants' experiences with legalizing and stocking
  4. Participants' experiences with body acceptance guidelines
B. Identifying Fullness
C. Handling Emotional/Mouth Hunger
  1. Explanation of the translation of the language of feelings into the language of food and fat
  2. How to end the yelling and develop a compassionate response

# Week 5

A. Check-In
  1. Participants' experiences with physiological/stomach hunger
  2. Participants' experiences with making the match
  3. Participants' experiences with fullness
  4. Participants' experiences with legalizing and stocking
  5. Participants experiences responding to emotional/mouth hunger
  6. Participants experiences with body acceptance guidelines
B. Decoding Negative Body Thoughts
  1. Hirschmann and Munter's four steps (p. 215)
  2. Examples of participants' negative body thoughts
     a. Consider a more compassionate attitude
     b. Decode the negative body thought

# Week 6

A. Check-In
  1. Participants' overall experiences with what is going well
  2. Participants' concerns and obstacles with any of the guidelines

B. Where Do I Go from Here?
1. Present information regarding ongoing support
2. Discuss this approach as a process rather than a set of rigid rules
3. Explain expectations regarding weight loss (use visualization regarding ambivalence toward weight loss, p. 234)
4. Reiterate the importance of ending deprivation and building attuned eating before exploring any emotional factors

# FEEDING OUR CHILDREN

Here are some dos and don'ts to encourage healthy eating patterns and body images for children. This handout is useful when speaking with parents.

## DO:

- Trust your child to listen to his or her own internal cues about eating
- Encourage your child to eat in response to physical hunger
- Provide a wide variety of all types of food to your child
- Allow your child to stop eating when he or she reports fullness
- Teach your child to love his or her body at any size and shape
- Facilitate physical activity for pleasure
- Help your child find ways to deal with feelings or boredom other than by reaching for food

## DON'T:

- Use food as a reward
- Coax you child to eat foods he or she does not want
- Make any foods forbidden, such as sweets
- Restrict the amount of food your child eats
- Criticize your child's body size
- Speak negatively about your own body
- Promote dieting behavior

# SAMPLE LETTER

Dear Dr. _____,

I wanted to write you a letter before we meet at my first scheduled appointment. In the past, my experiences with the medical establishment have been, for the most part, painfully difficult. I wanted to let you know my thoughts on how the doctor/patient relationship can be improved.

First, I want you to know that I am fat. I say this without apology. For most of my childhood, and all of my adult life, I have struggled to lose weight. I have been encouraged to do this by doctors, family members, and friends. I have tried more diets than I care to count, and have been prescribed diet pills and liquid fasts in the past. While I lost weight on all of these programs and regimens, I, like most people, have regained the weight each time. In fact, I firmly believe I have dieted my way up to my present size. My conclusion is that diets don't work. The fact that the majority of people who lose weight on a diet regain the pounds adds to my conviction. From what I understand of the research, this type of yo-yo dieting creates a host of medical issues, and I am better off keeping a steady weight than cycling up and down. If I am to be your patient, I ask you to respect my decision not to diet. For my part, I vow to treat my body with care, and to work toward health and fitness regardless of my body size.

Second, if I have a particular health concern, I don't want my size offered as the problem and weight loss as the solution. Please don't dismiss me, but tell me about other ways I might improve my condition even if my weight stays the same. If I come in with a sinus infection or a broken thumb, there is no reason to weigh me or discuss my size. If a health concern *is* related to my weight, as partners, we can strategize non-diet behaviors that can improve the quality of my health.

Third, I want you to see me as a person worthy of respect and not be treated as a moral failure. I have been subjected to humiliation in this culture because my body size differs from the exalted ideal. Bodies come in different shapes and sizes and are due, in large part, to genetics. I come from a family with many fat people through the generations, including my parents. The fact that I have gained weight beyond my natural full size body type is due, in large part, to the years of yo-yo dieting that cycled my weight upward. I am not lazy, immoral, or psychologically unstable, as many have stereotypically concluded, just because I am fat. So please, when you meet me, see me in my fullness and in my wholeness, and I promise I will do the same for you. Working together as partners, with open, honest communication and mutual respect, I will do all I can to contribute to my good health, with your expertise guiding the way. If you have any questions or concerns before we meet, please call me.

I look forward to meeting and working with you.

Sincerely,

Terri

# ASSESSING YOUR SIZE ATTITUDES

This behavior assessment can be used to evaluate your support for the health and well-being of large people. Use the following scale to indicate the frequency of each behavior.

1=never        2=rarely        3=occasionally
4=frequently   5=daily

## How Often Do You:

### NEVER–DAILY

1. Make negative comments about your fatness    1 2 3 4 5

2. Make negative comments about someone
   else's fatness                              1 2 3 4 5

3. Directly or indirectly support the
   assumption that no one should be fat         1 2 3 4 5

4. Disapprove of fatness (in general)           1 2 3 4 5

5. Say or assume that someone is "looking
   good" because s/he has lost weight           1 2 3 4 5

*Assessing Your Size Attitudes* 377

6. Say something that presumes that a fat
   person(s) wants to lose weight          1 2 3 4 5

7. Say something that presumes that fat
   people should lose weight               1 2 3 4 5

8. Say something that presumes that fat
   people eat too much                     1 2 3 4 5

9. Admire or approve of someone for
   losing weight                           1 2 3 4 5

10. Disapprove of someone for gaining weight   1 2 3 4 5

11. Assume that something is wrong when
    someone gains weight                   1 2 3 4 5

12. Admire weight loss                     1 2 3 4 5

13. Admire rigidly controlled eating       1 2 3 4 5

14. Admire compulsive or excessive exercising   1 2 3 4 5

15. Tease or admonish someone about their
    eating (habits/choices)                1 2 3 4 5

16. Criticize someone's eating to a third person
    ("so-and-so eats way too much junk")   1 2 3 4 5

17. Discuss food in terms of "good/bad"    1 2 3 4 5

18. Talk about "being good" and "being bad" in
    reference to eating behavior           1 2 3 4 5

19. Talk about calories (in the usual dieter's
    fashion)                               1 2 3 4 5

20. Say something that presumes being thin is
    better (or more attractive) than being fat   1 2 3 4 5

21. Comment that you don't wear a certain style
    because "it makes you look fat"        1 2 3 4 5

22. Comment that you love certain clothing
    because "it makes you look thin"       1 2 3 4 5

23. Say something that presumes that fatness
    is unattractive                        1 2 3 4 5

24. Participate in a "fat joke" by telling one or
    laughing/smiling at one                1 2 3 4 5

25. Support the diet industry by buying their
    services and/or products               1 2 3 4 5

26. Undereat and/or exercise obsessively to
    maintain an unnaturally low weight        1 2 3 4 5

27. Say something that presumes being fat is
    unhealthy                                 1 2 3 4 5

28. Say something that presumes that being
    thin is healthy                           1 2 3 4 5

29. Encourage someone to let go of guilt      1 2 3 4 5

30. Encourage or admire self-acceptance and
    self-appreciation/love                    1 2 3 4 5

31. Encourage someone to feel good about
    his/her body as is                        1 2 3 4 5

32. Openly admire a fat person's appearance   1 2 3 4 5

33. Openly admire a fat person's character,
    personality, or actions                   1 2 3 4 5

34. Oppose/challenge fattism verbally         1 2 3 4 5

35. Oppose/challenge fattism in writing       1 2 3 4 5

36. Challenge or voice disapproval of a
    "fat joke"                                1 2 3 4 5

37. Challenge myths about fatness and eating  1 2 3 4 5

38. Compliment ideas, behavior, character, etc.
    more often than appearance                1 2 3 4 5

39. Support organizations that advance fat
    acceptance (with your time or money)      1 2 3 4 5

Behaviors 1 to 28 are unhelpful or harmful; look over areas that need improvement and strive to avoid these and similar behaviors in the future. Behaviors 29 to 38 help and support size acceptance; re-read items you marked "never" (1) or rarely (2); make a list of realistic goals for increasing supportive behavior.

(Excerpt from *Making Peace with Food* by Susan Kano. Copyright© 1989 by Susan Kano. Reprinted by permission of HarperCollins Publishers Inc., New York, NY.)

# WEIGHT LOSS MYTHS

This list of myths, facts, and positive steps can be used at workshops for adolescents or adults.

1) *Myth*: Dieting is a good way for me to lose weight.

*Fact*: 95 to 98% of people who go on a diet gain back all the weight they lose *plus more*, according to a National Institute of Health study. If you talk to someone you know who is a long-term dieter, chances are they will tell you that they weigh more now than before they started dieting.

*Positive Step*: The key to a healthy relationship with food is to eat when you are hungry, eat exactly what you are hungry for, and stop when you are satisfied. When you eat in this way, your body will stabilize at its natural weight.

2) *Myth*: I can stop my body from adding fat cells by eating less.

*Fact*: Around puberty, girls will find that their bodies develop fat around their hips, thighs, and buttocks. *This is supposed to happen*, even though there is much pressure in our culture to stay thin. When you try to stop this process by restricting your food intake, especially during adolescence, your body is programmed to think that you will not be prepared for child-bearing years. As a result, you will have a physiological response in which you will produce *more* fat cells and *larger* fat cells that will be with you for life.

*Positive Step*: Accept the fact that your body will naturally change throughout your life cycle. Celebrate the health and capacities of your body rather than trying to attain cultural ideals that are unrealistic.

3) *Myth*: I should only eat healthy foods.

*Fact*: Although it is important to include healthy foods in your diet, we all like a variety of foods and we live in a society where food is abundant. When you tell yourself you can't have a certain food, such as a cookie, you feel a sense of deprivation. Eventually, you will rebel against the deprivation and eat more cookies than your body needs. While you may feel out of control, *this is a normal reaction to restricting foods.*

*Positive Step*: Keep all foods "legal." When you eat a wide variety of foods in response to physiological hunger, your diet will be nutritionally balanced. Everyone likes to eat all types of foods, and allowing yourself to do so will help you avoid the trap of the diet/binge cycle.

4) *Myth*: The more I exercise, the better off I'll be.

*Fact*: Exercise is an excellent way to keep your body healthy and strong. However, exercise can become a compulsive activity causing physical and emotional problems. If you must exercise every day in order to feel okay, exercise for hours at a time, or if exercise gets in the way of other activities, you have probably become a compulsive exerciser.

*Positive Step*: Focus on exercise as a way to stay fit rather than as a way to lose weight. If you choose to develop a regular exercise schedule, make sure that it enhances your lifestyle rather than becoming an obsession.

5) *Myth*: People who are thinner are healthier.

*Fact*: People who are fit are healthier. In fact, a recent study found that it is healthier to be larger and fit than to be thin and unfit.

*Positive Step*: Consider a reasonable plan for movement or exercise at your current size that feels comfortable to you.

There are now many programs that offer classes for larger people in a safe, accepting environment with an emphasis on fitness rather than weight loss.

6) *Myth*: I can't be happy unless I'm thin.

*Fact*: There are happy and unhappy people at all sizes. Research shows that the key to having a high self-esteem is for you and your family to value who you are and respect your body, no matter what your size.

*Positive Step*: Some important things you can do for yourself, no matter what shape or body size you have, are to stay fit, eat according to your physical hunger, and develop a loving attitude toward your body. If you overeat because of emotional reasons, or generally feel unhappy, consider getting help from a therapist so that you can deal directly with the issues in your life that make you unhappy.

7) *Myth*: Losing weight is a matter of willpower.

*Fact*: A *Consumer Reports* study found that the promises of commercial weight loss programs are false. The Federal Trade Commission now requires programs to qualify their results. This indicates that individual dieters are not at fault for failures. Rather, regaining weight after initial losses is the norm.

*Positive Step*: Stop beating yourself up for the difficulties you encounter in maintaining weight loss. Rather than feeling shame, try to become compassionate with yourself. It is tough to live in a society that tells you that you are not okay just the way you are. Instead of trying to change the shape of your body, consider trying to change the messages that you've internalized.

8) *Myth*: People who are fat eat more than people who are thin.

*Fact*: Studies do not find this to necessarily be the case. Large people often eat the same amount of food as people considered to be average size.

*Positive Step*: Remember that your genetics plays the greatest role in determining your size, followed by changes in your physiology due to yo-yo dieting. If you find yourself bingeing, it is likely that you are responding to deprivation as the result of dieting. This behavior will diminish as you normalize your relationship with food.

9) *Myth*: If I understand the emotional causes of my overeating, it will stop.

*Fact*: Understanding the reasons you overeat will not change your relationship with food. While you may solve some of the other difficulties in your life, compulsive eating behaviors require direct intervention.

*Positive Step*: Read books, attend workshops, or seek the help of a professional who can help you deal directly with your overeating by teaching you how to stop dieting and become attuned to your natural hunger. Once you take this step, you will be in a much stronger position to intervene with the emotional triggers of your overeating.

10) *Myth*: Compulsive eating is an addiction that must be controlled.

*Fact*: Compulsive eating can take the form of an addiction for many people who use food to regulate their emotions. However, compulsive eating can be cured.

*Positive Step*: Unlike other addictions including cigarettes, alcohol, and drugs, you cannot live without food. Therefore, rather than trying to control overeating by giving up certain types of food, the key is for you to relearn how to put food back where it belongs. When you can do this, you will outgrow the need to eat compulsively.

# THE TENETS OF HEALTH AT EVERY SIZE

The Health At Every Size (HAES) paradigm continues to gain momentum across health professions and among groups concerned with the consequences of dieting and fat prejudice. The following list of tenets, developed by numerous professionals, provides a framework for therapists in their treatment of compulsive eating.

1) Health Enhancement — attention to emotional, physical, and spiritual well-being, without focus on weight loss or achieving a specific "ideal weight."
2) Size and self-acceptance — respect and appreciation for the wonderful diversity of body shapes and size (including one's own!), rather than the pursuit of an idealized weight or shape.
3) The pleasure of eating well — eating based on internal cues of hunger, satiety, and appetite, rather than on external food plans or diets.
4) The joy of movement — encouraging all physical activities for the associated pleasure and health benefits, rather than following a specific routine of regimented exercise for the primary purpose of weight loss.

5) An end to weight bias — recognition that body shape, size, and weight are not evidence of any particular way of eating, level of physical activity, personality, psychological issue, or moral character; confirmation that there is beauty and worth in EVERY body.[1]

# ENDNOTE

1. Kratina K., King N., & Hayes, D. *Moving away from diets: Healing eating problems and exercise resistance.* Lake Dallas, TX: Helm Publishing, 2003.

# RECOMMENDED READING

The following list includes resources that we have found to be invaluable, but it is by no means exhaustive.

## NON-DIET PARADIGM

Bloom, C., Gitter, A., Gutwill, S., Kogel, L., & Zaphiropoulos, L. (1994). *Eating problems.* New York: Basic Books.

Hirschmann, J., & Munter, C. (1988). *Overcoming overeating.* New York: Fawcett Columbine.

Hirschmann, J., & Munter, C. (1995). *When women stop hating their bodies.* New York: Fawcett.

Kratina, K., King, N.L., & Hayes, D. (2002). *Moving away from diets.* Lake Dallas, TX: Helm Publishing.

Normandy, C. E., and Roark, L. (1998). *It's not about food.* New York: Grosset/Putnam.

Orbach, S. (1986). *Fat is a feminist issue.* New York: Berkley Books.

Roth, G. (1984). *Breaking free from compulsive eating.* New York: Signet.

Roth, G. (1982). *Feeding the hungry heart: The experience of compulsive eating.* New York: Signet.

Tribole, E., & Resch, E. (1996). *Intuitive eating.* New York: St. Martin's Press.

## BODY IMAGE/SIZE ACCEPTANCE

Erdman, C. (1996). *Nothing to lose.* New York: HarperSanFrancisco.

Erdman, C. (2003). *Live large: Idea, affirmations, and actions for sane living in a larger body.* Carlsbad, CA: Gurze Books.

Hutchinson, M. (1985). *Transforming body image: learning to love the body you have.* Trumansburg, NY: The Crossing Press.

Johnson, C. (2001). *Self-esteem comes in all sizes.* Carlsbad, CA: Gurze Books.

Manheim, C. (1999). *Wake up, I'm fat!* New York: Broadway Books.

## CULTURAL INFLUENCES

Campos, P. (2004). *The obesity myth.* New York: Gotham Books.

Fraser, L. (1997) *Losing it: America's obsession with weight and the industry that feeds on it.* New York: Dutton.

Goodman, C. W. (1995). *The invisible woman: confronting weight prejudice in America.* Carlsbad, CA: Gurze Books.

Kilbourne, J. (1995). *Slim hopes: Advertising and the obsession with thinness.* Northhampton, MA: Media Education Foundation.

Wolf, N. (1991). *The beauty myth: how images of beauty are used against women.* New York: Anchor Books.

## CHILDREN AND TEENS

Berg, F. (2001). *Children and teens afraid to eat: Helping youth in today's weight-obsessed world.* Hettinger, ND: Healthy Weight Network.

Hirschmann, J., & Zaphiropoulos, L. (1993). *Preventing childhood eating problems.* Carlsbad, CA: Gurze Books.

Waterhouse, D. (1997). *Like mother, like daughter: How women are influenced by their mothers' relationship with food — and how to break the pattern.* New York: Hyperion.

## HEALTH AT EVERY SIZE

Berg, F. (2000). *Women afraid to eat: Breaking free in today's weight-obsessed world.* Hettinger, ND: Health Weight Network.

Gaesser, G. (2002). *Big fat lies: The truth about your weight and your health.* Carlsbad, CA: Gurze Books.

Lyons, P., & Burgard, D. (1988). *Great shape.* New York: W. Morrow.

Waterhouse, D. (1995). *Why women need chocolate.* New York: Hyperion.

# OTHER RESOURCES

Abundia Retreats
Barbara Spaulding (contact person)
(847) 705-9256

Amplestuff
P.O. Box 116
Bearsville, NY 12409-0116
amplestuff@aol.com
www.amplestuff.com

Association for Size Diversity and Health (ASDAH)
Claudia Clark, Director
320 Saddlemire Building
Bowling Green State University
Bowling Green, OH 43403
(419) 372-2081
caclark@bgnet.bgsu.edu

BBW Magazine Online
www.bbwmagazine.com

Body Positive
Deb Burgard (contact person)
www.bodypositive.com

Chicago Center for Overcoming Overeating, Inc.
Judith Matz, Director
P.O. Box 108
Deerfield, IL 60015
(847) 267-1200

Council on Size and Weight Discrimination
P.O. Box 305
Mt. Marion, NY 12456
miriam@cswd.org
www.cswd.org

Gurze Books
(800) 756-7533
www.bulimia.com

*Health at Every Size*
Wayne C. Miller and Jon Robison, editors
(800) 568-7281
www.bcdecker.com

Healthy Weight Network
402 South 14th Street
Hettinger, ND 58639
(701) 567-2646
www.healthyweightnetwork.com

Holistic Health Promotion/Health at Every Size
Jon Robison (contact person)
www.jonrobison.net

International Size-Acceptance Association (ISAA)
P.O. Box 82126
Austin, TX 78758
director@size-acceptance.org
www.size-acceptance.org

Largely Positive, Inc.
Carol Johnson, Director
P.O. Box 170223
Glendale, WI 53217
(414) 299-9295
positive@execpc.com
www.largelypositive.com

Largesse
largesse@eskimo.com
www.eskimo.com~largesse

Massachusetts Eating Disorder Association, Inc. (MEDA)
92 Pearl Street
Newton, MA 02158
(617) 558-1881
www.medainc.org

National Association to Advance Fat Acceptance (NAAFA)
P.O. Box 188620
Sacramento, CA 95919
(916) 558-6880
naafa@naafa.org
www.naafa.org

National Center for Overcoming Overeating
Jane Hirschmann and Carol Munter, Directors
P.O. Box 1257
Old Chelsea Station
New York, NY 10113-0920
(212) 875-0442
www.overcomingovereating.com

National Eating Disorders Association (NEDA)
603 Stewart Street, Suite 803
Seattle, WA 98101
(206) 382-3587
www.nationaleatingdisorders.org

Radiance Magazine Online
www.radiancemagazine.com

The Renfrew Center Foundation
475 Spring Lane
Philadelphia, PA 19128
(877) 367-3383
www.renfrew.org

## BEYOND A SHADOW OF A DIET™

We are available for seminars, workshops and
professional training.
Visit our website at beyondashadowofadiet.com
Contact us at:
jmatz@beyondashadowofadiet.com
efrankel@beyondashadowofadiet.com

# INDEX